Pragmatist Democracy

Pragmatist Democracy

Evolutionary Learning as Public Philosophy

CHRISTOPHER K. ANSELL

OXFORD
UNIVERSITY PRESS

OXFORD
UNIVERSITY PRESS

Oxford University Press, Inc., publishes works that further
Oxford University's objective of excellence
in research, scholarship, and education.

Oxford   New York
Auckland   Cape Town   Dar es Salaam   Hong Kong   Karachi
Kuala Lumpur   Madrid   Melbourne   Mexico City   Nairobi
New Delhi   Shanghai   Taipei   Toronto

With offices in
Argentina   Austria   Brazil   Chile   Czech Republic   France   Greece
Guatemala   Hungary   Italy   Japan   Poland   Portugal   Singapore
South Korea   Switzerland   Thailand   Turkey   Ukraine   Vietnam

Published by Oxford University Press, Inc.
198 Madison Avenue, New York, New York 10016

www.oup.com

Oxford is a registered trademark of Oxford University Press

Library of Congress Cataloging-in-Publication Data
Ansell, Christopher K., 1957-
Pragmatist democracy : evolutionary learning as public philosophy / Christopher K. Ansell.
    p.   cm.
Includes bibliographical references and index.
ISBN 978-0-19-977243-8 (hardback) — ISBN 978-0-19-977244-5 (pbk.)
1. Political participation—Philosophy. 2. Public administration—Philosophy.
3. Pragmatism. I. Title.
JF799.A57   2011
320.01—dc22   2011001556

9 8 7 6 5 4 3 2 1

Printed in the United States of America
on acid-free paper

For Ella, Lillian, and Suzanne

CONTENTS

PREFACE

This project has its roots in my earlier work on cooperation and conflict in the French labor movement. In that project, I found that the schism-prone French working class was able to build broad-based solidarity when it could overcome the ideological dualities that divided union from party and revolutionary from reformist. I discovered that overcoming these dualisms required not only a fundamental change in organizational strategy but also a change in mindset. After that project, I began working on more contemporary topics related to European integration and to new forms of "networked" institutions designed to promote regional economic development. But again, I became fascinated with how institutional transformations were accompanied by new ways of thinking. Teaching an undergraduate course on public administration, I realized that this was also true of attempts to reform bureaucracies. Successful reform, I came to understand, depends on changing people's perception of how they think about public problems.

I no longer remember how I first became familiar with the body of philosophy called "Pragmatism." I like to think I first learned of Pragmatism as a research assistant working for the late David Greenstone on his book on American political culture. I do remember being struck by the parallel between Pragmatism's antidualism and the attempt of the French working class to overcome the divisions that divided them. But the more I read about Pragmatism, the more I began trying to imagine how it might open up new ways of thinking about organization. In particular, I wondered whether it might help change the way we think about and structure public organizations, which often seem caught in a trap between the competing demands of democratic accountability and effective governance. If my earlier work was right, successful change would require both new organizational logics and new ways of thinking.

I began to read the organization theory literature from a Pragmatist perspective and I noticed that several theorists adopted a Pragmatist orientation, sometimes making specific reference to Pragmatism. I decided to write a paper that would synthesize this Pragmatist perspective on organization theory. The result was a long and unwieldy paper that I first presented over a regular lunch with three close colleagues at Berkeley—Todd LaPorte, David Leonard, and the late Judy Gruber. They acknowledged that the ideas were intriguing but suggested that I needed to better demonstrate their real-world implications. They also suggested that this long and unwieldy paper might be expanded a bit and made into a short book.

That same paper circulated around the Internet for awhile and I began to discover that I wasn't alone in my interest in Pragmatism. Marc Ventresca invited me over to Stanford to give the paper at the Scandinavian Committee on Organizational Research (SCANCOR); and Peter Bogason, a public administration scholar, invited me to visit the Centre for Democratic Network Governance at Roskilde University in Copenhagen. I also gave a paper at the Interdisciplinary Committee on Organizational Studies (ICOS) at the University of Michigan, and Mayer Zald made sure that Michael Cohen and I knew of our mutual interest in Pragmatism. That fortunate meeting eventually led Michael, Karl Weick, and me to organize a small conference at Michigan on John Dewey and organization studies. I also participated for several years in an annual conference on Organizations and Knowledge Management organized by David Obstfeld and Paul Carlile, where I met a number of organization theory scholars interested in Pragmatism. I also began to meet others who shared my interest in Pragmatism and social science. Satoshi Miura, an international relations scholar, spent a sabbatical at Berkeley where we had many good discussions about Pragmatism. I also had some great lunches with the late Ernie Haas, who was developing a "pragmatist constructivism" for international relations. A Harvard conference on Pragmatism and the social sciences organized by Chris Winship, Archon Fung, and Neil Gross, and a University of Oregon conference on institutional change organized by Gerry Berk, Dennis Galvan, and Vicky Hattam, brought together a number of Pragmatist-oriented scholars. It has been particularly nice to interact with Gerry and Dennis as they developed their own Pragmatist perspective on institutions. Over the years, I've also had valuable exchanges about Pragmatism with Arjen Boin, Moshe Farjoun, Neil Fligstein, Mark Granovetter, Chuck Sabel, David Stark, and Norb Wiley. In addition, I was fortunate enough to meet and discuss this project with one of the central figures of the book, the late Philip Selznick. Since I often felt like I was working in the wilderness, the support and camaraderie of these scholars has been extremely valuable to me.

A number of colleagues have been critical to the development of this project. Beppe DiPalma and Todd LaPorte provided continuing mentorship and friendship, even when I'm sure they wondered if the book would ever materialize. And despite his gentle skepticism about the project, John Padgett's intellectual support and friendship have been invaluable to me. Mark Bevir has been a continuous source of support and inspiration and did me the great favor of constructively reading a terrible early draft of the manuscript. Rick Kern, in the French Department at Berkeley, is my unofficial academic "life coach" and I hope to return the favor. So many others have also inspired me over the years, shaping my understanding of institutions, organizations, public administration, and politics. In addition to those already mentioned, I want to especially acknowledge Jörg Balsiger, Renata Bichir, Mathilde Bourrier, Arthur Burris, Dan Carpenter, Martha Feldman, Steve Fish, Marc Flandreau, Ken Foster, the late John Freeman, Gary Herrigel, Alison Gash, Jane Gingrich, Vanna Gonzales, Matt Grossman, Judy Innes, Nicolas Jabko, Bob Kagan, Ann Keller, Dan Kronenfeld, Loren Landau, Madeleine Landau, the late Martin Landau, Taeku Lee, Jonah Levy, Eduardo Marques, PerOla Öberg, Shirin Ahlbäck Öberg, Kevin O'Brien, Conor O'Dwyer, Craig Parsons, Sarah Reckhow, Rod Rhodes, Lloyd Rudolph, Susanne Rudolph, Paul Schulman, Eckhard Shröeter, Bernie Silberman, Eva Sørenson, Masayuki Susai, Craig Thomas, Jacob Torfing, David Vogel, Steve Weber, Steve Weiner, Margaret Weir, Hal Wilensky, Daniel Ziblatt, and Nick Ziegler.

I would also like to thank my editor, David McBride, and two anonymous reviewers for Oxford University Press. The reviewers provided a deep and constructive analysis of the draft manuscript, which allowed me to greatly improve the final manuscript. I sincerely thank them. And a note of thanks to my neighbor, graphic artist Grégoire Vion, for suggesting the Escher cover illustration.

My family probably never realized that they were evidence and inspiration for the book. Through his example, my father-in-law, Bill Ryan, demonstrated a central premise of Pragmatism—that it is possible for people of widely different political opinions to engage in intelligent discussion. As public servants of various stripes, my sisters Julie and Lynn, my sister-in-law Orla, my brother-in-law Mark, and my stepfather Paul all personally demonstrated the reality and potential of intelligent, honest, and committed public service. Through her art, my sister Barb provided evidence of the Pragmatist philosopher John Dewey's argument for the deep connections of art and science. The rest of the extended clan—my mom, my mother-in-law Barb, Kristen, Court, Stacey and Tom—demonstrated over and over that the citizenry is well endowed with what Pragmatist philosopher Charles Peirce called "critical commonsense." I owe my greatest debt to those who have had to live with this project on a daily basis. My wife Suzanne Ryan became a diehard supporter of the book as soon as she learned that John Dewey was born and bred in her beloved home state of Vermont. My daughters, Ella and Lillian Ansell, may look back later in life and recall that this was the project their Dad worked on for a good part of their childhood. Whether they resent that or remember it fondly, they should know that they provided the ultimate proof of what Peirce called "evolutionary love."

Pragmatist Democracy

CHAPTER 1

Democratic Governance in a Pragmatist Key

A simple and elegant logic defines the relationship between democracy and governance. Through fair and competitive elections, citizens signal how they would like to handle public concerns. Elected representatives then deliberate among themselves, crafting laws and programs to address those concerns; and public agencies then faithfully execute these laws and programs, effectively managing public problems. In theory, this logic creates a tight chain linking popular sovereignty to effective governance. In practice, the machinery of democratic governance is complex, and there is often considerable slippage from the civic ideal. When intractable public problems collide with the acrimony and distrust that characterize contemporary politics, the gears of effective democratic governance can become jammed.

Quite often this gnashing of gears seems to occur when public agencies must implement public policies. For different reasons, classical liberals, populists, and progressives are all critical of the administrative state. With their concern about limited government and upholding the rule of law, classical liberals are ever-vigilant against the tendencies of bureaucracies to take matters into their own hands and to turn their prerogatives into private gain. For populists, the problem is that delegation of public authority to bureaucracy threatens to subvert the public will with the cold and impersonal logic of faceless experts and bureaucrats. Progressives decry the politicization of bureaucracy and the tendency to subvert good science and rational decision-making to "partisan" politics. Across the political spectrum, people seem to believe that the bureaucracy is out of control, hidebound, politicized, democratically unresponsive, and morally vacuous (cf. Goodsell 1985; du Gay 2000).

Public agencies are at the nexus of democracy and governance. Democracy is the representative process of generating a legitimate mandate to rule, while governance is the management of specific public problems. Public agencies are on the tail end of the chain of representation but on the front end of problem solving. In theory, these agencies carry out the will of the people, and we impose a range of organizational and legal constraints on them to guarantee their responsiveness. At the same time, we expect them to respond flexibly and efficiently to public problems. Public agencies are the democratic institutions that face the largest gap between discretion (low) and responsibility (high).

These tensions are manageable when agencies have clear political support for their mission and when their tasks are relatively straightforward. Three very general kinds of challenges have made the management of these tensions less tenable. The first challenge is the inexorable pluralization of politics and social life, which presents public agencies with highly differentiated constituencies and new demands for access and representation (Kooiman 2003). The second challenge is adversarial politics, driven by the high stakes of elections and the expansion of the advocacy sector (Kagan 2003; Dalton 2004). Agencies must now manage their business in an environment of divisive politics, in which their actions are scrutinized and challenged by opposing sides. The third challenge is the complexification of public problems, driven by the pace of technological change, the power and reach of markets, the scarcity of resources, and our tendency to layer new institutions upon the old (Stoker 2006). Complexity creates crosscutting and unpredictable forms of political and administrative interdependence, yielding increasingly "wicked" problems (Rittel and Webber 1973).

The combination of these factors leads to unproductive spirals of distrust.[1] As agencies try to cope with complex problems, they must work with plural and mobilized publics who demand greater bureaucratic responsiveness to their concerns. These demands for responsiveness lead to attempts to increase political control over agencies, often reducing their discretion to cope with complex problems (Moe 1989). Their subsequent ineffectiveness undermines our faith that public institutions can solve problems. Failure is understood to be the result of poor management, conflicts of interest, bureaucratic sloth, or "red tape"—not the difficulty of coping with politically contentious publics and complex problems under significant constraints. The remedy has been to shift to "results-oriented" management, to greater transparency and accountability, or, ultimately, to privatization and markets. Since these "solutions" respond only to the symptoms of the deeper problem, it is not surprising that they rarely increase our trust in government.

To ameliorate these unproductive spirals of distrust, it is necessary to take a counterintuitive step for those who regard bureaucracy as the cause of these problems. It is necessary, in fact, to make a transition from seeing public agencies as the central problem to seeing them as a key part of the solution. Because they are at the nexus of democracy and governance, they must play a more active role in managing the tension between representation and problem solving.[2] Public agencies must become a central linchpin in building consent for public problem-solving.

To play this role, it is necessary to broadly rethink how administrative organizations function within democratic societies. Reconstructing this relationship requires a particular understanding of how institutions and organizations currently function and how they relate to the society around them. This process also requires intellectual resources for overcoming recurrent tensions between apparently incompatible alternatives and values. To do this reimagining, this book draws inspiration and guidance from the philosophy of Pragmatism.[3] As a philosophy created to reconcile competing claims, Pragmatism provides intellectual resources and insights for managing the tensions between democracy and governance.

The book explores how the philosophy of Pragmatism can help us to confront the contemporary tension between democracy and governance. The last two decades have witnessed a major revival of the philosophy of Pragmatism, influenced by the work of Richard Bernstein, Jurgen Habermas, Hans Joas, Hilary Putnam, and Richard Rorty, among many others (Dickstein 1998). This revival has led to renewed interest in the work of the founders of Pragmatist philosophy and to the resurrection of John Dewey as a major philosopher.[4] This revival has also caught the attention of social scientists and led to the resurfacing of a considerable, though fragmented, tradition of Pragmatist thinking in the social sciences and professions (see the excursus on this tradition at the end of this chapter). Derived largely from the work of Charles Peirce, William James, John Dewey, and George Herbert Mead, this amalgam of Pragmatist philosophy and Pragmatist social science offers the basis for a powerful public philosophy.

Democratic Experimentalism

Pragmatism is a wide-ranging philosophy that encompasses logic, epistemology, aesthetics, political theory, psychology, education, and many other topics. Not surprisingly, it is difficult to encapsulate its essence in a few choice principles. Nevertheless, as will be developed in detail later in this chapter, Pragmatism is usefully described as a philosophy of evolutionary learning. It emphasizes the ability of both individuals and communities to improve their knowledge and problem-solving capacity over time through continuous inquiry, reflection, deliberation, and experimentation.

To describe the generic philosophical commitments of Pragmatism is one matter, but demonstrating how these elements might lead to a restructuring of the relationship between governance and democracy is another. Luckily, this book can build on the work of many others in exploring the application of Pragmatist ideas to public affairs. Perhaps the most significant recent attempt to apply Pragmatism to the relationship between democracy and governance is the work of Charles Sabel, Michael Dorf, and others who have developed what they call "democratic experimentalism." In the broadest statement of these ideas, Dorf and Sabel (1998) describe a system of governance that builds on the lessons learned from Japanese firms about continuous quality improvement. Interpreting these lessons in a Pragmatist light and transposing them to the public sphere, Dorf and Sabel describe public agencies engaged in continuous problem-solving experimentation that is characterized by benchmarking, collaboration, and reciprocal information-sharing and monitoring to reduce error ("learning by monitoring").

To support this democratic experimentalism, Dorf and Sabel reinterpret the Madisonian theory of separation of powers. Public agencies operate in a federal system that enhances the pooling and sharing of information across jurisdictions, which is essential for effective benchmarking. The decentralized character of this federal system facilitates the direct, deliberative engagement of citizens in agency problem-solving (which Dorf and Sabel call "directly deliberative polyarchy"). Legislatures fund and authorize this experimentalism on the condition that agencies establish clear metrics against which to measure their success or failure. Courts ensure that these agencies meet constitutional and legal standards, guarantee human rights, and provide information necessary for citizens to judge experimental outcomes. Sabel and his colleagues have shown that what they call "democratic experimentalism" is already functioning in a number of public sectors, including American drug treatment courts (Dorf and Sabel 2000), child welfare agencies (Noonan, Sabel, and Simon 2009), and the European Union (Sabel and Zeitlin 2008).

To understand how this Pragmatist approach restructures the relationship between democracy and governance, consider an example that Dorf and Sabel use to illustrate democratic experimentalism—the Chicago Alternative Policing Strategy (CAPS). The CAPS refocused rank-and-file policing on problem solving at the community level, forming "beat teams" to work closely with neighborhoods in the identification of crime problems and solutions. These decentralized activities reported their problem-solving efforts to police headquarters, creating a mechanism for information pooling and benchmarking across neighborhoods (Dorf and Sabel 1998). Further analysis of this case of democratic experimentalism by Archon Fung (2001, 2004) argues that CAPS empowered ordinary citizens to directly and continuously participate in deliberative problem-solving. The "deep structure" of CAPS, according to Fung, is "accountable autonomy": neighborhood efforts must have autonomy to flexibly engage in problem solving, but they must also be held accountable by police headquarters.

A comprehensive thirteen-year review of CAPS (Chicago Community Policing Evaluation Consortium 2004; Skogan 2006) found that participation at neighborhood "beat meetings" increased dramatically in the early years of the program and then continued to increase gradually over the rest of the period. Observational studies also found that the quality of meetings improved over this period. The evaluation gives high marks to CAPS for increasing problem-solving accountability within the police force and for fostering active partnerships between the police and other city agencies. African American neighborhoods that had been plagued with problems at the beginning of the experiment reported significant improvements in neighborhood conditions over the period. Surveys also found that confidence in the fairness and effectiveness of the police increased significantly during the program. These gains in legitimacy increased across all racial and ethnic groups. By creating a new problem-solving strategy and a new relationship with the public, CAPS has produced a more virtuous cycle of trust building between the public and the police force.[5]

The Chicago police probably did not read Charles Peirce or John Dewey before inventing CAPS. Instead, their experiment grew out of a unique configuration of pressures, people, and institutions. Yet there are good reasons for interpreting CAPS against the wider backdrop of a philosophy like Pragmatism. To move beyond the unique conditions that produce such experiments, it is useful to identify the broader set of institutional and democratic mechanisms underpinning them. It is also important to articulate the broader ideas, principles, and values that might guide these experiments' extension and refinement and that set standards for evaluating their success or failure. It is important to provide a more general intellectual framework in which the lessons learned from local experiments like CAPS can be absorbed and built on. Expanding on the literature on democratic experimentalism, as well as on many works of other scholars inspired by Pragmatism, this book tries to carve out and elaborate a distinctively Pragmatist public philosophy.

Pragmatism as Public Philosophy

Public philosophy stands somewhere between general philosophy and concrete engagement in public affairs. It is more concrete than general philosophy, because it searches for how to apply general ideas and principles to specific public issues. Yet it does not provide a detailed recipe for public action but rather aims to clarify the values and ideas that guide civic engagement. Articulating this public philosophy requires showing that abstract ideas are concretely applicable, but also that the values and ideas inherent in public affairs are drawn out so they can be better expressed, understood, and debated.

To understand the logic of this book it is necessary to understand how carving out a space for a Pragmatist public philosophy requires not only distilling real-world lessons from Pragmatist philosophy but also articulating what is distinctly Pragmatist about the ways that scholars and practitioners already think about governance and democracy. In other words, Pragmatist public philosophy has to be pitched at the right level of generality in order to foster a conversation between general philosophical ideas and concrete public engagement. In moving from the abstract to the concrete, the test of these ideas is relevance and realism. Does this public philosophy have relevance for public affairs? And can we really imagine these ideas being useful in the world we live in? In identifying a Pragmatist interpretation of what scholars and practitioners are already saying about governance and democracy, the key criterion of success is conceptual coherence. Does the Pragmatist interpretation hold together in a reasonable and mutually reinforcing way?

Pragmatism has a family relationship with at least three other prominent public philosophies—Liberalism, Republicanism, and Communitarianism.[6] In one sense, Pragmatism is compatible with all three of them, because it does not prescribe the specific ends (e.g., certain conceptions of distributive justice or equality) or means (e.g., state, market, or association) of our shared political life. Individual Pragmatists, of course, will not be neutral with respect to these values. But Pragmatism places greater value on the open-ended process of refining values and knowledge than on specifying timeless principles of what is right, just, or efficient. In this sense, it is possible to be a Liberal, Republican, or Communitarian Pragmatist. In another sense, this emphasis on the open-ended process of refining values and knowledge is precisely what makes Pragmatism distinctive. The three other public philosophies certainly do not preclude the value of learning and inquiry, but none of them make it a central or explicit feature of their public philosophy.

The value that Pragmatism places on continuing inquiry and learning ultimately encourages an alliance with social science.[7] A public philosophy that takes inquiry seriously must be prepared to learn from social-scientific efforts to understand the social and political world. However, the orienting assumptions and concerns of different schools of social science are themselves suffused with public and private values.[8] This is often desirable, because social science would otherwise have little meaning or relevance for public affairs. While public philosophy and social science should not be subordinated to one another, they need to be in conversation and this means that they have to speak each other's language. One of the tasks of constructing a Pragmatist public philosophy is therefore to articulate and distill some of the orienting assumptions and ideas of a Pragmatist social science. This means calling attention to the traditions of Pragmatist social science that already exist, while advancing new concepts and ideas that can enrich this tradition.

Thus, this book has the intertwined and reinforcing goals of articulating a Pragmatist public philosophy, applying it to the contemporary tensions between democracy and governance, and building a larger platform for a Pragmatist social science. These three goals are linked by Pragmatism's distinctive model of evolutionary learning, which emphasizes the problem-driven, reflexive, and deliberative quality of social action. A Pragmatist public philosophy applies this model of evolutionary learning to public affairs, using it as an open-ended resource for reimagining the relationship between institutions, governance, and democracy. Evolutionary learning can also provide the orienting assumptions and concerns of a Pragmatist social science, thereby guiding and deepening inquiry into how individuals, institutions, and societies refine and improve their values and knowledge in a continuous fashion.

Pragmatism as Evolutionary Learning

The term "evolutionary learning" is used to call attention to Pragmatism's distinctive melding of evolutionary ideas with a theory of learning.[9] Pragmatism's embrace of an evolutionary perspective is well known (Menand 2001), but its precise stance toward evolution is not always well appreciated (Hausman 1997; Popp 2007). Darwin had considerable influence on Pragmatism, but the Pragmatist model of evolution does not primarily emphasize natural selection and it opposes Social Darwinism.[10] There is in Pragmatism, to be sure, the notion that evolution occurs through successful adaptation to the environment. But consistent with a learning model, Pragmatist evolution bears at least as strong a resemblance to Lamarckian as to Darwinian evolution.[11] Pragmatism also appreciates evolutionary feedback effects (known as the "Baldwin Effect") and emphasizes the cumulative nature of evolution.[12]

Pragmatism's learning model builds on Peirce's model of semiotics and inquiry and James's and Dewey's psychology (Kivinen and Ristelä 2003; Colapietro, Midtgarden, and Strand 2005). Many of Peirce's investigations focused on how humans use signs to communicate and produce knowledge. Learning, for Peirce, took place in communities of inquiry that were self-conscious about how they used signs to structure inquiry. Peirce, James, and Dewey also stressed the experiential basis of learning, which arises from confrontation with concrete problems. They understood much experiential knowledge to be habitual and not subject to conscious reflection. However, experiential learning is enhanced when people become reflexive about their own habitual knowledge, something Peirce dubbed "critical" commonsense. When this reflexivity is cultivated, it could become the basis for an experimental and inquiring approach to problem solving. When individuals and groups learn to use experimentation and inquiry to "reconstruct" their experiential knowledge and skills, this approach can lead to continuous learning or growth—to evolutionary learning.

It is one thing to value evolutionary learning and another thing to identify the conditions that support it. Much of Pragmatism is an exploration of the cognitive and social conditions that enable evolutionary learning. Historically, this exploration grew out of an attempt to break down the opposition between the two rival theories of knowledge—rationalism and empiricism. To do this, Pragmatism had to overcome a set of dualisms erected by this opposition—mind versus body, subject versus object, theory versus practice, and many others. This antidualism is a fundamental aspect of Pragmatism.[13] Evolutionary learning is produced when different, even opposing, orders of things are yoked together in a synergistic manner.

Pragmatism suggests at least three strategies for yoking together opposing orders in a creative tension that Dewey called a "transaction" (Dewey and Bentley 1949; Garrison 2001; Vanderstraeten 2002). The first strategy is to emphasize the continuousness of phenomena. Peirce developed the idea of continuousness to reject what he called the "law of the excluded middle." He argued that the boundary that marked one thing from another was ill-defined and phenomena were continuous rather than discrete.[14] Perhaps the most well-known description of continuousness in the Pragmatist corpus is James's description of consciousness as a continuous stream (the "stream of consciousness"). By emphasizing continuousness, a dualistic opposition is often transformed into a whole-part or a figure-ground relationship.

The second way that Pragmatism overcomes dualism is to introduce a third dimension that sets up a mediated relationship between opposing elements. Peirce's theory of categories, signs, and semiotics is well known for introducing this third dimension (Hookway 1985, 130–134; 2000, 97–103).[15] In the same spirit, Dewey emphasized the role of habit as a form of mediation between impulse and intelligence; and Mead uses the idea of the "generalized other" to describe the dynamic interaction between self and society. All three Pragmatists regarded triadic intermediation as producing a developmental dynamic.[16]

The most important way Pragmatism yokes opposing elements together is to insist on a tight coupling between meaning and action. Contemporary social science often confronts us with a choice between the utilitarian and consequentialist approach of rational choice theory and the ideational and symbolic approach of constructivism and postmodernism. Like rational choice theory, pragmatism emphasizes the instrumental "problem-solving" nature of human behavior (Knight and Johnson 1999). Yet like constructivism and postmodernism, Pragmatism perceives human activity as fundamentally "symbolic" in nature (Blumer 1969; Rochberg-Halton 1986). To align the practical and the symbolic, Pragmatism emphasizes that meaning is discovered through action, not in timeless foundations prior to action.[17]

Pragmatism's antidualism identifies three generative conditions for evolutionary learning: a problem-driven perspective, reflexivity, and deliberation.

Problem-Driven Perspective. Problems disrupt existing assumptions and call for fresh discovery. They pin disputes about knowledge, principles, and values down to particulars (the problematic situation is the triadic dimension) and they focus our attention on action and consequences. Although received wisdom guides us in problem solving, meaning is never fully determined prior to action. Problem solving must be probative, exploring the relevance and value of inherited ideas while anticipating the discovery of new meaning. The uncertainty inherent in problem solving calls for creative action.[18] A "problem-solving" attitude is not merely practical; it drives evolutionary learning by subjecting received knowledge, principles, and values to continuous revision.

Reflexivity. Problems also prompt critical and self-conscious reflection. For Peirce and Dewey, reflexive learning occurs when people are able to critically scrutinize their own common sense or habits. The most sophisticated form of reflexivity occurs when individuals or groups come to appreciate how their choices shape the subsequent development of their own character and competence. This requires attention to how the choice of "means" shapes subsequent "ends" and to how present problem solving can "scaffold" competencies for future problem solving.[19] It also requires increasing sensitivity to how problem solving creates opportunities to discover and refine value. A Pragmatist model of evolutionary learning calls for us to become increasingly reflexive about the trajectory of our own experience.

These ideas help us appreciate how Pragmatism departs from a strictly utilitarian or consequentialist model.[20] For Pragmatism, what ultimately counts is not narrowly "what works" but the meaningfulness of action. As Steven Feshmire describes the Pragmatist stance: "What is most at stake in moral life is not some quantifiable pleasure and pain but what kind of person one is to become and what kind of world one is to develop" (2003, 76). Actions take on enhanced meaning through the cultivation of an emergent sense of purpose. As Hugh McDonald writes in his discussion of a Pragmatist environmental ethics: "The goals of action give meaning to present activity" (2004, 94). These ideas are central to Pragmatism's attitude toward human growth and progress.[21]

Deliberation. The term "deliberation" has two interrelated meanings for Pragmatism. The first refers to the reflexive inquiry produced by the clash of different, sometimes incommensurate, perspectives (Bohman 1999; Misak 2000).[22] The second is related to the centrality of communication for creating new knowledge and intersubjective meaning (Duncan 1968; Vanderstraeten and Biesta 2006; Carey 2009). Pragmatist deliberation emphasizes the role of communication in probing, adjudicating, and bridging these differences. In problematic situations, communication coordinates joint action and inquiry, and this communication can produce jointly constructed meanings that can reshape prior beliefs and goals of the communicators (Talisse 2005; Englund 2006; Vanderstraeten and Biesta 2006; Russill 2008).

Two important aspects of Pragmatist deliberation are rarely sufficiently juxtaposed. The first aspect is well known: the stress on communication leads Pragmatists to showcase the communal or public basis of inquiry. Peirce's ideas about "communities of inquiry" and Dewey's analysis of "publics" exemplify this aspect. Both philosophers point to the value of widening the community or public—Peirce in his *law of large numbers* (Menand 2001) and Dewey in his inclusion of those indirectly affected by the consequences of others' actions in his definition of a public. The second aspect is the value placed on the directness of communication, which celebrates the deliberative value of *face-to-face* communication. This is the real meaning behind Dewey's valorization of small communities, which is sometimes treated as anachronistic by his critics. Small-town life merely exemplifies direct, face-to-face communication.

Evolutionary learning occurs when these three generative conditions—a problem-driven perspective, reflexivity, and deliberation—work together in a recursive cycle. Problems generate reflection, which generates deliberation, which may produce a refined definition of the problem. When individuals or collectivities take control of this learning cycle, we can refer to it as "experimentalism." As the debate over Campbell's "experimenting society" suggests, the assumptions behind an "experimental" approach to public affairs are controversial and frequently criticized as overly positivistic or unrealistic (Campbell 1969, 1970, 1982; Shaver and Staines 1971; Dunn 1982, 2002). Pragmatism, however, understands "experimental" quite broadly to mean a self-conscious and purposeful approach to learning, rather than in the more restrictive sense of a randomized controlled experiment.[23] Pragmatist experimentation treats problems as deliberate opportunities for learning.

Pragmatism departs from a strictly positivist view of experimentation by emphasizing the provisional, probative, creative, and jointly constructed character of social experimentation. Pragmatism acknowledges the uncertainty and ambiguity inherent in problems and the partial perspectives we bring to bear on them.[24] The results of inquiry are treated as fallible and, therefore, as provisional. Recognition of uncertainty and ambiguity leads to a probative stance: much of what inquiry does is to structure and define problems in such a way that we can make progress on them. This calls for skill and creativity. Dewey's account of reflexivity, for example, stresses that experimentation is often a form of "dramatic rehearsal" in which possible lines of action are imagined and tentatively evaluated. Pragmatism also stresses how symbols mediate the process of inquiry, implying that experimentation often requires the invention of new concepts. Peirce's account of experimentation, for example, emphasizes the value of forming new hypotheses—abductions—in uncertain situations. As a form of deliberative inquiry, Pragmatist experiments produce jointly constructed hypotheses and "metrics" that allow different parties to judge whether the experiment has been a success. To structure a problem as an experiment therefore requires a deliberative and creative process of forming hypotheses and metrics that can be evaluated in reference to the outcomes of specific problem-solving strategies.

Drawing antidualism together with problem orientation, reflexivity, and deliberation, Pragmatist evolutionary learning is characterized by four seemingly paradoxical principles: progressive conservatism, cosmopolitan localism, analytical holism, and processual structuralism.

Progressive Conservatism. For Pragmatism, meaning is both cumulative and continuously revised.[25] New principles and values discovered in action are integrated into received wisdom or used to reconstruct it. Pragmatism's progressive credentials are often celebrated (West 1989), notably in the form of Dewey's progressive model of education, Peirce's faith in science, James's claims for meliorism, and Mead's developmental model of the child. But the Pragmatists also stressed the central importance of habit, which conserves past experience. Evolutionary learning requires the continuous refinement of habit. As Koopman writes of the Pragmatist view of progress (meliorism): "[it] consists in simultaneously accepting and criticizing our inherited traditions" (2006, 109).

Cosmopolitan Localism. Learning is produced by shifting back and forth between local and cosmopolitan perspectives. Reflexivity, for example, implies the adoption of a "meta-perspective" from which people can evaluate their own habits and beliefs. The cosmopolitan level is associated with more abstract principles and ideas; the local level is associated with the concrete and continuous experience of action. However, no sharp separation of theory and practice is implied but rather a cycling between local and cosmopolitan perspectives. We see this same principle at work in Pragmatist communication, which juxtaposes broad public and face-to-face communication.

Analytical Holism. Pragmatism joins analysis and synthesis closely together. In *How We Think*, Dewey writes: "Synthesis is the operation that gives extension and generality to an idea, as analysis makes meaning distinct. Synthesis is correlative to analysis" (1910, 158). Learning occurs when greater situational specificity of meaning and action (analysis) advances in concert with wider integration of meaning and action (synthesis). Analytical holism is an important feature of Pragmatist problem-solving. Problem solving is not merely the pursuit of an (analytical) solution to a single problem but also a probing (synthetic) exploration of a larger set of values.[26] Thus, problem solving leads not only to a solution but also to the ongoing reconstruction and integration of this knowledge.

Processual Structuralism. Structure is emergent from process, but processes are scaffolded by structure.[27] Pragmatism's focus on action and activity and on the continuous revision of meaning leads to an emphasis on process, while the focus on cumulative knowledge, on habit, and on mediated action lead to an emphasis on structure. James provided the most enduring metaphor for processual structuralism in his description of life as a set of "flights and perchings." But Dewey provided the most concrete and practical version in his discussion of the ongoing development of habit. For Dewey, a habit is a structure upon which higher-order processes (reflective intelligence) can build. But these higher-order processes can then actively reconstruct habit. Veblen's cumulative causation and Baldwin's feedback effects become important here: reflexive intelligence means that we judge present action and anticipated consequences in terms of how they will structure our future selves.

To conclude, Pragmatism conceptualizes evolutionary learning in a particular way. Evolutionary learning is both experiential *and* mediated by symbols. Meaning is linked closely to action by focusing on problem solving. Symbols are tools for problem solving, but the uncertainty of problems means that they are treated as provisional (fallible). Problem solving is probative (oriented toward discovery of value through action) and creative (hypothesis-forming or abductive), traits that lead to an experimental and inquiring approach to problems. The lessons, skills, and values learned in problem solving are cumulative, but they are also constantly tested, investigated, and revised (*progressive conservatism*). Learning requires us to shift perspectives in order to reflect critically upon our own experiences and ideas (*cosmopolitan localism*); to move back and forth between analysis and synthesis (*analytical holism*); and to become self-conscious about how habits, experience, and ideas scaffold future learning and growth (*processual structuralism*). Taken together, these features encourage us to cultivate our own character and competence and to view problems as opportunities to enhance the meaningfulness of our actions. Hereafter, this distinctive conception of evolutionary learning will be referred to as "Pragmatist learning." The rest of the book will be devoted to exploring how this concept can help us to reimagine the relationship between democracy and governance.

An Overview of the Book

In the chapters that follow, the ideas of evolutionary learning are applied to three core aspects of the relationship between democracy and governance: public learning, bureaucratic organization, and political accountability and consent. As suggested by the CAPS experiment described above, public learning is possible where public agencies can engage in joint problem-solving with society. A joint problem-solving approach, however, is quite difficult to achieve under status quo conditions. The bureaucratic and hierarchical structure of most public agencies may be designed to make them responsive to the public will but it is ill-suited for meaningful problem-solving engagement with the public. Our conception of public agencies as lying on the receiving end of a long chain of democratic representation makes it difficult to relax these bureaucratic and hierarchical constraints. For public agencies to serve as focal points for public learning, they have to function differently as organizations. To do this, new strategies for achieving democratic accountability and consent have to be developed and expanded.

As stated above, this work seeks to establish a wide intellectual vantage point from which to examine these issues. The book begins with a general discussion of institutions, with chapters 2 and 3 arguing that institutions are a critical medium of public learning. Institutions are repositories of experience and knowledge as well as tools for collective action and problem solving. Our current theoretical frameworks for thinking about institutions, however, are more likely to point to how institutions inhibit learning than to how they can support it. Building on a substantial Pragmatist tradition of studying institutions, chapters 2 and 3 conceive of an institutional theory in terms that help to capture the mechanisms and dynamics of Pragmatist learning. Institutions are defined in terms of an interaction between concepts and experience. This interaction can be both conservative and progressive. Concepts and experience accumulate; but they can also be continually revised as people confront new situations and problems. From the perspective of Pragmatist learning, institutions can neither be viewed as simply subject to "rational design," where institutions are treated as objects that can be manipulated without regard for how they are embedded in social life, nor, conversely, as "congealed taste," where institutions represent timeless customs and values. Institutions are subject to collective control and revision, but processes of institutional design must be closely attentive to way that institutions are complexly "scaffolded" by webs of related institutions.

Chapters 4 ("Organization") and 5 ("Problem Solving") extend this institutional learning model by developing a Pragmatist approach to individual and organizational problem-solving. As described in chapter 4, a problem-solving view of institutions is explicit in Philip Selznick's work, particularly in his book on "responsive law" (Nonet and Selznick 2001). But problem solving has rarely been developed into an explicit aspect of institutional theory.[28] While institutions must all routinely confront problems, a Pragmatist approach would suggest that many institutions are not systematically oriented toward problem solving and are often significantly constrained in their ability to engage in *creative* problem-solving. Public organizations *have* problems, but they are not particularly oriented toward *solving* them. Even when they solve problems on an ad hoc basis, problem solving is rarely developed into a more systematic strategy. Chapter 5 builds on current work on policing and regulation to argue that problem solving can be strategically developed as an approach to public management.

Joint problem-solving between public agencies and the public must be supported by a transformation of the hierarchical and bureaucratic character of large-scale organizations. As described in chapter 4, hierarchy implies a situation where decisions are made in a top-down, command-oriented way. Bureaucracy is an organization that relies on impersonal rules to achieve coordination and control. The model of bureaucracy described by sociologist Max Weber combines both hierarchy and bureaucracy into a single bureaucratic organization, which is often seen as exemplifying how modern public administration works. Much of the contemporary public administration and governance literature suggests the need to break away from Weberian bureaucracy (Barzelay 1992; Osborne and Gaebler 1992; cf. Lynn 2001; Olsen 2006). Moving from hierarchy to markets and networks or from bureaucracy to "post-bureaucracy" and "public entrepreneurialism" is seen as an antidote to red tape. Results should take precedence over rules.

The desire to escape the pathologies of bureaucratic organization, however, potentially throws out the proverbial baby with the bathwater. Organization theorists have argued for a long time that there are many forms of hierarchy and more than one way that rules can relate to action (Gouldner 1955a; Burns and Stalker 1961; Chandler 1962; Simon 1962; Landau and Stout 1979; Sabel 1994, 1999; Adler and Borys 1996; Stinchcombe 2001). Instead of arguing to replace top-down bureaucracy with bottom-up entrepreneurialism, this book uses Pragmatism to think about whether public administration can achieve a creative synthesis between them. Fortunately, this book can stand on the shoulders of giants. Chapter 4 argues that Mary Parker Follett and Philip Selznick anchor a powerful Pragmatist tradition in the study of large-scale organization. Selznick's important contribution is to help us think about how informal and formal elements of organizations must be fused together to make bureaucratic institutions into effective communities. He argues, in a Pragmatist spirit, that such a fusion requires the cultivation of organizational purpose through the development of a meaningful mission. Follett's contribution is to describe a type of "relational" authority that differs from top-down command.

Pragmatism does not merely seek to replace "hierarchy" or "bureaucracy" with flat, entrepreneurial organization but rather to harness the values of decentralization and bottom-up initiative to the values of centralization and hierarchical steering. Cosmopolitan localism, as introduced in the discussion of Pragmatist learning, suggests that relational authority can work, recursively, by moving back and forth between a bottom-up and a top-down perspective. This logic leads to a model of "constitutional hierarchy," where organizational leaders specialize in setting broad policy goals and guarding organizational values but do so in constant and direct interaction with the street-level bureaucrats who implement policy. Building on Dewey's discussion of the relationship between reflective intelligence, habit, and impulse in *Human Nature and Conduct*, chapter 6 ("Recursiveness") describes how agencies can expand their capacities for problem solving by bringing top-level executives into close and direct communication with street-level bureaucrats. The New York Police Department's Compstat system is used as an example of this recursive process.

Pragmatist learning values the growth of problem-solving competence and capacity. Building on the work of Selznick and Follett, the Pragmatist model of large-scale organization greatly values the cultivation of individual and organizational problem-solving competencies. Too often, we think of administrative agencies in accounting terms, as allocations of resources to achieve narrowly delimited functions. Building on the Pragmatist idea of learning as the growth of capacity and competence, we can think of agencies as "skill sets" and "problem-solving capacities" that may need to be mobilized for a range of tasks not always delimited ahead of time.[29] This does not mean that agencies should receive unlimited grants of resources to expand skills and capabilities. But our conception of agencies as bundles of skills must be made more robust. We must think of agencies in historical terms as communities that have developed complex skills and strategies based on prior learning.

Organizational transformation of public agencies cannot easily occur without a fundamental change in the relationship between agencies and democratic publics. As described at the outset of this chapter, the traditional model of representation regards public agencies as the final link in a chain of representation that begins with the electorate, moves on to the legislature, then to appointed agency officials, and finally reaches the street-level bureaucrat. As an exclusive model of consent, this logic creates many of our current governance problems. Pragmatism suggests a complementary model of democratic consent that mirrors the pattern of problem solving.

Pragmatists like John Dewey, Mary Parker Follett, and Jane Addams all argued that elections and majoritarianism are not a sufficient basis of democratic consent. To say that representative institutions are insufficient, however, is not to say that they are unnecessary. The point is to *complement* traditional channels of representation with more direct and deliberative forms of consent building focused on problem solving. Although public agencies are not the sole site of deliberation, participation, expertise, or problem solving, they comprise a relatively unique place where these values can be brought together. They are the linchpin between popular sovereignty expressed through elections and local problem-solving efforts.

Public agencies can serve as a linchpin of democracy because they can build up societal consent for policies through effective local problem solving and institutional revision. The book does not claim that they do this alone or exclusively, only that they are well positioned to play this role. As Bohman writes of Pragmatist deliberation:

> Dewey does not believe that merely introducing genuine public debate and discussion within individualist methods will be sufficient to overcome the crisis of democracy. Unorganized discussion alone, no matter how free and open, generates only the class of opposite opinions. (1999, 593)

Public organizations working on solving specific public problems, however, create opportunities for focused and organized civic engagement. They are focal points for the creation of problem-solving publics.

For some, assigning public agencies a consent-building role will be regarded as advocating "administrative corporatism" and will raise the specter of "private" law-making (Lowi 1969). Such a charge stems from an ideal view of popular sovereignty as unitary and indivisible. By contrast, Pragmatism envisions the possibility of building up consent more organically, in an evolutionary fashion, around overlapping problem-solving efforts. This argument is developed in detail in the chapter on consent (chapter 8).

Armed with the idea that agencies must be problem-solving communities and that their role is, in part, to expand societal consent for creative problem-solving and widen the sphere of responsibility for problems, we are brought to the idea of collaborative governance. In models of collaborative governance, public agencies directly engage stakeholders in agency decision-making in order to better solve public problems and to create broad-based consent for agency policy. Chapter 9 develops a Pragmatist interpretation of collaborative governance as a strategy for creating problem-solving publics.

To grant public agencies discretion to engage in problem solving and to change their relationship with external publics, we must entertain the problem of bureaucratic power and accountability. While not unmindful that power needs to be checked, this book works against the popular clamor for greater bureaucratic oversight and accountability. While some measures of oversight, accountability, and transparency are certainly necessary, these measures can easily produce more costs than benefits. And while often portrayed as anti-dotes to citizen mistrust of government, they often deepen our distrust. As argued in chapter 7 ("Power and Responsibility"), Pragmatism would place more emphasis on cultivating responsibility than on ensuring accountability.

Responsibility is not a Kantian imperative. From a Pragmatist perspective, responsibility has to be built and institutionalized, which means that there is no escaping the issue of political power. Chapter 7 builds a Pragmatist per-spective on power, which focuses on how power is tamed or civilized. While a Pragmatist view of power has some affinity with a Madisonian model of the separation of powers, it would add a triadic element—a third party that can adjudicate the countervailing claims of separate powers. Following Dewey, this third party is envisioned to be a "public" that can deliberate about shared values and goals. Civilizing power calls for building up the capacity of publics to deliberate and adjudicate (Dewey 1927; Fung 2002).

If we draw these ideas about public agencies and democracy together, they add up to a distinctive Pragmatist approach to democracy that the concluding chapter will call "problem-solving democracy." To make public agencies a linchpin of this problem-solving democracy may seem a very radical shift. Yet it is important to realize that public agencies are thrust into this role anyway. The real tension is between our constitutional and democratic theory of pop-ular sovereignty and the way public life works in practice, albeit in a less than optimal fashion. The tension between theory and practice is expressed in the spiraling distrust between citizens and the state. As a framework for social sci-ence and public philosophy, Pragmatism helps us imagine how to bring theory and practice together.

Excursus: Pragmatism, Social Science, and the Applied Professions

Beyond Pragmatism as philosophy, there is a deep—if ultimately unfo-cused—tradition of Pragmatist thinking in the social sciences and in the pro-fessions (Joas 1993). James's *Principles of Psychology* was once the leading textbook on psychology; and Dewey's article "The Reflex Arc Concept in Psy-chology" was once one of the most frequently cited articles in that field. So it is not surprising to find a Pragmatist tradition in psychology.[30] Yet, arguably, Dewey and Mead had even more influence in sociology, where they were a central influence in the development of the Chicago School of Sociology and symbolic interactionism.[31] In economics, American institutional economics was fundamentally shaped by Pragmatism (Tool 1977; Mirowski 1987; Bush 1989; Liebhafsky 1993). One of the towering figures of that tradition, Thorstein Veblen, was a student of Peirce's at Johns Hopkins (Hall and Whybrow 2008). Other leading institutional economists, including John Commons, Wesley Mitchell, and Clarence Ayres, were strongly influenced by Dewey (Pickens 1987; Smith 1994; Webb 2002).[32] In anthropology, systematic influence is harder to find, but major figures like Franz Boas (Lewis 2001) and Victor Turner (Turner 1986) were influenced by Pragmatism.

In political science, one of the founders of modern political science, Arthur Bentley, collaborated closely with Dewey (Dewey and Bentley 1949; Ratner, Altman, and Wheeler 1964). Other important figures in early American political science, like Herbert Croly and Charles Merriam, were also influenced by Pragmatism (Neblo 2004). More contemporary exponents of Pragmatist ideas include Charles Lindblom (Lindblom and Cohen 1979) and Charles Sabel (Dorf and Sabel 1998). Pragmatism has also had a strong influence on political theory, in part through the work of Harold Laski (Da Silva 2008), Sidney Hook (Talisse 2001), Jurgen Habermas (Aboulafia, Bookman, and Kemp 2002), and Roberto Unger (2004). Democratic theorists have expressed great interest in Dewey's work in recent years.[33]

In more applied disciplines, Pragmatism has always had some important influences.[34] In legal theory, Oliver Wendell Holmes was one of the original members of the famous Metaphysical Club, along with Peirce and James (Menand 2001; Haack 2005). But Pragmatism also had an important influence on legal theorists like Roscoe Pound and on important practitioners like Louis Brandeis (Wang 2005; Berk 2009) and Benjamin Cardozo.[35]

There has been significant discussion about the influence of Pragmatism on public administration.[36] Waldo's classic discussion of the philosophical bases of American public administration suggested limited exposure (Waldo 1948), and Snider (2000a, 2000b) has explored the reasons for this limited influence. Other authors, however, have seen more influence (McSwite 1997).[37] Whatever the basis for Pragmatism's historical influence, there has been a flurry of recent interest in Pragmatism in public administration.[38]

The impressive breadth of this influence across the social sciences and professional disciplines suggests that Pragmatism could serve as a powerful platform for engagement across the fragmented social sciences, linking the social sciences to a public philosophy that values social learning, civic communication, and democracy.[39] A close examination of these influences, however, suggests that the different disciplines draw quite selectively on Pragmatism. The democratic theorists, for instance, rely primarily on Dewey's *The Public and Its Problems*, fashioning him as either a deliberative (Bohman 1999), participatory

(Shields 2003), or radical democrat (Knight and Johnson 2007). Others focus on Dewey's "science of democracy," emphasizing the link between science and democracy (Smiley 1989; Morris 1999; Festenstein 2001) or his "experimentalism" (Dorf and Sabel 1998; MacGilvray 1999). It is less clear whether democratic theorists have much in common with scholars in other disciplines who, for example, stress the importance of Peirce's semiotics (Kevelson 1990), Dewey's model of habit (Cohen 2007), or Mead's theory of the self (Wiley 1994).

The very richness of Pragmatism is therefore sometimes a barrier to wider traffic among disciplines. The Pragmatist genealogy is also uneven. In some areas, Pragmatist influences are largely of historical interest; in other cases, these influences have been marginalized or subsumed by other disciplinary developments; and in still others, there has been a strong revival of Pragmatist thinking or a quite recent recognition of the potential value of a Pragmatist perspective. To understand this unevenness, it is useful to see it in a broader political context. Pragmatism had an influence not only on the social sciences and professions but also on broader reform movements. It is sometimes understood to be "the philosophy" of the American progressive movement (Kloppenberg 1986). World War I, however, was a critical watershed for Pragmatism. Afterward, it was attacked from both the right and the left (Diggins 1994).[40] Many of these critiques created "myths" about Pragmatism that continue to survive today (MacGilvray 2000; Westbrook 2005).

As both public philosophy and social science, the revival of Pragmatism carries valuable intellectual resources and baggage from the past. The fragmented character of the intellectual community is probably the most limiting factor for Pragmatism. In response, this book advances a synthetic reading that proposes to make Pragmatist learning the common platform for social science and public philosophy.

CHAPTER 2

Institutions

■

If Pragmatism places evolutionary learning at the center of its public philosophy, how should we apply it to public affairs? What is the right level-of-analysis for thinking about how publics, as opposed to individuals, learn? There is no shortage of possible answers to these questions, but some responses express the ideas and potential of Pragmatism better than others. This chapter begins by arguing that "institutions" is the best answer to these questions, better than possible alternatives like "culture" or "technology." This answer places Pragmatism squarely within the institutionalist tradition in the social sciences. The chapter then demonstrates Pragmatism's historical place within that tradition. However, neither the broader tradition of institutionalism nor its Pragmatist variant fully supports the Pragmatist conception of evolutionary learning. Beginning with a consideration of how the term "institution" is defined and continuing with an analysis of the dynamics of institutionalization, this chapter clears a path to thinking about institutions as a basic medium of evolutionary learning.

How should we describe social environments that result from, but also shape, our subsequent choices and actions? And how should we describe the products of joint social interactions that represent collective learning? Ordinary language offers a choice of at least three grand terms: "culture," "technology," and "institutions." While the choice between them may seem merely academic, a moment's reflection on each term suggests important implications for public philosophy.

In ordinary language, the term "culture" typically refers to the set of beliefs, values, practices, and symbols shared by a group of people. Culture connotes an all-encompassing set of taken-for-granted meanings fundamentally constitutive of identity and behavior. From a Pragmatist perspective, this attention to meaning is a clear advantage of using a term like "culture" to think about evolutionary learning. However, the emphasis on all-encompassing, shared, and taken-for-granted meaning implies that most cultural accounts do not stress the reflexive or deliberative qualities of meaning. Although scholars of culture have argued that these are not necessary assumptions or conclusions, the colloquial meaning of culture is an important consideration for any public philosophy.

The term "technology" has nearly the opposite set of advantages and disadvantages. In ordinary language, the term refers to socially constructed objects used to achieve instrumental goals. From a Pragmatist perspective, this instrumentalism has useful connotations for problem solving.[1] Technologies are deployed to solve specific problems, implying a level of critical self-reflection about their use and design. Although scholars of technology have shown that they are expressions of culture and can themselves become constitutive of thought and identity, technologies are popularly conceived as "means" rather than "ends." Again, this colloquial meaning is an important consideration for public philosophy.

As pointed out in chapter 1, Pragmatism attempts to draw meaning and action—and, by extension, culture and technology—closely together. Dewey's philosophy has, in fact, been characterized as "cultural instrumentalism" (Eldridge 1998). The term "institution" captures this dualism of meaning and action better than either of the alternatives. In colloquial terms, it is common to talk about an institution as representing and embodying the beliefs and values of a community. We speak of a beloved organization or practice in our community by saying "that's a real institution here." But it would not be unusual to hear a politician say, "We have created a new institution to solve the debt crisis." Academic debate also tends to divide over whether institutions embody cultural meaning or are primarily tools for achieving instrumental purposes.[2]

An institution can be both a cultural framework *and* a technology and it is this Janus-faced perspective that makes institutions good candidates for evolutionary learning. As cultural frameworks, institutions sustain and accumulate meaning; as technologies, they are used to address concrete problems. Potentially, they sustain and accumulate the lessons from past problem solving while subjecting those lessons to the test of contemporary problems. While a less productive relationship between culture and technology often prevails in institutions, this is still an important potential.

If we treat institutions as the medium of evolutionary learning in public affairs, then we can build directly on a tradition of institutional thought inspired by Pragmatism.

Pragmatist Institutionalism

Contemporary institutionalism has broad interdisciplinary reach across the social sciences. To advance this book's goal of developing a social science informed by Pragmatism, the book begins by revisiting a rich tradition of

Pragmatist institutionalism largely overlooked by current discussions of institutionalism. It is true that the founding Pragmatist philosophers—Charles Peirce, William James, John Dewey, and George Herbert Mead—did not themselves have a well-developed theory of institutions. James is sometimes even seen as an anti-institutionalist (Weinstein 1971). But Mead and Dewey, in particular, understood that institutions stand at the center of public life. Mead viewed society as "institutionalized social action" (Athens 2005, 307). Dewey mentioned institutions repeatedly in his work, calling institutions "the only means by which positive freedom in action can be secured" (1957, 166). Although the founding Pragmatists lacked a theory of institutions, they inspired a number of attempts to develop one.[3]

There are three recognizable branches of this institutionalist tradition: a sociological version developed by Charles Cooley and Everett Hughes, and advanced by the "Chicago School" of Sociology and symbolic interactionism; an economic version, associated with Thorstein Veblen, John Commons, Claude Ayres, and other institutional economists; and an organizational theory version, powerfully expressed by authors like Mary Follett and Philip Selznick.[4]

Taken together, the work of the Pragmatist institutionalists is rich but not as powerfully synergistic as it might be. It is not straightforward to find common theoretical touchstones that unify all three branches. However, by triangulating among the founding Pragmatist philosophers and these different schools of thought, it is possible to advance four foundational claims for this tradition. Pragmatist institutionalism is based on and motivated by (1) a Pragmatist model of psychology; (2) an emphasis on the interpretation and production of meaning; (3) an understanding of institutional life as a dynamic "going concern"; and (4) a naturalistic stance toward institutions, one that understands them in situ. Each claim is developed in greater detail below.

PRAGMATIST PSYCHOLOGY

The founding Pragmatists toiled at the boundaries of philosophy and psychology. Peirce sought to understand the cognitive basis of belief and reason, and James's *Principles of Psychology* was the leading psychology text of his era. On these foundations, Dewey and Mead elaborated distinctive perspectives on individual and social psychology. The early Pragmatist institutionalists drew heavily on this Pragmatist psychology,[5] which featured a multitiered view of mind that stressed the interaction between emotion, habit, and reflexive intelligence.[6] Habit, or what we might today more broadly call "learned behavior," was central to the Pragmatist psychology of Peirce, James, Dewey, and Mead (Baldwin 1988; Lawlor 2006; Cohen 2007; Hausman 2008)[7] and was particularly important to Veblen and the institutional economists (Hodgson 2004, 2007).[8]

It is worth noting that Herbert Simon's idea of routine was inspired by William James's interpretation of habit as a way of economizing energy (Barbalet 2008). However, Simon's concept of routine veered away from the Pragmatist understanding of habit by treating routine as an automatic response distinct from cognition or emotion. By contrast, Pragmatism understands habit, cognition, and emotion as closely intertwined (Cohen 2007; Baldwin 1988). Whereas Simon's concept of routine makes it analogous to automatic machinery, Pragmatist institutionalism associates habit with what today we might more readily call "skill" (Barbalet 2008).[9] For Pragmatism, a habit is a competency or a capacity, a view exemplified by Veblen's study of craftsmanship.[10] For James and Dewey, habits also shape ends and are not simply means (Lawlor 2006). In fact, Dewey understood "character" as a bundle of moral habits—a perspective that influenced Selznick's (1957) argument about institutional character.

For Pragmatists, habit and creativity are also entwined. In his essay "Fixation of Belief," Peirce argued that we draw inferences habitually; and, as developed in his concept of abduction, he also suggested that these habitual inferences could be creative.[11] Peirce thought that we arrived at hypotheses through educated guesses and that our capacity to guess was partially innate. He distinguished learned and unlearned innateness, with habits being a form of learned innateness.[12] Recent work in the Pragmatist tradition emphasizes this close interaction between habit and creativity. Sabel (2006) describes the way that continuous revision of "routines" provides the foundation for highly productive and innovative organization. Berk (2009) and Berk and Galvan (2009) emphasize the creativity inherent in recombining existing habits to confront novel problems, a process they call "creative syncretism."

THE INTERPRETATION AND PRODUCTION
OF MEANING

Pragmatism is centrally interested in meaning and stresses the role of symbols in the mediation of social life. Building on Dewey and Mead, Herbert Blumer summarized this perspective in his articulation of the three core principles for symbolic interactionism: (1) "human beings act towards things on the basis of the meaning that the things have for them"; (2) "the meaning of such things is derived from, or arises out of, the social interaction that one has with one's fellows"; and (3) "these meanings are handled in, and modified through, an interpretative process used by the person in dealing with the things he encounters" (Blumer 1969, 2). These orienting principles express the way that Pragmatists place the continuous interpretation and production of meaning at the center of institutional processes.

Mead understood institutions as arising from a process whereby individuals engage in interaction through the mediation of symbols. As Athens writes: "According to [Mead], whenever and wherever people use common maxims to organize their joint actions, they are engaging in institutional social action" (2005, 307). Mead's understanding of institutions included the idea of a "social object," which "is the common attitude that participants assume toward a prospective social act's construction." Participants may thereby "simultaneously form a 'common plan of action' for its subsequent execution" (Athens 2005, 311).

Pragmatism closely links meaning to action. Therefore, meanings are not constructed once and for all, but they are continuously constructed and reconstructed through action. This leads to a situational view of meaning, which W. I. Thomas expressed by coining the phrase the "definition of the situation." He argued that the definition of the situation was a central concern of sociology and it assumed a central place for the Chicago School of Sociology. Everett Hughes later built his approach to institutions around this situational view of meaning (Helmes-Hayes 1998).[13]

While stressing the meaningful character of institutions, the Pragmatist institutionalists also saw institutions in instrumental terms. Building on Dewey's ideas of instrumentalism, the institutional economist Claude Ayres developed a view of institutions as "technologies" (Ayres 1951, 50–51). As discussed in the introduction to this chapter, however, it is important to appreciate how Pragmatism links this instrumental view of institutions to a more cultural understanding of how institutions embody meaning (again, this follows from the stress on the close link between meaning and action).[14] Selznick (1957), for example, argues that organizations, as social technologies, only become institutions when they become valued in their own right. In making this argument, he draws directly on Dewey's discussion of the continuous interaction of means and ends.[15]

DYNAMIC, GOING CONCERNS

One of the strongest and most important commonalities among the Pragmatist institutionalists is the idea that an institution is a "going concern"—a social order that develops a reflexive concern about its own survival and functioning. Everett Hughes coined the term, which was later picked up by Commons and Selznick (Helmes-Hayes 1998). The idea of an institution as a "going concern" was at the core of Hughes's understanding of institutions and captured his dynamic, ecological, and experiential approach to institutions, as he described in the preface to *The Sociological Eye*:

> In any society there are certain mobilizations of people for expression or action. They are "going concerns"; some people keep them going. Other people get moved by them or to them from time to time and they also keep them going. . . . If we are to study human society, we must attend to the going concerns, which are subject to moral, social, and ecological contingencies. (Hughes 1993, xviii)[16]

As can be seen from Mead's concern with social maxims and Hughes's idea of an institution as a going concern, Pragmatist institutionalism associates institutions with collective action. Commons was the most explicit in this focus on collective action, defining an institution as "collective action in control, liberation and expansion of individual action" (1931, 649). Collective action, he elaborated, "ranges all the way from unorganized custom to the many going concerns, such as the family, the corporation, the trade association, the trade union, the reserve system, the state" (1931, 649).

The term "going concern" suggests more than mere collective action. It implies a form of collective action that has become self-conscious. Distinguishing a group from an institution, Cooley, for example, wrote that an institution is "a continuous organic activity with a social heritage of its own and with methods of cooperation which it imparts to the persons who enter into it" (1927, 318). Seventy years later, Selznick makes almost the same point: "To see the corporation 'as an institution' is to view the enterprise as a going concern, taking account of relevant stakeholders, attending to long-run interests, being sensitive to the operative structure of authority" (Selznick 1996, 272). Note that this argument does not mean that the institution merely reproduces itself in an identical form, but rather that it develops an awareness of its own value. Survival—for example, reproduction—typically requires adaptation rather than stasis. Commons expressed this idea of reproduction and adaptation in terms of the continuous revision of the "working rules" of enterprises. For Selznick, it was the "character" of the institution and its "distinctive competence" that adapts (Selznick 1957).[17]

Pragmatist institutionalism emphasizes the dynamism of institutional change. Rather than understand institutions in equilibrium terms, they are better understood as continuous processes—a philosophic point stressed by James and embraced by Mary Parker Follett (1919) and Charles Cooley. Cooley described institutions as a "distinct organic process" (1927, 318). Symbolic interactionism also stresses this processualism, arguing that institutions are best understood from the perspective of social interaction that produces a continuously negotiated order (Strauss 1988).[18]

NATURALISM

Consistent with the idea that institutions are dynamic going concerns, Pragmatist institutionalism emphasizes the importance of seeing them as "lived in." Jane Addams, who had a strong influence on the early Chicago School and on Dewey, strongly emphasized this idea of the lived experience of institutions. She criticized municipal reform that focused on the institutional machinery of government to the neglect of how these institutions were rooted in the lived experience of the community (Shields 2006). Everett Hughes and the symbolic interactionists followed in this tradition, envisioning institutions as "arenas" of social interaction, an idea made explicit in Anselm Strauss's "social worlds model" (Strauss 1993). As Hallet and Ventresca (2006) argue, one of the values of symbolic interactionism is its emphasis on seeing these arenas as "inhabited." An important implication of this naturalistic perspective is that institutions must be studied in situ—that is, from the perspective of the lived experience of institutional inhabitants.

This image of social arenas inhabited by people having concrete interactions and experiences supports an ecological perspective of institutions.[19] Drawing on the Chicago tradition of sociology, Hughes made the first explicit description of the ecological character of institutions.[20] He emphasized the specifically territorial or spatial meaning of the term "ecological."[21] Building on Hughes's concept of institutional ecology, Star and Griesemer (1989) demonstrated how it helps reveal opportunities for institutional cooperation and conflict.

If we combine these four foundational ideas of Pragmatist institutionalism—Pragmatist psychology, the interpretation and production of meaning, dynamic going concerns, and naturalism—the rudiments of evolutionary learning come into view. The emphasis on habit as learned behavior conserves the lessons of experience.[22] These lessons are continually reinterpreted and revised as new situations arise that require creative response. As institutions become more self-reflexive about their own survival and functioning, they can engage in more self-conscious and systematic revision of these habits. The contexts for this evolutionary learning are situated action and interaction linked together ecologically. As Chisholm (1995, 2001) has argued, Pragmatist institutionalism is a problem-driven model of institutional evolution.

This model of institutional evolution is both progressive and conservative, as suggested by Veblen's interpretation of how institutions evolve:

The habitual element of human life changes unremittingly and cumulatively, resulting in a continued proliferous growth of institutions.
Changes in the institutional structure are continually taking place in
response to the altered discipline of living under changing cultural
conditions, but human nature remains specifically the same. (Veblen
1914, 18; cited by Cordes 2005)[23]

Commons also had a view of institutional evolution, which he envisioned as
working something like the evolution of common law:

The decision, by becoming precedents, become the working rules, for
the time being, of the particular organized concern. The historic
"common law" of Anglo-American jurisprudence is only a special
case of the universal principle common to all concerns that survive, of
making new law by deciding conflicts of interest, and thus giving
greater precision and organized compulsion to the unorganized
working rules of custom. (1931, 651)

Although it is scarcely recognized in the organization theory literature, Selznick also had a view of institutional evolution. His later work on "responsive"
law developed a valuable perspective on the implications of reflexiveness for
the ongoing evolution of institutional processes (Nonet and Selznick 2001).

The tradition of Pragmatist institutionalism is without a doubt a rich one,
but it is also rather fragmented. Although the traditions of institutional economics associated with Veblen and Commons, Blumer's symbolic interactionism, and Follett and Selznick's organization theory were all influenced by the
philosophical tradition of Pragmatism, they drew on rather different sources
of inspiration from that tradition. Veblen drew heavily on the idea of habit and
evolution, as developed by Peirce, while Blumer drew most explicitly on
Mead's model of social psychology. Follet was clearly influenced by James's
processualism and pluralism, while Selznick drew on Dewey's analysis of the
continuous interaction of means and ends. There are deep affinities among
these perspectives, but the very richness of the Pragmatist tradition makes a
Pragmatist institutionalism difficult to unify.

The next section returns to basics. A good way to elevate what is common in
the Pragmatist tradition is to reconstruct a basic definition of institutions that
might serve as a common platform for further research and investigation.
While definition is a mundane task, it is an important one. Institutionalists
often neglect to define what they mean by their most fundamental term ("institution"), and when they do attempt definition it is often clear that different
varieties of institutional theory begin from different starting assumptions. The

discussion that follows supports the goal of treating institutions as a medium of evolutionary learning.

A Transactional View of Institutions

Good definitions signal key dimensions of a phenomenon but avoid defining what should be explained. With this dictum in mind and inspired by the discussion above, we can begin with the following very general definition of institutions: *Institutions are relationships between the symbolic artifacts that mediate social life and people's experience of those artifacts.* The use of the term "artifact" signals that institutions have an objective quality in that we treat them as having an existence outside our minds.[24] To say that these artifacts are symbolic is to say that they embody subjective and intersubjective meaning. To say that institutions mediate social life indicates that we call symbolic artifacts "institutions" when we are referring to their role in mediating social interaction. To say that an institution is a relationship between people's experience and symbolic artifacts is to emphasize that an institution is not the artifact per se, but the meaning the artifact has for people. By this broad definition, art, language, music, law, organizations, technology, and social conventions may all be institutions.

This very broad definition captures some of the essential ideas of Pragmatism. To think of an institution as an artifact endowed with meaning is to follow Pragmatism in trying to bridge the divide between subject and object.[25] To focus on the meaning of artifacts is to emphasize the essentially interpretative quality of institutions. And to emphasize their social mediating role is to call attention to Pragmatist institutionalism's emphasis on collective action. The reference to "people's experience" highlights the "lived in" character of institutions. Experience is cumulatively carried forward from the past, even as people have fresh experiences in the present.

This Pragmatism-inspired definition of institutions can be made more specific. We are interested primarily in the *conceptual* aspect of symbolic artifacts. Concepts structure thought and social life, helping to reveal the bridge between "mind" and "society." Free-floating concepts are not institutions per se. They become institutionalized only as their meaning becomes partially "fixed" (to use Peirce's metaphor) in three senses. First, since Pragmatism insists on the "lived" character of institutions, the meaning of a concept depends on how it is concretely *grounded* in experience. Second, since concepts take part of their meaning from their relationship to other concepts, meaning is shaped by *ecological* relationships to other concepts. Finally, the meaning of concepts is bestowed not only by those who use them but also by third-party *audiences* who arbitrate their use. Institutions can therefore be defined as *grounded conceptual ecologies with audiences*. A detailed justification of this definition is provided in an excursus at the end of this chapter.

Although the meaning of an institutional concept is partially "fixed" in this way, Pragmatism would locate the dynamism of institutions in indeterminacy. The meaning of an institutional concept is never fully fixed by past experience, ecological association, or third parties. Instead, the meaning of an institutional concept is ultimately "fixed" (for now) by its use in the present situation. Indeterminacy allows us to place institutions in a larger processual context that Dewey called "transactional." A transactional approach rejects the idea of a fixed starting perspective and instead places elements in a larger field of action and examines their subsequent interaction (Dewey and Bentley 1949; Abowitz 2000; Garrison 2001).[26] A transactional approach to institutions would focus on the interaction of concepts and experience over time as individuals and groups use them to respond to situational problems.

Variants of contemporary institutionalism that assume that institutions are "taken-for-granted" norms, "logics of appropriateness" or "stable equilibriums" often have trouble explaining institutional change. An analysis of the institutional process as a repeated transaction between concepts, experiences, and situations offers, therefore, some distinct advantages. In these transactions, individuals may utilize established concepts and experiences to confront situations in a way that simply reproduces institutions across time. When confronted with problematic situations, however, people may "abductively" create new institutional concepts (hypotheses).[27] This logic is consistent with arguments about the importance of "ideas" for institutional change (Weir 1992; Parsons 2003). New concepts, however, often arise from a creative recombination of existing experience and concepts (Berk 2009; Berk and Galvan 2009).

A transactional view suggests that experiences with concepts will accumulate over time as they are used. A concept becomes more institutionalized as people develop a richer inventory of associations with it. As these experiences become dense, a kind of "lock-in" might occur, leading to path-dependent consequences (Arthur 1989; Pierson 2004). As research on expertise suggests, a rich set of associations between experience and concepts may lead to the ability to utilize concepts and experience in a skillful and strategic fashion sensitive to the logic of specific situations (Fligstein 1997; Klein 1999). In this sense, dense experiential associations may narrow the bandwidth of institutional behavior but they may also enhance freedom of maneuver within these bounds (experts are anything but arbitrary or random in the deployment of their experience). Much the same thing can be said about the ecological level. As concepts and experience become embedded in wider ecologies, their meaning is constrained by their relationship to other concepts and experience. But freedom of maneuver may be enhanced as the ecology becomes more complex.

The final point about institutional processes follows from the argument about audiences. Pragmatist institutionalism regards institutionalization as a process whereby groups become self-reflective about the meanings they attribute to certain concepts. We can call an audience that has become collectively self-reflective a *public*. A *public* is an audience that communicates among itself and deliberates about the meaning of concepts and experiences. A *community* is a public that can act collectively to arbitrate the interpretation of concepts and control their meaning.[28] The idea of communities as third-party arbiters of institutional meaning is at the heart of Selznick's institutionalism (Selznick 1957, 1992).

Building on this definition of institutions and on the transactional perspective advanced here, evolutionary learning can be said to take shape through the following types of processes: (1) when experience is conceptualized or new concepts are articulated (conceptualization); (2) when concepts become grounded in concrete experience (contextualization); (3) when concepts and experiences become articulated in relation to other concepts and experiences (elaboration); and (4) when audiences form around the use of concepts and experiences (reflexivity). Recall that when we are referring to institutional concepts, we are assuming that they play a role in mediating social relations.

From any baseline situation, evolutionary learning can be said to occur at the institutional level when these processes of conceptualization, contextualization, elaboration, and reflexivity allow groups to more skillfully act together to understand and solve subsequent problems. For this to occur, we should expect to see socially mediating concepts being used more precisely or comprehensively or see them drawing on a richer set of experiences. We should also expect to see greater articulation and consistency in relationships between concepts. And we would expect to see audiences exhibiting greater competence and capacity to act reflexively about social concepts and experiences. Whether learning has occurred has to be judged from the point of view of a particular institutional audience.

As these indicators make clear, not all institutional change is evolutionary learning. Faddish new concepts may be developed that actually reduce the precision or comprehensiveness of situational action. These new concepts may ignore past experience or spawn unnecessary complexity. Institutional audiences may lose their capacity to act reflexively. As the next section argues, in judging whether evolutionary learning has occurred, we should also never lose sight of the role of power.

Institutions, Politics, and Power

A criticism frequently leveled at Pragmatists is that they ignore politics and power. Therefore, we should consider how the definition of institutions as "grounded conceptual ecologies with audiences" lends itself to thinking about politics and power. It does so in several ways. First and foremost, politics and power exert themselves through the control of concepts. We may think of this control as the power of framing and agenda setting in specific situations or, more broadly, as the ability to control the discursive field of concepts. In any case, this is consistent with thinking about the institutional process as a transactional process, because framing, agenda setting, and discursive power all control the "premises of decision" (March and Simon 1958).

Second, politics and power are refracted through the experiential basis of concepts. Power is exercised by controlling the experiential associations that people develop with concepts and by controlling the associations between concepts. But even the powerful must work through or around the matrix of historically grounded meaning that concepts have for people.[29] Powerful actors are often skillful in mobilizing these sentiments for their own purposes. But they must contend with audiences who have power to arbitrate the use and meaning of concepts. The power of audiences varies depending on their resources, organization, and unity.

The evolution of the concept "organic agriculture" offers an example of just how political and contentious processes of institutionalization and institutional change can be. In the 1930s, an international movement developed to reject the increasing reliance of farming on synthetic fertilizers and pesticides. The term "organic farming" was first coined in 1940 by a British agriculturalist, Lord Northbourne, to capture his idea that the farm is an "organism" (Johnson 2006). He argued that a farm should be managed holistically and self-sufficiently, and he contrasted organic farming with "chemical farming." In the 1960s, the counterculture movement embraced organic farming as a more "natural" relationship between humans and nature. Organic farming came to be understood as a challenge to "industrial farming," with all that it implied about large-scale production, mechanization, reliance on imported energy and chemicals, monocropping, and commodification of products.

Although organic food was originally a small niche market, market size expanded dramatically in the 1990s, setting the stage for the current battles over the meaning of the concept (Guthman 1998). As production scale expanded, organic food was increasingly produced on an industrial scale, using industrial techniques and mass marketing. After a series of food scares, consumers (one important audience) saw "organic production" as a sign of safe food, and food producers came to recognize the value conferred by the label "organic."

Marketing strategies increasingly exploited the natural image of organic food and governments stepped in to set organic standards (Pollan 2006). These standards focused on the production of food without the use of synthetic fertilizers or pesticides. Critics of these developments argue that organic food production has been industrialized and commodified and that the meaning of "organic" has been gutted. Instead of meaning a sustainable, holistic practice of farming (farm as organism), the meaning of the term "organic" has increasingly come to mean "no pesticides or synthetic fertilizers used."

The example of organic agriculture illustrates that the process of institutionalization can be a contested one that is shaped by the power of different actors to control the meaning of a concept. It also illustrates how institutional change takes shape through creation of new concepts (the concept of "organic") and through subsequent elaboration or contraction of the meaning of these concepts. The meaning of organic farming has always meant farming without synthetic fertilizers or pesticides. But for many it means something more than that—a more holistic and natural way of farming. From the perspective of this latter audience, recent consumerist trends in organic production certainly do not appear to represent evolutionary learning; they appear to erode the basic concepts and values of the organic movement.

The conclusion that evolutionary learning must be judged from the perspective of particular audiences is consistent with arguments made about "advocacy coalitions" in public policy studies. Those arguments assert that policy learning typically occurs within, but not across, advocacy coalitions (Sabatier 1988). Chapter 10 on collaborative governance will argue, however, that wider learning can be fostered by creating publics that bring stakeholders from different advocacy communities together.

Between Rational Design and Congealed Taste

To explore some of the implications of this conception of institutions, we can return to the discussion of the Janus-faced quality of institutions. Are institutions cultures or technologies or both? In some respects, this is a very old discussion. One of the founders of sociology, Max Weber, observed that tradition and modernity (*gesellschaft* and *gemeinschaft*) produced very different types of institutions. Traditional institutions are based on custom, while modern institutions are based on instrumental rationality. Yet because tradition and modernity are viewed as developmental stages, it has not always been fully appreciated how both patterns of institutionalization can be simultaneously at work in many "modern" institutions.[30] One dynamic of institutionalization is a process of increasing *context-dependence*.

Institutionalization occurs through a process of pinning down institutions in a certain local context—embedding them in local understandings and social relations. The other dynamic of institutionalization, by contrast, is a process by which institutions become increasingly *context-independent*. The influential work of John Meyers, for instance, regards the institutionalization of science as a process whereby it becomes increasingly independent of any local context (Meyer, Boli, Thomas, and Ramirez 1997).

Context-independence is equivalent to treating institutions as free-floating concepts, while context-dependence is equivalent to treating them as densely grounded in experience. Gouldner's (1955a) classic description of a gypsum plant illustrates both forms of institutionalization working at cross-purposes. He describes an "indulgency" pattern of management rooted in customary notions of work and supported by dense social relations. This highly context-dependent pattern of institutionalization creates a tangle of special social relationships, roles, and cultural practices. After the death of the chief executive "Old Doug," a new management team brings a different dynamic of institutionalization to the plant. They seek to bureaucratize the management relationship, substituting formal for informal relationships and codified rules for customary understandings. As illustrated by Gouldner, context-independent institutionalization works by destroying context-dependent institutionalization.

Pragmatism, as you might now expect, would reject the dominance of either context-independence or context-dependence. Instead, it sees evolutionary learning as a productive transaction between the local and the cosmopolitan. The introduction of the Balanced Literacy Approach into school reform in the United States offers one example of how this relationship can be productive. Balanced Literacy is a theory of learning that can be taught to teachers. As a codified method, it is independent of the context of any specific classroom. The term "balanced" is the key to understanding the method. It refers to the balance between "mutually reinforcing ways of supporting students' development as readers: reading *to* them, reading *with* them, and supporting them as they learn to read *by* themselves" (Stein, Hubbard, and Mehan 2004, 179). However, successful application of the balanced literacy approach is highly context-dependent. It requires teachers to tailor the method to specific student needs and classroom contexts, which can be difficult and require a mastery of certain skills. As Stein, Hubbard, and Mehan observe: "For most teachers, learning to implement programs such as Balanced Literacy involves shifting from a practice grounded in routine demonstrations of decontextualized, often low-level skills to a practice that incorporates improvisation within a loosely structured overall plan" (2004, 176). The production of this loosely structured improvisation actually presupposes much contextual scaffolding to be successful, as school reformers learned when they tried to extend the method from where it was successfully developed (District #2 in New York City) to a larger school district (San Diego School District).

This example points directly to a fundamental tension in contemporary institutionalism about whether institutions can be rationally designed or whether they are so intricately embedded in the historically rooted experience of particular communities ("congealed taste") that attempts to "design" them are doomed to failure. A rational design approach tends to treat institutional elements as context-independent technologies (and hence as modular units easily transported from one context to another), while the congealed taste approach sees them as thoroughly embedded in and dependent upon local cultures (and hence neither modular nor transportable). Experience with the balanced literacy approach shows that it is modular and transportable, but that successful implementation requires attending to the contextual scaffolds that support or hinder successful implantation.

Although rational choice institutionalism is the most explicit version of rational design, the assumption that institutions can be intentionally, consciously, and explicitly designed for specific purposes is widespread in the planning and policy professions (Pierson 2004). From this broader perspective, rational designs are essentially ideal forms. The assumption is that they can be described, specified, and evaluated in ways that are independent of specific contexts. It is this ability to describe institutions as ideal forms that allows the rational design approach to think about institutions as being subject to comprehensive engineering and reengineering. Design choices are understood to be synoptic: they are made at a particular moment in time and are comprehensive. An ideal form allows rational designers to conceive of how to optimize designs. Institutions are seen as concepts that exist independently of any social context. Although rational design may be quite successful, the limits of the rational design approach are suggested when we think of institutions as "congealed taste."

The congealed taste perspective also has a long history in the social sciences as well as its own popular expression.[31] It is colloquially expressed whenever someone says, "That's not the way we do it here" or when cynics call reforms like the balanced literacy approach "fads." The congealed taste perspective perceives institutions as resulting from the gradual accretion of action that establishes institutions on a habitual or customary basis. By contrast with the rational design perspective, the congealed taste perspective can scarcely conceive of institutions based in custom and habit outside of their social context. Congealed taste institutions are nearly synonymous with informal culture and tradition and part and parcel of the lifeworlds of people who inhabit them. Congealed taste institutions may be functional and they may be greatly valued, but it is difficult to conceive of them as objects of conscious design. They accrete in response to a variety of local situations and are evaluated by the test of time. They are chosen, but not designed in the sense implied by rational design, and the choice is never comprehensive or synoptic. Moreover, they are part of a skein of practices, values, and loyalties that are essential to the very meaning of the institutions. To abstract a social object from these practices, values, and loyalties is to commit an error of reification. The danger of reification is that rational designers will believe that abstract social forms are self-actualizing, when in fact they depend on values and understandings accreted historically.

Pragmatism does not reject either perspective but instead seeks to harness them together. Dewey uses the metaphor of posture to make this point. He argues that we cannot simply will ourselves to stand up straight (i.e., rational design), if we have not developed the basic set of muscles (i.e., congealed tastes) that allow us to exercise good posture. However, it is possible to consciously improve our posture (i.e., rational design) over time through the conscientious development of these basic muscles (i.e., congealed taste). This posture metaphor for dynamic institutional evolution can be taken further. Consistent with Dewey's philosophy of the environmental grounding of action, the posture metaphor suggests that higher-order skills (posture) are scaffolded by the refinement of lower-order skills (muscles). This skein of lower-order habits can easily become a constraint on higher-level performance. We can develop bad habits. Thus, the development of lower-order skills must be guided toward the achievement of higher-order purposes. They must be guided by a conscious (rational) image of posture as a desirable state. The general point of this Pragmatist perspective can be stated in terms of the metaphor of "scaffolding." First, there is upward scaffolding, in which broader and more ambitious institutional goals can be conceived and institutionalized on the scaffolding of more basic institutional competencies. And second, there is downward scaffolding, in which more general or more comprehensive concepts guide the development of specific concepts and practices.

If the rational design perspective regards institutions as subject to comprehensive, planned change, the congealed taste approach regards change as an incremental affair that lacks an overarching design. The key to the Pragmatist position is to appreciate that lower-order institutions (concepts and dispositions) become scaffolds for higher-order institutional change. Thus, a Pragmatist might be skeptical of comprehensive, planned change because it often removes existing scaffolding without introducing sufficient scaffolding to support the reformed institutional design. On the other hand, a Pragmatist might be equally skeptical of incremental change as leading to either directionless drift or to reinforcing the status quo. The Pragmatist position on institutional reform is that reformers must first build the institutional scaffolding to support more comprehensive change. To give direction to this change, however, the direction has to be envisioned (e.g., envisioning better posture), and this envisioning will occur via concepts that are somewhat independent and autonomous of existing practices. But with the end point of comprehensive change envisioned, the change strategy is approached more incrementally, building toward more comprehensive change by focusing on building up the necessary scaffolding.[32]

Institutional change in the Finnish system of labor protection inspections can partially illustrate this dynamic interaction between congealed taste and rational design. As described by Virkkunnen and Kuutti (2000), Finnish labor protection inspectors found the traditional inspection system unable to adequately cope with the task of inspecting firms (the problem). A close analysis of inspections identified the limits to inspection as arising from the individualized division of labor, where each inspector was assigned a set of firms to inspect using standardized inspection procedures. The analysis led to a rational design for a team-based inspection system to replace the individualized division of labor along with a priority-setting tool to replace the standardized inspection procedure. These new concepts were then tested in a particular context: one inspection district. But this was not the end of change, because the success of the new inspection system had to be supported by changes in management structure (new scaffolding), which in turn required a series of other institutional changes. These changes came into conflict with some of the supporting elements of the prior system of inspection (prior scaffolding). "What we see here," Virkkunnen and Kuutti write, "is not a unified learning process of an organization but interacting learning processes in a network of dependent activities" (2000, 313). Change, in this case, was a combination of the incremental and the systemic.

Conclusion

Pragmatist institutionalism has a rich heritage largely overlooked by contemporary institutionalism. Institutional economists inspired by Veblen and Commons (Hodgson 2004, 2006, 2007; Bromley 2006) continue to argue that Pragmatist philosophy and psychology provides useful foundations for institutional economics. Dewey and Mead also remain an important touchstone for symbolic interactionists (Strauss 1988; Maines 2001) and for political institutionalists (Chisholm 1995, 2001; Whitford 2002; Berk 2009; Berk and Galvan 2010). In organization theory, there is also an increasing recognition that Pragmatism offers some distinctive contributions for understanding how organizations work (Sabel 2006; Cohen 2007; Ansell 2009).

This chapter tries to provide foundations for a more extensive conversation among these groups. It argues that Pragmatist institutionalisms share at least four common premises. First, a Pragmatist institutionalism is rooted in a

Pragmatist model of social psychology. Second, a Pragmatist institutionalism understands institutional formation and change as the interpretation and elaboration of meaning. Third, a Pragmatist institutionalism understands institutional life as a dynamic "going concern." Fourth, a Pragmatist institutionalism adopts a naturalistic stance toward institutions, emphasizing "lived experience."

Another way to build a broader platform for a Pragmatist institutionalism is to begin with common definitions. This chapter argued that institutions are relationships between the symbolic artifacts that mediate social life and people's experience of those artifacts. The key symbolic artifacts are *concepts*. These concepts become institutionalized when they are *grounded* in experience, when they develop *ecological* associations with other concepts, and when *audiences* form around them. This definition of institutions as *grounded conceptual ecologies with audiences* provides a useful orienting framework for analyzing the potential for institutional evolution and learning.

Pragmatist philosophy steers us away from seeing institutions as static "things" (e.g., "objective" rules in rational choice institutionalism; "subjective" taken-for-granted beliefs in sociological institutionalism). Instead, it encourages us to think about institutions *transactionally* as dynamic, ongoing interactions between concepts, experience, and situations. This approach suggests that we can understand each institutional transaction as a form of active inquiry, which is deductive, inductive, or abductive. The abductive, hypothesis-generating aspect of inquiry adds an important element of creative action to institutionalism.

Finally, Pragmatist institutionalism rejects the extreme views that institutions are either straightforwardly the product of rational design or the result of a process of historical sedimentation. Instead, based on the definition of institutions as both conceptual and experiential, evolutionary learning arises from a dynamic tension between context-independent concepts and context-dependent experiences. From this perspective follows an emphasis on both the upward and downward *scaffolding* of institutional change. Rational designs are necessary for guiding purposeful institutional evolution, but successful design requires attention to its scaffolding by context-dependent dispositions. Thus, Pragmatist institutionalism calls attention to both the progressive and the conservative aspects of institutional change.

Excursus on a Pragmatist Definition of Institutions

This chapter advances a definition of institutions as *grounded conceptual ecologies with audiences*. This excursus unpacks this definition, providing a more detailed justification for each of its key terms.

The term "conceptual" anchors the definition. The term is used to give more specificity to the phrase "symbolic artifact." From a Pragmatist perspective, we want a term that points to how symbols are related to knowledge, inquiry, communication, cognition, categorization, and action. "Concept" is a good term for doing that. Concepts are mental representations that are abstract categories.[33] Philosophers of concepts often use examples like "dog" or "red" to illustrate concepts, but "judge" or "court" serve as better examples of how concepts might form the basis of institutions. Concepts are fundamental building blocks of knowledge and are the key element in propositional statements, including rules (if concept x, then concept y). Mead called propositions that mediate social interaction "social maxims" and he liked to use the rules of baseball as an illustration—for example, "four balls and you walk" (Athens 2005, 312). "Balls" and "walks" are concepts that create a rule when linked together.

It is common in contemporary institutionalism to equate institutions with rules. "Concept," however, better captures the communicational and constitutive role of institutions than does "rule."[34] Concept also better captures the "categorical" nature of institutions, as described by Mary Douglas (1986), and the central role of institutions in *naming*. Institutions start as named objects, to which more complex propositions like rules are then attached. It is difficult to imagine central bank rules without first naming the "European Central Bank."

"Concept" is also more elemental than "discourse" or "narrative," which are typically complex bundles of concepts. But like these terms, "concept" calls attention to the linguistic aspects of institutions. It is through this linguistic (or Peirce would say "semiotic") view of institutions that we understand how they are linked to meaning and interpretation. Concepts enter into our communication and reasoning.[35] Thus, understanding institutions as concepts, and not simply as habits or rules, allows us to appreciate how institutions become part our reflexive intelligence.[36]

A concept itself is not an institution. A concept that mediates social interaction becomes institutionalized when it becomes *grounded* in concrete human experience. Concepts are grounded to the extent that there is an accumulation of emotions, values, meanings, and habits oriented toward them or triggered by them. An experiential view sees institutions as products of concrete historical events; institutions are "inhabited" or "lived in." Note that the definition of institutions advanced here does not define them in terms of habit, as do some Pragmatists. As learned behaviors, habits are a critical aspect of institutions, but the term "habit" is too narrow to define institutions. Experience is a wider term, around which James, Dewey, and Mead developed a considerable philosophical framework.[37] However, consistent with the idea of habit, we can refer to the action-oriented attitude that derives from experience as "dispositions," a term that Dewey often used interchangeably with the term "habit."

Given their past experience (accumulated emotions, values, meanings, and attitudes), people have a disposition to interpret concepts and situations in a particular way in the present. A "disposition" implies a nondeterministic tendency to respond in a particular way.[38]

Institutions are grounded in a second sense. Dispositions link concepts to specific situations and hence to particular contexts. The meaning of a concept is not inherent in the concept itself or in the object it represents (Gabora, Rosch, and Aerts 2008). Nor can an institution be fully described by the generic dispositions associated with a concept, though this may be a reasonable and useful approximation. Rather, consistent with a Pragmatist view of action, dispositions are triggered or "fixed" (to use Peirce's term) by other contextual information.[39] Hence, we can say that an institution is really an interaction between concepts, dispositions, and situations. A certain disposition toward a social concept is invoked by a certain situation. From a Pragmatist perspective, a *problematic* situation (for Peirce, a situation of doubt) leads to reflection on both concepts and dispositions.

To focus on how institutions are concepts *and* experiences is to try to overcome a deeply rooted dualism. Put in the language of cognitive science, the Pragmatist definition of institutions advanced here is both representational (conceptual) and associational (aggregating upward from sensory experience).[40] To put it in the language of epistemology, it is both rational (stressing the importance of a priori concepts) and empirical (concepts as generalizations from sensory experience). Some paradigms similar in spirit to Pragmatism, like ethnomethodology and some versions of cognitive science, see action as preconceptual (Garfinkel 1967; Suchman 1987).[41] But Dewey's model of action emphasizes the interaction between the experiential and the conceptual.[42]

Finally, institutions are *ecological* in the sense that grounded concepts form patterned relationships. Socially mediating concepts do not exist in isolation, but in broader ecologies of concepts and experience from which they take part of their significance and function and through which they create human environments. The term "ecological" implies that institutions are bundles of grounded concepts that exist in some interdependent relationship with one another. The term is largely interchangeable with the term "institutional field," though "ecology" calls more attention to relationships while "field" calls attention to the landscape.[43]

One of the important implications of an ecological perspective is that it focuses our attention on the intersections and interpenetrations of social life. In their important work on "boundary objects," Star and Griesemer (1989) advocate an ecological perspective on institutions. As they point out, one of the advantages of an ecological perspective is that it allows us to focus on the intersecting character of social worlds. An ecological perspective also suggests that we think about institutions as *embedded* in at least three specific senses. First, webs of grounded concepts typically develop within specific spatial-temporal environments (which, however, are not easily bounded by space or time).[44] Second, an ecological approach means that the formation of new institutions typically assumes and builds on the existence of other institutions. Thus, any use of a particular concept typically invokes and depends on the existence of other concepts. The concept "court" often depends on the concepts of "judge," "lawyer," and "law." Third, an ecological approach suggests that the use of institutions will link a specific set of people together (recall the point that institutions are "inhabited").

Finally, an "institution" is not simply a bilateral relationship between person and concept or even simply an interaction between two persons mediated by a concept. Pragmatism's triadic logic suggests the importance of third parties—*audiences*. An audience is the collective third party that looks on as a person uses or evokes the meaning of a concept. The idea of "institutional audience" builds on Mead's discussion of the "generalized other," in which socialization occurs when people "take the perspective of others." Though the audience may be a silent partner in any transaction, it can become an arbiter in the ongoing attempt of parties to create intersubjective alignment around concepts. The audience's role as arbiter is crucial for understanding what the Weberian tradition calls "legitimacy." An audience with a strong disposition toward a particular interpretation will bestow a strong legitimacy effect. However, just as there is no presumption here that an institution is based on shared values and meanings, there is no presumption that audiences are monolithic or that they will converge on the same dispositions. Conflict in institutional transactions may be reinforced and sustained when the parties take the perspective of others with different expectations.

CHAPTER 3

Large-Scale Institutional Change

Chapter 2 argued that institutions are a critical medium of evolutionary learning. Institutions are collective frameworks that retain the lessons of past experience and orient us to current problems. They express and shape our fundamental cultural commitments as communities and are tools for addressing the social and political problems we confront. The last chapter envisioned evolutionary learning as the ability to subject our institutions to the test of new problematic situations, revising and elaborating them so that they can be more skillfully used. The previous chapter, however, said nothing about the scale of institutions in question. Although it is relatively easy to imagine institutional learning occurring on a small scale, is it possible to imagine evolutionary learning on a much grander scale?

Evolutionary learning on a grand scale might be conceived of as the aggregation and accumulation of many small-scale institutional changes. Indeed, this is the Darwinian view of natural evolution, as well as the perspective of incrementalism in the social sciences (Lindblom 1959). This is an attractive position, because small-scale changes are often more politically manageable and realistic than large-scale changes. However, the success of incremental change is often significantly constrained by the larger institutional contexts in which it occurs.[1] As critics have suggested, incremental change often merely reinforces the status quo or leads to directionless drift. While Pragmatism certainly supports the value of continuous small-scale learning, large-scale institutional change may often be necessary for evolutionary learning to advance.

Large-scale institutional change is more often explained by "punctuated equilibrium" than by gradualism. Wars, natural disasters, major economic crises, or revolutions provide the external shocks necessary to disrupt old institutional patterns. New institutions are formed in the vacuum created by these shocks. Incremental change reigns during non-crisis periods, while more far-reaching and fundamental change only becomes possible during periodic crises (Baumgartner and Jones 1993). This dichotomy of incremental and punctuated change seems to capture much of our experience with institutional change. The goal here is not to deny this dichotomy.[2] Rather, just as the last chapter explored the terrain between "congealed taste" and "rational design," this chapter explores the possibility for more positive interaction between incremental and large-scale institutional change.

Evolutionary learning on a grand scale depends on such mutually supportive interactions between incremental and large-scale institutional change. If incremental change is to be anything but directionless, it must be cumulative—it must add up to something. This accumulation must be guided by large-scale institutions. Yet large-scale institutions are notoriously inertial. Only incremental changes that support the status quo are selected. Learning, therefore, may take place within an existing institutional framework while the overarching framework is itself inertial. By contrast, evolutionary learning on a grand scale requires a situation where large-scale institutions can guide the accumulation of small-scale changes but where these incremental changes can also drive large-scale institutional change forward.

In *Mountains beyond Mountains*, Tracy Kidder's (2009) biography of Dr. Paul Farmer, we find a powerful example of a positive interaction between small-scale and large-scale institutional change. In the early 1990s, the World Health Organization (WHO) was conducting a major campaign to control tuberculosis (TB) using a powerful treatment protocol known as DOTS, which stood for "directly observed short-course chemotherapy." This treatment protocol was institutionalized on a global scale and the program had begun to achieve impressive results. As Farmer learned in local clinics in Haiti and Peru, however, a negative side-effect of DOTS was that it produced drug resistance to multiple TB drugs in some patients (multiple drug resistance or MDR). To the extent that the DOTS establishment acknowledged the link between DOTS and MDR, they regarded it as an unfortunate but untreatable byproduct of a very valuable public health program. Concerned by the growing number of MDR cases, Farmer and his colleagues conducted a small-scale experiment in Peru to demonstrate that people with MDR were effectively treatable. The experiment demonstrated that MDR patients could be successfully treated. Pressing their findings in international forums on TB, Farmer and his colleagues ultimately succeeded in getting the WHO to modify its treatment recommendations. The revised program was dubbed "DOTS-plus" and, after drug prices were brought down, the new WHO regimen included treatment for MDR.

As Kidder's book makes clear, this process of change was neither smooth nor conflict-free. But, on the whole, the revision of the DOTS drug protocol represented movement toward a more effective global treatment for TB.

Learning had occurred. This chapter will explore the idea that positive interaction between local experimentation and large-scale institutional change is the basis for evolutionary learning on a grand scale. This interaction is conceived of as a "constitutional process," a metaphor that captures the multilevel character of this interaction and the development of institutional publics. The chapter concludes with an examination of whether the movement for sustainable development can be described as such a process.

Institutional Change as a Constitutional Process

The image of a constitutional process is an apt metaphor for a dynamic, multilevel image of institutional evolution and learning. A constitution is typically a set of meta-norms that guide and constrain more fundamental practices and actions (in the TB example, DOTS is a meta-norm). Meta-norms are often quite general, expressing generic ideas, values, or guidelines. Because of their generality, their application to specific cases may be ambiguous and often requires interpretation. Events and issues will arise that test the meaning of meta-norms (MDR challenges DOTS), leading to a body of interpretation that elaborates and specifies how these ideas, values, or guidelines are to be applied in specific cases. If meta-norms are taken seriously, they will have real consequences for specific applications (much to Farmer's chagrin, the DOTS protocol was strictly observed at the local level). However, it is not always obvious how meta-norms should be applied to specific cases. In those cases, local action may establish critical precedents for constitutional interpretation.

As a metaphor for institutional evolution and learning, a constitutional process describes a continuous coevolution between meta-norms and concrete local action (DOTS → Farmer's Peruvian Experiment → DOTS-plus). The metaphor also implies the existence of a public that is concerned about the body of interpretation that develops around meta-norms. Consistent with the Pragmatist idea of institutions as "going concerns," a public is a collective bound together by thick communication and joint deliberation about means and ends (e.g., the international medical community working on TB). A public communicates or deliberates against the backdrop of an informed and engaged audience.

This ongoing public deliberation about meta-norms and their application to specific cases is a good model for institutional evolution and learning. A constitutional process is an ongoing negotiation about the meaning of particular concepts and their use.[3] Such processes may be cooperative or conflictual. In a cooperative constitutional process, participants align the meanings that they attribute to a concept in order to coordinate their behaviors. In a competitive constitutional process, participants seek to strategically bind others to particular precedential meanings. Whether cooperative or conflictual, the important point is that people remain bound together as a going concern—mutually concerned about the meanings of concepts without necessarily agreeing on the foundational meaning of those concepts.[4] A highly developed public will care about the consistency, coherence, and integrity of its meta-norms. It will be concerned about not only how to uphold the values inherent in existing meta-norms but also how to apply and learn from the application of these meta-norms to new situations.

The image of institutions as constitutional processes has many implications for studying institutional evolution. Selznick, for example, has argued that the constitutionalization of institutions leads them to develop a code of rights, laws, and self-government. Selznick summarizes his perspective as follows:

> In *Law, Society, and Industrial Justice* (1969) I studied institutionalization in a context I thought should be of special interest to the sociology of law, which had become my main preoccupation. I showed how the bureaucratic character of the large firm encourages managerial self-restraint and the recognition of employee rights. Here institutionalization takes the form of "legalization," understood as infusing a mode of governance with the constraints and aspiration of a legal order. The outcome is "private government" and, with it, something akin to the rule of law. (Selznick 1996, 272)

From Selznick's perspective, constitutionalization occurs when an institution gradually develops a series of meta-rules to govern itself internally.[5] Charles Sabel (1999) has developed a similar kind of constitutional perspective to describe organizations. He contrasts "constitutional orders" to markets and hierarchies and suggests that constitutional orders are composed of "constituent units" and a "superintendent." As the metaphor of national constitutions suggests, and as the perspectives of both Selznick and Sabel imply, a constitution is a higher-order process that both governs and responds to lower-order processes. Learning occurs through the formation of meta-norms that can guide local action in a consistent and responsive fashion, but local action can also produce a revision and refinement of meta-norms.

Both Selznick and Sabel are talking about constitutional processes at the scale of a single organization. But we can imagine something like a constitutional process operating on a much larger institutional scale—a policy sector, an entire infrastructure, or even global governance. Building on the definition of institutions as grounded conceptual ecologies, we can think of large-scale constitutional processes as taking shape around "meta-concepts"—higher-order concepts that guide local action. These concepts may interact with much more localized "experiments" that put part or all of the meta-concept to test. If successful experiments diffuse and proliferate, broader publics may develop that can then support the further refinement and elaboration of the meta-concept. This process of interaction between meta-concepts, local experiments, and the development of publics may ultimately culminate in large-scale institutional change.

Before describing this constitutional process in more detail, the next section introduces the idea of meta-concepts and investigates their power to catalyze large-scale institutional change.

Meta-Concepts

George Herbert Mead is known for his theory that the "self" develops in relation to the construction of a "generalized other" that symbolically represents the perspective of the broader community. Analogously, dynamic institutional evolution can take shape around a meta-concept or meta-concepts.[6] Just as the self develops in relation to the generalized other, local institutional action can take shape in reference to meta-concepts. Meta-concepts are powerful because publics can form around them. They are often ambiguous, however, because like Mead's generalized other, they can operate at a high level of generality. They often do not specify practices in detail and in this sense they can be relatively decontextualized.

Ansell (1997, 2001) showed how the general strike became a symbol that nineteenth-century French labor unions rallied around. The meaning of the general strike was not empty, but it was highly multivocal. Different working-class audiences read different meanings into the general strike. Despite the ambiguity, alignment of unions around this meta-concept led to a dramatic realignment of working-class institutions—transforming a fragmented union movement into a much more unified movement. As a meta-concept, the general strike helped to create a new public that became the basis for a new institutional order.

More contemporary examples are readily available. In fact, scratch below the surface of nearly any contemporary policy area and you will find various "meta-concepts" at work. "Community policing" is a good example. Though there are ongoing disputes about what it means, community policing has been gradually institutionalized. Oliver (2000) describes the first phase of community policing between 1979 and 1986 as a period of "innovation." Large police departments conducted a series of experiments and demonstration projects with foot patrols, community substations, and problem-solving strategies that came to be grouped under the meta-concept "community policing." The period

1987 through 1994 was then a period of "diffusion," in which the concept of community policing diffused rapidly through the police community, touching 8,000 police departments by 1994 and 13,000 by 1996. During this period, Oliver argues that the meaning of the concept itself expanded to cover a wider range of practices and came to indicate a more thoroughgoing revision of the traditional policing paradigm. After 1994, Oliver argues that community policing entered an "institutionalization" phase. During this phase, federal, state, and local grant programs developed to encourage the implementation of community policing in both urban and rural departments.

Nearly every policy area has a concept like "community policing" that comes along and leads to a shift in the institutional paradigm. Opponents see these meta-concepts as faddish and hollow; proponents see them as promising to correct all the ills of the previous institutional regime. Some meta-concepts never take off; others fizzle out quickly. They sometimes function as a form of "symbolic politics," masking business-as-usual, but they sometimes fundamentally reorient business. Whatever the career of specific meta-concepts like community policing, they are often the focus of a constitutional process that mediates and expresses how publics think about their own basic commitments and practices. To understand their constitutive role, we can examine some of the properties that make them powerful mechanisms of social mediation.

META-CONCEPTS AS BOUNDARY OBJECTS

Meta-concepts often act like "boundary objects." Star and Griesemer developed the concept of boundary objects to explore patterns of coordination in complex institutional ecologies. They define boundary objects as "objects which are both plastic enough to adapt to local needs and the constraints of the several parties employing them, yet robust enough to maintain a common identity across sites" (1989, 393). The boundary objects are used to align meaning across intersecting but semiautonomous social worlds.[7] Carlile (2002) distinguishes among the syntactical, semantic, and pragmatic features of successful boundary objects. Syntactically, he writes, a boundary object "establishes a shared syntax or language for individuals to represent their knowledge." Semantically, it "provides a concrete means for individuals to specify and learn about their difference and dependencies across a given boundary." Pragmatically, a boundary object can facilitate "a process where individuals can jointly transform their knowledge" (451–452).

The boundary object idea helps us to understand how processes of institutionalization can do two things simultaneously. First, boundary objects facilitate communication and interaction across boundaries. Second, boundary objects maintain a space for "localized, embedded, and invested" practice

(Carlile 2002). Recalling the argument that a Pragmatist institutionalism emphasizes the ability to move back and forth between decontextualization and contextualization, we see that boundary objects facilitate just this kind of transaction. Community policing, for example, was able to mediate between the contextual embeddedness of specific police departments and the wider community of national and international policing. Meta-concepts that operate as boundary objects in this way can help to generate an emerging public or galvanize a latent public that becomes the basis for a highly dynamic pattern of institutional evolution.

Wilson and Herndl (2007) describe the way that boundary objects can transform "demarcation" events (boundary work demarcating different communities) into "exchange" events (trading zones where people work out the commensurability of their commitments). Yet there are serious constraints on the ability of boundary objects to facilitate this communication. Sapsed and Salter (2004) argue that when interdependence is limited, the boundary object will be marginal to the activity of each decentralized unit. Moreover, they point out that boundary objects will fail if they become a form of unilateral control of one unit over others, because that leads the controlled unit to evade the boundary object. "[A] boundary objects stands or falls," they write, "on its capacity to accommodate local 'dialects.'"[8] D'Adderio's (2004) study of software systems usage shows that product and database structures failed to perform as boundary objects because they did not flexibly allow localization. Virtual prototyping technologies, by contrast, worked as effective boundary objects because of their plasticity, encouraging cycles of local to global exchange. In this successful case, tools developed as a common platform were "reappropriated" by local design groups, eliciting their tacit input into the codified product definition and enabling engineering benefits downstream. The translation routines between the global and the local helped to coordinate the diverse communities of practice.

A successful meta-concept, however, is more than simply a good boundary object. It also tends to entail a "soft" teleology.

META-CONCEPTS AS TELEOLOGY

In classical Aristotelian philosophy, teleology is a form of explanation that attributes causation to "final" causes rather than to "mechanical" (proximate) causes. An acorn grows into an oak tree because that is its destiny and it is programmed to do so, not because of the soil, water, and sun that are the proximate causes of growth. Although modern social science tends to be deeply suspicious of teleological explanation, "goal-directed" behavior is sometimes understood as teleological, with a goal being the "final cause" that explains the behavior of actors. Charles Peirce, for example, took this position (Hulswit 1996). Following Peirce, Bromley distinguishes between "mechanical" and "final" causes in explaining institutional change. A mechanical cause means judging potential institutional change in terms of the present, whereas a final cause means to judge it in terms of where you want to be in the future (2006, 13).

Peirce had a very specific view of how "goals" operated as final causes. Goals are general rather than concrete. They are not concrete future events. As Hulswit writes of Peirce's view of teleology: "The final cause is not a concrete thing, but it is a type, a mere possibility; it is nothing but an ideal end state which a process tends toward" (Hulswit 1996, 186). Cooper describes Peirce's view of teleology as akin to an "attractor" in modern complexity theory (2008, 754).[9] This idea of an attractor is also implicit in James's view of attention as having a teleological function. According to James, concepts are a "teleological weapon of the mind" (Bourdeaux 1972, 340). Dewey built on James's idea that the process of conceptualizing was teleological.[10] Meta-concepts are equivalent to what Dewey called "ends-in-view" and teleological in that sense (Garrison 2001). Pragmatism adopts a "soft" teleology that must be distinguished from the more essentialist Aristotelian interpretation.

Successful meta-concepts typically have a teleological element: they set up an attraction toward some ideal end state. In talking about another fashionable policing concept—Compstat—Firman gives us a glimpse of the teleological quality of "community policing":

> The publicity about Compstat in many ways parallels the early days of community oriented policing. Who would not want to work closely with the community? Now, who would not want to address management and problem solving in such an innovative manner? In policing, and many other professions, this kind of "buzz," often in advance of measurable outcomes, helps programs and ideas move rapidly into the field. (2003, 457)

As multivocal boundary objects that set up a "soft" teleology, meta-concepts can often serve as a powerful rallying point and banner for large-scale institutional change.

Large-Scale Institutional Change as a Constitutional Process

Now let's draw these ideas together to describe large-scale institutional change. The first point is that we want to draw an analogy between large-scale institutional change and constitutional processes. Meta-concepts represent the cosmopolitan level of this constitutional process, while local experiments represent the local level. A constitutional process is an ongoing interaction over time between meta-concepts and local experiments. These interactions can produce change by linking people together in new, sometimes crosscutting networks and by creating and expanding publics. Large-scale institutional change occurs when networks and public are reinforcing and expanding. Figure 1 provides a graphical summary of these ideas.

Large-scale institutional change is typically not "designed." There will be advocates and entrepreneurs who push change forward, but no synoptic designer (Schickler 2001). Instead, large-scale institutional change will result from many projects and goals converging to produce change. Meta-concepts often become the touchstone that guides this plurality of projects and goals in a common direction. The boundary-spanning and multivocal quality of meta-concepts helps to knit different projects and goals together. Early in an episode of large-scale institutional change, the ambiguous quality of meta-concepts is an advantage because it enables them to have a wide appeal. The soft teleology inherent in meta-concepts becomes a banner that temporarily unites the marginalized and disgruntled forces internal to the existing institutional ecology with new allies outside it.

We can imagine several different types of contexts in which meta-concepts are likely to guide large-scale institutional change:

1. Institutional "greenfields": Sometimes, new spaces for institutionalization are opened up by technological change, by the creation of new alliances, through the recognition of new problems, or by the creation of a new policy arena. In institutional greenfields, there is no struggle against the existing institutional ecology for recognition and legitimacy.
2. Institutional "brownfields": More often, however, projects for large-scale change are hatched within or at the margins of existing institutional ecologies and they must then typically confront resistance from those insti-

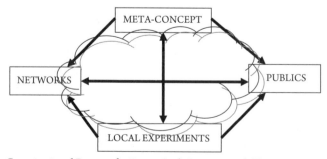

Figure 1. Constitutional Process for Large-Scale Institutional Change.

tutions. We can imagine at least four types of outcomes that result from large-scale institutional change projects in this context:

(a) *Failure*: New ideas and institutions come and go and most of them probably fail.

(b) *Syncretism*: New ideas and institutions are absorbed by, integrated with, or layered on top of existing ideas and institutions (Orren and Skowronek 1994; Schickler 2001; Berk 2009; Berk and Galvan 2010).

(c) *Realignment*: New ideas and institutions lead to a reorganization of the existing institutional ecology (Ansell 1997, 2001).

(d) *Parallelism*: New ideas and institutions are established outside of and independent of existing institutional ecologies.

In both institutional greenfields and brownfields, it is common to see change occur through this interaction between the very general and the very specific. In the greenfield case, this is because many things are possible, but there is little prior structure upon which to build. Therefore, guiding ideas are likely to be quite underspecified, and structuration will gradually take shape through specific efforts. In the brownfield case, the interaction of cosmopolitan and local occurs because change tends to develop at the margins of existing institutions. The institutional powers-that-be will only accept change at the margins, with innovation limited to small experiments or with experiments arising only where local conditions or problems are most conducive to change.

The relationship between meta-concepts and local experiments runs in both directions. Meta-concepts often arise in the first place out of local experiments, as they did in the case of community policing. However, once meta-concepts have been articulated, they can rarely be implemented whole cloth. Instead, groups experiment with the application of these concepts, usually in a very local way and then, if the local experiments are successful, perhaps in a more ambitious way. Experiments are important because they can provide local "proofs of concept." As local experiments proliferate, they often do so under different local conditions and for different motives. The meta-concept is the boundary object around which local experiments accumulate and knowledge and experience is shared.

How does large-scale institutional change gather steam? The metaphor of institutional change as a constitutional process calls attention to the interaction between top-down processes and bottom-up processes. As described in chapter 2, we need to be attentive to the way that small-scale changes provide the scaffolding for larger-scale changes. In the example of TB, the demonstration of effective treatment of multidrug resistant TB in a small experiment in Peru ultimately prompted the revision of the World Health Organization's drug treatment protocol. Yet we also need to be attentive to the way that the revision and elaboration of meta-concepts provides top-down scaffolding for subsequent experimentation. The WHO's adoption of DOTS-plus was not the end of the TB story but rather a platform for a new round of experimentation. So both bottom-up scaffolding and top-down scaffolding are necessary to support large-scale institutional change.

Two types of interaction between top-down and bottom-up processes are probably essential for large-scale institutional change: networks and audiences. Networks that link particular people and groups together provide the political backbone for large-scale institutional change. Both meta-concepts and local experiments shape these networks. The bridging and multivocal character of meta-concepts facilitates bringing people together in new ways. However, they bring people together around an abstract idea. Local experiments are a powerful source of realigning potential, because they bring people and groups together more concretely under the banner of a meta-concept. From a political standpoint, "experiments" are often an acceptable way to permit innovation and they may allow temporary realignments in established networks. If experiments fail, they often tarnish the promise of meta-concepts. But if they succeed, they may reinforce these new networks, which can become the basis for more ambitious experiments.

Institutional change can also gather steam by expanding the audience for reform. The audience for local experiments may be quite narrow and only include those who are involved in it or affected by it. A successful experiment, however, can often create a wider audience. Consider the experiment in participatory budgeting in Porte Alegre, Brazil. This experiment has become iconic around the world for those advocating more participatory or collaborative strategies of policymaking. Local experiments and meta-concepts often interact to widen audiences. Wider audiences are often only interested in local developments if they can be interpreted as events of general interest. Meta-concepts serve this "framing" role. Audiences also lose interest in broad-change ideas unless evidence emerges for their potential. This interaction between meta-concept and local experiment can widen the receptive audience, leading to diffusion of experimentation.

Networks and audiences can reinforce each other. Wider audiences may support local network realignments, providing them with the legitimacy and perhaps resources to conduct local experiments. Local network realignments may help to consolidate local audiences that are receptive to the lessons learned in other locales. Wider audiences, however, can also dampen enthusiasm for institutional change if they judge local experiments a failure or undesirable. Therefore, in the formative period of large-scale institutional change, we will often see groups trying to establish wider networks with more receptive audiences. Wider audiences and more expansive network connections are created in order to support innovation. The broad banner of a meta-concept, such as community policy or participatory budgeting, can help to link these distributed efforts together in a common cause.

By putting meta-concepts into practice, local experiments will link the meta-concept to specific secondary concepts, which may be either new or existing concepts. As networks and audiences reinforce one another, a public may begin to emerge that is capable of deliberating about these concepts. As a result, the meta-concept may become less ambiguous in meaning and a codified body of knowledge, practice, and experience may develop around it. As the meta-concept becomes more specified, some of the original audience may lose interest or even turn against the idea. Or a fracturing may occur, with competing publics developing competing interpretations of an idea. If audiences decline, or become marginalized, the meta-concept will probably be seen as a passing fad. If strong publics develop around the meta-concept, then institutional change can develop in a parallel, syncretic, or realigning fashion, depending on the resistance and power of existing institutional ecologies and on whether new networks and publics conform to or cut across existing alignments.

Certainly not every new meta-concept that comes along will be judged as progress. Most large-scale institutional change will undermine someone's cherished beliefs and values. But evolutionary learning on a societal scale is probably not possible without large-scale institutional change. To illustrate this point, and to demonstrate the utility of this model of large-scale institutional change, the last section of this chapter examines the institutionalization of the idea of "sustainable development."

Sustainable Development

The term "sustainable development" is clearly a powerful slogan. But standing between the slogan and real consequences lies "mountains beyond mountains" of institutional challenges. For development to become sustainable, nations, firms, and other social institutions often have to fundamentally transform their way of doing business. In fact, the slogan imagines institutional change on the largest scale possible, seeking to fundamentally realign how the forces of economic production and consumption relate to the goals of environmental protection. An examination of the trajectory of this concept of sustainable development as a constitutional process illuminates both the possibilities and the challenges of large-scale institutional change.

"Sustainable development" exemplifies the idea of a meta-concept. By any measure, it is a blockbuster concept that has changed the way we think and talk about the relationship between economic development and environmental protection. At the same time, doubts persist about whether sustainable development has been fully institutionalized or about whether it has really transformed practices of development or environmental protection (Tarlock 2001). The concept first emerged out of a series of overlapping debates and discussions that began in the late 1960s.[11] According to Kidd (1992), the term "sustainability" first appeared as an important theme in a 1972 book, *Blueprint for Survival*, and in the *1972 Yearbook of the International Union for the Conservation of Nature*. The concept then appeared in a number of books during the later 1970s. In 1976, the term "sustainable yields" was used in the U.S. Magnuson Act of 1976 to refer to the capacity of ecosystems to maintain fishery yields. However, scholars generally agree that the critical watershed for the concept of sustainable development was the 1987 report by the World Commission on Environment and Development, *Our Common Future*, chaired by Gro Harlem Brundtland (Mebratu 1998; Aguirre 2002; Jordan 2008).[12]

As a meta-concept, sustainable development has some important properties. First, it clearly operates as a boundary object. Part of the power of this concept is that it creates a bridge between environmental protection and economic development—two concepts in sharp conflict, particularly in the developing world (Boehmer 2002; Robinson 2004, 370). As Lafferty writes, the Brundtland report "made a conscious effort . . . to conceptually link (and morally bind) environment *and* development" (1999, 123). In fact, Robinson observes that "[t]he term 'sustainable development' has been seen by some as amounting to a contradiction in terms, between the opposing imperatives of growth and development, on the one hand, and ecological (and perhaps social and economic) sustainability on the other" (2004, 369–370).

A second property of this meta-concept is its multivocality. As formulated by the Brundtland report, sustainable development was clearly not a "plan" for action. Scholars universally point to the vagueness of sustainable development as a concept (Mebratu 1998, 502–503). And Robinson observes that "[o]ne of the most striking characteristics of the term sustainable development is that it means so many different things to so many different people and organizations" (2004, 373). Harding agrees: "We seem unable to agree on exactly what sustainability means and how the concept should be interpreted in particular situations" (2006, 229).

Scholars, however, also note that this ambiguity has been fruitful.[13] Robinson writes that the term profits from "constructive ambiguity" (2004, 374). Kates, Parris, and Leiserowitz call the definition of sustainable development "creatively ambiguous":

Each definitional attempt is an important part of an ongoing dialogue. In fact, sustainable development draws much of its resonance, power, and creativity from its very ambiguity. The concrete challenges of sustainable development are at least as heterogeneous and complex as the diversity of human societies and natural ecosystems around the world. As a concept, its malleability allows it to remain an open, dynamic, and evolving idea that can be adapted to fit these very different situations and contexts across space and time. (2005, 20)

Aguirre writes that "[s]ustainable development is an umbrella concept, a flag around which different constituencies can rally. It is a very useful symbol, like liberty or democracy, around which a number of interpretations are possible" (2002, 106).

Despite this ambiguity, sustainable development generates enthusiasm because, like "community policing," it establishes a soft teleology that invokes an emotional response. Aguirre describes the "enthusiastic endorsement of scientists" despite the lack of any consensus among them about what it means (2002, 109). Levy and Wissenburg argue that sustainable development is a "policy telos," which they define as "shared conceptions giving direction to cooperative political ventures" (2004, 786).

Building on these features of bridging, multivocality, and soft teleology, the idea of sustainable development has captured a wide audience. It has generated a discursive public around the idea of balancing economic development and environmental protection by encouraging a significant debate about what it means to be sustainable.[14] As Sneddon, Howarth, and Norgaard observe of the original Brundtland report:

> *Our Common Future* marked, anchored, and guided the rise of a remarkable political debate, indeed a whole new political discourse across contesting interests, from grounded practitioners to philosophical academics, from indigenous peoples to multinational corporations. It is clear it is a contested concept. But it becomes a touchstone for further development. At the very least, the staying power of SD can be explained by its propensity for providing some common ground for discussion among a range of development and environmental actors who are frequently at odds. (2006, 254)

Instead of producing convergence on clear definitions, diffusion has led to a proliferation of interpretations and definitions.[15] The concept of sustainability has also created endless riffs on the common theme, as exemplified by the proliferation of "sustainable" as an adjective: sustainable construction, sustainable mineral development, sustainable tourism, sustainable forestry, the sustainable city. The list goes on and on.

The ability of the concept of sustainable development to play these roles faces real limits. The multivocal quality of the concept can foster creativity, but if it is too multivocal it can become meaningless.[16] A meta-concept can also easily die if dialogue becomes too polarized. In the case of sustainable development, there is an ongoing threat of repolarization around the different priorities of development and environmental protection. Vogler, for example, notes that the Johannesburg Conference confirmed a trend that began with the Rio Conference to emphasize the socioeconomic pillars of sustainable development over the environmental pillars (2007, 438).

The ability of a meta-concept to induce dialogue depends on both sides of the dialogue treating it as an accepted point of reference, while arguing about its precise meaning. Sustainable development is a powerful contested concept because it binds people who might ultimately be ignoring each other into a conversation. However, dialogue is undercut if one side rejects the concept altogether and poses an alternative concept. There is, indeed, a vocal minority of people who reject the concept of sustainable development altogether. They reject the idea that both environmental protection and economic development can ever be compatible goals.

Whether sustainable development remains a "robust" concept or is added to the dustbin of conceptual history will depend on how it is put into practice. If the concept of sustainable development can become a guide to concrete action, then it may be "sustainable." However, if it fails to guide local action, it will gradually lose meaning and ultimately be replaced. The evidence is, in fact, mixed, which suggests both the potential and the limits of institutional evolution.

There is little doubt that the concept of sustainable development spread internationally at an enormous speed, becoming a point of reference for powerful organizations and governments like the World Bank and the European Union (Boehmer-Christiansen 2002; Baker 2007; European Commission 2007).[17] Many institutions, like the World Bank, rapidly adopted explicit references to sustainable development in their policy documents (Goodland 1995, 9). Sustainable development has encouraged an ever-expanding institutionalization (Vogler 2007).[18] Sneddon, Howarth, and Norgaard observe that "the concept is now firmly entrenched within many government offices, corporate boardrooms, and the hallways of international NGOs and financial institutions" (2006, 259). Even Aguirre (2002), who views the rapid diffusion of sustainable development ideas as a fad, admits that it has achieved a significant level of institutionalization.[19]

Many, however, have noted an implementation gap with sustainable development (Harding 2006; Sneddon, Howarth, and Norgaard 2006; Volkery et al. 2006; Jordan 2008). Meadowcroft puts this implementation gap into perspective:

Information collected by the UN Division for Sustainable Development . . . indicated that just over a third of all countries had at least initiated the development of SD strategies by the end of 2003. With almost 70 states reporting some activity, the phenomenon is not insignificant. On the other hand, evidence suggests that even when SD strategy processes get underway, they typically remain marginal to the core activities of government and to the real exercise of political and administrative power. (2007, 153)

Although implementation progress may be limited, we do see the fairly extensive development of specific principles for development of National Sustainable Development Plans (NSDPs) (George and Kirkpatrick 2006). Even in Europe, however, where enthusiasm has been strongest, implementation of NSDPs has often lacked high-level political support (Steurer and Martinuzzi 2005).

The development of an important global sustainable development program, Local Agenda 21, helps to further illustrate both the possibilities and limits for sustainable development as a process of large-scale institutional change. After the publication of *Our Common Future* in 1987, the world community met in 1992 in Rio de Janeiro for the "Earth Summit." One of the products of that meeting was an ambitious set of goals dubbed "Agenda 21" ("21" standing for the twenty-first century). One of the most important features of Agenda 21 was a process known as Local Agenda 21 (or LA 21), which envisioned local governments as critical agents for moving the sustainable development agenda forward. The LA 21 encouraged communities to mobilize around bottom-up strategic planning processes in order to create local action plans for sustainable development.

In many respects, LA 21 exemplifies the idea of large-scale institutional change as a constitutional process. Local Agenda 21 recommended quite general goals and procedures to guide strategic planning processes, but local implementation was quite experimental (Freeman 1996; Selman 1998; Mercer and Jotkowitz 2000; Yanarella and Bartilow 2000; Feichtinger and Pregernig 2005).[20] Even local governments within the same country interpreted these processes and the meaning of sustainable development in quite different ways (Gibbs, Longhurst, and Braithwaite 1998; Mercer and Jotkowitz 2000). Local Agenda 21 spread rapidly, but unevenly, around the world.[21] This diffusion created many local learning processes, loosely linked together by various regional, national, and international networks operating under the banner of the global LA 21 process.[22]

In trying to put the general goals and procedures of LA 21 into practice, local authorities had to develop their own concepts and ideas about sustainable development. A local leader of the Agenda 21 process in the city of Leicester in the United Kingdom wrote of the experience:

It is fair to say that we experienced some difficulty in defining precisely what is meant by the phrase "sustainable development." In Leicester, in the past decade, considerable time has been spent reflecting on definitions of sustainable development, deriving policies and principles linked to it and formulating action plans. (Roberts 2000, 10)

Local learning occurred through the elaboration of the meaning of sustainable development. Leicester, for instance, learned to prevent the polarization of environmental and development constituencies by stressing the link between sustainable development and the local quality-of-life.

Local Agenda 21 tries to catalyze local change by bringing people together in new ways, enhancing local dialogue, and expanding local participation. By emphasizing multisectoral planning, LA 21 processes encourage conversation and action among existing institutions and programs (Jörby 2002; Sancassiani 2005). In many cases, it has also opened up new space for public discussion about sustainability at the local level (Jörby 2002; Khakee 2002) and has expanded the range of stakeholders involved in sustainability planning.[23] These actions seek to expand public engagement with the goals of sustainable development (Macnaghten and Jacobs 1997).

Local Agenda 21 processes have paid particular attention to the development of sustainability "indicators" (Scipioni et al. 2009).[24] Because new indicators can reveal and illuminate problems that were previously only poorly perceived, they provide a natural mechanism for expanding the audience for sustainable development (Macnaghten and Jacobs 1997).[25] The original Rio description of local processes stressed the importance for local authorities to engage directly with citizens and community stakeholders. Networks have also been shown to be very important in the diffusion and support of LA 21, as well as other sustainability efforts.[26] These networks have proliferated in recent years (Keiner and Kim 2007).

How did these LA 21 experiments interact with existing institutional structures? As might be expected, Local Agenda 21 processes often encountered resistance from existing local and national institutions (Barrett and Mikoto 2002; Evans and Thebald 2003). To organize multisectoral planning and to mobilize new stakeholders, these processes were sometimes organized as "parallel" institutions at arm's-length from existing institutions, which then makes it difficult to mainstream LA 21 projects (International Council for Local Environmental Initiatives 2002). The opposite complaint is also heard: sustainability planning sometimes falls to environmental ministries and thus fails to become truly multisectoral (International Council for Local Environmental Initiatives 2002; Echebarria, Barrutia, and Aguado 2004; Lagarde 2006).[27] Local communities may also lack the local institutional and civic capacity to effectively support sustainable development planning (Evans et al. 2006; Kessler 2008).

Local Agenda 21 has had modest effects on local sustainable development. Implementation has been poor, and LA 21 programs have often been politically marginalized (Geissel 2009). Selman argues that LA 21 processes have found it difficult to produce "visible outputs" that generate interest in sustainability (2000, 49). Insufficient funding has been a common complaint (Mercer and Jotkowitz 2000; International Council for Local Environmental Initiatives 2002; Sancassiani 2005; Schmidt, Nave, and Guerra 2006). However, the results have not been negligible either. For example, in Italy, one of the countries in Europe to more slowly embrace LA 21, 100 action plans have been produced and 1,300 local projects have been implemented (Sancassiani 2005).[28]

Although LA 21 has not produced the "sustainability transition" that many hoped for, revolutionary change was probably never a realistic expectation. The more appropriate question is whether LA 21 has contributed to a process of self-sustaining learning that will gradually deepen our commitment to and our understanding of strategies for sustainable development.[29] At present, the evidence is mixed. In the past, the LA 21 movement has certainly shown signs of being able to renew and sustain itself. At the World Summit on Sustainable Development in Johannesburg in 2002, for example, the slogan "Local Action 21" was coined to carry the movement forward into its second decade and to encourage a transition from planning to implementation (Otto-Zimmerman 2002). However, as the movement nears the end of its second decade, some scholars suggest that LA 21 processes have begun to lose steam (Geissel 2009). Whether this means that local authorities have lost interest in sustainable development altogether, or whether they have simply outgrown the LA 21 planning process, is difficult to say.

The scale and scope of activity aiming to usher in a new era of "sustainable development" is really quite remarkable, especially given the fundamental ambiguity and multivocality of the concept. While this ambiguity and multivocality is not always constructive, it has anchored a dialogue between opposing interests that has lasted for over two decades. It has promoted institution-building activity at every scale of government as well as in the private sector. In addition, it has successfully created processes for reflecting on existing practices, deliberating about alternative futures, and initiating widespread experimentation and innovation. Without a doubt, the sustainable development movement has encountered institutional resistance, lacked financial resources, and suffered from political neglect. However imperfect, the movement that began with the publication of *Our Common Future* has shown the *potential* for global learning about how to bring the often competing objectives of environmental protection and economic development together.

Conclusion

This chapter began by contrasting incremental and punctuated models of institutional change. Incremental change often has the advantage of being politically feasible, but it also has the disadvantage of drifting aimlessly or of reinforcing the status quo established by larger institutions. The punctuated equilibrium model, however, assumes that large-scale institutions are resistant to change and only large external shocks will produce change. The incremental and punctuated models of institutional change are useful for describing the approximate limits on evolutionary learning—aimless drift and reproduction of the status quo on the one hand and inertial institutions and external shocks on the other. Evolutionary learning on a grand scale, by contrast, is only possible if small- and large-scale institutional change work in tandem. Large-scale institutions must be able to guide the accumulation of incremental changes in a productive direction, while this accumulated incremental change must be able to transform large-scale institutions.

This chapter imagines this mutually supportive interaction between small- and large-scale institutional change as a multilevel "constitutional process" in which local experiments interact with broad overarching meta-norms. These meta-norms guide the accumulation of lessons learned from local experiments, while feedback from these experiments leads to elaboration and transformation of meta-norms. This perspective is consistent with the multilevel model of "experimentalist governance" described by Dorf and Sabel (1998) and Sabel and Zeitlin (2008) and builds directly on Sabel's earlier work on "constitutional orders" (Sabel 1999).

What this chapter adds to the literature on experimentalist governance is the idea of "meta-concepts." No one can fully design or control evolutionary learning on a grand scale, and experimentalist governance is a highly distributed activity. Building on the discussion of institutions in chapter 2, this chapter argues that "meta-concepts" can serve as the focal points that give shape and direction to this distributed activity. They provide a bridge between distributed local experiments, facilitating communication and the collective accumulation of experience and knowledge. In this way, they help to anchor the development of large-scale publics that can interpret and adjudicate the meaning of lessons learned from local experiments. The multivocal, boundary-spanning, and soft teleological quality of certain meta-concepts allows them to play this role.

The meta-concept "sustainable development" is used to give realism to these ideas and to explore the possibilities for evolutionary learning on a grand scale. As a powerful multivocal and boundary-spanning idea that presents an attractive teleology, the idea of sustainable development has become a touchstone for dialogue between communities that once rarely spoke. By linking together discussions about economic development and environmental protection, sustainable development has also partially rewired the ways in which organizations and governments think about and develop their activities. In doing this, sustainable development has created a "constitutional process" that has guided local, regional, and national experimentation on a global scale. This process has created new publics that support sustainable development goals, culminating in the widespread institutionalization of sustainable development ideas. However, the idea of sustainable development also points to the challenges that all efforts to create evolutionary learning on a grand scale must confront. Given the ambitions of the movement for sustainable development, it is not surprising that the transition to sustainability has been hindered by resistance from existing institutional structures, by financial limitations, and by political marginalization. Although the movement for sustainable development has been going strong for over two decades, it remains to be seen whether this movement can continue to provide a platform for evolutionary learning in the future.

CHAPTER 4

Organizations

▨

This chapter builds on the last two chapters by extending a Pragmatist analysis to organizations. As understood here, organizations are special-purpose associations with established institutions that allow them to act in a concerted fashion to develop and carry out collective goals.[1] Because they are able to act collectively, develop goals, and create institutions, organizations are centrally important for evolutionary learning. If institutions are the medium of evolutionary learning at the societal level, organizations are the agents. This chapter establishes a general theoretical framework for thinking about organizations as agents of evolutionary learning. These ideas are further developed in chapters 5 and 6, where the analysis focuses more directly on public agencies.

Several scholars have argued that the Pragmatists, and Dewey in particular, failed to understand the implications of the rise of large-scale organizations.[2] Whether or not this is true, it is possible to construct a Pragmatist framework for thinking about large-scale organizations by building on the work of two organization theorists with a Pragmatist vision, Mary Parker Follett and Philip Selznick. Follett was an early management theorist and a contemporary of Dewey and Mead who developed a distinctive view of authority and power in modern organizations. Selznick was a sociologist who was directly influenced by Dewey. He developed a powerful framework for understanding organizational leadership as well as many other aspects of how organizations function. This chapter focuses on Selznick, bringing in Follett in a more supportive role.

What purpose does it serve to return to the work of Selznick? The first purpose is to anchor a tradition of Pragmatist organization theory. From the perspective of evolutionary learning, intellectual traditions are important because they help to bring communities of inquiry together and also improve the chances for accumulation of knowledge. Selznick already has a prominent place in the study of organizations, but the Pragmatist character of his thought is not well known. A conventional reading of his work interprets him as a structural-functionalist or culturalist.[3] Therefore, the second purpose of this chapter is to draw out a Pragmatist interpretation of Selznick's work. The third purpose of returning to Selznick, however, is the most important one. Interpreted in a Pragmatist light, Selznick's work provides a foundational Pragmatist account of large-scale organization that can complement Charles Sabel's (2006) recent analysis of Pragmatist organization, as well as other contemporary perspectives on organizational learning.

Selznick is not typically seen as a progenitor of the extensive contemporary body of work on organizational learning (Argyris and Schon 1978; Nelson and Winter 1985; Levitt and March 1988; March 1991; Sabel 2006; Senge 2006). This literature addresses the question of how organizations learn or fail to learn far more directly than does Selznick and is therefore fundamental for understanding evolutionary learning in organizations. Selznick does not even specifically use the terms "evolution" or "learning"; nevertheless, his work complements these more specific accounts of organizational learning. By linking together ideas of organizations as cultures, self-regulating polities, and problem-solving systems, Selznick (with help from Follett) captures what might be called the "constitutional basis" for evolutionary learning in large-scale organizations. The main themes of his work can be expressed according to the main points of the evolutionary learning model described in chapter 1, summarized below.

Antidualism: Selznick analyzes the way large-scale organizations can overcome the tensions between formal and informal and centralized and decentralized organization.

Problem-focused: His analysis of how organizations can become "responsive" to societal circumstances and his attention to organizational competencies provides a basis for thinking about how organizations become active problem-solvers.

Reflexivity: His analysis of how organizations become communities and how organizational leaders shape the character of organization through attention to how meaning is institutionalized provides a framework for thinking about organizations as reflexive communities.

Deliberation: Selznick's analysis of how organizational communities become self-regulating polities offers a basis for thinking about deliberation in organizations.

The chapter begins by directly contrasting Selznick's view of organization with Max Weber's understanding of bureaucracy. As the great theorist of modern bureaucracy, Weber is well known for his pessimism that bureaucracy—as the ultimate embodiment of rational-legal authority—would leave us in an "iron cage" of dehumanized efficiency. Although organization theorists have long been critical of Weber's notion that bureaucracy is the most efficient of institutions, his work remains a touchstone for organization theory and public administration. Indeed, his insights into rationalization, bureaucratization, and authority are foundational for much of the social sciences. Selznick himself was deeply influenced by the work of Max Weber through the influence of his teacher, Robert Merton. However, a contrast between Weber and Selznick helps to illuminate a different view of modernity and modern organization.

The widespread contemporary condemnation of bureaucracy and the preference for "flexible" markets and networks over "rigid" hierarchy draws heavily on Weber's image of bureaucracy. Du Gay argues that the contemporary push to "entrepreneurial governance" defines itself in opposition to the "impersonal, procedural, hierarchical and technical organization of the Weberian bureau" (2000, 6). While Selznick's work anticipates some of the themes of "post-bureaucratic organization," his analysis is less skeptical about large-scale organization than Weber's, but for that reason it is also less likely to try to merely replace it with what Sabel calls the "twin" of hierarchy—informality and flexibility (Sabel 2006). By breaking with the dualisms bequeathed by the Weberian legacy, Selznick creates a Pragmatist vision of modern organizations that combines control and flexibility. The chapter concludes with a discussion of one of the important implications of Selznick's model for current reform of public organization—its emphasis on cultivating the competencies and "character" of public organizations.

Antidualism I: The Pragmatist Marriage of Formal and Informal Organization

To argue that Weber's analysis of modern institutions is pessimistic is not to say that he was not prophetic in his understanding of institutions. He was. But his analysis was also limited by the very categories he used to analyze institutions. Weber's sociology is neo-Kantian; as MacKinnon writes, "There was no more devoted Kantian than Max Weber" (2001, 335). It is in Weber's analysis of the autonomy of reason and ideas—rationality—that we most clearly see the influence of Kant. This autonomy, as ultimately embodied in bureaucracy, required sharply dualistic categories. Most importantly, Weber built his concept of bureaucracy on sharp distinctions between the formal and the informal and the personal and the impersonal. In fact, it was precisely the formal impersonalism of bureaucracy that led Weber to his pessimism about the iron cage. This formal impersonalism led to the conception of bureaucracy as an institution being an "object," separated from its "subjects."[4]

The concept of authority at the heart of Weber's institutional sociology is the empirical interpretation of Kant's idea of the categorical imperative. As MacKinnon writes: "Kant's categorical imperative is a command in itself disinterested in ends. . . . Similarly so for Weber's value rationality, which 'always' involves 'commands' or 'demands' that are binding on the subject" (2001, 343). Weber's concept of authority is the linchpin of his argument about bureaucracy, because authority is the link between power and legitimacy. It is not accidental that Weber's analysis of bureaucracy linked formality and impersonalism with authority and legitimacy. These features of bureaucracy are strongly reinforcing logics, and they are linked to the clear separation of person from office (and hence the separation of subject and object).[5] If office is separated from person, it becomes an object, which allows it to be assigned a general grant of authority. The more general this grant, the more this authority must be regarded as sacred and autonomous—hence the importance of legitimacy. This legitimacy is "objective" (accountable to public standards) and input-oriented rather than output-oriented. In rational-legal authority, authority resides in rules; formality and impersonalism bestow legitimacy on rules.[6]

Pragmatism also grew out of neo-Kantianism. However, it broke with Kant precisely around the issue of dualism. Pragmatists reject any sharp dualism between subject and object. Building on James and Mead, Dewey sought to overcome subject–object dualism through his notions of experience, instrumentalism, and experimentalism. Habit and custom, he argued, can be reflexively reconstructed in an evolutionary manner. Although Dewey had concerns about large-scale organization, he was not anti-organizational (Stever 1993). As Dewey wrote in *Freedom and Culture*:

> The predicament is that individuality demands association to develop and sustain and association requires arrangement and coordination of its elements, or organization—since otherwise it is formless and devoid of power. But we have now a kind of molluscan organization, soft individuals within and hard constrictive shells without. . . . No small part of the democratic problem is to achieve associations whose ordering of parts provides the strength that comes with stability, while they promote flexibility of response to change. (1989, 127)

Dewey embraced an idea of ordered liberty, which required organization. In fact, as Stever argues, "It is a reasonable extrapolation of [Dewey's] thinking that value creation must inevitably be performed within organizational settings" (1993, 431). Dewey clearly understood that organization could curtail freedom and lead to tyranny and technocracy, but organization did not inevitably lead to this result.

Selznick was influenced by both Weber and Dewey. His classic *TVA and the Grassroots*, for example, was a study in goal displacement inspired by Roberto

Michels's "iron law of oligarchy" (Michels was a student of Weber's). Selznick also acknowledged Dewey's influence in various footnotes and references, though these scattered footnotes and references do not really do justice to the way that Selznick's larger body of work on institutions embodies a Pragmatist conception. Selznick is quite aware of Dewey's battles against "pernicious dualism" and finds this antidualism particularly relevant to overcoming the dualism of freedom and discipline (2002, 136–137). For Selznick, as for Dewey, self-government requires discipline, which is partly habitual and learned (2002, 137).[7]

In contrast with Weber's analysis of bureaucracy, Selznick's work on large-scale organization rejected sharp dichotomies between personal/impersonal and formal/informal. These ideas are most explicitly developed in his great work, *Leadership in Administration.* Consider Weber again. His analysis of bureaucracy as an iron cage was built upon his analysis of the routinization of charisma. A charismatic figure is a prophet, a visionary, who is able to mobilize a following through the force of his or her vision. Yet, in Weber's view, an organization based on charismatic authority is not stable. The routinization of charisma leads to rational-legal authority as the basis of a more stable organization. Weber despaired for this loss of charisma, because he saw charisma as a creative force, but bureaucratization represents a transition from creativity to mundane routine.

By contrast, in Selznick's analysis, the role of leadership is to institutionalize organization by assisting in the "infusion of value." Leaders help to articulate a powerful mission for their organization and then help to create a social structure and community that can support this mission.[8] This emphasis on the role of leadership in institutionalizing a mission does not insist on a sharp separation between personalism and impersonalism. In fact, as Jowitt (1993) has emphasized, Selznick's theory can be described as "charismatic impersonalism." In Pragmatist terms, the role of leaders is to develop a close alignment between meaning and action. Selznick's focus on a leader's role in articulating and developing an organizational mission embodies the Pragmatist idea of cultivating purpose and principle.

The Pragmatist sociologist Charles Horton Cooley was among the first to call attention to the importance of informal organization in modern institutions. He regarded "primary groups"—groups bound together by face-to-face communication and cooperation—as the heart of social institutions (Cooley 1962).[9] Jane Addams and Mary Parker Follett, both leaders of the settlement movement, also stressed the informal, intersubjective nature of institutions (Seigfried 1999; Stivers 2002). Building on Chester Barnard, Mary Parker Follett, and the early human relations school in organization theory, Selznick departed from Weber in emphasizing the continuing importance of informal organization in large-scale organization.[10]

For Weber, the impersonalism of the bureaucracy drives out informal organization. But for Selznick, formal and informal organization are not diametrically opposed. In his analysis of institutional leadership, Selznick emphasized that the role of leadership is to align formal and informal organization. His conception of informal organization was built around a conception of community that mirrors the Pragmatist's emphasis on community as face-to-face relations.[11] Rather than being suppressed, informal organization could be harnessed to the broader mission of the organization. Through the cultivation of organizational purpose and the meaningfulness of work, leaders can encourage the development of informal organization around the central purposes of the organization.

One of Selznick's best-known arguments is that institutionalization is equivalent to transforming an organization from an "instrument" into a "community"—from a thing valued only as a means into an end-in-itself. The role of leadership is to cultivate the purpose of organization through the articulation of mission and to support this mission by encouraging the creation of a community committed to it. In fact, Selznick's argument about institutionalization built directly on Dewey's theory of valuation. Dewey argued that ends could only be defined in conjunction with available means.[12] Technology, for Dewey, is never merely an "instrument"; it is also the embodiment of meaning (Hickman 1992). Selznick's theory of institutionalization is built on this idea of the continuous iteration between ends and means and the view that organizations (as technologies) come to be treated as ends-in-themselves.

By contrast, Weber's theory of bureaucracy understood rationalization in general, and bureaucratization in particular, as a process whereby ends and means were distinctly separated from one another. Bureaucracy therefore could serve as a neutral instrument (means), and this view was indeed powerful because it supported the notion of the neutral competence of bureaucrats and the separation of politics (value) and administration. The ideas of neutral expertise and a politics–administration dichotomy are casualties of the Dewey-Selznick logic of valuation. In Selznick's view, institutionalization builds bias into organizations—bias that has consequences for the downstream articulation of ends.

Selznick called the bias built into organizations "the institutional embodiment of purpose" and it affords another glimpse of the parallel between Selznick and Dewey. As developed in the last chapter, Dewey understood much of human behavior as habit-based, and he understood "character" to be a bundle of interpenetrating habits. This "character" could be ethical, and much of Dewey's moral theory focused on how individuals can cultivate good ethical characters. In *Leadership in Administration*, Selznick develops a model of organizational character, drawing a close association between character and competence. For

Dewey, habit is a predisposition to action, a learned skill similar to the skill of a craftsperson. For Selznick, character—as an "institutional embodiment of purpose"—aligns mission (purpose), competence (skill), and commitment (value). Character is defined by Selznick as a *distinctive competence.*

Antidualism II: Moving beyond Command and Obedience

If, in contrast to Weber's model of bureaucracy, Selznick would encourage a productive marriage of formal and informal organization, Mary Parker Follett would offer an alternative to Weber's model of authority and control. Follett was a contemporary of Dewey's and shared many of his basic philosophical and public commitments (Ansell 2009). She was a student of Josiah Royce and William James at Harvard, and her work sought to integrate Royce's Idealism and James's Pragmatism. Her varied career as a scholar, social activist, and management consultant gave her an unusual ability to bridge the worlds of theory and practice in an insightful and creative way and led her to develop a fresh perspective on authority, conflict, and cooperation in organizations (Tonn 2003). She provides the closet thing we have to a Pragmatist account of authority and control.

Among Follett's most famous essays is "The Giving of Orders," in which she lays out a model of authority that requires integration between supervisor and subordinates. Follett argues that the extremes of what she calls "bossism" (linear command) and no orders at all (anarchism) are to be avoided (1941, 58). She asks us to understand the "experience" that employees have when they are issued a linear order, which undercuts both their independent judgment and their motivation. Instead of conceiving the relationship between supervisor and subordinate as linear and unidirectional, she described the relationship as interactive: "I should say that the giving of orders and the receiving of orders ought to be a matter of integration through circular behavior" (Follett 1941, 54).

To achieve that balance between top-down command and bottom-up initiative, she articulates what she calls the "law of the situation." The key to the law of the situation is to "depersonalize the giving of orders" (Follett 1941, 58): "One *person* should not give orders to another *person*, but both should agree to take their orders from the situation" (ibid., 59). For Follett, the situation has "authority." In arguing for depersonalizing the giving of orders, she clarifies that the goal is not actually to depersonalize organization but rather to repersonalize the relationship by stripping it of personalized control.[13] Like Dewey, Follett emphasized the importance of "face-to-face" relations and the immediacy of the specific situational context. Face-to-face relations are important because they facilitate the "joint" study of the situation.[14]

Follett's revision of the concept of authority, as expressed by the law of the situation, is closely related to the stress she lays on the idea of responsibility. "How can you expect people merely to obey orders," she writes, "and at the same time to take that degree of responsibility which they should take?" (Follett 1941, 63).[15] Moreover, responsibility is difficult to fix, and hence assign, because it grows organically out of the process of interweaving the task situations of different people. Although she recognizes the need to assign authority and responsibility a priori and to hold people accountable, she observes that "in the ideal organization authority is always fresh, always being distilled anew"(ibid., 151). Her goal is to draw attention to the authority and responsibility of people lower in the organizational hierarchy.

What is the role of leadership in Follett's model of organization? She vigorously rejected the idea that the leader's role is to command and the follower's role is to obey. Arguing against a command-oriented view of leadership, she writes that "group activity, organized group activity, should aim: to incorporate and express the desires, the experiences, the ideals of individual members of the group."[16] Follett emphasizes that leadership is a process of increasing the power and individuality of employees.

Follett does not object to the idea of authority, as such, but only to the idea of "ultimate" authority, from which lesser authority is derived (1941, 154). She proposes that instead of thinking about "ultimate" authority, we ought to think about "cumulative responsibility." Some people do have more cumulative responsibility than others. But, she writes:

> The best method of organization is not that which works out most meticulously or most logically the place for "finals" and "ultimates," but that which provides possibilities for a cumulative responsibility, which provides for gathering together all the responsibility there actually is in the plant, which provides for making various individual and group responsibilities more effective by the working out of a system of cross-relations. (1941, 154–155).

Her sense of coordination is typically a form of collegial governance, often through the organizational vehicle of what today might be called "project teams."[17] She repeatedly emphasizes the importance of cross-functional coordination and stresses that early and continuous coordination are essential (Follett 1941, 157–158).[18] Ultimately, integration can only be successful if it builds up from organic coordination among separate tasks.[19] Control, she argues, arises out of the interactive coordination that produces unity: "The activity of self-creating coherence *is* the controlling activity" (204). The implication, she tells us, is that the more "highly integrated" an organization is, the more control it will have (205).[20] However, this does not imply that the group controls the individual. Rather, an integrated group encourages a form of self-control, which is what Follett means by responsibility. Parker summarizes Follett's theory of control: "The group-oriented process of shared self-control therefore constituted the major aspect of the Follett behavioral model of control" (1984, 740).[21]

Antidualism III: Neither Centralization or Decentralization

Selznick's marriage of the formal and informal and the personal and impersonal, and Follett's "situational" model of authority and idea of cumulative responsibility, are mutually reinforcing ideas. Taken together, they can help organizations to successfully manage the inherent tension in large-scale endeavors between centralization and decentralization. Among the most valuable lessons of Follett's conception of authority is that centralization or decentralization are not alternatives: "That centralization and decentralization are not opposed is the central lesson for business administration to learn" (1941, 80). Clearly, she favors a form of decentralization, because she writes that "I know no one who believes more strongly in decentralization than I do, but I believe that collective responsibility and decentralized responsibility must go hand in hand" (79). She provides multiple examples of the benefit of pushing initiative down into the operational ranks, and she argues that there should be no "sharp line" between planning and executing (88).

To fully see how Follett would overcome the pulls of centralization and decentralization, we have to further investigate her analysis of power and leadership. Complementing her "law of the situation," Follett suggests a distinction between "power-over"—as exemplified by traditional command relationships—and "power-with," which is a "co-active" or "joint" power (Follett 1941, 100). Follett regards "legitimate power" as power-with and she sees it as produced through the circular relations of integration. She distinguishes the idea of "balance of power" from the idea of "power-with" or joint power (e.g., power-with is a form of integration). A balance of power constrains the power of each party through countervailing power. By contrast, Follett argues in favor of increasing the power of each party by increasing their joint power (1941, 110). Furthermore, she argues that power cannot be delegated because it is a capacity (109). She writes: "To confer authority where capacity has not been developed is fatal to both government and business" (111).[22]

A powerful implication of Selznick's approach to organizations is that the successful creation of a committed community around a mission creates conditions for successful decentralization. When employees or members share a common commitment to the organization, they can be granted greater latitude in decision making, trusting that they will make decisions in the spirit of the general mission. Organizations with a strong institutional embodiment of purpose can grant frontline workers significant discretion, a very valuable asset in many organizations and a de facto situation in many public organizations (like police agencies). Yet "decentralized" would be a misleading description for an organization that adopts Selznick's brand of institutionalization. Such organizations actually exhibit combined properties of both centralization and decentralization. In a classic study partially inspired by Selznick, Herbert Kaufman (1967) shows how organizations that develop a strong institutional embodiment of purpose can achieve strong central control in combination with strong decentralization.

Selznick drew another idea from Barnard, Follett, and the human relations school that is closely connected with this property of centralization-decentralization: relational authority. Rather than conceiving of authority as a command and control relationship, as Weber does in his model of bureaucracy, Selznick's conceives of leadership as requiring consent from below. Barnard, of course, gave the classic statement of this view in *The Functions of the Executive* (Barnard 1968).[23] Consent from below does not mean either "poll democracy" or "transactional" leadership (Burns 1982). For both Barnard and Selznick, leadership must put a firm and distinctive stamp on the organization. But leadership will be enhanced when organizational members develop their own personal commitment to the leader's articulation of purpose. Nor is leadership a simple principal-agent relationship. Leaders enhance their authority by enhancing the commitment of members to their vision. Members enhance their own autonomy by enhancing the leader's capacity to direct and integrate the organization around a common mission. The idea of relational authority is consistent with Dewey's notion that increased organization does not necessarily lead to a loss of freedom.

Relational authority is a linchpin in the reconciliation of formal and informal rule. On the one hand, informal organization may imply only personalistic particularism—a patronage relationship created to motivate employees who have little incentive to perform otherwise. On the other hand, formal controls are often seen as ineffective—as "mock bureaucracy"—or as a way to achieve control where informal relationships are conflictual or poorly developed (Gouldner 1955a). Relational authority affords leaders the ability to use formal controls effectively, if they can effectively align formal controls with informal support from below. In his study of the Federal Bureau of Prisons, Boin (2001) shows how this kind of relational authority can mutually enhance compliance with formal rule on the one hand, and expand informal commitment on the other.[24]

Organizations as Political Communities

One of Selznick's most famous books—*TVA and the Grassroots*—has strong affinities with a Weberian approach. This book is a case study of what came to be known as "goal displacement," an idea implicit in Weber's theory of the "routinization of charisma" and elaborated by his protégé, Roberto Michels, in his classic book *Political Parties*.[25] Michels examined the bureaucratization of the German Social Democratic Party and German trade unions and developed an argument that has come to be known as the "iron law of oligarchy." Building on Weber's analysis of bureaucratization, Michels argued that bureaucracy leads to elite control over the masses (oligarchy). While efficient and therefore indispensable, bureaucracy allowed elites to become more concerned about their own livelihood and organizational survival than about the goals of the masses. When challenged from below, these elites perpetuate themselves through co-optation of dissenters into their ranks. Oligarchy displaced the original democratic goals of the socialist movement in Germany.

Michels's idea of goal displacement provided the central framework for Selznick's analysis of the Tennessee Valley Authority (TVA). As a novel experiment in grassroots planning, the TVA confronted a political crisis. The TVA threatened powerful agricultural interests within the Tennessee Valley. To guarantee the survival of the TVA, its leadership sought out an accommodation with these interests, incorporating them into the TVA through a process of both formal and informal cooptation. In the process, the original idealist vision of grassroots planning became a myth, emptied of its more radical promise, but still serving the purpose of providing a political justification. Alvin Gouldner (1955b) famously took Selznick to task for the "pessimism" of this vision of organization, which was in the very same vein as Weber's pessimism about the iron cage of bureaucracy. Gouldner challenged Selznick to develop a more democratically constructive analysis, which Selznick did in his next book, *Leadership in Administration*.

The TVA may have been Selznick's most Weberian book, but it is worth pointing out how even in this book he was guided by Dewey.[26] In one sense, the TVA experiment itself could be said to embody a Pragmatist vision: a community-based concept of regional planning that would seek to enhance the capacity of the grassroots to democratically decide their own future. From this perspective, the TVA can be read as a cautionary note. The decentralized, participatory vision that the TVA embodied was, to borrow words from Selznick's later work on responsive law, a "high risk strategy." Although the idea of goal displacement came from Michels (via Merton), Selznick's analysis of the fate of this decentralized, participatory vision builds explicitly on Dewey's model of valuation and the means–ends continuum.

Selznick argued that the problem of grassroots planning was that it began as an "unanalyzed abstraction." For Pragmatism, ungrounded idealism is problematic and can lead to serious unintended consequences (this point is similar to the critique of "rational design" discussed in chapter 2). Pragmatism emphasizes a close alignment of ideas and action. Goal displacement occurred in the TVA case at least partly because of the ungrounded idealism of the original concept. With Dewey, Selznick emphasizes that ends only become defined through interaction with means.[27]

Selznick's affinity for both Michels and Dewey can also be looked at from another angle. Michels's analysis bears a strong Aristotelian stamp. Aristotle was the first great scholar of comparative politics and he described the political community as having different regimes—monarchy, democracy, and aristocracy. Aristotle's view of the community as first and foremost "political"—as polities—is deeply embedded in the civic republican tradition that strongly influenced both Selznick and Dewey. For Selznick and Michels, and for Pragmatism more generally, the organization can be understood as a polity.

Selznick's emphasis on the organization as a polity can be seen in all his works. However, in later work on the law, he began to elaborate an argument that institutionalization as value infusion—the development of community—develops in conjunction with the emergence of a polity. Community and polity are, in fact, two sides of the same dynamic. With value infusion, a group of people will develop a sense of being a community, and one expression of this sense of community is the creation of a political order that can regulate the internal life of the community. In his work on law, Selznick was particularly interested in how organizations, as polities, can develop an emergent legal system. As pointed out in chapter 2, this process can be thought of as a process of constitutionalization, which creates rights and duties and a sense of citizenship. The implications of this view are important. Whether they are police officers, teachers, or forest rangers, Selznick would expect the "citizens" of a healthy developing institution to claim ownership over it—that is, to develop a vested interest in it.[28] This is, in part, what it means for an institution to become a "going concern."

While "vested interests" often have a negative connotation, Selznick understood their potential value. An engaged organizational citizenry will be concerned about the integrity of the institution and its guiding principles and values. It will have developed a strong sense of what Follett called "cumulative responsibility." When an organizational citizenry has the motivation (vested interests), the opportunity (a community operating in a framework of relational authority), and a sense of ownership over organizational principles and values (cumulative responsibility), then it is possible for them to become a reflective and deliberative community.

From Political Community to Problem-Solving Community

Although Selznick is widely acknowledged as a theorist of institutions and institutionalization, the power of his approach for understanding "emergent" phenomena is not widely appreciated. In *Law, Society, and Industrial Justice*, Selznick argues that a sociological approach to law focuses specifically on the "emergent, system-forming nature of institutions" (1969, 44). Selznick, however, did not fully explicate this idea until he wrote *Responsive Law* with Philippe Nonet. In this work, Nonet and Selznick elaborate three different forms of law: repressive, autonomous, and responsive. In repressive law, there is no separation between politics and law. Law is used as a political weapon to achieve the purposes of rulers, often in a coercive way. In a second phase, autonomous law develops, which is characterized by a strong demarcation between politics and law. The implicit bargain that allows law and courts autonomy from politics is that they content themselves with procedural interpretation and avoid interference with substantive content (e.g., politics). In the third phase, the law ventures past this boundary beyond politics and law. It becomes concerned not only with procedural integrity but also with broader questions of societal justice. Judges and courts become "responsive" to larger societal issues. Nonet and Selznick's concept of responsive law is exemplified by the "problem-solving courts" that have developed in the United States in the last few decades.

The distinction between autonomous and responsive law is ideal-typical and rarely represented in pure form. Nevertheless, Nonet and Selznick suggest that there is a developmental relationship between them and that responsive law can only effectively develop upon a strong base of autonomous law. As law becomes responsive, however, it becomes less concerned with autonomy and independence per se and more concerned about societal problem-solving. They note the parallel between this argument and Deweyian Pragmatism: "The more wide ranging legal inquiry becomes, the more it encourages a more sophisticated pragmatism, in the spirit of John Dewey, which regards ends as problematic and subject to reconstruction in light of their costs" (2001, 84–85).

The move toward responsive law entails "high risks," but these risks, they argue, must be weighed against the possible drawbacks of autonomous law.[29]

"Legality understood as close accountability to rules is the promise of autonomous law," Nonet and Selznick write, "legalism is its affliction" (2001, 64). "Legalism," they further observe, is an "imposition to rely on legal authority to the detriment of practical problem-solving." Nonet and Selznick note the parallel between autonomous law and bureaucracy and responsive law and "post-bureaucracy": "Bureaucracy is not a dynamic institution committed to solving problems and attaining objectives. Rather it is a relatively passive and conservative system preoccupied with the detailed implementation of received policies" (2001, 65).

From a Weberian perspective, many of the current changes in political life—networks, decentralization, public-sector entrepreneurialism—are by definition a form of deinstituitonalization.[30] However, for Selznick, they *may be* developmental. In Selznick's three forms of law—repressive, autonomous, and responsive—a shift away from autonomous law could be a regression toward the arbitrary form of law that he calls repressive. But Selznick's analysis of law also suggests that what to some eyes is "deinstitutionalization" can be a movement toward responsive law. The comparison between Weber and Selznick is useful precisely because it highlights these possibilities.

Responsive institutions are threatening because they blur boundaries: a judge goes beyond the letter of the law to engage in "therapeutic" action with a repeat offender; a public agency forms a partnership with private stakeholders to redevelop a declining shopping district; beat officers develop close relationships with the communities they patrol. Each relationship demands the flexibility to tailor solutions to situationally specific problems. But both the relationship and the flexibility it entails can jeopardize the prized autonomy, independence, and public ethics of public organizations. The key to understanding how institutions can maintain their integrity while engaging in flexible problem-solving is to understand the "cultivation of public purpose" that must attend a shift toward greater openness and flexibility. As Nonet and Selznick write: "Only when an institution is truly purposive can there be a combination of integrity and openness, rule and discretion" (2001, 77).[31]

As organizations develop their own internal rules and sense of citizenship, they will also develop a tendency toward self-regulating autonomy. This striving toward autonomy may reflect the fact that organizations wish to act according to their own institutionalized values, but it also suggests that they wish to act in a responsive fashion according to their own understanding of public needs and problems. This self-regulating autonomy is a serious problem if public officials are self-regarding rather than public-regarding. Selznick, however, suggests that the public character of organizations may be reinforced by wider institutionalization in the political community: "Characteristically," he writes, "an institution . . . is valued for the special place it has in a larger

social system" (1969, 44).[32] It is when organizations institu
tively "public" character—reinforced by both organizati
external publics—that they can be granted greater autonc
"responsive" manner.

It is the institutionalization of character and competen
the larger field of meaning of liberal-democratic society th
stand how public organizations can combine autonomy, openness, integrity,
and flexibility. Character and competence must be cultivated not with narrow
reference to the parochial needs and interests of an organizational community
but in a fashion that is responsive to the broader needs and principles of a larger
liberal and democratic community. Good leaders can help public organizations to evolve in this direction.

Competence and Character

Selznick's theory of organizations seeks to overcome many of the dualisms inherent in Weber's theory of bureaucracy and rationality. For Selznick, informal
organization must be harnessed to support formal organization; personal
identification with the purposes of the organization must be brought together
within an impersonal institutional framework that supports and governs these
purposes. By overcoming these dualisms, Selznick (along with Follett)
describes the conditions necessary for successful decentralization, a relational
form of authority, and emergent self-regulation. These organizational features,
in turn, support what Selznick calls a "responsive" organization—one that can
flexibly respond to public problems. From a democratic perspective, this flexibility is potentially problematic. But rather than keeping this responsiveness in
check by a system of external rules or incentives, Selznick's vision is to channel
it toward public-regarding purposes (creating "public value" in Mark Moore's
terms) by cultivating the organization's competency and character. In his
essay, "Institutionalism Old and New," Selznick (1992) says that his work has
been about understanding the "competence" and "character" of institutions.
Competence allows organizations to be effective problem-solvers; character
harnesses this competence to larger public purposes.[33]

Selznick's emphasis on organizational competencies is consistent with the
larger tradition of Pragmatist institutionalism. Pragmatism emphasizes the
central value of skills, with basic skills serving as scaffolding for more complex
and sophisticated skills. These ideas can be seen in Veblen's description of the
"workmanlike" qualities of organization, in Hughes's focus on occupations
and professions, and in Dewey's understanding of habit. If we take these points
together, Pragmatist institutionalism suggests that we pay special attention to

tions as repositories of specific competences and that these competences need to be cultivated. The idea of organizations as going concerns—as partially self-governing institutions or communities that persist through time—suggests that organizations are communities bound together by the cultivation of these competences.[34]

The focus on competence and character in Selznick's work embodies a powerful approach to achieving successful organizational reform. His theory points to the enhancement of competence and character as a distinctive path toward organizational improvement. For his model to work, competence and character have to be mutually supporting. As an organizational ethos, the character of the organization has to continuously mold professional and personal values toward a distinctive public mission. Competence is the skill and capacity to act on these values, but it also contains within it the pride of personal achievement and public worth.[35] There is a tight loop of mutual causality implied here. Character sets the terms under which competence can be productively used; competence gives meaning and efficacy to character. In contrast, to Weber's model of "neutral competence," Selznick's model calls for every organization to have a "distinctive competence."[36] Organizational members will be imbued with this distinctive competence and will seek to protect and advance the values it represents.[37]

Selznick's model departs significantly from the approach prescribed in recent years by New Public Management (NPM). Inspired by modern economics and principal-agent models, NPM aims to align and optimize performance through the use of incentive systems. By contrast, Selznick would have us *enhance the problem-solving capacity of organizations through investment in greater competence.* Both Selznick and NPM value greater organizational autonomy and decentralization, but they differ sharply on what permits that autonomy and decentralization. While NPM would suggest that it is critical "to get the incentives right," Selznick would counter with the importance of a strong organizational ethos rooted in commitment and competence. And, in contrast to NPM, Selznick does not try to deregulate on the "input" (rule-oriented) side of public management. Although his model departs from the formal, impersonal, rule-oriented approach of Weberian bureaucracy, Selznick's model does not seek to replace rules with incentives (although a Pragmatist approach does suggest that successful rules will have a different character, a point taken up in chapter 6). To be clear here, a Pragmatist would no more reject "getting the incentives right" than an NPM advocate would reject "investing in competence." The difference is a matter of emphasis but one that can lead to very different strategies for organizational reform.

An initial response to a competence-based approach may be "yes, but. . . ." Yes, institutions may be bundles of competences, but does this actually have any implications beyond recognizing the point?[38] Actually, a competence-based perspective requires a rather fundamental shift in perspective. In our traditional view of public agencies, the focus is on programs and program outputs, not competences. Competences are required to produce programs and program outputs, but they are merely instrumental to producing these results. A competence-based approach requires that we devote more attention and resources to building competences than a narrowly instrumental view of competences might appear to justify. Obviously, a competency-based perspective requires a balance. Monasteries are concerned about the cultivation of a certain kind of competency and character, but they probably make poor models (at least in their pure form) for public agencies.[39] The production and reproduction of competences is expensive, and the public cannot afford to support monasteries dedicated to the cultivation of their own competence.[40] The public-serving character of agencies places limits on investment in organizational competences.

The cultivation of competences, however, may actually be cost-effective. An organization that is highly efficient in the short term may also be ineffective, and hence ultimately inefficient, in the long run. To illustrate (but not prove) this point, we can compare two different versions of school reform—one of them focused on the cultivation of competences and the other focused on holding schools accountable for results.[41]

The results-oriented model, inspired by work in New Public Management, is the model of "high stakes testing" that lies at the core of the No Child Left Behind program in U.S. education. Schools are held accountable for "results," which are defined as standards-referenced test results. It is clear that schools do respond to this model of performance measurement and that there have been improvements in test scores. But the depth of student learning or school improvement is less clear. One familiar problem is "teaching to the test" in which teachers and school administrators engage in a range of strategies to maximize test results. Whether test results produce educated students who can reason critically and think creatively is another question altogether. Another problem is trying to hold weak schools accountable for results when they lack the basic competence to perform at high levels. The "results" model assumes that school failure is a lack of effort rather than a lack of competence. It tries to provide the "right incentives" to motivate teachers and schools.

By contrast, another approach to school reform, made famous by New York City's District #2, focuses on refining the competences of teachers. The core philosophy is that children will learn if adults have the competence to teach effectively. This strategy emphasizes putting scarce resources into professional development and the development of a sophisticated system of mentorship and teaching support, which provides teachers with constant feedback aimed at improving their teaching practice. Of course, even competent teachers can "shirk," as the principal-agent approach would emphasize. So the Pragmatist model would insist that competence must be infused with a strong sense of public purpose. Highly competent teachers must be committed to the belief that teaching has public value. It is this "character" of commitment to this public purpose that solves the shirking problem, not "high-stakes" testing.[42] From this perspective, teaching will be effective if highly committed teachers are provided with sophisticated teaching skills.

Scholarship on firms has explored the importance of firm-based competences for comparative market advantage (e.g., Prahalad and Hamel 1990; Teece, Pisano, and Shuen 1997; Zollo and Winter 2003).[43] This literature notes that while firms may produce a range of products, innovative firms focus on core competences rather than products per se.[44] Fowler et al. offer the following example: "Consider Canon's success in developing a stream of different products (including cameras, printers, fax machines, and cell analyzers) based on its core competencies in precision mechanics, fine optics, and microelectronics" (2000, 368). Lei, Hitt, and Bettis define core capacities as "a central set of problem-defining and problem-solving insights that enable the firm to create potentially idiosyncratic strategic growth alternatives and to enact, at least partially, its environment" (1996, 550). The literature on "core competencies" and "dynamic capabilities" builds on a "resource view" of firms, which stresses the importance of skills in high-performing organizations.[45]

The idea of focusing on competences rather than on products or programs leads to the need to think about organization in terms of costs. Competences can be expensive to develop and maintain. How do you justify building up organizational competences in a world of fiscal constraint? Innovative firms produce profitable cutting-edge products. But is there an equivalent political market for highly competent, innovative public agencies? The public demand for highly competent public agencies is surely more uneven than it is for firms. Is the public actually willing to pay for highly competent teachers? Unfortunately, in the public world, competence is often valued post hoc only after the costs of organizational failure become known. Kettl (1993) provides a good example of these costs in his study of the U.S. toxic waste cleanup program called "Superfund." The program relied primarily on contracting out cleanup work to remain administratively lean. But leanness had a cost, because the EPA failed to develop the internal competences to negotiate and oversee these contracts. The result was highly wasteful and ineffective cleanup projects.

Despite the apparently high up-front investment of a competence-based approach, one possible rationale for a competence-based approach is that it is ultimately more cost-effective than program-based budgeting. Public organizations are rooted in a strong policy-program linkage that structures organizational behavior and usually resists flexible "retooling" as new challenges and needs arise. Programs are relatively fixed budget lines with high over-head. Anyone who has ever worked in a public agency knows the high cost of maintaining underemployed employees allocated to one program, while other programs struggle to meet their responsibilities because of lack of personnel.[46] A budgeting process that prioritizes competence over programs, however, could more easily reallocate personnel where they are needed. Case studies like the NASA Mars Pathfinder mission suggest that projects with the right mix of highly skilled personnel and effective team management can achieve very impressive results with many fewer people. A competence-based approach may sound expensive, but savings come from flexible reallocation of skills and assets.

A second possible rationale for budgeting around competences is that it can facilitate cross-functional coordination within organizations. The ability to organize competences across program lines is not generally supported by program management or by budgeting systems. It is common for failures to occur because of lack of dedicated funding for projects that cross boundaries. Organizations structured around programs establish incentive systems that make cross-program coordination nearly impossible.[47] One possible benefit of competence-based government is that organizations would see coordination with other organizations as a possibility of expanding and refining skills.

A possible third rationale for budgeting around competences is that it can provide a more transparent view of what it costs to maintain a high-performing agency. If you want an agency like the U.S. Federal Emergency Management Agency (FEMA) to perform at high levels, it would be quite useful to place the real costs of keeping its employees at high skill and readiness levels front and center. The cost of maintaining personnel is typically included in program budgets, but the point is that the cost of maintaining and refining organizational competences is not obvious in most budgeting processes. Therefore it is possible that "costing" competences rather than programs might actually yield a more transparent view of organizational budgeting.

Conclusion

Large-scale organizations have become central to modern life. Whether we are protecting populations from pandemics or natural disasters or teaching children to read or exploring space, organizations are vital mechanisms for coordinating social action on a large scale. But in recent years, we have witnessed a major disenchantment with large-scale organizations. This disenchantment arises, in part, from our dismay with the apparent inflexibility, inefficiency, and ineffectiveness of bureaucracy, which has fueled demands for alternative forms of organization that are more nimble, entrepreneurial, and results-oriented. This chapter engages this issue from a Pragmatist perspective, arguing that large-scale organization does not necessarily lead to Weber's "iron cage." Building on the work of Mary Parker Follett and Philip Selznick, this chapter develops a Pragmatist alternative to Weberian bureaucracy.

This Pragmatist alternative would try to overcome any sharp separation between formal/ informal or personal/ impersonal organization, with the aim of developing strong informal and personal commitment to general organizational principles and values. In place of hierarchical command, Pragmatism would substitute a more relational model of authority. Leaders would build consent for guiding principles and values and infuse them into the institutional fabric of the organization. If successful, these steps can facilitate greater decentralization within organizations without loss of central direction. Decentralization, in turn, allows organizations to engage more responsively in problem solving. Granting public organizations discretion and autonomy to engage in problem solving, however, is inherently risky, since this discretion and autonomy may be used in undesirable ways. Such discretion and autonomy can only be granted when organizations have institutionalized a powerful organizational ethos that binds organizational members to public purposes. To do this, organizations must develop distinctive competences that link the professionalism of employees to strong public missions and values.

Selznick's model supports the broader goal of evolutionary learning. The competences and character of organizations are themselves the result of evolutionary processes in which certain values and skills become institutionalized. As the organization becomes a "going concern," developing through time, competence and character reflect the experiences and lessons of organizational life. As the organization becomes a more autonomous and self-regulating community, it is able to act reflexively toward its own distinctive competence. Relational authority permits and encourages the community to act in a deliberative fashion to improve and refine its own competences and character. Distinctive competence, self-regulation, and relational authority allow public organizations to act in a more responsive, problem-driven fashion, which accelerates learning and refinement of competences.

This Pragmatist model of organization offers a powerful alternative to contemporary attempts to reform bureaucratic organizations to make them more flexible, entrepreneurial, and results-oriented. A Pragmatist approach to reform would place greater emphasis on building competences rather than on designing incentive systems or program structures. Although a competency-oriented approach to reform might require up-front investment, it can also provide the basis for a more flexible and adaptive use of organizational resources. A competence-oriented approach can also facilitate a more coordinated approach to problem solving by breaking down the institutional barriers to interunit and interorganizational cooperation associated with program structures. The next two chapters build on this organizational analysis by elaborating a Pragmatist approach to problem solving.

5

Problem Solving

One of the core ideas of Pragmatism, as set out in chapter 1, is that evolutionary learning is "problem-driven." Pragmatism's focus on problems and on problem solving is, in fact, a central theme, linking many different ideas together. A problem-driven perspective reflects, in part, the evolutionary turn of Pragmatism, with its emphasis on the adaptive relationship between humans and their natural and cultural environment. It also captures the Pragmatist emphasis on action and on the concrete and situated nature of this action. By challenging established knowledge and experience, problems also provide critical opportunities for learning. They prompt inquiry and push people to develop creative strategies for problem solving.[1] The focus on concrete problems also serves as a fruitful strategy for productive political interaction. While a problem-driven approach does not magically dissolve political differences or values and replace them with rational inquiry (Festenstein 2001), a focus on problems does help opposing parties avoid unproductive and dogmatic disputes.

Problem solving operates on many different levels, from the individual to the societal. The main purpose of this chapter is to develop a framework for institutional-level problem-solving. All collective problem-solving depends, of course, on individual-level problem-solving, which is tantamount to a theory of individual rationality. Pragmatism has much to say about individual rationality and argues that individual problem-solving builds on practical reason and pattern recognition. In the interest of getting more quickly to the main topic, however, this topic of individual rationality and problem solving is discussed at length in an excursus at the end of the chapter.

This chapter focuses on how we can translate the philosophical orientation of Pragmatism toward problems into a problem-solving approach suitable for public affairs and useful for public agencies. The core idea for doing this is what chapter 1 called "analytical holism"—the interactive relationship of analysis and synthesis. As applied to problem solving, the term "analytical" refers to the need to break up more complex problems into their constituent parts, attacking them in a highly focused way. It also refers to the need to invest in analysis of the causes and consequences of problems. The term "holism" refers to the need to fully consider the context in which problems occur and the need to devise customized solutions that take this context into account. It also refers to the recognition of the complex interdependence that links problems together.

With the concept of analytical holism as a guide, the chapter builds directly on previous work on public problem-solving. Inspiration for developing a problem-solving model for public affairs comes from several sources—Goldstein's (1990) work on problem-oriented policing, Sparrow's (2000) analysis of regulatory problem-solving, Berman and Feinblatt's (2005) and Dorf and Sabel's (2000) analysis of problem-solving courts, and Chisholm's (1992, 1995, 2001) work on institutional problem-solving.[2] While building on their work, the goal is to set out the general features of a problem-solving model that reflects Pragmatist ideas. To do this, we must begin with an investigation of the character of public problems.

An Ecological Approach to Problems

A problem-solving approach should take very seriously the character of problems, because not all problems are created equal. The literature on problem solving contains any number of useful typologies for characterizing problems, but problems can be broadly clumped into two opposing groups: simple, tame, neat, tractable, and structured problems on one side; and complex, wicked, messy, intractable, and ill-structured problems on the other.[3] Governance problems tend to fall on the more difficult side of this spectrum, and the literature has done a good job of identifying why this is the case. A central theme of this literature is that you have to have some idea of what kind of problem you are dealing with before you set out to solve it.

This literature cautions that you won't solve an ill-structured or a wicked problem if you set about solving it as if it were a garden-variety "structured" or "tame" problem. Specific kinds of problems require distinctive problem-solving approaches. For example, it is hazardous to approach an ill-structured problem as if it is well-structured, because this can lead to what Mitroff (1998) calls "Type 3 errors": "solving the wrong problem precisely." Mitroff and colleagues (Mitroff, Emshoff, and Kilmann 1979) have argued that ill-structured problem-solving requires a dialectical approach and a focus on the assumptions that different stakeholders bring to problem definition and problem solving.[4] This discussion of ill-structured problems ultimately leads to the much wider discussion of "problem definition," which emphasizes that problems are socially constructed (Rochefort and Cobb 1993).[5]

Since complex, wicked, messy, or ill-structured problems are multidimensional, poorly bounded, and vaguely formulated, they tend to create what Dunn (1988) calls "a problem of problems"—the problem of how they will be simplified, focused, bounded, or more precisely formulated.[6] While mindful that there are no magical solutions, this chapter constructs an "ecological" approach to problem solving that respects and responds to the character of difficult problems. As described in chapter 2, this ecological conception is implicit in Pragmatist philosophy and explicit in Pragmatist institutionalism. To motivate the core ideas behind this ecological approach, it is useful to begin with an examination of Herbert Simon's classic statement about "problem decomposition."

Simon's work is a touchstone here, because there is a very close affinity between Pragmatism and the behavioral tradition of decision making and organization theory that Simon's work spawned.[7] This section, however, reflects on both the value and the limitations of Simon's model from a Pragmatist perspective. In a famous essay, "The Architecture of Complexity," Simon (1962) argued that boundedly rational individuals can increase their capacity to solve complex problems through what he calls "problem decomposition." Problems are simplified by decomposing them into smaller, more limited problems—an "analytical" (as opposed to "synthetic") strategy for gaining leverage over a problem. Simon extended this logic to organization by developing the concept of modularity. He argued that organizations can handle complex problems by decomposing the organization into modules that parallel decomposed problems. Through this combination of problem decomposition and modularity, Simon developed a powerful argument for hierarchy. However, Simon's hierarchy is not a command-and-control system in the Weberian mold, but rather a set of nested subsystems with strong interdependence within subsystems and weak interdependence across subsystems. This view of hierarchy as a "nearly decomposable" system captures, in many respects, the idea of an ecology.[8]

The ecological quality of problem solving is further revealed in Donald Chisholm's (1992) provocative analysis of the San Francisco Bay Area transit system. Chisholm's analysis begins with the premise that the Bay Area transit system is a multiorganizational system with only weak hierarchical coordination. Yet it appears to function fairly well. He argues that it achieves effectiveness via informal networks that coordinate across the institutional boundaries of different transit operators. These informal networks help to reduce the transaction costs associated with formal hierarchical coordination (in the command-and-control sense). The network concept is Chisholm's own, but he links it in an intriguing way to Simon's argument about problem decomposition. The problem with hierarchy, says Chisholm, is that it links problems together that in fact do not need to be linked. Instead, following Simon, he argues that interdependence needs to be "localized" (decomposed). A multiorganizational system allows for such a localization by encouraging direct interaction only between those operators that share a direct, common problem. Coordination is not necessary where natural interdependence is not present. Hence, a nearly decomposable system linked together by networks closely mirrors the pattern of actual operating interdependence.[9]

Simon's concept of a nearly decomposable system is *analytical,* in the sense that it attempts to achieve leverage over a problem by dividing and separating it into tractable subsystems. Yet he has a much weaker conception of how to put Humpty Dumpty back together again. In Simon's model, hierarchy puts the pieces back together, but it does so in a mechanically aggregative fashion. Chisholm's idea of putting the pieces together through informal, horizontal networks is useful here. The decomposed Bay Area transit system is recomposed through informal social networks that mirror the pattern of direct operational interdependence.

Some problems, however, are not so easily decomposed (Sabel 2006). Russell Ackoff (1974) developed the concept of "messy problems" to describe such problems, while others have called them "high interaction" problems (Nicherson and Zenger 2004) or "compound" problems (Gerson 2009). Paul Schulman (1975) has similarly pointed out that certain policy problems are not easily decomposable.[10] Although some problems may be dealt with through analytical strategies of decomposition, others may require a more synthetic strategy. In a study of distributed problem-solving in software development, Bruun and Sierla (2008) found that well-defined problems were solved using modular (decomposition) strategies, but that ill-defined problems were solved using an "integral" strategy—a strategy that brings together heterogeneous knowledge into direct (unmediated) contact for the purpose of joint problem-solving.[11]

The ecological approach developed here seeks to bring together the "analytical" and the "synthetic" aspects of problem solving. As suggested by the literature on complex and wicked problems, problems often come in bundles. On the one hand, it is difficult to take these problems on all at once. So, following Simon, we try to decompose these problems into more tractable and manageable chunks. On the other hand, we do not forget that complex and wicked problems, in particular, will be difficult to fully decompose. Making this assumption, in fact, is likely to lead to problem-solving failures. Therefore, an ecological approach is highly sensitive to patterns of interdependence among sets of problems. Problem solving may start with chunks of problems, but it consciously tries to work outward along the lines of interdependence between related problems.

Ecological problem-solving can be characterized as a mode of discovery. Rarely is there a unique place from which to begin solving complex and wicked problems. Instead, institutional problem-solvers must experiment with where they have leverage over problems by trying different strategies of decomposition. In a complex problem ecology, the solution to one aspect of a multidimensional problem will often lead to the manifestation of another dimension of the problem elsewhere. Therefore, building on partial solutions, the goal is to widen problem solving to cover a wider sphere of the problem ecology. This synthetic process also requires discovery. Just as institutional problem-solvers must discover where they can get tractable analytical leverage over a complex problem, they must also discover the wider pattern of problem interdependence. Rarely is there a unique path of synthetic discovery, though some will certainly be better than others. Nor does the process end with discovery of the wider problem ecology, because institutional problem-solvers must then iteratively adapt their original strategy of analytical decomposition.[12]

Ecological problem-solving supports a wider process of evolutionary learning. In a massive historical study of the evolution of the U.S. Navy personnel system, Chisholm (2001) demonstrates how an integrated system evolved that was able to able to meet multiple objectives at a high level of performance. The outcome was never globally and synoptically designed. Rather, it evolved in the ecological manner just described: the solution to one problem revealed subsequent problems; the solutions to these problems, in turn, led to still others. Building explicitly on a Deweyian model of problem solving, Chisholm shows that the Navy continued to widen the scope of problem solving, learning as they went along, and then revising basic personnel strategies over time to align them with more comprehensive strategies. The training of officers evolved to support the Navy's ability to effectively conduct specific operations. Then institutionalized recruitment and career structures were gradually adapted to deliver an appropriate number of officers to man the Navy organization. Recruitment, training, and career mobility were gradually calibrated into a mutually supportive personnel system.

The concept of scaffolding, as introduced in chapter 2, is useful for thinking about ecological problem-solving. The idea of "scaffolding" was first explicitly developed by Jerome Bruner and colleagues to describe the ability of a teacher to support ("scaffold") the learning processes of a pupil (Wood, Bruner, and Ross 1976). Early in the learning process, students cannot solve problems on their own. Teachers can facilitate independent problem-solving by providing *some* of the structure—the scaffolding—for the final solution.[13] The work on scaffolding has focused on individual problem-solving. However, as suggested in chapter 2, scaffolding can also be used to think about institutional processes. Scaffolding is simply a metaphor. But it calls attention to the following questions: How can the solutions to localized problems provide support for more ambitious or comprehensive problem-solving? And how can these more comprehensive problem-solving efforts support more refined local problem-solving strategies?

Key Characteristics of Pragmatist Problem-Solving

The remainder of the chapter elaborates on this Pragmatist approach to problem solving. Building on the framework of the ecological approach just described, Pragmatist problem-solving should be *focused, holistic*, and *proactive*. Problem-solving strategies ought to be situationally focused and operate as closely to concrete and immediate problems as they can. However, as argued above, highly focused problem-solving strategies are rarely sufficient. Public problems are multidimensional and complexly linked; therefore, effective problem-solving typically requires a more holistic approach. Furthermore, as suggested by Dewey's discussions of experimentation, inquiry, and reflective intelligence, problem solving is ultimately not a reactive enterprise. Through a progressive discovery of problem ecologies, institutional problem-solvers should develop the capacity to proactively anticipate problems.

The ecological approach also suggests that problem solving is a *distributed* activity that occurs at *multiple scales*. Most public problems cannot be fixed by individuals or even organizations working alone. Problem solving can therefore be expected to require cooperation among different professionals, organizations, and stakeholders. Moreover, many problems do not manifest themselves in a single place with a delimited scope. Successful problem-solving often requires that public problems be confronted simultaneously at different spatial and temporal scales. These ideas are derived from not only the analytical holism of Pragmatism but also its concern with the way that successful learning and growth develop from bringing multiple perspectives into fruitful conflict.

In addition to being distributed and multilevel, Pragmatist problem-solving should also *build capacity*. On the one hand, Dewey understood problem solving as any situation in which someone tries to resolve uncertainty. On the other hand, as developed in Dewey's models of learning and education, problem solving is a cultivated skill that can be learned and refined.

Finally, a Pragmatist approach to problem solving is inherently *communicative* and *identity-conferring*. These points are derived from the discussion in chapter 1 of the limits of a narrowly consequentialist interpretation of Pragmatism. Problem solving is not just about consequences; it is also about cultivating purpose and principle. Every problem is an opportunity for interrogating the larger sense of purpose that animates our behavior. Our definition of problems and our creative attempts to solve problems signal the meaningfulness of our action to ourselves and others. As an activity that contributes to our cultivation of purpose and principle, problem solving confers identity.

The remainder of this chapter develops these traits of a Pragmatist problem-solving approach in more detail.

PROBLEM SOLVING IS SITUATIONALLY FOCUSED AND EXPERIMENTAL

Situationally focused problem-solving is highly attentive to the contextual specificity of problems. Getting people and agencies to focus on the contextual particulars of public problems has several benefits. First, focusing attention on the situationally specific can help to concentrate energy on pressing concerns, thereby avoiding ritualized efforts to solve problems.[14] Second, situationally focused activity can be an aid to fruitful conflict, helping groups to get past the kind of ideological debate that can prevent creative problem-solving.[15] Third, relevant knowledge for problem solving is often contextually and situationally specific (Tyre and von Hippel 1997). Fourth, a problem-solving strategy that focuses on local contexts can generate highly customized solutions.

To say that problem solving should be situationally focused means that problem-solving strategies have to respect the circumstantial and contextual character of problems. However, this does not necessarily mean that the scale and scope of problem solving has to be local. In his book *Imposing Duties*, Sparrow emphasizes that problems must be defined in the "appropriate dimensions and at the right level of aggregation" (1994, 52).

The Boston Gun Project provides a good example of situationally focused problem-solving. In attempting to control gang violence and homicides, a co-ordinated effort of local, state, and federal agencies publicized a strategy of bringing the coordinated energies of the multi-organizational project to bear on any *specific* violation of a declared ceasefire. As Sparrow writes: "The threat was that law enforcement, by pooling its resources and focusing on one gang, could invariably impose serious sanctions on that gang" (2000, 174). When a struggle broke out within one gang—the Vamp Hill Kings—the task force organized a powerful, focused response. Sparrow notes that the Boston Gun Project's success "stems in part from the researchers' success in identifying a core concentration within the more general problem" (2000, 176).

It may seem odd to be recommending a problem-solving approach to public agencies. After all, they have a surfeit of problems. Do they really have to be advised to focus on concrete problems? Isn't this nearly all they do? Yet this is where the problem-solving approach links up with the larger critique of Weberian bureaucracy, because program imperatives, formal rules, and budget incentives often direct attention and energy away from concrete and immediate circumstances. As Sparrow writes: "A problem-solving operation organizes the tools around the work, rather than organizing the work around the tools" (2000, 131).[16]

Public agencies do indeed confront problems all the time, but the problem-solving approach recommends a self-conscious attitude toward problems, encouraging us to acknowledge life as a stream of problematic situations that require attentiveness to the immediate problem inherent in each situation. Police agencies obviously encounter crime all the time. However, they often respond habitually or procedurally, without due regard for the crime as a problem. Problem-oriented policing encourages police to look at each crime as a problem that could be solved. While a police agency might constantly deal with problematic situations, this does not necessarily mean that it will adopt an orientation of problem *solving*. William Bratton provides a good story that exemplifies the problem:

> A classic 911 story came up back when I was working in Southie at District 6. In one year, 1,300 calls came in regarding the corner of I Street and East Seventh Street. A gang of kids was hanging out on that corner and an old-timer was living in an apartment with a window right next to where these kids were drinking and acting up. The old man called constantly. We would send a two-man sector car, get there in five minutes, kick the kids off the corner, notify the dispatcher, and leave. The kids would come back, the old man would call—always anonymously—we would arrive ... 1,300 times. Nobody ever tried to locate the caller or solve the problem. (1998, 93)

This story exemplifies the distinction made in the policing literature between "incident-oriented policing" versus "problem-oriented policing" (Braga 2002, 12–13). Incident-oriented policing is a reactive strategy of policing that does not try to understand the causes of the incident. In essence, the police respond to the problem routinely, and even ritualistically, but only superficially "solve" the problem.[17] Berman and Feinblatt draw a similar conclusion about problem-solving courts, writing that "problem-solving courts seek to gain a deeper understanding of the issues that are fueling court caseloads, on the theory that more information leads to better judicial decisionmaking" (2005, 36).

In fact, part of the rationale for staying focused on situational problem-solving is that organizations can otherwise become overly attentive to a procedural rationality that can lead to goal displacement. In Bratton's example, the police might have been quite conscientious about responding quickly to calls, but they had lost sight of the goal of solving problems or never had that goal to begin with. Problem solving shifts attention to consequences and results. As Sparrow writes: "One of the basic lessons of a problem-oriented strategy is this: *organize the resources around the problem* and avoid the temptation to force the problem into machinery created for another purpose" (2000, 218).

In the case of problem-solving courts, Berman and Feinblatt write, "No longer is it enough for judges and attorneys to focus exclusively on process and precedents. Instead, problem-solving justice demands that courts think deeply about the outcomes they achieve for victims, for offenders, and for society" (2005, 34). Each crime is therefore meaningful as an event that requires inquiry. The meaning of a case must be understood in terms of the specific and concrete circumstances in which it arose and how it is linked to other similar problems (neighborhood decay, gangs, etc.).[18] Thus, an institutional problem-solving model parallels a "pattern recognition" model of individual practical reasoning (see the excursus at the end of the chapter). Problem solving requires self-conscious recognition of the specific pattern of features inherent in a problematic situation.

Focused problem-solving implies a customized response to problems. Berman and Feinblatt write that problem-solving courts are a "tailored approach," which "disaggregates the criminal caseload, making sure that judicial resources match the special needs of each case" (2005, 5).[19] Although the focused perspective of problem solving suggests the relevance of circumstances, this does not mean that problems are merely given by the environment. For Dewey, a problem is a blockage of human purposes. Constraint on action therefore requires inquiry and reflection into the nature of the problem itself. Sparrow emphasizes that problem solving requires increased commitment to the "analytical problem of picking a problem apart—understanding its components and precursors, it causes and consequences" (2000, 225; see also Sparrow 1994, xxi). In a review of problem-solving policing, Cherney (2006) notes that crime problem-solving must be an interaction between a working "theory" of crime and context-specific problem solving. Theory helps to shape the interpretation of crime data and guide strategic interventions.

As a situationally focused approach moves through time, it facilitates an experimental approach to problem solving.[20] An experimental approach encourages us to ask, in a detailed fashion: "How would we recognize success if it happened" (Sparrow 2000, 150). In their analysis of drug treatment courts as "experimentalist institutions," Dorf and Sabel (2000) show how courts have developed criteria to track the progress of court-sanctioned drug treatment regimens over time, iteratively updating their instructions to offenders in light of their successes and failures.

PROBLEM SOLVING IS HOLISTIC

Pragmatist problem-solving would suggest that we make complex problems more tractable by focusing on the specific situations and contexts in which they occur. This strategy is broadly in the spirit of Simon's analytic strategy of "decomposing" complex problems into simpler problems. However, Pragmatist problem-solving would also treat problems in more holistic terms. This holism would start by treating the problems singled out for focused attention in a holistic way. Thus, a Pragmatist problem-solving strategy might start with the tractable youth homicide problem rather than the more "wicked" youth gang problem. However, it would treat the youth homicide problem, as did the Boston Gun Project, in holistic terms, bringing a wide range of techniques and resources to bear on this delimited problem. Once this more tractable problem is under control, the Pragmatist problem-solving strategy would build outward to other related problems, using upstream solutions as scaffolds for downstream problem-solving. Ultimately, Pragmatist problem-solving would build toward more holistic solutions to more complex problems, following pathways of interdependence between problems. The youth homicide solution would become the first step to a youth gang solution.

A situationally focused approach to problem solving permits problems to be treated holistically (Blanco 1994, 66). To the extent that it recognizes the contextual character of problems, situational thinking encourages us to think of the full and integrative specificity of a particular problem. An overly analytical approach to specific "cases" can undermine the integrative aspect of problem solving. Minow, for example, argues that the typical proceduralism of courts tends to greatly narrow the consideration of cases as problems. By contrast, she describes Judge Jack Weinstein's commitment to "the whole problem" (Minow 1997, 2013).

A holistic approach to problems often depends on perceiving the ecological character of problems.[21] In *Good Cops*, Harris describes an example of effective problem-solving:

> Problem-oriented policing, with its focus on taking a holistic view of troubled situations, is central to preventive policing, and Lindsay and her colleagues put this approach to work in Los Angeles County. Instead of attacking a jumble of discrete crimes on an ad hoc basis, teams of police officers and their allies—residents, property managers, and other city service providers—would examine each housing project as a whole, seeking to eliminate entire patterns of incidents using a range of approaches in addition to arrest. (2005, 71)

Situationally focused problem-solving is naturally focused on contextual particulars, but it must be encouraged to go beyond particulars through more holistic action.

Pragmatist problem-solving must move beyond immediate context in an attempt to understand and solve problems. Sparrow, for example, argues that innovative regulatory programs will "move beyond individual problems, risks, or patterns of non-compliance to establish dynamic systems or mechanisms for identifying high risk areas, quantifying them, comparing them, selecting focus areas, and then managing them on a continuing basis" (Sparrow 2000, 89). Problems often do not have clear boundaries and they are linked to other problems in complex, interdependent relationships.[22] While it is important to focus on contextual details, by itself this approach can lead to an overly narrow approach to wider problem ecologies. As Mitroff (1998) argues, problem solving often fails because it draws the boundaries of problem-definition too narrowly.[23]

To cope with the interconnectedness of problems, Pragmatist problem-solving is therefore expansive (or "progressive" in Sparrow's terms). Sparrow argues that problem solving needs to "consider the interconnectedness of systems" (2000, 148). It may build, for example, from small successes toward larger successes. In describing the successful Boston Gun Project, Sparrow notes that: "The Operation Ceasefire strategy also demonstrates the possibility of focusing on particular behaviors and eliminating them one by one (but across the board), successively moving to less and less serious behaviors in what Kennedy calls a 'strategically serial fashion' (2000, 179)". This example suggests movement from most serious to less serious offenses, building more comprehensive solutions to problems in the process. However, problem solving may also move from more tractable problems outward to those less tractable, gradually developing the scaffolding to solve more wicked problems.

A holistic orientation is also important to avoid merely displacing problems from one location to another or to avoid problem solutions that create subsequent problems. As Gary Alan Fine observes: "Each solution sets the terms for later problems and constrains their solutions" (2006, 8).[24] The problem-oriented policing model suggests that rather than treat each incident as unique, the goal is to identify broader patterns of crime. For Goldstein, a problem is "a cluster of similar, related, or recurring incidents" (Goldstein 1990, 66). The problem-oriented policing model uses this strategy of systemic pattern recognition to motivate more situational crime-prevention strategies (Braga 2002, 16–22). Holistic thinking probes the deeper causes of problems.

PROBLEM SOLVING IS PROACTIVE

Problems, of course, arise naturally all the time. But as the previous discussion of focused and holistic problem-solving suggests, Pragmatism would have us change our relationship to problems. Not only should we adopt a perspective that emphasizes solving problems and try to solve them in more holistic ways; Pragmatism would also have us get out in front of problems. Instead of merely reacting to problems, we ought to anticipate them and adopt strategies that prevent problems from occurring in the first place. A proactive strategy is, in fact, a natural complement to a strategy that reflects on the deeper causes of problems and then seeks more holistic solutions. Public agencies are often continuously responding to problems. However, problem response is quite often reactive. Pragmatism suggests that the desire to cultivate purpose and principle should encourage a more proactive stance toward problems—one that tries to solve them before they occur. Such a stance, however, creates challenges for institutions, which must be specifically designed for a proactive approach.

Again, problem-oriented policing provides one of the best examples of the attempt to shift from reactive to proactive problem-solving. Problem-solving policing seeks to prevent crime before it occurs, rather than simply react to it after it has occurred (Goldstein 1990). In describing a preventive approach to policing, Harris writes:

> A problem-solving approach focuses police work on keeping public safety issues from arising or at least on minimizing them by forcing police to look for patterns in crime and disorder. This means that police begin to view each incident as a symptom of a larger problem. Solving the larger problem will be the most effective possible option for minimizing future problems. (2005, 28–29)

Preventive policing, Harris argues, requires "building connections and partnerships between the police and the communities they serve" (2005, 28). In part, this changing relationship with the community is based on informational needs required by a preventive approach. Getting out in front of an issue requires an understanding of causes, so that it is possible to get beyond merely responding to symptoms (the reactive approach). Preventive problem-solving also increases the requirements for coordination, both within an agency and between the agency and the public, creating a "reciprocal interdependence." Preventive problem-solving requires achieving some sense of upstream agreement that certain problems are worth solving preventively.[25]

Part of the problem with reactive problem-solving is that it tends to be punitive. In child welfare, for example, strategies that "react" to cases of child abuse often adopt a highly punitive strategy to parents that have abused their children. This punitive approach can lead to a very sour relationship between child protective services and the communities in which they intervene. By contrast, a family preservation strategy, which seeks to prevent abuse in the first place, requires or allows the development of a more positive relationship with families and communities (Hagedorn 1996).[26] Moving regulation from end-of-pipe "pollution control" toward a strategy of "pollution prevention" is another example of a shift toward a proactive strategy. (See Mayer, Brown, and Linder 2002; also see O'Rourke and Lee 2004 on the Massachusetts Toxic Use Reduction Act.) Moving toward a proactive stance often requires shifting attention to the design phase of activities.[27]

As scholars of problem-oriented policing note, a shift from reactive to proactive strategies does not mean that the police do not have to respond to crime. Obviously, they need to remain focused on problems and respond to them. But there is a danger in shifting from reactive to proactive strategies. As Sparrow notes: "What I did not realize in 1994 was how quickly and easily rejection of reactive *strategies* leads to the decimation of reactive capabilities" (2000, 183).[28] Yet even with actions that follow rather than precede the crime, the police can better anticipate how to respond more effectively. By collecting information and analyzing problem patterns, proactive problem-solving is not at all antithetical to "effective response" to problems after they have occurred.[29]

PROBLEM SOLVING IS KNOWLEDGE- AND SKILL-INTENSIVE AND BUILDS CAPACITY

Pragmatism suggests that problem solving is a form of inquiry.[30] Problems require investigation. Although agencies may confront a continuous stream of problems, investigation of these problems is often superficial. In police work, for instance, Braga, McDevitt, and Pierce note that "research has demonstrated that problem analysis is usually shallow. Police officers often conduct only superficial analysis of problems and then rush to implement responses" (2006, 21). Even in a police agency committed to problem-oriented policing, such as the San Diego Police Department, Cordner and Biebel (2005) found the glass "half-full." They found that police officers did engage in problem solving but not in sophisticated or extensive analysis.[31]

Problem inquiry of the type envisioned by Pragmatism is likely to be knowledge- and skill-intensive.[32] What kind of knowledge and skills are necessary? Consistent with a Pragmatist perspective on individual problem-solving (see the excursus at the end of this chapter), problem solving will draw on various kinds of knowledge and skill, including both theoretical knowledge and craft skill, as well as tacit knowledge.[33] As Cherney writes of policing:

> Problem solving requires various types of knowledge—from technical skills (crime analysis and auditing) to know-how knowledge . . . that is, insights into local politics and capacity to manage diverse organizational

demands and negotiate consensus between different personalities that participate in a crime prevention partnership. Building such competencies is important to broadening the knowledge base around effective local practice that is of direct relevance to police and practitioners involved in the problem-solving process. (2006, 4)

As this statement suggests, the problem-solving model would build on the competency-based organizational model introduced in chapter 4. Problem solving is a capacity that can be built up by cultivating and enlarging the skills and experiences of an agency.[34]

As will become clear in later chapters, a Pragmatist model is not content with building problem-solving capacity in agencies alone. It would also build capacity in the wider public. In recent years, a number of examples of building community problem-solving capacity have developed. The U.S. Environmental Protection Agency (EPA), for example, has experimented with enhancing community problem-solving capacity by funding community-based organizations to develop collaborative local research programs (Wilson, Wilson, Heaney, and Cooper 2007).[35]

Problem solving requires capacity, but it also builds capacity for future problem-solving.[36] Part of the way that Pragmatism departs from a narrow consequentialism is that it offers a developmental view: action is taken not only to solve the immediate problems but also to build future problem-solving capacity. As Dewey argues in his philosophy of education, a problem is an opportunity for development. The Pragmatist idea of development is linked to continuous learning and the idea that each action is in some sense an experiment. Weber, Lovrich, and Gaffney (2005) provide one of the few studies investigating how problem solving can affect the development of problem-solving capacity. They show that the problem-solving process can either enhance or degrade problem-solving capacities.

Drawing on an evolutionary learning perspective, capacity is increased when institutions or publics develop the ability to: (1) develop highly customized responses to problems; (2) experiment; (3) critically reflect upon their own problem-solving strategies; (4) internalize the externalities of their own problem-solving activities; and (5) prevent rather than react to problems.

PROBLEM SOLVING IS DISTRIBUTED AND MULTILEVEL

One important consequence of an ecological approach to problem solving is the expectation that problem solving will require coordination between many parties distributed across multiple scales of activity. An exclusive focus on problems at one level-of-analysis is likely to lead agencies and publics to over-look related problems occurring at other levels-of-analysis. William Bratton, for example, writes of the shift in perspective that occurred when he was assigned as a young sergeant to work in the Boston police commissioner's office: "As beat cops or sergeants assigned to individual districts we were inclined to deal with the situations immediately at hand, but in the commissioner's office we were taught to approach problems citywide" (1998, 81). Lack of coordination across such different perspectives increases the chance of problem-solving failure.

Pragmatism values the learning potential inherent in bringing different perspectives together, whether they come from different units in the same or-ganization, different levels of government or from diverse stakeholders.[37] Wicked or messy problems, in particular, can only be resolved by bringing multiple stakeholders together (Roberts 2000; Bryson, Cunningham, and Lokkesmoe 2002; Calton and Payne 2003; Van Bueren, Klijn, and Koppenjan 2003; Lach, Rayner, and Ingram 2005). However, the organizational require-ments to support distributed and multilevel problem-solving are not trivial.[38] An example from New Zealand provides a sense of the challenge:

> When a problem emerges the instinct of Kiwi managers, following de-cades of reform, is to seek ever greater specification of performance goals and output measures. . . . [However] [m]ore problems involve shared responsibility for results, which conflicts with the instinct to-ward ever-greater specification of every manager's responsibility. (Kettl, 1997, 452)

Sparrow observes that the limitation of most organizational problem-solving is that it tends to be localized and does not become a systematic practice of the entire organization (2005, 133). He argues that if you do not systematize a problem-solving orientation to the whole organization, including middle man-agement, it will remain ad hoc (2005, 155–156).

Successful problem-solving often requires mobilization of activities across institutional boundaries. Buntrock (2008), for example, describes how the European Commission successfully dealt with the problem of steel industry crises after several previous failures. He argues that it was critical that the com-mission created strong horizontal links to steel firms and developed mecha-nisms for consultation and negotiation with and between the firms. He concludes that " effective problem-solving requires a shift in previous power relations within the original institutional context of the organization. This is achieved by activating and structuring diffuse resources for which an addi-tional, more subtle and problem-oriented institutional structure is needed" (2008, 291–292).[39]

There is both a horizontal and vertical dimension to widening the institutional scope of problem solving. Horizontally, programs and polices often create "closed," "sectoral," or "stove-piped" organizations.[40] Therefore, a problem-solving orientation typically requires some degree of institutional change. Miettinen and Virkkunen describe how Finnish occupational health and safety inspectors shifted toward a problem-solving strategy:

> Instead of single individual inspectors focusing on a fixed set of workplaces to enforce the legislation and improve safety, the inspectors would work in teams on general and important safety problems, analyse their causes, and subsequently plan interventions to change the situation. The new model thus comprised a new concept concerning the object of the inspection activity and a new logic to guide it, as well as an idea of the kinds of artifact that would be needed as instruments to realize this logic and also a novel concept for the subject of the activity: the problem-oriented team. (2005, 447)[41]

Operationally, problem solving that moves across functional boundaries or across levels of analysis must create institutional mechanisms like teams that facilitate mutual adaptation between units and levels.[42] Since problem solving is often non-linear, these mechanisms must encourage a mutual "openness to problem redefinition" as the problem solving process unfolds (Sparrow 2000, 176). Therefore, mutual adaptation is by necessity a deliberative process, especially in the case of wicked problems (Durant and Legge 2006).

PROBLEM SOLVING COMMUNICATES AND DEEPENS VALUES

A final feature of problem solving implied by Pragmatism is that good problem-solving is not merely about achieving desirable "consequences." A well-crafted approach to a problem always communicates something about the status and meaning of the problem itself. It also confers identity on the problem-solving community itself, often in the form of an identity of competence. These features of Pragmatist problem-solving are motivated by the idea that Pragmatist action seeks to cultivate purpose and principle.

The Boston Gun Project provides a concrete example. After initially publicizing their intention to bring a coordinated and focused response to acts of gang violence, the Project brought its energy to bear on a particular gang—the Vamp Hill Kings. This gang was the first to violate the ceasefire established by Operation Ceasefire. Targeting the Vamp Hill Kings, however, communicated a message to other gangs. As Sparrow notes: "The message essentially was,

'Look what enforcement agencies can do to you if they focus on you,' coupled with 'The Kings didn't listen. Look what happened to them. You do violence, and you can be next'" (2000, 175). The ability to send this clear signal reflected the clarity of purpose and the coordination of action that the Project had achieved prior to its intervention.

Effective problem-solving often positively expresses and confers identity. In many cases, problem solving confers identity on the problem-solvers themselves, often by reinforcing or enhancing their sense of competence. Dutton and Dukerich (1991), for example, describe how the growing problem of homelessness challenged the "can do" spirit of the New York Port Authority. With their image threatened, the Port Authority ultimately developed a strategy that reinforced their reputation for competent management. However, problem solving can also confer identity on wider communities affected by problem solving. The "broken window" approach to policing provides a good example. In this approach, community problem-solving is linked to the idea of enhancing the sense of pride in the community commons. Tackling small aesthetic problems like graffiti are seen as a first step toward more comprehensive crime control. Addressing graffiti rather than more high-profile crime might appear misguided. But the approach calls attention to the way that solving a small tangible problem can provide the scaffolding that signals the larger possibilities of problem solving. Concern for quality-of-life issues reinforces the identity of the community as a place that people care about.

Pragmatist problem-solving should therefore deepen and extend collective values. Nonet and Selznick point this out in their study of responsible law: "This notion of 'fixed' due process contrasts with a more 'flexible' interpretation that sees rules as bound to specific problems and contexts, and undertakes to identify the values at stake in procedural protection" (2001, 79). Thus, problem solving becomes linked to the goal of cultivating the purpose and principles inherent in joint action.

Conclusion

Problem solving is a core theme of Pragmatism, but a strategy for applying these ideas to public affairs has not been systematically developed. This chapter suggests that a Pragmatist approach to problem solving would adopt an ecological approach to problems and that this approach yields important insights for public affairs. To deal with complex problems, ecological problem-solving decomposes problems into simpler and more tractable problems but also seeks to discover and respond to the interconnectedness of problems. Ecological problem-solving emphasizes the importance of developing a highly focused problem-solving strategy as well as seeking to deal with problems holistic and proactive way. The success of this approach will typically depen. on effective coordination across different groups and scales of institutional activity. Problem-solving strategies should be designed to promote continuous learning and should, over time, build capacity for problem solving. Not only does problem solving require intensive communication among stakeholders, but it is itself a form of communication that can signal intention and meaning. By conferring identity on problem-solvers and affected communities, problem solving can become a vehicle for cultivating purpose and principle.

Excursus on Problem Solving as Practical Reason and Pattern Recognition

This section briefly sketches a Pragmatist perspective on how to think about individual-level problem-solving. Very much in the Aristotelian tradition, Pragmatism embraces a model of "practical reason."[43] Practical reason suggests that individuals do act in an intentional and purposeful manner but that the cognitive process often departs from contemporary textbook accounts of analytical rationality.[44] While there is a broad affinity here between this point and Herbert Simon's model of "bounded rationality," Simon's model has misdirected our attention in some respects. The point is not that people are constrained and imperfect models of a logic machine but rather that "practical reason" works in quite different ways than suggested by analytical rationality.[45] These departures suggest that practical reason may be inferior to analytical rationality under certain circumstances but can be superior in others.

Practical reason suggests that people make decisions in situationally specific contexts under conditions heavily laden with the associations drawn from past experience. Hence, practical reason draws on a "situational rationality."[46] People are variably "skilled" decision-makers who exercise reasoned judgment in situations in which they draw heavily on these past experiences.[47] Skillful judgment comes, in part, through pattern recognition, analogical reason, and intuition, with a more limited (though not negligible) place for more classical analytical reason and logic.[48] Skillful judgment draws on craft knowledge, which is both learned and partially tacit.[49] However, Pragmatism avoids dichotomizing theoretical and practical knowledge and hence embraces a position similar to that expressed by Aristotle's concept of *phronesis* (practical wisdom as derived from knowledge of particulars).[50] Finally, this model of skillful craft judgment emphasizes the ability to "improvise"—the ability to refashion prior solutions or bits of solutions for use in new situations (Weick 1993; Forester 2000; Berk and Galvan 2009).[51]

practical reason is close in spirit to the "naturalistic decision-" developed by Klein (1999). Studying firefighters and other confronted with the need to make rapid decisions, Klein e decision makers draw on a variety of capabilities to make ding deductive logical analysis. But studying these decision makers in situ, they found that decision makers rely more heavily on intuition, mental simulation, metaphor, and storytelling than on logic. Intuition allows rapid appraisal of situations; mental simulation permits the imagining and evaluation of different scenarios; metaphor facilitates the drawing of analogies between situations; and storytelling reinforces experiences and lessons and reproduces them for future use (Klein 1999, 3). This model—Klein calls it the *recognition primed decision model*—draws heavily on past decision-making experience by focusing on how decision makers identify situations as prototypical.[52] For example, the firefighter classifies the fire as a "vertical fire" and knows how to fight a vertical fire: you "get above it" (Klein 1999, 15–20).[53] Klein's model provides a concrete model of practical reason as it might be applied to everyday problem-solving.

Pragmatism also suggests that individuals are *selectively attentive* to features of their environment. In fact, Herbert Simon's early description of cognitive limitations was built in part upon James's and Dewey's psychological analysis of attention. However, Pragmatism also combines selective attention with what has become better known as the central insight of gestalt psychology: that the mind actively and holistically organizes perception into meaningful schemas.[54]

In contrast to the "propositional logic" underlying analytical rationality, this emphasis on the gestalt quality of perception suggests the importance of images in cognitive reasoning.[55] Though the precise role of images in cognition remains a matter of debate, Kosslyn notes: "Imagery is a basic form of cognition, and plays a central role in many human activities—ranging from navigation to memory to creative problem solving" (1994, 1).[56] In addition to its role in "imagination," imagistic processing is closely linked to both tacit (hence unspoken) knowledge and to the emotional valences we associate with situations.[57]

Analytical rationality treats reason and emotion as inherently antagonistic.[58] Practical reason, however, sees reason and emotion as potentially complementary.[59] Our experiences have emotional valences that become associated with our tacit or commonsense knowledge. Philosophers and psychologists have recently begun to demonstrate the physiological and cognitive basis of this complementary relationship. In *Descartes' Error*, for example, Damasio (1994) argues that patients who have lost the ability to feel emotions because of brain injuries also have a great deal of trouble reasoning.[60] Pragmatists would agree with Forester that "emotional sensitivity" is an important component of judgment (Forester 2000).

Pragmatist problem-solving, however, goes beyond skilled craft knowledge built upon habit, experience, tacit knowledge, and emotional sensitivity. It should also be reflexive or experimental, which suggests that individuals or groups treat prospective action as a hypothesis to be tested against experience. As Dewey saw it, experimentalism was the core of a scientific attitude toward knowledge. Schön and Rein (1995) suggest that Charles Lindblom's incrementalist model was inspired by Dewey's experimentalism. As a model of evolutionary (as opposed to deductive) rationality, Lindblom argued that "successive incremental comparison"—incremental modification from preexisting conditions—is superior to "synoptic rationality" (Lindblom 1959).[61] Although incrementalism fits well with the local, situational rationality advocated by Pragmatism, it misses the more imaginative and reflexive aspects.[62] Forester (1993) makes exactly this point, calling for a "critical pragmatism" that balances a local, situated rationality with vision and imagination. Joas describes Pragmatism, in fact, as "a theory of situated creativity" (1996, 133).[63]

To summarize, Pragmatism imagines that individuals will approach problems with different levels of skill and different funds (or burdens) of experience and emotion. Problem solving will be grounded in concrete situations perceived as a gestalt. However, Pragmatism also suggests that problem solving has a "trans-situational" logic that triangulates between past experiences, the present situation, and an imagined future. For Pragmatism, problem solving requires an element of imagination or creativity that requires problem solvers to get outside—and to reflect back upon—local knowledge and experience. Just as actors are variably skilled, Pragmatism would expect them to vary in the degree to which they can be reflective.

CHAPTER 6

Recursiveness

Activity is creative in so far as it moves to its own enrichment as activity, that is, bringing along with itself a release of further activities.
—John Dewey, *Human Nature and Conduct*

By creating a critical mass of creativity, innovation, and dedication at the executive level as well as in middle management and among the rank-and-file, the police chief executive can tip the balance to create an "epidemic" of organizational creativity, innovation, and dedication that yields remarkable results.
—Vincent Henry, *The Compstat Paradigm*

We live in an age where hidebound bureaucracies are supposed to give way to flexible and entrepreneurial networks, where hierarchical control and planning ought to be replaced by self-organization, and where decentralization is regarded as preferable to centralization. In fact, this state of affairs is just the current round of an old debate between freedom and constraint well known to Dewey, who wrote: "To view institutions as enemies of freedom, and all conventions as slaveries, is to deny the only means by which positive freedom in action can be secured" (1957, 166). Resolving the tension between top-down and bottom-up organization, however, is no trivial matter. The irrationalities of centralized and standardized rule-making are well known and lead us to celebrate bottom-up initiative and local knowledge. But then events like the beating of Rodney King, Hurricane Katrina, or Abu Ghraib come along to renew our sensitivity to the value of "command and control." Consequently, public organizations seem to cycle between demands for decentralization and centralization.

This chapter explores the *recursive* quality of evolutionary learning for insights into how to more effectively manage these institutional tugs-of-war. Recursiveness is defined here as a *continuous and interlocking cycle of perspectives*. Although recursiveness is not a term explicitly used by the founding

Pragmatists, the idea runs throughout their work.[1] As developed in detail in an excursus at the end of this chapter, for example, Dewey analyzed human psychology as a continuous and interlocking cycle of impulse, habit, and reflective intelligence. In much the same way, the tug-of-war between centralization and decentralization can be reconceived as a recursive process.

Applied to organizations, recursiveness is analogous to Follett's concept of "circular integration," as described in the previous chapter. However, one of the advantages of using the concept of recu rsiveness is that it allows us to draw a connection to complexity theory, via Douglas Hofstadter's analysis of recursiveness. In his provocative book, *Gödel, Escher, Bach*, Hofstadter related recursiveness to the idea of "strange loops" and he analyzes these loops in terms of the concepts of "nesting" and "entangled hierarchy." These ideas allow us to "loop back" to Herbert Simon and his conception of hierarchy as nested subassemblies.

Finally, armed with an elaborated model of recursiveness, this chapter explores its applicability to the tension between centralization and decentralization. Building on the analysis in chapters 4 and 5, the Compstat system developed by the New York Police Department (NYPD) is examined as a concrete case of organizational recursiveness. Developed during the tenure of Chief William Bratton, Compstat was part of a larger structural reform that decentralized decision-making discretion to precinct commanders. However, through the use of "real-time" crime statistics and frequent strategy meetings, Compstat allowed NYPD headquarters to actively steer and guide organizational problem-solving.

Elaborating the Model of Recursiveness

A number of scholars have developed models of recursiveness.[2] Anthony Giddens's model of structuration, for example, uses the concept in a manner quite compatible with Pragmatism. In *Central Problems in Social Theory*, Giddens writes:

> In place of each of these dualisms, as a single conceptual move, the theory of structuration substitutes the central notion of the duality of structure. By duality of structure, I mean the essential recursiveness of social life, as constituted in social practices: structure is both medium and outcome of the reproduction of practices. Structure enters simultaneously into the constitution of the agent and social practices, and "exists" in the generating moments of this constitution. (1979, 5)

Gregory Bateson also developed a recursive model of life in his later work (Harries-Jones 1995). Bateson's view of recursion sought to understand not only how the parts composed the whole but also how the whole "reentered" the parts. In one account, Bateson regarded recursion as a form of causal looping: "a system of causation turned in upon itself and controls itself" (Harries-Jones 1995, 186).[3]

From the perspective of trying to overcome the dualism of centralization and decentralization, however, we can turn to an important theorist of complexity, the computer scientist Douglas Hofstadter. Recursiveness is a central concept in his wonderful analysis of the deeper linkages among art, language, and mathematics (Hofstadter 1979). The core idea of Hofstadter's concept of recursiveness is the phenomenon of "strange loops," which are graphically illustrated by M. C. Escher's paintings that continuously loop back to where they started (or that shift back and forth in perspective from figure to ground). Hofstadter argues that recursion occurs in two basic types of structural context—a context of levels or "nesting" and a context of tangled hierarchies or "heterarchy." It is analytically useful to point out that these two ideas exist in a fundamental tension to one other. It is this tension that allows recursion to occur.[4]

Let's begin this discussion with Herbert Simon's analysis of hierarchy as a nearly decomposable system, which was mentioned in the previous chapter. His argument suggests that hierarchy is a nested system, much like a Russian doll.[5] The idea of nesting in both Simon (1962) and Hofstadter (1979) implies a clear ordering of the relationship between superordinate and subordinate levels: the superordinate level fully contains the subordinate level within it. Federations, for example, have a clear nested structure. The state of California is encompassed by the larger association of the United States of America. Furthermore, the jurisdictions of each of the states are mutually exclusive. California does not share territory with Nevada.

Since this concept of nesting is so pervasive, there is a tendency for analysts to see this kind of nested hierarchy as a universal principle of all organization (Koestler 1967). Yet nested relationships are not always so clear. Sometimes the nesting does not have such a well-defined ordering. This is where heterarchy comes in. From a set-theoretic perspective, the units of the heterarchy overlap, both vertically and horizontally—imagine California and Nevada sharing authority over a patch of territory. The units of a heterarchy are interpenetrating. In network-theoretic terms, the heterarchy is an organization structured according to the principle of many-to-many rather than many-to-one ties (Kontopolous 1993; Ansell 2000) (see fig. 2). In a heterarchy, both units and levels can still be observed, though they are less distinct than in the nearly decomposable hierarchy imagined by Simon. As a network of relationships becomes more spaghetti-like—"entangled" in Hofstadter's terms—the distinctiveness of both levels and units is lost.

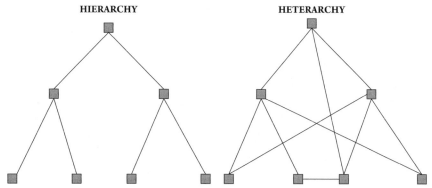

Figure 2. Hierarchy and Heterarchy Compared.

Before proceeding, it is perhaps useful to draw a distinction between structural and behavioral organization. In terms of formal authority, the United States is a nested, clearly ordered hierarchy. However, when it comes to dealing with a tricky problem like control over water from the Colorado River, this nested ordering can often become less distinct. In behavioral terms, the relationship between California and Nevada probably looks more heterarchical, though structurally their jurisdictions are clearly demarcated.

In dynamic terms, the strange loops described by Hofstadter occur when a subordinate level (e.g., nested within a more encompassing level) flips over to become the superordinate level. The prior ordering is *inverted*. This cannot easily occur in a strictly hierarchical organization, with a clear ordering of relations between the whole and its parts.[6] It is more likely to occur in a heterarchical organization, where the relationship between the whole and the parts is not as well defined. On the other hand, an inversion has no meaning in organizations without nested levels. When an organization becomes completely entangled—a spaghetti-like network—there are no distinct levels.

When a level of organization shifts back and forth between being superordinate (the nesting level) and subordinate (the nested level), you have the possibility of a powerful form of recursiveness that possibly overcomes the tension between top-down and bottom-up organization. In most contemporary organizations, this is likely to happen on the behavioral rather than on the structural level. In Dewey's recursive model of habit, impulse, and intelligence, the inversion is the temporary reordering of perspective. Intelligence, for Dewey, may temporarily stand above and outside habit and impulse, but then perspective shifts back to habit and impulse as one engages in action.[7] An "inversion" flips over hierarchy, placing the previously subordinate role in a (temporarily) superordinate position.[8] Such temporary inversions of perspective and even command occur, behaviorally, all the time in hierarchies. Rochlin, La Porte, and Roberts

(1987) offer a good example in the aircraft carriers they studied. They found that a naval officer will defer to an enlisted person when the situation is a technical one and the enlisted person has greater technical or contextual knowledge.

To summarize, a recursive system can develop where organization—structural or behavioral—is heterarchical. This system should have some recognizable units and levels (a relationship of nesting), but these levels will be reciprocally embedded in each other. Under these conditions, recursive "strange loops" are possible. These loops work according to "inversions" in which subordinate levels flip over to become temporarily superordinate levels, only to flip back into a subordinate role. These ideas are consistent with the initial definition of recursiveness as a continuous and interlocking cycle of perspectives.

The NYPD and Compstat

With these ideas about how to describe recursiveness, we can analyze a concrete example—the NYPD's Compstat system. Compstat, which stands for "compare statistics," is a crime-fighting strategy developed by the NYPD under the leadership of former NYPD Police Chief William Bratton and refined and extended by subsequent chiefs (Howard Safir and Raymond Kelly). The centerpiece of Compstat is the use of real-time statistics to analyze crime patterns and to develop customized crime control strategies. It is often credited with a dramatic reduction of crime that led to New York's current claim to be the "safest big city in America," though the precise causal relationship between Compstat and crime reduction is contested.[9] This chapter treats Compstat as an "existence proof" that recursiveness is a plausible mechanism for describing organizational life. The recursive qualities of Compstat helped the NYPD overcome persistent bureaucratic pathologies.

In his introduction to Phyllis McDonald's study of Compstat, former NYPD Police Chief William Bratton succinctly describes the problem of hierarchy in the pre-Compstat NYPD:

> The CompStat system and its results reflect a sea change in the way the New York Police Department does business. Like many large bureaucracies, the NYPD had been organized around avoiding risk and failure. For years, precinct commanders had been constrained on every side by regulations and procedures. Many police operations, such as prostitution sweeps and executing search warrants, could only be conducted by centralized units, reflecting an abiding distrust of precinct personnel and resources. Yet, despite all the micromanagement, the department was providing very little in the way of strategic direction. It was clear what precinct commanders and personnel weren't

allowed to do, but much less clear what they *ought* to be doing to combat crime, disorder, and fear. (McDonald 2002, xiii)

Earlier attempts to deal with these bureaucratic pathologies sought to decentralize discretion to "beat cops," a strategy closely linked to the NYPD's broader agenda of encouraging community policing. Bratton also sought to partially decentralize decision making, but the beneficiaries of this decentralization were middle managers rather than street-level bureaucrats. Precinct commanders were given much greater authority and responsibility, while being held accountable to top police executives through the Compstat process.[10] From one perspective, the Compstat process looks almost like a Tayloristic centralization of decision making. But as Greenberg notes: "The crime control model is not a contradiction to the 'bottom-up' theory espoused in community policing. Rather this model is where the 'bottom-up' and 'top-down' theories meet" (McDonald 2002, 50).

Within the literatures on policing, the Compstat model is often described from the perspective of problem-oriented policing, "broken windows" policing, or community policing; within the management literature, it shares some features with management-by-objectives, total quality management, strategic planning, and process reengineering. Compstat's emphasis on performance measures and results-oriented accountability means that it also shares a family resemblance to New Public Management. Additionally, Compstat's reliance on computer technology leads some people to view it as primarily a management information system.[11] These descriptions are often apt, but from a recursiveness perspective they often overstress the use of Compstat to achieve top-down accountability.[12]

Overall, the Compstat process has some striking similarities with Dewey's analysis of the relationship between habit, impulse, and intelligence. The Compstat meetings operate like high-level reflective intelligence, aiming to reorganize the routines of local units. Much traditional policing is incident-oriented and reactive, leading patrol officers (and others) to work according to rather unreflective routines.[13] The Compstat meetings add the kind of reflective intelligence into the mix that Dewey describes as essential for continuous readaptation of habit. As McDonald writes:

The questioning is also designed to ensure that the patrol commander is evaluating all these tactics and strategies for effectiveness and altering them or experimenting with different applications if the desired results are not being achieved. In addition, the questions should provide the patrol commander with new approaches to consider in designing solutions to problems, ensure that needed specialized units are cooperating with patrol, and ensure that the crime reduction objectives are being adequately addressed. (McDonald 2002, 44)

Compstat's four basic principles—accurate, timely intelligence; rapid deployment; effective tactics; and relentless follow-up and assessment—call for a continuous looping cycle of experimentation.[14]

The core technology of Compstat—real-time crime statistics analyzed collectively in frequent Compstat meetings—is by no means a completely novel strategy in policing. Police departments have long collected and used crime statistics, and they have also used push-pin maps.[15] Command meetings to plan crime control strategies are certainly not a novelty. But traditionally, crime control statistics became available after a long delay (say, six months), and command meetings were more infrequent and exclusive (limited to top executives). Most importantly, real-time data were not closely integrated into time-sensitive operational decision-making. The Compstat process uses real-time data collated several times a week to refine operational strategies in frequent, elaborate, and inclusive strategy meetings.[16]

Dewey's analysis of habit, impulse, and intelligence can be read as an attempt to overcome the dualities of theory/practice and thought/ action. The equivalent in policing is to overcome the duality between central command planning (theory, intellectual work) versus street-level operations (practice, experience, routine).[17] In fact, this tension was expressed as a tension between the administrative (program maintenance) role of executives and middle-level managers and the active on-the-ground role of beat officers. As McDonald notes:

> In the past, most commanders in patrol viewed their job as primarily administrative. Their administrative roles were reinforced by community policing as the beat officer became the central element of problem solving and crime resolution in the police department while community policing encouraged partnership with the community, but it also reinforced an isolation from the patrol commander. (McDonald 2002, 73)

Like Dewey in *Human Nature and Conduct*, Compstat adopts an action-oriented attitude. The goal is to shift attention from program maintenance to active crime-fighting. For example, McDonald notes the bias against creating standing programs to deal with crime problems:

> Too often in the past, both police and government have established "programs" to attack a specific problem. The programs then tended to go on indefinitely, as routines were established, personnel became wedded to new positions, and results were not checked. One impact

of continuous and ongoing feedback is a new urgency that produces dramatic results. (McDonald 2002, 80)

Compstat helps to overcome a division of labor that keeps top police executives and precinct commanders focused on either very high-level planning or on administrative details and keeps local patrol cops acting in a reactive, incident-oriented way.[18]

Having broadly described the affinity between Dewey's analysis of the recursive loop between habit, impulse, and intelligence and Compstat's continuous reconstruction of crime control strategy, let's broaden the analysis to consider the more elaborated model of recursiveness. In terms of the organizational chart, the NYPD was, and is, a neatly organized hierarchy. Specialized police units (e.g., investigation, patrol, etc.) are clearly demarcated and nested within a traditional hierarchical structure. However, the Compstat reforms created a new kind of nesting that responds to some of the traditional "stovepiping" problems of police departments. As with many large police agencies, the NYPD suffered from the lack of cooperation between specialized police units. Jack Maple, one of Bratton's top aides, provides a vivid example:

A borough-wide narcotics commander might assure me his people worked closely with homicide investigators to solve shootings and murders. But if I said, "Then tell me, what is the name of your counterpart in Homicide?" he could draw a blank. Drug trafficking was responsible for 30 to 50 percent of the city's murders ... but narcotics and detectives didn't get together to compare notes. (Maple 1999, 23)[19]

The reforms made the geographic patrol unit—the precinct—the fundamental unit of policing, subordinating specialized units to the precinct commander (McDonald 2002 13, 58). Speaking about the failure of detectives and narcotics to cooperate, Maple provides a good example of the reformed structure:

We couldn't just present this evidence [on drug-related homicides] to the detectives and Narcotics and ask them to play nice together; we forced the issue. Into each borough's homicide squad, we introduced a "narcotics module," consisting of a supervisor, six narcotics investigators, and two undercover officers, who could do buy-and-busts into the drug crews targeted by the investigators for questioning about the homicides. (Maple 1999, 104)

Although the actual structure of the NYPD did not need to change drastically, units based on geographical area (precincts) were given a priority over specialized units.[20] This was symbolized by the Compstat meetings themselves, where precinct commanders made the primary presentations about crime in their precinct while the chiefs and relevant personnel from more specialized waited in the wings (Silverman 1999, 118).

The shift to geographic-based policing led to a corresponding shift from hierarchical (many-to-one) to heterarchical (many-to-many) relations among the units. Operationally, this took the form of small teams assembled for specific crime-fighting projects, which linked specialized units as well as different precincts.[21] Henry describes how task forces cut across jurisdictional boundaries:

> Small, fluid and flexible task forces were used throughout the NYPD's transformation, from the reengineering committees to the task forces that developed each crime strategy to the focus groups and policy advisory groups that defined and offered suggestions for the problems facing the agency. In the operational sphere, innumerable small, fluid and committed task forces were established to deal with problems that spanned precinct or patrol borough borders. (Henry 2002, 160)

This heterarchical style operated not only within the NYPD but also between the NYPD and the many other public agencies with which it had to cooperate. Although the NYPD always had relationships with these other agencies, Henry notes that the number of linkages became much more extensive after Compstat, so that "a schematic depiction of all the lines of communication and interaction among these agencies would resemble a web, with multiple interconnecting lines extending from each agency to every other agency" (Henry 2002, 8).

Heterarchy is vividly present in the Compsat meetings themselves. In these meetings:

> The Commander can respond directly and publicly to the executive asking the question, and an atmosphere of transparency and fairness is created because everyone in the room is privy to the same information and everyone is held to the same standard. As we'll see, this arrangement altered the ineffective traditional system of hierarchical communication (that is, communication up and down the established linear channels of a traditional organizational chart), transforming it into a communications model that resembled what Bratton has called a "seamless web" . . . rather than a pyramid. (Henry 2002, 264)

The Compstat meetings bring executives, precinct commanders, and various units into a small, transparent, and consequently highly energized arena (Henry 2002, 17–18).[22] The transparency inherent in these meetings is an important energizer of cross-functional cooperation (Henry 2002, 20, 270). As Silverman notes, Compstat brings jurisdictional disputes "out in the open" (Silverman 1999, 111).

Although in many respects the Compstat system appears to operate like a centralized accountability mechanism, it actually works to create a continuous cycle of learning between executives, middle managers, and street-level operatives.[23] Precinct commanders learn that the Compstat meetings provide a forum for them to communicate with top executives and make direct requests for resources and cooperation (inverting the traditional top-down relationship). Prior to Compstat, precinct commanders would have had to navigate many bureaucratic layers to gain the audience of top brass (Henry 2002, 109). But with Compstat, they have developed a much more direct relationship. Henry describes the value of Compstat to commanders:

> This is the commander's chance to bring problems and issues (especially those concerning the adequacy of resources and crime patterns that cross precinct boundaries) to the attention of executive staff—in essence to publicly communicate their needs and, in doing so, to place some of the responsibility and some of the accountability on the executives. It is also the commander's chance to impress his or her peers, and the motivational power of peer pressure is an important dynamic in Compstat. . . . In other words, commanders feel accountable to their peers as well as to the executive corps. (Henry 2002, 267)

Thus, the increasing transparency of information and decision making is a two-way street.

Compstat meetings encourage the development of shared ownership of problems across hierarchical levels. After the probing questioning of the Compstat meeting and the direct cooperation in strategy formation, top executives cannot plausibly deny knowledge or responsibility for operational strategies (or constraints imposed by resources or lack of cooperation). The Compstat system therefore empowers precinct-level officers, which they use to claim resources and support unavailable in the traditional NYPD.[24] One good example offered by Henry describes a beat cop, Michael Kelley, who was trying to rid a tough neighborhood of drug dealing. Kelley tried arresting individual dealers but discovered that they were replaced as quickly as he arrested them:

Kelley approached his precinct commander, whose position, power, rank, and authority provided access to the kind of personnel and other resources necessary to effectively address the problem in its entirety. The precinct commander then mobilized the resources of other patrol officers, narcotics investigators, and homicide detectives, along with the DA's office personnel to pursue the problem (Henry 2002, 140). This same "inverted" logic can then work its way back up the hierarchy, with precinct commanders making claims on resources and support from higher levels and other units.

It is therefore a mistake to narrowly think of Compstat as a system of top-down accountability or management by results. Clearly, it has strong elements of accountability and performance measurement built into it. But these features can only be seen in proper context by interpreting Compstat as a recursive process of evolutionary learning, as summarized below.

1. Compstat is built upon a framework of problem-oriented policing. Real-time statistics and mapping technologies are an important part of this framework, but deep "pattern recognition" of crime problems rather than technology is the key to success. A deeply contextual understanding of crime problems must be linked to the development of customized problem-solving strategies (e.g., focused problem-solving).
2. Problems must be understood in context, but problems are multidimensional and interdependent. Therefore, effective problem-solving requires vertical and horizontal coordination that aligns different perspectives, skills, and resources. Compstat meetings provide the mechanism for aligning different perspectives, skills, and resources around customized problem-solving strategies. They provide a mechanism for voicing the views of precincts, specialist units, and headquarters.
3. The Compstat meeting is a mechanism for probing the meaning of problems and the usefulness of existing tactics (reflexivity). It is also a mechanism for brainstorming about new problem-solving tactics. Through the joint analysis of problems and problem-solving tactics, precincts develop joint ownership of problems with headquarters and shared responsibility for outcomes. As a mechanism that allows immediate and rapid cycling between different perspectives, direct, face-to-face communication (deliberation) is the key to joint ownership and shared responsibility.
4. Frequent Compstat meetings provide a mechanism for continuous tracking and assessment of problems and problem-solving strategies. Only continuous tracking and assessment can provide for continual refinement of customized tactics (experimentation).
5. Compstat was merely the centerpiece of a broader institutional reform that altered both the structure and the process of problem solving. Structurally, the reform decentralized discretion to the precinct level, while creating a more heterarchical project-based structure for problem solving.

Thus, Compstat integrates two interlocking cycles of perspectives. First, there is a cycle of problem solving (problem analysis, development of problem-solving strategies, application of these tactics, assessment of tactics, problem analysis, etc.). Second, there is a recursive cycle that aligns the perspectives of precinct commanders and "beat" officers with the perspectives of other specialized units and top police officials at headquarters. The central problem with reform ideas that narrowly emphasize top-down accountability or performance management is that they encourage a distancing of top leadership, middle managers, and the rank-in-file—with leaders higher up the hierarchy standing in judgment of the problem-solving efforts of those lower in the hierarchy. Compstat suggests that whole organizations can only be mobilized around creative problem-solving if leaders are directly engaged in, and share ownership of, problem-solving strategies. Even then, there is nothing magical about Compstat. It can only be effective to the extent that it produces high-quality, innovative, and continuously improved problem-solving strategies.

Finally, it is also worth noting the strong resemblance between Compstat and Mary Parker Follet's system of coordination and authority, as described in the last chapter. Recall that she stressed the "circular integration" of superordinates and subordinates, whose actions are aligned by the "law of the situation" (problem solving). She also stressed the development of "cumulative responsibility" produced by the "jointness" of activity.

Linking Pin Organization

The whole logic of Compstat eventually got pushed down the NYPD hierarchy. Mini-Compstat processes were created at the precinct level, motivated in part by the need for precinct commanders to develop information and strategy with their own staffs before being grilled in top-level Compstat meetings (Henry 2002, 273). Silverman quotes Inspector Joanne Jaffe, who observed: "The meetings have forced me to try to know everything that I can. If I have to know everything, I will make sure all my bosses and cops know everything, too" (Silverman 1999, 174). Precinct commanders are forced by Compstat to develop a detailed understanding of crime patterns in their precinct (Henry 2002, 257). Mini-Compstat processes, in turn, are pushed down to even the operational level below the precinct (Silverman 1999, 167). This diffusion of the Compstat process suggests that organizations like the NYPD might be better thought of as interconnected networks of recursive processes rather than a single large loop suggested by a Compstat meeting.

Rensis Likert's (1967) concept of a "linking pin organization" suggests a way of thinking about how an organization can be structurally conceived as an interconnected network of recursive processes. Likert developed the concept of a "linking pin organization" to describe a structural pattern in which a supervisor is a member of the team she supervises and a member of other management groups where she represents her team. The supervisor is a linking pin because she links different parts of the organization together. Ackoff (1987) developed the model further, emphasizing the circularity inherent in the linking pin model. He suggested the creation of "boards" at each managing level that included representatives from higher and lower levels in the organization. This structure, he argued, can create circular responsibility across levels.

Romme (1996, 1997) points out that the Likert and Ackoff models are two of the most prominent attempts to integrate the values of hierarchies and teams.[25] The linking pin model can be said to embody at least two structural principles: interpenetration of groups (via overlapping membership) and short circuits of interaction across levels. Romme suggests a "double linking" between vertically ordered teams in which those with local information join the higher-level team (producing an upward flow of critical information) and a manager from the higher-level team joins the local team (to provide guidance on higher-order objectives). Romme and Witteloostuijn (1999) argue that double linking increases double- and triple-loop learning. The heterarchical model discussed above suggests that the organization needs to be linked horizontally (linking groups at the same hierarchical level) and vertically (linking groups across hierarchical levels).

Although Compstat is often understood to be a strategy for achieving accountability, this analysis suggests that it is better understood as having strong affinities with managerial models of learning and continuous process improvement.[26] The linking pin model suggests that organizations are not a single loop of evolutionary learning but instead a network of overlapping loops.

One of the implications of the problem-solving model developed in the previous chapter is that the problem-solving strategy is continuously *emergent* and *simultaneously engineered*. In organization theory, the concept "emergent strategy" has two meanings. The first meaning is that strategy emerges from interaction among many participants and is not simply imposed hierarchically (Mintzberg and Waters 1985); the second meaning is that strategy is continuously being adapted to changing environmental conditions. Carr, Durant, and Downs write that "emergent strategy is undertaken by an organization that analyzes its environment and implements its strategy simultaneously" (2004, 80).[27] Compstat offers examples of both meanings: it emerges vertically through the interaction of precincts and headquarters and horizontally through the interaction of multiple divisions; and it adapts in real time to changing patterns of crime. Simultaneous engineering means that the process of organizational adaptation is a nonlinear one. An organizational unit must continuously adapt its local action to the outputs of other units, which must in turn adapt their own local actions. In other words, simultaneous engineering is a recursive process of mutual adaptation. To avoid the drift and reactive decision-making that may plague emergent and simultaneously engineered problem-solving strategies, both vertical and horizontal problem-solving activities must be aligned. The linking pin model provides a structural basis for this alignment.

An Alternative Model of Hierarchy

The model of recursiveness and the example of Compstat suggest an alternative model of hierarchy, which complements ideas about institutions and organization developed in chapters 3 and 4. Much of the current "post-Weberian" discourse identifies "hierarchy" as the problem. We are told that we have a choice between markets, hierarchies, or networks. Yet the problem is not exactly hierarchy, but rather a certain aspect of the conception of hierarchy: the sharp separation of planning from execution combined with a tight coupling of these antipodes through vertical chains of command and work by rule. The pathologies of this kind of hierarchy are typically seen from the perspective of street-level bureaucrats, who face cumbersome and dysfunctional rules that they must ignore in practice because they are so out of step with actual task imperatives. But it is less often appreciated that top executives also suffer serious constraints in this kind of hierarchy. After all, aren't they in charge? Don't they get to do the planning? Don't they get to take the broad view? From their perspective, however, they are constantly fighting fires. For their top-level control system to work, they must continuously monitor the effect of their rules on their subordinates. Otherwise, they confront resistance from street-level bureaucrats whose "workarounds" make a mockery of their rules. But in devoting their attention to the detailed operational implementation of their rules, executives become embroiled in administrative minutiae. They are accused of micromanaging details, though this micromanagement appears necessary to achieve vertical control over the organization. From the top executives' point of view, the cost is to the breadth of their perspective. Rather than focusing on the big picture, they become mired in administrative detail.

At some level, organization theory long ago noticed this dilemma and proposed alternatives, which were discovered in practice. For example, in the structural contingency tradition, Chandler described the multidivisional (M-form) organization, Stinchcombe described the craft organization, and Burns and Stalker described the organic organization. Perhaps Chandler's description of an M-form as it developed under Dupont (as opposed to GM) is most telling.[28] Rather than creating a tight coupling of planning and operations, the Dupont family gradually separated a high-level planning body from its semi-independent divisions. This allowed the planning body to truly plan and allowed the divisions to focus on how to best achieve their goals. In many respects, the move to the M-form is the original version of "management by results"—the shift from control by inputs (operational rules) to control by outputs (production results). Yet what sometimes gets lost in this contemporary discussion—especially as interpreted by New Public Management and by a principal-agent perspective—is something that Chandler noticed: this separation allowed the Dupont board to focus on high-quality planning.

Pragmatism leads toward some of the same conclusions as the principal-agent model and New Public Management, but like Chandler it notices different features of the resulting system. Chandler's M-form model, however, also tends to miss some of the important features of a Pragmatist-inspired approach. For example, if a high-level planning board develops general policy, and semi-independent divisions focus on the details of running their operations, then how do the two levels get aligned? How does the planning level, for example, know what it wants in the form of "results" without a detailed understanding of what is happening on the ground? And if they don't understand the context in which their policy will be implemented, don't they run into the same kinds of mismatch problems that their Weberian predecessors encountered? Pragmatism points to the value of an intermediary third level—a problem-focused level—that can intermediate between the top and the bottom.

Ironically, perhaps, we find an interesting and concrete example of this tripartite system in the development of the Tennessee Valley Authority (TVA), which Selznick critically studied. The TVA was run by a three-member board that operated like a high-level planning body. Below this board was a series of semi-independent operational divisions. As described in detail by Hargrove (1994), the key institution that mediated between the board and the semi-independent divisions was the general manager system. The general manager was a two-way communication conduit between the board and the divisions, often running shuttle diplomacy between the two and ultimately developing a measure of independent power because of this powerful brokerage role.

Compstat is a similar type of intermediary institution between high-level planning and street-level operations. Even more than a general manager system, Compstat provides the interface between policy planning and street-level operations. This interface is built on the concept of a strong role for precinct commanders, those archetypal "middle managers."[29] New Public Management, by contrast, often reduces the role of these middle managers, who are understood to be cogs in an input-oriented bureaucratic rule system. For Compstat—as for the TVA—these middle managers are the critical link in communicating between planning and operations. The Compstat interface itself allows top-level planners to understand the street-level context in which they work. It allows middle managers to directly communicate street-level conditions.

A Constitutional Model of Hierarchy

Based on this introduction, we can further elaborate a theoretical model of Pragmatist hierarchy. This model is based on the idea, just introduced, that by freeing up top executives from detailed operational control, they can not only more fruitfully engage in strategic planning but also focus on giving the organization a clear and consistent policy direction. They do not do this by engaging in planning from a lofty and isolated position, freed from the cares of actual operations. Rather they engage in their role of shaping strategy and policy through closer engagement with the concrete problem-solving dilemmas of street-level bureaucrats.

The organizational levels of this hierarchy are loosely coupled and semiautonomous. The top level of this hierarchy can be thought of as the "constitutional level."[30] This level focuses on setting the overall policy direction of the organization and defining the central purposes of the organization. In other words, this top-level body is consistent with Selznick's notion of leadership as defining the mission and purpose of the organization. It is also compatible with the idea in the governance literature of steering or what Sørenson and Torfing (2007) call "meta-governance." It also parallels the discussion in chapter 3 of institutional learning as a constitutional process.

As in the M-form, this organization is also composed of a level of semiautonomous subunits engaged in operations. These subunits, however, are also engaged in planning to the extent that they must plan for their own operations. In fact, there is no sharp separation of planning and operations in this organization. Subunits must plan their own operations. There is a distinction between operational planning and policy planning. But, as described in the Compstat system, the top level must be intimately familiar with operations and operational planning. A middle-level interface between top-level executives and the subunits is necessary. Rather than being simply a command system from top to bottom, high-level goals and operational practice are aligned through this interface. Here is where we see a major distinction between the Pragmatist hierarchy and a New Public Management (NPM)/principal-agent hierarchy. In shifting to a "results-orientation," NPM suggests that the top and bottom can be aligned through performance measures, which will allow bureaucracy to escape from the pathologies of "input-oriented" (rule-driven) control. In fact, the problems of input-oriented control—the mismatch between general rules and action situations—persist for performance measurement. Performance measurement only works when the measures are meaningful measures of productive work—for example, "a test worth teaching to." Otherwise, all sorts of pathologies develop. In the constitutional hierarchy proposed here, managers do not merely shift from inputs to outputs. They must remain engaged in operations and input-oriented details, just as they must remain concerned about how to measure outputs.

Another point needs to be made here about the relationship between rule and action. Part of the criticism of Weberian hierarchy is that it leads to a stifling set of bureaucratic rules, ultimately leading to workarounds. The "results-oriented" New Public Management seeks to dispense with coordination-by-rule and replace it with coordination-by-incentives. The middle ground that Pragmatism adopts is that rules ought to be closely aligned to action. Thus, by implication, we should expect fewer rules, and rules that constrain and guide, but do not prevent judgment; and in return, we should expect these rules to be meaningfully expressed in concrete action.[31] In other words, organizations should strive to continuously align rules with action. Mathilde Bourrier (1996) has described maintenance operations in two U.S. nuclear power plants. She expected to find that operators would consistently work around rules. However, she found that operators in both plants consistently applied and respected rules because those rules were regarded as important safety measures.

Continuous alignment of rule to action (this is Dewey's continuous read-aptation of habit again!) means that institutions ought to be restrained in the promulgation of rules. And they need mechanisms to continuously adjust and delete unused or inapplicable rules (see Bourrier 1996 for examples). Of course, every organization has such mechanisms in place to some degree. The constitutional model suggests that such institutional mechanisms for revising rules to align them with action ought to be enhanced. Rule align-ment and revision is, however, difficult in organizations where top executives must use daily operational rules to gain vertical control over detailed actions of subordinates.

It is worth noting a changed meaning of centralization and decentralization in this model. These terms have the most meaning in a Weberian hierarchy. In a centralized bureaucracy, for instance, decision making takes place at the top of the organization and then flows vertically down the bureaucracy through a system of command and control. Thus, the pathologies of such a system are seen as problems of centralized control. Within this system, decentralization is seen as a useful corrective to these problems, which means relocating decision making to lower-level units. The Pragmatist hierarchy described here weakens this dichotomy between centralization and decentralization. Like the Forest Service organization described by Kaufman (1967), organizations can be simultaneously centralized and decentralized. This is possible because planning and operations are not sharply delineated.

This constitutional model of hierarchy supports recursive alignments among strategic planning, rule making, and operations. It also supports cross-functional problem-solving, which is essential for focused but comprehensive solutions to problems (e.g., the Boston Gun Project described in the previous chapter) as well as more systematic problem-solving. With its emphasis on creating efficiency through specialization and its strong vertical emphasis on tight chains of command, the Weberian or "mechanistic" hierarchy tends to create vertical "silos" that constrain lateral coordination. With its more loosely coupled levels, by contrast, the constitutional hierarchy allows for greater lateral coordination, which is essential to Pragmatist problem-solving.

If silo relationships are created by vertical and segmental tendencies in organizations, relaxing the tight coupling between levels should create new opportunities for cross-functional integration or communication. This argument is already implicit in the description that has been so far given of the Pragmatist hierarchy. For example, the constitutional-policy level of the organization is freed from the administrative minutiae of controlling vertical chains of command. As this task is relaxed, top executives can focus on the broader issues facing the organization. When administrative boundary issues are no longer the focus of so much daily attention, it will be easier to see patterns of relevance that exist across functional areas. The same is true for lower-level units. As they become less focused on meeting the myriad segmental reporting and administrative requirements coming from above—and the more that they focus on solving concrete problems—the more they can be freed to develop lateral coordination with other units. One of the advantages of problem-focused action is that cross-functional coordination can be achieved at the point of need.

Conclusion

This chapter has argued that a continuous and interlocking cycle of perspectives—recursiveness—can help to overcome or manage some of the institutional tensions that exist in large-scale organizations and that discourage effective problem-solving. Building on Hofstadter's understanding of recursiveness as "strange loops" that occur under heterarchical or fuzzily nested conditions, recursiveness is useful for understanding a pattern of iterative exchange across hierarchical levels. In a strange loop, the subordinate can temporarily become the superordinate, inverting normal status or scale orderings. This model of inversion helps us to imagine how recursiveness processes in hierarchical organizations might create conditions for more fruitful coordination across organizational levels and scales.

The Compstat case provides an example of recursiveness in practice. By creating a mechanism that brings precinct commanders into direct face-to-face contact with headquarters brass, a Compstat meeting creates the conditions for continuous exchange and mutual adaptation between local problem-solving efforts and citywide strategy. Compstat meetings create top-down and peer-based pressures to engage in vigorous local problem-solving. But they also allow precinct commanders to demand resources from top brass and to develop shared responsibility for problem-solving strategies. The creation of "mini-Compstats" at the precinct level suggests that organizations can be thought of as many linked recursive cycles rather than a single loop. Likert's linking pin organization provides a model for how these recursive cycles might be structurally linked together.

Drawing together this recursive model of organization with the discussion of "constitutional processes" in chapter 3 and the Selznick-Follet model of organization developed in chapter 4, this chapter concludes by describing a "constitutional" model of hierarchy. Higher levels of organization set broad strategies, guiding principles, and organizational values while granting considerable operational discretion to lower-level units. While the levels of the constitutional hierarchy are relatively autonomous from one another, the levels must be in continuous direct contact through the mediation of middle managers. However, rather than replacing "input-oriented" controls (bureaucratic rules) with "output-oriented" controls (New Public Management's results), the constitutional hierarchy requires recursive alignment and improvement of problem-solving strategies, guiding principles, and organizational values.

Excursus: A Brief Analysis of Dewey's *Human Nature and Conduct*

In a series of remarkable books—notably, *Experience and Nature, Human Nature and Conduct, Art and Experience,* and *Logic: The Theory of Inquiry*—John Dewey sought to overcome the philosophical dualisms that he saw poisoning modern thought and life: individual and society, subject and object, mind and body, thought and action, and reason and emotion, among others. Read as a strategy to overcome philosophical dualism, these books are not just a series of treatises on important philosophical concepts but rather a cumulative "reconstruction" of how we think about the human condition. Building on the work of other Pragmatist philosophers—Charles Peirce, William James, and George Herbert Mead—Dewey's basic strategy was to reconstruct the basic concepts of philosophy so that the two sides of the dualism are continuous rather than dichotomous. But how did he do this? Did he have a particular technique? If so, an understanding of this technique might help us to think through other related problems. Yet Dewey never fully articulated the overarching technique he used to overcome dualism, though his magnum opus on logic certainly provides a general description of how he thought we ought to engage in inquiry. This excursus examines Dewey's overarching technique as a continuous looping "recursiveness."

The technique of recursiveness is implicit in the model of iterative and organic growth that the Pragmatists, in their different ways, advocated (e.g., Peirce's abductive method, James's meliorism, Mead's model of socialization, Dewey's educational philosophy, etc.).[32] This excursus analyzes one important Pragmatist work: John Dewey's classic work on social psychology, *Human Nature and Conduct* (1957; hereafter, HNC), to provide one systematic illustration of the recursive nature of Pragmatist argumentation.[33] This choice is relevant from an organization-theoretic perspective because, along with James's *Principles of Psychology*, HNC was an important influence on Herbert Simon's important analysis of organizational routine (Cohen 2007).

Dewey's classic treatise on social psychology reads like an analytical dissection of three foundational concepts of human behavior: habit, impulse (or what we might today call "instinct"), and intelligence. Part I of the book is devoted to habit, part II focuses on impulse, and part III analyzes intelligence. Yet taken together, Dewey describes a recursive relationship between these three aspects of social psychology. In its simplest form, his argument is that habit, as organized impulse, shapes intelligence, while intelligence, via reflection, reconstructs habit. Development and creativity call for a continuous recursive cycle between habit, impulse, and intelligence.

What is the mechanism that drives this continuous loop between habit, impulse, and intelligence? It is this meta-analytic description of recursiveness that remains largely implicit in Dewey's work, though he uses an equivalent strategy in other works (particularly, *Experience and Nature* and *Art and Experience*). To create a looping action, Dewey adopts at least six basic strategies. These are presented below with selected quotes from HNC to illustrate the point:

1. *Dewey and the other Pragmatists overcome dualisms by introducing a third mediating term.* In HNC, that third term is "habit," which mediates between impulse (instinct) and intelligence: "Like most opposite extremes in philosophic theories, the two theories suffer from a common mistake. Both of them ignore the projective force of habit and the implications of habits in one another. Hence they separate the unified deed into two disjoined parts, an inner called motive and outer called act" (Dewey 1957, 43).

2. *For each term, Dewey stresses its direct, immediate orientation toward action or activity:* "Over and over again, one point has recurred for criticism;— the subordination of activity to a result outside itself. . . . Memory of the past, observation of the present, foresight of the future are indispensable.

But they are indispensable to a present liberation, an enriching growth of action" (Dewey 1957, 265). This direct, immediate orientation to action is what propels the recursive cycle forward. The Pragmatism orientation toward action is well known and is captured by Morton White's (1949) description of Pragmatism as a "revolt against formalism."

3. *Although each term is oriented toward direct, immediate action, it also mediates between the other two terms.* He makes this point in reference to overcoming the dualism of ends and means: "Means are means; they are intermediaries, middle terms. To grasp this fact is to have done with the ordinary dualism of means and ends. The 'end' is merely a series of acts viewed at a remote stage; and a means is merely the series viewed at an earlier one. The distinction between means and ends arises in surveying the *course* of a proposed *line* of action, a connected series in time" (Dewey 1957, 34). The treatment of a term as simultaneously "immediate" and "intermediate" is characteristic of Pragmatist attempts to overcome dualisms.

4. *Each term has its own advantages and its own limitations.* Value creation and creativity comes from harnessing them together, such that the advantages of one term overcome the limitations of the next term.

5. *The loop between habit, impulse, and intelligence is continuous and the focus is on the process rather than a final destination.* This recursive activity builds upon itself, leading to an expansion of capacity: "Yet the choice is not between throwing away rules previously developed and sticking obstinately by them. The intelligent alternative is to revise, adapt, expand and alter them. The problem is one of continuous vital readaptation" (Dewey 1957, 239–240).

6. *The activity-oriented quality of Pragmatist thinking regards the present as a point of synthesis.* Dewey writes that "'Present' activity is not a sharp knifeblade in time. The present is complex, containing within itself a multitude of habits and impulses" (Dewey 1957, 281).

Dewey does not place priority status on habit, impulse, or intelligence. But habit has a special role in his analysis because he sees it as the missing term in a dualism that pits the primacy of instinct against the primacy of reason. As Dewey emphasizes in the quote above, he sees habit as "projective," by which he means oriented toward action. Habits are "active means that project themselves, energetic and dominating ways of acting" (HNC, 25). At the same time, habits are also intermediate terms that mediate the expression and execution of thought. Our ideas and our purposes work through the "refracting medium of bodily and moral habits" (Dewey 1957, 32).

Habits, however, run into problems. They may run up against environmental constraints or they may conflict with each other. And it is when they run into problems—when their action-oriented style is thwarted—that they create opportunities for impulse. For Dewey, impulses are our native instincts. They come from within us rather than from our interaction with the environment and they can be in tension with habit. Impulses are also action-oriented. They demand expression and become pathological when suppressed. The action-orientation of impulse, however, is directed at habit (and by extension, at custom and institutions). Thus, Dewey argues that they are potentially creative: "Impulses are the pivots upon which the re-organization of activities turn, they are agencies of deviation, for giving new directions to old habits and changing their quality" (Dewey 1957, 93). Rather than suppress impulse, Dewey argues that it ought to be used intelligently to reorganize habit, custom, and institutions (Dewey 1957, 130).

Ultimately, impulses mediate the relationship between habit and thought. "The position of impulse in conduct is intermediary," he writes, and goes on to say: "Thought is born as the twin of impulse in every moment of impeded habit" (Dewey 1957, 169, 171). For Dewey, thought means the capacity to reflect upon your own behavior. This capacity to reflect is a form of imagination that Dewey calls "dramatic rehearsal." It arises from conflict or tension between habit and impulse, but it is also action-oriented:

> We begin with the summary assertion that deliberation is a dramatic rehearsal (in imagination) of various competing possible lines of action. It starts from the blocking of efficient overt action, due to that conflict of prior habit and newly released impulse to which reference has been made. Then each habit, each impulse, involved in the temporary suspense of overt action takes its turn in being tried out. (Dewey 1957, 190)

Dramatic rehearsal (reflection) allows us to imagine action without actually acting. Like habit and impulse, however, reflection is also a mediating term. Reflection (or what he sometimes calls "deliberation") uses ideas, goals, and principles to reconstruct habits, impulses, and their relationship. This argument comes out in Dewey's experimentalist view. From this perspective, ideas and principles are hypotheses that reshape our basic premises of action. They complete the cycle that began with habit, but they also begin a new cycle.

CHAPTER 7

Power and Responsibility

This chapter takes up the theme of power and then considers how a Pragmatist might approach the question of institutional design in a way that takes power into account. Pragmatism is commonly accused of ignoring power relations (Hoch 1984a, 1984b). Although reasonable objections might be made to such an accusation, the fundamental criticism is probably just. And if it is just, then this is particularly problematic from the perspective of a theory of democratic politics and institutions. This chapter therefore offers one account of a Pragmatist view of power and then considers how institutional design might incorporate a consideration of power.

One response to the critique that Pragmatism ignores power is that the whole point of Pragmatism is to challenge a particular kind of power—the power of conventions that claim to be foundational. As Knight and Johnson write: "Pragmatists are non-foundationalists and so deny that some nonpolitical vantage point exists from which we might render and assess political judgments" (2007, 49). Peirce's view of science and Dewey's defense of democracy are techniques for challenging foundational claims, whether in religion, politics, or science.[1] Allen (2008) argues that Pragmatism shifts the basis of power from foundational claims to shared experience, which makes power "radically contingent"—that is, contextually dependent on human relationships and experiences.[2] Another view of power that might arise from Pragmatism's critique of foundationalism is that power is exerted through the "power to define the situation" (Fine 1984).

The early Pragmatists' reform agenda also sought to create frameworks of countervailing power that would counterbalance the rise of powerful corporate and state actors. Dewey's argument in *The Public and Its Problems* is that the increasing scale and interdependence of modern capitalism and politics undercuts the power of citizens to actively represent themselves. Organized publics are a necessary compensation for this new situation. Jane Addams and

Mary Parker Follett saw local institutions as essential for mobilizing the voice and citizenship of citizens in order to counter the power of machine politics (for Addams) and national political parties (Follett) (Whipps 2004). The Pragmatist claim for the value of science, knowledge, and education might also be understood as not just a claim for "rationality" over "politics" but also as a political counterweight to other kinds of politics.[3]

Although Pragmatism is in these ways a constructive engagement *with* power, the critique holds that it has little explicit treatment *of* power (with the partial exception of Mary Parker Follett, to be discussed). Any discussion of the design of political institutions, however, clearly needs to consider how power will be managed. As a pluralist philosophy, Pragmatism might prefer a situation where power is widely distributed and diffused so that no single person or institutional role has a large power advantage. However, institutions often concentrate power. In this case, Pragmatism might embrace a separation-of-powers strategy for taming power and channeling it in positive directions. But it might also go beyond the dyadic logic of countervailing power to emphasize the importance of third parties as arbitrators and integrators.

Pragmatism might also imagine power in terms of evolutionary learning, looking for how power can evolve to become more self-restraining. This perspective leads to a discussion of "responsibility" as a form of self-restraining power with important implications for institutional design. A presumption of responsibility is often the basis for granting both greater autonomy and discretion to public organizations. Unfortunately, the contemporary relationship between accountability and responsibility is often a negative one, leading to a vicious cycle. When a person or institution is not trusted to act in a responsible fashion, more externally imposed accountability is presumed necessary. But externally imposed accountability often inadvertently undermines self-actualizing responsibility, resulting in demands for greater externally imposed accountability. An evolutionary learning perspective encourages us to look for opportunities to create more virtuous cycles that enhance responsibility while granting institutions more autonomy and discretion.

A Transactional View of Power

It is possible to develop a distinctly Pragmatist approach to power by drawing on some of the same logics used in previous sections to analyze institutions and authority. First, building on Peirce's three categories, we can think of power in monadic, dyadic, and triadic terms. Second, we can think of power in semiotic terms and thus analyze power in terms of Peirce's three categories of signs. This symbolic treatment of power insists that power is always a communicative act. Finally, an evolutionary learning approach to power can be constructed around Dewey's transactional logic.

Peirce constructed his philosophy around three categories distinguished by their monadic, dyadic, and triadic qualities. He uses this categorization to order many of his ideas, including his concept of signs. Iconic signs are monadic and directly and immediately express their meaning. Indexical signs are dyadic; they point to their meaning, often expressing cause and effect. And symbolic signs are triadic, establishing their meaning by reference to systems of signs. Building on Peirce's philosophical categories and his distinction between different types of signs, we can distinguish three basic types of power: monadic, dyadic, and triadic. One of the advantages of this scheme is that it calls attention to the communicative, and hence social, dimensions of power.

Monadic power is attributional. It is power that arises from the individual attributes of a person or an institution, like physical strength, intelligence, or wealth. As a sign, monadic power is iconic: power is communicated as a direct representation of the very attributes from which power is derived. The gilding of bank buildings and military parades of armaments unmistakably convey this iconic power. Iconic power is communicated as an *inherent* power of the person or institution.[4]

Most "modern" views of power are dyadic. In a classic sociological treatment of power, Emerson (1962) criticized "attributional" views of power and developed an alternative "power-dependence" perspective. He argued that the power of A over B depends on how dependent B is on A to realize her goals. In other words, power is a function of dyadic interdependence.[5] A similar dyadic view of power was developed in political science by Robert Dahl (1957). In Dahl's definition of power, power is the ability to get someone to do something that they don't want to do. Although neither Emerson nor Dahl analyzed the semiotic dimensions of power, dyadic power uses indexical signs to communicate. Unlike an iconic sign, an indexical sign points to something beyond the person or institution communicating power, typically signaling the potential consequences of that power to the parties receiving the message.

A triadic view of power introduces a third element that mediates dyadic power relations. Follett introduced a triadic view of power in her "law of the situation." In the context of understanding authority relationships within organizations, Follett suggested that power should be depersonalized by replacing the "power over" inherent in command situations (dyadic power) and instead allow both superior and subordinate to take their commands from the facts inherent in the situation. Another triadic approach that follows from Dewey's discussion of publics is to treat dyadic power relationships as mediated by an audience. The audience interprets and arbitrates the claims made by one person or institution on others.[6]

Triadic power is communicated by symbols—signs that refer to other signs for meaning. When these symbolic fields are interpreted by a stable audience, they tend to become codified into social orders, creating what Mary Douglas (1970) called "grids" and "groups." Status orders like caste systems, feudal hierarchies, and clans bestow symbolic power on particular roles and positions. Such "premodern" systems like caste systems, feudal hierarchies, and clans are easy for us "moderns" to spot as symbolic social orders. Yet a similar triadic logic is also at work in "modern" organization charts or in professional credentialing.

We can now make an initial statement of a Pragmatist orientation to power. Pragmatism would seek to transform more "raw" forms of monadic and dyadic power into triadic power by subjecting them to or empowering third-party audiences. However, Pragmatism clearly rejects the creation of social orders that erect foundational values or conventions. It would seek to "destabilize" (but not destroy) these values or conventions by subjecting them to a situational logic of consequences and to knowledge claims about consequences. Third-party audiences (a "community of inquiry" in Peircean terminology; a "public" in Dewey's terms) would arbitrate these claims.[7] Building on the discussion of organizational competencies in chapter 4 and problem-solving skills in chapters 5 and 6, Pragmatism would value the competency and skill of these third parties. But while valuing competency and skill, it would also place a positive value on expanding the size of these publics. Pragmatism would acknowledge a tradeoff between small groups of highly competent "experts" and a larger, but less competent "public." Pragmatism would not try to settle this tradeoff once and for all but would make the tradeoff on a situational basis. However, it would have a general bias for broadening publics by "empowering" more people to make competent decisions. Education is among the best (though not only) means of empowerment. Thus, power is tamed through a democratization of decision making and knowledge, though it is a democratization contingent upon competency.

Beyond this preliminary statement of a Pragmatist approach to power, Pragmatism would also encourage us to understand power in processual or transactional terms. In *Knowing and the Known*, Dewey and Bentley (1949) distinguished between "self-actional" (monadic), "interactional" (dyadic), and "transactional" (triadic) perspectives. Consistent with the semiotic approach described above, a self-actional logic of power suggests that power is an inherent capacity of a person or institution. An interactional logic of power builds on these capacities but focuses attention on their consequences for others. A's actions have consequences for B; B's actions in turn have an impact on A. As developed by Emerson and later by power-dependence theory, this dyadic logic leads to an exchange perspective on power. A transactional view builds on both the self-actional and the interactional, but again it shifts perspective. Parallel with the triadic logic described above, a transactional perspective on the relationship between A and B views them in the larger context in which they operate. This is very similar to what organizational sociologists call a "field" perspective, and power is therefore understood to be situationally contingent on this context.[8] A transactional perspective is also dynamic. Power is no longer a fixed attribute of one party that it wields against another party, but capacities and exchange relations are transformed through the transactional process. Because a transactional view treats power as contingent, emergent, and relational, it provides a basis for thinking about power in terms of evolutionary learning.[9]

Mary Parker Follett provides a transactional view of power. Her "law of the situation" locates the play of power in the shared context of interaction. She argues that the law of situation mediates power relations, depersonalizing power. She also distinguishes "power over" from "power with." "Power over" is the dyadic power that A has over B to command obedience. "Power with" is relational power that emerges in a situationally contingent way. This emergent, relational power is a shared or joint power; it is not simply a compromise between the interests of party A and party B but rather a situational discovery of their joint interests. "Power with" lies in this discovery of joint interests, which Follett calls "integration" to distinguish it from "compromise." In contrast with "power over," "power with" does not have the same need to constrain the capacities of others. "Power with" encourages joint empowerment. The transactional relationship Follett describes between situationally contingent action, interest integration, shared power, and joint empowerment provides one framework for thinking about how power is tamed through evolutionary learning.

Another transactional view of power is suggested by Norbert Elias's (1982) work on "civilizing" processes.[10] Elias studied how courtly manners developed and violence declined as a result of the centralization of monarchies. Manners, he shows, develop as a form of self-restraint, a form of learned behavior that is eventually institutionalized. Elias relates this development to power. Much like Emerson's power-dependence model, Elias's work emphasizes that power is a function of interdependence.[11] However, he goes beyond the power-dependence model by emphasizing how growing webs of interdependence lead to a transformation of subjectivity. Elias understood power as an evolving relationship between what he called "socio-genesis" and "psychogenesis." Based on this logic, Elias argued that "power-ratios" between people declined as the complexity of their webs of interdependence grows, something Elias called "functional democratization." Thus, like the transactional approach, Elias understands power relations in terms of larger "fields" of relations, and not simply dyadically.

Follett's and Elias's transactional perspective adds substance to the Pragmatist perspective on power described earlier. Following Follett, Pragmatism would seek to "civilize" power by designing institutions to encourage "power with" and "integration" rather than "power over" and "compromise." Following Elias, Pragmatism would encourage the development of "self-restraint" (and "responsiveness") that internalizes wider fields of interdependence. Taken together, we can speculate that movement toward Follett's shared power model might evolve along with our recognition of our interdependence on others.

Drawing inspiration from this Pragmatist approach to power, the remainder of this chapter explores some concrete institutional design issues that are at the center of contemporary debates about governance.

Accountability and Autonomy

One way to control the discretionary power of public servants is to create a system of accountability. Our traditional model of accountability is powerful because it reconciles popular sovereignty with the need to delegate technical functions and operational details to public agencies. This traditional model of accountability asserts not only that agencies are bound by the rule of law but also that, through political appointment and hierarchical command, the wishes of the electorate will be translated into concrete administrative outcomes (Behn 2001). Yet this model is also deeply problematic in practice. First, it presumes—and reinforces—a sharp distinction between politics and administration that is not easily sustained when the technical details of policy or administration are complex. Second, it presumes—and reinforces—a hierarchical "command and control" structure in public agencies. Although such structures have the advantage of delimiting jurisdictions and assigning responsibility, such attributions are often superficial. In fact, they often obscure the de facto responsibility of certain individuals or fail to acknowledge the diffuse and shared responsibility within organizations. Third, accountability as a concept of formal control, typically seeks control through the use of rules. While these rules may, in fact, achieve their purpose, they often become a form of what Alvin Gouldner (1955a) famously called "mock" bureaucracy. Moreover, the vacuous nature of the rules often leads to a vicious cycle, where the failure of existing rules is met with new systems of rule-oriented control. The new rules only add to the complexity of the formal environment and create new opportunities to "game" the system. Thus, the imposition of new rules becomes largely a symbolic affair, designed to assuage the public. However, within the agency, such rules create what Brunsson (1989) calls "organized hypocrisy," because organizations are bedeviled by contradictory needs to satisfy task imperatives and rule-oriented accountability.

Market-oriented utilitarians have responded to these problems in various ways and have in many respects transformed the debate about accountability. For example, rational choice advocates have conceived of the traditional accountability problem as a principal-agent problem. Doing so enables them to address the gulf that often exists between the preferences of principals and agents. In light of the traditional model of accountability, they accept that alignment of the preferences of principal and agent might occur through the use of rules. However, they prefer to structure alignment by means of incentives. According to this view, agencies will not comply with rules unless there are adequate incentives to motivate them to do so. These ideas are embodied in the New Public Management view that agencies and their managers can be held accountable for "results" rather than holding them accountable for detailed operational rules (Hood 1991, 1995; Dubnick 2005). This incentive-based logic allows principal-agent theorists to conceive of possibilities for more decentralized management forms.[12]

The contemporary "liberal" version of accountability, by contrast, insists on transparency and openness as a strategy to hold agencies accountable. Citizens may not have direct access to the decision-making process, but light must be allowed to shine on all the decision-making processes of the agency. Secrecy is therefore inherently a violation of this stance. This is a form of indirect accountability. By opening up the agency and making it transparent, the result is that citizens can be vigilant and provide a check on negative behavior. Although transparent decision making sounds quite attractive, in practice it can drive actual decision making underground and encourage a system of risk-averse, superficial agency behavior.

To a large extent, the traditional hierarchical model of rule-oriented accountability, the market-oriented utilitarian emphasis on incentive-based accountability, and the liberal model of transparency all share what Dewey (1928) called the "Quest for Certainty." They all assume that organizations can be controlled with precision through external control. By contrast, Pragmatism points to the idea that, within limits, we must accept, and even cultivate, the autonomy of public agencies.[13] As Sparrow argues, problem solving requires the autonomy to "pick the important problems" ("The Right to Choose *What* to Work On") and the autonomy to experiment with different solutions ("The Right to Choose *How* to Work on It") (Sparrow 2000, 246–250).

From the perspective of the traditional model of accountability, the idea of agency autonomy is a troubling thought, because the traditional model seeks to establish clear lines of democratic control over public agencies. Although quite valuable in this respect, the traditional model of accountability can be counterproductive when applied in a heavy-handed way. Agencies need a significant degree of autonomy to function well, though certainly not absolute autonomy.[14] But we should give up on the quest for certainty entailed by the desire to perfect the external control of agencies. To say this is to recognize a tradeoff. External control might be desirable if it were possible and had no negative side consequences. There is no principled reason that agencies should not be held accountable to rules, incentives, or standards. Yet the costs of control strategies must also be recognized (Behn 2001). Most importantly, the pursuit of perfect external accountability often feeds spirals of public distrust.[15]

Drawing on some of the ideas about power described above, it is possible to describe a Pragmatist-inspired model of accountability with autonomy.[16] This Pragmatist model is more like to the "let the managers manage" strategy advocated in some of the contemporary governance literature, and less like the "make the managers manage" strategy of the principal-agent literature.[17] The model suggests that we need to allow agencies greater discretion, though only to the extent that they can progressively demonstrate the capacity to act in a public-spirited and competent manner. Self-restraining responsibility is an important element of this autonomy, which grants agencies discretion for the active creation of value (Moore 1995). This discretion can only be granted to organizations who have cultivated a strong organizational ethos. External control, therefore, ought to focus on whether agencies have developed a strong, meaningful ethos that demonstrates the capacity to increasingly accept responsibility for solving difficult problems. In *The Communitarian Persuasion*, Selznick writes: "Accountability imposes an external standard. Responsibility internalizes standards by building them into the self-conceptions, motivations, and habits of individuals and into the organization's premises and routines" (2002, 100). Rules, incentives, and transparency are fall-back positions where agencies are unable to demonstrate self-restraining responsibility.

While the current mantra of accountability appears to be tough, it fails to actually produce real responsibility. In complex organizations, it is difficult to assign or attribute responsibility (Bovens 1998). Strong external accountability standards are typically levied as post hoc assignments of responsibility for failure. These external controls can invigorate a blame game that typically produces strategies of responsibility avoidance and blame shifting (Weaver 1986).[18] Despite significant efforts to delimit accountability, most responsibility is assigned post hoc. Moreover, when agency employees are held to high standards of accountability, but given low degrees of discretion with which to control outcomes, blame shifting and avoidance are favored. To seriously assume responsibility for something, people and organizations must have flexibility to negotiate the terms of this responsibility.[19] In cases where complex coordination is necessary, such negotiation is particularly important for producing authentic shared responsibility.

Responsibility

Responsibility is different from accountability. People act responsibly when they exhibit a sense of obligation to themselves, to others, and to a particular situation. Responsibility is an expression of self-restraint guided by these obligations. By contrast, accountability is an external standard—for instance, someone is held accountable. Of course, accountability and responsibility are related. For example, President Clinton's attorney general, Janet Reno, took responsibility for the debacle in Waco, Texas—where an armed confrontation between the government and a religious cult ended in tragedy—because she was formally accountable as the top official in the Justice Department. Yet it is equally common for those who are ultimately held accountable to evade responsibility and often for good reason. Janet Reno was new to her job when the tragedy at Waco occurred and apparently she was misinformed about the situation by subordinate officials. Although she may ultimately have been accountable for the tragedy, it is far from clear that she was actually responsible for it.

The trend in political life is to insist on controlling responsibility by tightening the external standards of accountability. Yet the real problem of our public life is the failure of responsibility, not accountability. Increasing demands for accountability often obscure actual responsibility and enhance the gap between responsibility and accountability. Authentic responsibility arises out of personal and institutional values, which for Pragmatism are the "fruit of intelligently directed activity" (McDonald 2004, 114). Pragmatism links the cultivation of values to the autonomy and capacity for problem solving.[20] Hence, the development of responsibility requires the autonomy and discretion to engage in problem solving.[21] The trend toward heightened accountability, however, tends to reduce the autonomy and discretion of public officials. The strategy is to formally impose responsibility, often through punitive measures. Clearly, this works to a degree, often heightening the concern that individuals or organizations have about the impact of their actions. Yet the side effects are troubling. This heightened sense of accountability can lead to the evasion of responsibility. It can also lead to risk-averse behavior that reinforces the idea that public bureaucracies are rigid and hidebound.

In recent years, responsibility has often been a conservative theme. Neoconservatives have often argued, for instance, that tolerance can be just a way of not having any values or standards at all and of evading personal responsibility. Although it is not widely recognized, Pragmatism also stresses the theme of responsibility in our personal and public lives. Yet the Pragmatist interpretation of responsibility is different from the conservative view and is more suitable to our contemporary world.[22] The conservative view emphasizes personal responsibility; thus, there is little tension with the concept of accountability because most strategies of accountability seek to make attributions of responsibility to individuals. Yet the complexity of organizational life makes this difficult (Bovens 1998). In a complex world, responsibility is inherently shared and the "ultimate" responsibility is in practice quite diffuse.

To the extent that conservativism and an individualist ethic shade together, there is a strong emphasis on personal responsibility—for example, responsibility to oneself and for oneself. This conservative individualist ethic is deeply suspicious of any collective notions of responsibility, which are seen as undermining or obscuring personal responsibility. The Pragmatist vision of responsibility, by contrast, sees responsibility as starting with responsibility to the self, but gradually extending and deepening to include a sense of responsibility to others.[23] Conservative and individualist attitudes toward responsibility understand it as a kind of discipline driven by external "standards"—fixed external norms of behavior. Yet much of modern life is uncertain and ambiguous with regard to responsible moral behavior. For Pragmatism, there is no moral recipe from which you can read your ethical obligations. Pragmatism implies an *active and situational* orientation to the development of ethical obligations.[24]

The choice ethic of neoliberalism is also about personal responsibility. Basically, the logic of this ethic is that institutional situations ought to be structured so that if you do not act responsibly, you have only yourself to blame. The "results-oriented" management style of New Public Management (NPM) builds on this notion of responsibility. As Kettl claims about NPM:

> Governing the system requires developing new links between policymaking and policy implementation while simultaneously redefining existing roles. It requires that elected officials hold managers responsible for results—and it implies that voters will then be able to better hold officials responsible for the outcomes of public programs. (Kettl 1996, 456)

Managers are given an enlarged sphere of autonomy, but then held responsible for the "results" of their management. Unlike the conservative individualist ethic, this market-oriented logic is not worried about extending this sense of responsibility to the collective level. Teams can easily share collective responsibility for results. However, a key idea is that consequences should follow from failure to produce results: managers must be "made" to manage. This logic may work very well indeed to get managers to perform certain responsibilities very efficiently. It is easy to see, however, that it does not really produce an ethic of responsibility.

A Pragmatist interpretation of responsibility, by contrast, is that it must be both creative and integrative. Situations often pose difficult problems where multiple goals are at stake. Responsibility driven by rules or incentives, and enforced punitively, may be effective in encouraging a narrowly based responsibility. But civil servants must often reconcile multiple demands in an integrative and situationally sensitive way. They work primarily in a "shared responsibility" world where attempts to demarcate responsibility too narrowly merely encourage blame-shifting. Pragmatism would therefore support something closer to what Behn (2001) has called a "compact of mutual, collective responsibility" (2001, 125–140).

The problem of responsibility, however, is not limited to public servants. In one version of liberalism, the people cannot be trusted because they demand everything without being responsible for the tradeoffs.[25] The problem is that in democracy, the people are sovereigns without responsibility. Indeed this is the traditional liberal claim in favor of minimal democracy. Schumpeter claimed that since the people do not have a real sense of responsibility, they cannot be expected to act rationally. But responsibility is not possible because decisions are too remote from individual citizens (Held 2006, 168). One of the problems with the kind of elite democracy that Schumpeter advocates is that the democratic opposition has no responsibility for outcomes either. In fact, the opposition has every incentive for a government project to fail and to interpret the results of government projects as failures. The adversarialism inherent in Schumpeterian democracy encourages blame shifting.

Without accepting the conclusion drawn by elite theorists of democracy, we can see that we actually have a complex, interlinked problem of administrative and democratic responsibility, which is ultimately linked to a spiraling distrust in government. The public and interest groups make multiple, often contradictory demands on the state, bearing little responsibility for government success or failure. The adversarial system of interest representation, which is held accountable by elections, often encourages blame and problem shifting (Weaver 1986). Parties and legislatures may act "responsibly" (Schattschneider 1942), but often the difficult work of integrating competing demands is pushed down to public agencies, which inherit responsibility for making difficult political tradeoffs. The more that agencies are placed in this position, the more that the public and stakeholders unhappy with agency decision-making will come to regard them as bloated, ineffective, and corrupt. Demand will then grow for holding the bureaucracy accountable, which naturally reduces agency autonomy and discretion. Public agencies then become less able to respond to the multiple and contradictory demands placed upon them. In the traditional logic of democracy, the public makes demands, but shifts responsibility to elected officials; elected officials, in turn, make demands, but shift responsibility to the opposition and to the bureaucracy.

This dilemma calls for reimagining a new way to link the shared responsibility of citizens, stakeholders, elected representatives, and civil servants. The Pragmatist conception of responsibility would link responsibility to problem solving. As developed in the previous two chapters on problem solving and the next two chapters on consent and collaborative governance, agencies can engage citizens and stakeholders directly in focused problem-solving. Rather than making difficult tradeoffs for citizens, stakeholders, and legislators, the agency can become a focal point for developing joint responsibility for problems in much the same way that the Compstat system encouraged shared responsibility between top brass and precinct captains. The next section focuses on how responsibility is encouraged within public agencies.

Responsibility as Evolutionary Learning

If public agencies are to play a greater role as a focal point for more responsible public action, they must themselves have a highly developed organizational ethos of responsibility (Nonet and Selznick 2001). Building on the earlier discussion of power and on the more general model of evolutionary learning, a Pragmatist perspective can understand the cultivation of this ethos in terms of the development of organizational "publics" that act in a problem-driven, reflexive, and deliberative fashion. Instead of requiring compliance with a fixed set of standards, an organizational ethos of responsibility depends on an active and ongoing process of analysis and experimentation.

Chapter 4 described the development of organizations as self-regulating communities that develop a distinctive competence and character. This chapter describes the importance of third parties as arbiters of power relations. The idea of an organizational ethos draws on both of these ideas. An ethos of responsibility depends on the existence of a self-regulating community that can arbitrate the ethical behavior of individuals and groups within the organization. An ethos implies strong horizontal accountability to peers and therefore resembles professional accountability. An ethos is personal but not particularistic. Individuals make a personal choice to embrace an ethic, but an effective ethos of responsibility will be strongly connected to the distinctive competence of the organization.[26] The U.S. Marine ethic of responsibility for not leaving a fallen comrade on the field is a heroic example of such an ethos.

Responsibility is cultivated through the values learned from past problem-solving. But the problem in much of organizational life is that people avoid responsibility for problems in the first place. In Compstat meetings, for example, it is not uncommon to hear the question "Is anyone going to take ownership of this case?" (Silverman 1999, 97). A problem-driven perspective on responsibility emphasizes the process of taking "ownership of the problem," which means to enter into an obligation to yourself and others to work toward a solution to that problem. In much of organizational life, the problem is that people do not want to take ownership of problems and external accountability systems often discourage ownership. As Follett writes in her essay "The Giving of Orders": "How can you expect people merely to obey orders and at the same time to take that degree of responsibility which they should take?" (1940, 63).[27] Some organizational mechanisms, however, can enhance the likelihood that people will "take ownership." "Compstat," says one former precinct commander, "forces you back to basics—time and location of crimes, persons involved, hours we work, and strategies we use." While affixing responsibility, it "gives you the freedom to develop your own problem-solving approaches" (Silverman 1999, 97).[28]

By obscuring responsibility, organizational complexity can lead to a drift toward post hoc and punitive strategies of accountability. Post hoc strategies ceremonially preserve the sense of precise, analytical attribution of blame, often diagnosing chain-of-command problems as the root of the problem. The apparent clarity of post hoc attributions of blame leads to the sense that the problem has been fixed. The "hold them responsible" ethic at the heart of much of the contemporary accountability discourse may be well meaning, but parsing responsibility after the fact is difficult and often becomes ceremonial and partisan. As Sagan (1995) argues, the blame-avoidance game also undermines the ability of organizations to learn from their mistakes.

By contrast, the cultivation of responsibility is more proactive and analogous to Dewey's experimentalism.[29] He says people ought to be able to agree on what counts as a reasonable test of their argument and then they should commit themselves to the finding. The analogy is that people can make stronger up-front commitments to sharing responsibility for outcomes. To do this, they need to be able to actively participate in setting the standards of responsibility that will apply in a given situation. The main point, however, is not that a precise and itemized delineation of respective obligations is possible or even desirable. What is important is that people can develop a sense of shared responsibility based on reasonable expectations about the future.[30]

As Selznick notes, responsibility goes beyond accountability, because responsibility requires judgment and therefore it needs a measure of autonomy (2002, 29–30). It also depends on adequate competence and capacity. As Caspary observes, powerlessness has a negative effect on morals; it is difficult to feel responsible for what is outside of your control (2000, 158). In sum, an authentic sense of obligation depends on both a reasoned and emotional commitment to a problem—on "taking" ownership of a problem. Making this commitment depends, in turn, on whether people feel they have the competence, capacity, and freedom to actually meet their obligations.[31]

An important implication of this argument is that personal and collective responsibility cannot be imposed on an organization. Instead, organizations must go through a process of developing a commitment to "own" a problem. On a collective level, this process of commitment will depend on a process of deliberation about the meaning of shared responsibility in given situations.[32] A corollary of this argument is that responsibility is linked to knowledge. To be responsible, an organization must be able to collectively reflect in a realistic way upon the possible consequences of action.

Divided Power/Shared Power

Previous sections argued for a Pragmatist model of responsibility and suggested that where possible we should substitute a strong organizational ethos of responsibility for external accountability. Obviously, however, responsibility is a goal—not a condition—of political life. If responsibility is learned behavior, then we should not expect all people or organizations to have it. Thus, we clearly cannot depend upon an ethos of responsibility to resolve the problem of institutional power. But if responsibility is not the universal solution, we need to think about how Pragmatism ought to structure institutions and political life to deal with the problem of power.

In some respects, the transactional approach to power described in the first section of this chapter implies a separation-of-powers strategy for taming power. A separation-of-powers strategy has the advantage of checking power with power. As first elaborated by Montesquieu and the Federalist Papers, one of the dominant ways of thinking about how to constrain and tame power is the idea of checks and balances. In the United States, this concept not only is inscribed in the Constitutional order but also is infused in the institutional order. Everyone from Senators to police chiefs operates in a context of divided power.

No institutional arrangements are perfect, but the separation-of-powers model often leads to institutional stalemate, adversarialism, and serious coordination problems. As emphasized above, governance often requires a sharing of power and responsibility and divided powers often make this difficult to achieve. Divided powers are not the only model of organizing political power. As most fully explicated in the work of Arend Lijphart (1999), democratic theory also has a model of "shared power." As first elaborated to study consociational regimes, Lijphart describes a "consensus" model designed to manage serious societal conflicts. To compensate for this societal conflict, consensus-oriented institutions strive not to divide power but rather to generate regimes of shared power.

The issue of whether to share or divide powers is as relevant within organizations as it is for describing the constitutional order.[33] To understand the strengths and benefits of these logics, the next section explores the case of federalism, an area where the tradeoffs between divided and shared power strategies are highlighted.

DIVIDED—VERSUS SHARED-POWER FEDERALISM

Federalism offers good terrain for exploration of the issue of divided versus shared power. Although federalism is, by definition, a situation of divided power, there is still significant variance across federalist models in terms of how much power is shared across levels of government. The comparative federalism literature distinguishes between "separate" versus "shared" jurisdiction types of federalism, or following Börzel and Hosli (2003), between "power-separation" and "power-sharing" types of federalism. Braun summarizes:

> In the power separation model, the federal government has extensive powers to determine its strategies of revenue extraction and spending, but the member states also have the means to thwart the federal government's strategy. This is due to the principle that both types of governments have constitutionally guaranteed jurisdictional authority in a large number of policy matters. The accent is put in this system on autonomy and variation rather than on harmonization, solidarity and standardization. The power-sharing model is based on a functional division of labour between governments. While most of the decisions are taken at the federal level where both member states and the federal government have their say, implementation is almost completely in the hands of member states. Such a construction calls for a high degree of interdependence in policy-making and, hence consultation and bargaining. (2008, 5)

As this definition suggests, the power separation model adopts a sovereignty logic: each level of government carves out authority over a distinctive sphere of action. By contrast, in a shared-powers model of federalism, both levels of government have some degree of authority over the same sphere of action. Thus, the levels of government have what are sometimes referred to as "concurrent" powers. The United States and Germany are the archetypes, respectively, of the power-separation and power-sharing models of federalism (Börzel and Hosli 2003).

Both power-separation and power-sharing models have their strengths and weaknesses. The main strength of the power-separation model is that it creates a clear system of checks and balances. Its weakness is that it produces a more adversarial and negotiated style of interaction between levels of government. The advantages and disadvantages are the reverse for the power-sharing model: cooperation across levels of government is encouraged, but checks and balances are weakened. These are differences of degree rather than kind. Both systems are based on a constitutionally sanctioned division of powers across levels of government. In recent federalism reforms, power-separation federations have sought to introduce more collaboration between fragmented federal and state programs, while shared-power federations have sought to minimize the costs associated with a cooperative style. The strength of each model is also its defect.

Pragmatism has a more natural affinity with the power-sharing model, which is close in spirit to Follett's "power-with" model. Therefore, we should dwell for a moment on the critique of the power-sharing model. Perhaps the major critique of cooperative federalism is Scharpf's (1988) argument, which asserts that power-sharing countries face a "joint-decision trap," which can produce lowest-common-denominator policies, high transaction costs, and lengthy procedures. Concurrent powers do produce cooperation, but the quality of the outcomes and the efficiency of the process can be suboptimal. As Braun notes: "In all federal countries there is a common trend to turn the tide and avoid further centralization of competences by achieving a disentanglement of competencies in concurrent areas, though this trend has been more remarkable in the cooperative federal countries" (2008, 21). However, this "trend" is perhaps not as clear as Braun asserts. Bloms-Hansen (1999) suggests just the opposite: the trend is increasingly towards cooperative federalism. He argues that the cooperative relations do not produce joint-decision traps if the central government has "exit" options.

The transactional logic of power described earlier in this chapter suggested that it is often useful to think about power in triadic terms. In federal regimes, courts often play a key third-party role and judicial review is the mechanism by which courts arbitrate federal powers.[34] In revisiting his argument about the joint-decision trap, for example, Scharpf argued that the European Court of Justice helps to mitigate the worst problems of cooperative federalism in the European Union (Scharpf 2006). Other institutions may also play this third-party role. Scharpf, for example, also argues that the European Commission—as honest broker—can ameliorate the joint-decision trap in the European Union. Political parties can also be an important form of triadic intermediation between levels, as Martin Van Buren once argued in a United States strained by federal conflicts over slavery. Most broadly, the public is a third party that mediates between federal levels. Referring to the distinctive brand of national federalism advanced by the federalists in early U.S. history, Beer writes that "the influence between levels will pass from state to general government, but also from general government to state government." The "medium through which this influence will be transmitted," Beer writes, "will be the common electorate of the two sets of governments" (1993, 14).[35]

Whether courts, executive bodies, political parties, or the public or other third parties actually do help to mediate dyadic power relations in federal systems is an empirical question, but a Pragmatist perspective suggests that we at least pay serious attention to their possible role as arbiters and integrators. Another related strategy for thinking about managing federal power relations is suggested by the analysis of recursiveness developed in chapter 5. One interpretation of recursiveness emphasizes the importance of institutional interpenetration as a way to mediate between organizational levels.[36] Cooperative networks, for example, have been found to be a valuable form of interpenetration across levels of shared-power federations. As Swenden writes: "Federations which take the form of dividing functions, rather than dividing competencies require a dense network of intergovernmental collaboration. Without such networks, the federation would turn into the principal of general policy-making, the region into its agents" (2004, 381). Benz (2006) has argued that the joint-decision traps are often mitigated in practice by informal networks that facilitate coordination between levels.

This argument suggests that Pragmatism might adopt a separation-of-powers model broadly in the spirit of cooperative federalism. Although this example clearly does not provide a full analysis of federalism or cooperative power-sharing, it does point to some of the issues and mechanisms that such an analysis should consider. A cooperative regime creates "concurrent" powers rather than "dual" powers. This structure of authority can create suboptimal arrangements if it creates "joint decision traps" that produce least-common-denominator agreements and high negotiating costs. However, these decision traps can be ameliorated by third parties (courts, parties, publics) and by institutional designs that produce an interpenetration of representation. Informal institutions (e.g., social networks) may facilitate this interpenetration of representation. This is a mere sketch of the possibilities, but it begins to point toward how Pragmatists might think about managing power.

Conclusion

This chapter began by developing a Pragmatist approach to power, developing distinctions between monadic, dyadic, and triadic power. While recognizing monadic and dyadic forms of power, Pragmatism would try to "tame" power by emphasizing the role of third parties that can mediate between competing claims and demands of other parties (triadic power). Building on the work of Mary Parker Follett, Pragmatism would seek to design institutions that encourage "power with" rather than "power over." Following Norbert Elias, Pragmatism would tame power by designing institutions that deepen interdependence, while encouraging individuals to develop self-restraint responsive to this interdependence. The chapter then turns to the issue of accountability, arguing that increasing demand for external control of public agencies is often counterproductive. To ameliorate the need for strong external accountability, Pragmatism would support institutional strategies that cultivate individual and shared responsibility, which, following Elias, is understood as a form of self-restraint. This kind of responsibility, the chapter argues, requires the development of a strong organizational ethos oriented to public problem-solving. Public agencies (and units within agencies) should be granted greater autonomy in exchange for demonstrating their capacity and willingness to "take ownership of problems." While Pragmatism would encourage self-restraining (and self-actualizing) responsibility, the power of public agencies still needs to be checked. Pragmatism would adopt a pluralist view of power that supports "checks and balances." However, it would also support a more cooperative separation-of-powers model, as opposed to more adversarial approaches associated with divided-power models. The chapter concludes with an exploration of "cooperative federalism" as a useful model of power sharing.

CHAPTER 8

Consent

■

A whole series of contemporary phenomena—including loss of sovereignty, decentralization, networks, self-regulation, private authority, and public–private partnerships—suggest the disaggregation of the state, the decline of publicness, and the expansion of private power. What are we to make of these phenomena? The Pragmatist position is not, as you might expect, either-or, though it can acknowledge the danger in the blurring of public and private boundaries. After all, one of Dewey's most famous books—*The Public and Its Problems*—was a cry against the eclipse of the public and the rise of private power. How then should we face the challenge of maintaining the publicness of political life without erecting impenetrable boundaries between the public and the private?

A hallmark of the liberal conception of the state is a sharp demarcation between the public and the private. This demarcation protects the public sphere from colonization by private interests while also protecting the private sphere from the arbitrary power of the state. This liberal demarcation of public and private spheres is closely allied to our modern conception of democracy through a monistic conception of popular sovereignty. Duly constituted as a "public" by way of elections, the "people" as a single voice have democratic authority.

The concept of public that arises from this monistic conception of sovereignty is linked, in turn, to a sense of the law as a formal and autonomous sphere. The "people" do not act directly, but through the intermediary of the law and the state. To conserve the sovereignty of the people, and to express it precisely in a nonarbitrary way, we emphasize the importance of formal rules and procedures. These rules and procedures translate popular sovereignty into administrative action (or inaction). They ensure that popular sovereignty is paramount.

Thus, the classic model of liberal democracy depends on reinforcing concepts of law and representation. Popular sovereignty represented as a unitary will is expressed and safeguarded through a sharp distinction between public and private spheres; this public will is safeguarded and expressed by formal rules and procedures that derive their legitimacy from popular sovereignty. This is government by laws, not persons (the liberal credo), and law is the embodiment of popular sovereignty (the democratic credo). This marriage of impersonal law and popular sovereignty is an impressive and powerful achievement, but it is also where liberalism and democracy are being pulled apart.

An important consequence of the emphasis we place on safeguarding the unbroken chain of authority that runs from the people to formal rule is the high priority we place on procedural rationality. Public institutions make decisions by following procedures that require them to take certain democratically expressed values or goals into account. Procedural rationality protects the public integrity of decision-making processes and safeguards secondary concerns, like equity, safety, and probity, which attend any primary pursuit. But procedural rationality often suffers from legitimacy problems because it is always once removed from substantive outcomes. When procedural integrity clashes with other values and interests, the tensions between procedural and substantive rationality increase. To put it bluntly, we all detest bureaucratic red tape, but democracy (not mentally challenged bureaucrats) is the ultimate source of it. Bureaucracies are the place where the tensions between procedural and substantive rationality are most pronounced.

One way to reduce these tensions is for public agencies to engage with the public more directly. Building on previous chapters, public agencies can develop a shared understanding of responsibility by engaging in more joint problem-solving with the public. Public agencies can become the focal points of evolutionary learning in wider problem-solving communities. However, this wider engagement of public agencies with the public runs up against the trinity of separate public and private spheres, monistic popular sovereignty, and formal law. This chapter reexamines our assumptions about the monistic character of popular sovereignty and argues that it has to be complemented with a more pluralistic conception of consent. A more pluralistic conception of consent, in turn, allows us to imagine how to create a more productive relationship between public agencies and the public.

The remainder of the chapter works through a series of interlinked theoretical problems. The first section considers the issue of popular sovereignty in more detail, examining the pluralist alternative. The next section then examines the general problem of authority, setting out a Pragmatist framework for thinking about authority. The key point is that public agencies can develop their authority through effective problem-solving interaction with publics. The liberal conception of clearly demarcating public and private spheres, however, prefers to keep public agencies "closed" in order to buffer them from private influences. The third section of the chapter acknowledges this concern but argues that public agencies with a strongly institutionalized public mission can engage more openly with the public. This would allow them to play an important role in building democratic consent around problem solving. The fourth section of the chapter makes this argument in general, followed by a section that provides some examples of how this can work in practice. The last two sections of the chapter examine some of the challenges posed by allowing public agencies to become more "embedded" in society, arguing that it is possible for public agencies to uphold public values even in the face of greater contact with particularistic and private demands.

Monistic Sovereignty

It is not hard to see why a powerful justification for the state is necessary. Law and administration are often coercive and raise thorny issues of fairness and justice. Our consent to this intrusive state depends, in large part, upon our belief that the state serves us, the people. The idea that sovereignty—final authority—is derived from a unified popular will is a powerful requirement for the legitimation of a coercive state. One place to begin our examination of the problematic character of the current marriage of liberalism and democracy is with the conception of monistic sovereignty—the idea that popular sovereignty ought to be conceived as a single indivisible "will."[1] Although there is little faith anymore that there is a single "public interest" that transcends narrower private interests, we hold on to the idea that popular sovereignty ought to be conceived in unitary terms—once constituted, that is, through voting and legislatures, and then embodied in the rule of law.

The understanding of consent inherent in our contemporary liberal-democratic bargain is that popular sovereignty is constituted through election; legislators then make laws, which are administered by administrative agencies. While this hierarchical arrangement between the people, legislatures, and public agencies sounds entirely unexceptional—and indeed, normatively desirable—the practice of translating popular sovereignty into administrative action is fraught with difficulty. It assumes, for instance, that the relationship between policymaking and administration is straightforward and that public agencies restrict their role to administration. Yet nothing could be further from the truth. Public agencies are at the heart of policymaking in most contemporary democracies, yet our democratic theory suggests that we should pretend that is not true.

The idea of consent derived through voting and through a unitary popular will (constituted through the formation of majorities) also has many normatively desirable properties. Voting is an inclusive act and it formally translates the conception of political equality into practice. Thus, popular sovereignty expresses the powerful idea that consent is based on self-government, with each citizen given an equal voice in forming the laws that they will be governed by. But as we all know, there is a great deal of slippage in practice.[2] Informal processes of influence—exercised through campaign contributions and other means—skew the strategies of legislators in a less inclusive and egalitarian direction.

The shortcomings of our democratic system of representation are well known. However, our response to these shortcomings is to search for ways to tighten up the hierarchical connections between the people, legislatures, and public agencies and to prevent the slippage that occurs at each step in the process. An important problem with this response is that we regard voting as the "sole" means of establishing consent.[3] Any student of politics knows that the process of giving consent extends beyond the electoral process and is shaped by what has been called "output legitimacy." However, following from the monistic conception of sovereignty, any consent-building effort by public agencies not explicitly sanctioned by elected officials is regarded as entirely informal and sub rosa.[4]

English pluralism challenged this monistic conception of sovereignty. As the English pluralist, Harold Laski, observed:

> Unity, it is clear, there finds laudation enough. And the State as the expression of that unity enjoys a similar benediction. It, too, must be one and indivisible. Trade-unionists and capitalists alike must surrender the interests of their smaller and antithetic group-persons to the larger demands of that all-embracing One, the State. (1917, 8)

The English pluralists, however, were not only challenging the hierarchical authority of the state. They were also challenging the conception of legitimacy underpinning authority. This can be thought of in terms of the tensions between procedural and substantive rationality or between input and output legitimacy. As Hirst wrote of Laski: "Laski's pluralism 'denies, ultimately, the sovereignty of anything save right conduct'" (1994, 13). According to Hirst, pluralists believed that "law is not a pure voluntas, a positive sovereign will; rather, law must also embody reason attuned to the needs of society" (1994, 22). Thus, the English pluralists sound a lot like Selznick on responsive law, which may not be surprising because, as Hirst notes, Laski introduced "substantial elements of American pragmatism into his thought" (1994, 28).[5]

The English pluralists advocated a disaggregation of sovereignty, arguing for a parceling out of sovereignty to societal associations, and hence creating an "associative model" of sovereignty.[6] The associative model is in many respects congenial to Pragmatists. Follett's book *The New State* (1918), for example, explores these pluralist ideas in considerable detail. Ultimately, the English pluralists go too far in their advocacy of an associative model of sovereignty, undermining the sense of common association, and dissolving the whole into its parts. Pragmatism shares the concern expressed by pluralists about the problematic nature of unitary consent, but it would try to create a more positive relationship between the whole (monistic sovereignty) and its parts (associative sovereignty).

Emergent Authority

Since sovereignty can be defined as "final authority," we can further examine the tension between monistic and associative sovereignty as a conflict over the meaning of authority. Diggins (1994) has sensitively probed the issue of authority in Pragmatist thought, arguing that Pragmatism rejects traditional notions of authority but that it becomes unmoored because it cannot solve difficult social problems without such a concept. This Pragmatist rejection of the traditional notion of authority is closely related to its larger rejection of foundationalism—the idea that there is a set of a priori fundamental norms to guide behavior. These are indeed challenging issues philosophically and practically. The limited goal of this section is to link Pragmatist thinking about authority to the issue of consent.

Consider the relationships among authority, legitimacy, and rule as a disaggregation of "monistic sovereignty" occurs, or, to put it in another way, as the unitary and hierarchical character of states or organizations is relaxed. Weber's ideas linking authority, legitimacy, and hierarchy provide a useful starting point. For Weber, these concepts fit together closely. Hierarchy, as Weber argued, achieves coordination through command. To be effective, command requires compliance. It must therefore rest heavily on authority if it is not to be regarded as coercive—that is, on legitimate power. Thus, hierarchical command demands a highly developed justification of legitimacy, and a strong premium is thus placed on the nonarbitrary nature of power. Rule following—procedural legitimacy—is therefore one of the most powerful bases for constructing authority.[7]

Instead of rejecting "authority" altogether, Dewey sought to develop "experience" and "joint inquiry" as a new basis of authority. Dewey did clearly seek to break away from the mooring of foundational truths, located transcendentally in religion. But by the same token, he certainly did not reject an experience-based conception of morality or character. What Dewey says, in effect, is that we are the self-authors of our own moral universe. self-authorship is to decide how coercion can be used an legitimacy, and therefore, authority. Dewey's answer v "democracy." He saw science as a metaphor for authority collective-discovery. The idea was that we would be coerced we learned through our own process of discovery. Democra⌐, ..⌐⌐ ⌐.⌐ ⌐⌐⌐⌐⌐⌐ through which people could collectively engage in this joint inquiry.

Although a concept of authority may be extracted from Dewey's work, Diggins is correct that an explicit Pragmatist perspective on authority—that is, a conception of authority useful for politics and institutions—is not well developed. For a public philosophy, this failure to articulate a workable conception of authority is problematic. In *The Death of Character*, Hunter argues that the leveling of authority is corrosive of our collective life, and he places some of the intellectual blame for this corrosion on Dewey (2001, 181–182).[8] Ultimately, Pragmatists probably just differ with Diggins and Hunter on what counts as authority, but their criticisms make it clear that a more explicit statement of a Pragmatist conception of authority would be useful.

Authority is basically a form of influence. Persons or institutions have authority when they influence the behavior of others. What makes this influence distinctive is that it is based on socially shared symbols and meaning. To follow Max Weber, authority is power (influence) that is regarded as legitimate (based in socially shared symbols and meanings). Building on the discussion of power in the previous chapter, a Pragmatist framework for thinking about authority, and the closely related concept of legitimacy, can be constructed upon Peirce's tripartite model of signs as iconic, indexical, and symbolic. Peirce's tripartite model of signs corresponds to his three philosophical categories (firstness, secondness, and thirdness), which represent monadic, dyadic, and triadic logics, respectively. Iconic authority stands for itself (monadic). Indexical authority points to results (dyadic). And for symbolic authority, symbols point to other symbols, which point to still other symbols.[9]

When authority is iconic, it is fundamentally rooted in identity and the standard for legitimacy is authenticity. We all see countless examples in our daily life where people speak with authority because they are regarded—by themselves and others—as authentically representing a particular identity.[10] Authority is indexical when—as an instrument or tool—it points to the desirable results it has produced or will produce. This is a consequentialist notion of authority and similar to the idea of "output" legitimacy. A person or institution has indexical authority if their audience has an expectation that they will produce desirable results. Finally, symbolic authority is based on social conventions or norms that designate what is appropriate. Whether traditional or modern, conventions and norms achieve legitimacy through their claim to sent the group over and above narrower interests. Their power lies in their apparent autonomy from narrower interests.

Each of these three primitive types of authority is communicative: iconic authority communicates by signaling fidelity to identity ("I am this"); indexical authority communicates by signaling production of desired results ("I can achieve this"); and symbolic authority communicates by signaling its relationship to an autonomous code or third party ("I represent this").[11] Audiences interpret and judge these communicative claims in a similar tripartite manner.[12] The legitimacy of iconic authority depends on direct emotional identification ("She is one of us"). Indexical authority depends on expectations about desired results ("She will achieve this"). Symbolic authority depends on consistency with a skein of social conventions and moral obligations ("She represents this").[13]

If we follow the Pragmatist evolutionary learning model suggested in chapter 1, these primitive concepts of authority can be developmentally yoked together into more complex and sophisticated forms of authority that combine identity-based, results-based, and convention-based authority.[14] In this developmental model, the "results-based" (dyadic) logic mediates between the "identity-based" (monadic) and the "convention-based" (triadic) logics. Pragmatist authority is discovered through action—the production of results. But in a developmental model that combines all three forms of authority, production of "results" does not mean merely satisfying desires. "Results" must lead to a refinement and deepening of the meanings entailed by identity-based and convention-based claims.[15]

This brings us right back to Selznick and Nonet's concept of "responsive law" and to Selznick's claims about organizational leadership. Nonet and Selznick (2001) call straightforward conventionalism "autonomous law." By contrast, responsive law requires continuous discovery and reinforcement of the values inherent in law through the analysis of its consequences. Similarly, in Selznick's model of administrative leadership, the cultivation of missions (e.g., a results-based logic) reinforces the iconic identity of the organization as a community. This Pragmatist interpretation of Selznick's work suggests that a richer composite authority develops when leaders or institutions achieve results that simultaneously deepen the values inherent in broader social conventions and in their identity as a community.

This discussion of authority also brings us back to the concept of relational authority (discussed in chapter 4). Pragmatism rejects the idea that there are foundational claims to authority that transcend time and space; but it would accept that authority can be the cumulative product of evolutionary learning.[16] Leaders and institutions can build up their relational authority over time. One of the important consequences of this relational view of authority is that public agencies can build up consent for their actions, both with their own members and with external constituencies.[17] For a scholar of political science or public administration, this is hardly news. But for democratic theory, it is deeply problematic—the source of a possible distortion in the hierarchical chain of representation that runs from popular sovereignty to legislative representation to administrative implementation.

Closed Agencies

The emphasis on monistic sovereignty, on the constitution of formal public authority, and on erecting a strong distinction between public and private leads to a desire to keep public agencies separated from their environments. Pragmatism can grant that this demarcation of organizations from their environments may be critical under some conditions, particularly in the formative phase of organizational development. But Pragmatism would emphasize the development of relational authority within an agency and between the organization and its constituents. Stever argues that Dewey had a view of modern institutions that stresses that they should be "open to their environments" (2000, 18). Although relational authority already describes the relationship between some public agencies and their political environments—consider community policing—such activity is still often regarded skeptically.

From the perspective of monistic sovereignty, constituted exclusively through elections and then delegated to public agencies in a hierarchical manner, "responsiveness" to external constituencies is a slippery slope that leads to vocal or powerful community members asserting their minoritarian interests over the democratically sanctioned majority. The Progressive movement in the United States explicitly sought to create closed agencies in order to prevent the kind of corruption that was prevalent at the time—notably in organizations like the police. More broadly, to secure "public" authority from arbitrary power (either from private influences or via the arbitrary use of state power), liberalism tends to support formal and impersonal institutions, and formal and impersonal institutions tend to be closed. In supporting more open institutions, and more intensive relationships with external constituencies, Pragmatists must be aware of the concerns of both Progressives and liberals.

We also know that opening up agencies to external influence can lead to internal politicization. Encouraging an agency to be responsive to its external political environment can create, in fact, the worst of possible worlds: the procedural rationality safeguarded by formal and impersonal institutions could lose legitimacy, while substantive rationality becomes privatized or deeply politicized.

This problem parallels the one described by Nonet and Selznick (2001) in their argument in favor of the shift from autonomous to responsive law. For Nonet and Selznick, responsive law leads courts and judges to adopt a more open problem-solving attitude. But, as they note, increased openness is risky: "As institutions are opened to their constituencies, they become (1) more vulnerable to the imbalances of power in society and (2) more readily focused on a narrowing of concerns" (2001, 102). They argue that openness can destroy the integrity and distinctive competence of institutions (2001, 104). In *The Communitarian Persuasion*, Selznick suggests that openness must be counterbalanced by strong internal values: "Responsive institutions defend their distinctive values and missions, yet are open to voices and interests hitherto unheard or disregarded" (2002, 11). From a Pragmatist perspective, responsiveness should be understood within a developmental framework: only strong institutions can move toward greater responsiveness. As Boin and his colleagues have shown, it is quite possible for public agencies to become strong institutions (Boin 2001; Boin and Goodin 2007; Boin and Christensen 2008).

The Public–Private Divide

In the European Rechstaat tradition and the American Progressive tradition, the state is held up as the embodiment of publicness. This stance can drift toward an elitist view that regards civil servants or experts as best able to make decisions about the public interest. By contrast, in the populist tradition, value is derived from a "public" equated with the people (a version of the labor theory of value). From this perspective, the state represents a necessary evil, a possible source of corruption of popular sovereignty—either through private rent-seeking or through an elite cooptation.

The progressive/populist tension tends to be reinforced by a liberal/republican tension. From a classical liberal view, the best way to preserve public values is to sharply separate them from private values. Law—autonomous law—is the way to manifest publicness. A public institution is one codified by law and regulated by formal rules. Liberalism fears people because they represent private interests. It wants government by law, not men. If we think of the state as liberalism does, as a value-neutral means to the good life, then this creates a strong public/private split (Hickman 1990). Republicanism also fears men, but it sees virtue—not law—as the basis of publicness. Virtuous citizens are able to recognize the public interest and to transcend their own narrow private interests. Cultivation and socialization of this virtuous citizenry is the right strategy for securing publicness.

These traditions understand the "public" in such various ways that when combined they can produce pathologies for our contemporary democratic life. In the U.S. context, for example, we don't trust persons to represent the public, so we create legalistic, autonomous institutions; but we don't trust institutions either, so we check them with a separation of powers and multiple forms of accountability. We don't trust elites and minorities to represent the public, so we insist on strong majoritarian principles of representation; but we don't trust "the people" either, so we limit their voice through the creation of various forms of "counter-majoritarian" institutions. When this amalgam works, Americans attribute it to the genius of the founders or the spirit of compromise. But equally often, we end up with a legalistic and fragmented republic with contradictory tendencies to strengthen or curtail state or popular power. Lijphart's (1999) distinction between consensus and majoritarian democracy is a good one, but it misses the problems that arise when the formal legalism of liberalism, the separation-of-powers of republicanism, the majoritarian instinct of populism, and the executive-centered values of progressivism collide.

A central problem for each of these political theory traditions is their relatively exclusive view of what the public is. This exclusiveness makes it difficult to think of the relationship to the private sphere in anything but an antagonistic way. Somewhat counterintuitively, to deny a role for "private" influences is to tempt them to come in through the back door, allowing a multitude of private sins to hide under the guise of public principle, thereby reinforcing a desire to exclude private influences. By contrast, it is consistent with Dewey's notion of the public sphere to see publicness as an outgrowth of the interaction of private interests. The strategy is not to exclude private influences from public arenas but instead to engage private interests in an open manner.

Rather than keeping private interests separate, they must be engaged in a public process. Insisting on a "public" arena scrubbed free of private influence only tends to drive private interests underground. Emphasizing the transparency of public processes, for example, can push private concerns into the shadows. Publicness can be seen as illuminating private interests rather than excluding them. By the same token, a strong dichotomy between public and private also discourages us from seeing the "public" aspects of "private" behavior. A less dichotomous view of the public and the private might also allow us to recognize publicness in its partial manifestations so that it can be grasped and expanded. This less exalted form of publicness may actually serve us better. We could thereby cultivate the public-regarding nature of private interests.[18]

Building Consent from the Ground Up

Stever argues that modern organizational authority has come to rest on two pillars: science and consent. Our current notion of consent provides an unstable basis for administration, he argues, because "consent-based authority always leads to the view that administrative organization is exceeding its authority" (2000a, 136). Building on the critique of monistic sovereignty and the public/private dichotomy, we can begin to explore a more organic notion of consent. This exploration leads to the idea that public agencies can help to build up consent for their own activities and for the democratic state by engaging citizens and stakeholders in focused problem-solving and deliberation.[19]

Based on the idea of formal equality, a monistic view of sovereignty does not acknowledge that groups have very different stakes in outcomes. Yet without taking the intensity of preferences into account, groups with a lot at stake must use subterfuge to represent their interests. This subterranean strategy makes responsibility highly problematic, since the groups operating in the shadows care a great deal about outcomes, while groups operating in the light may be less invested. Clearly democracy cannot be simply about satisfying the interests of those with the most to gain or lose from policy outcomes. It must represent diffuse interests as well, which can easily be ignored if the intensity of preferences becomes the criteria of representation. To build a strong basis of consent for the state, democratic representation must manage the relationship between the formal equality of citizens and affected stakeholders. It must manage the relationship between strong and diffuse interests.

Consent based upon elections is powerful because it is broad-based and represents diffuse interests. But our traditional model of consent creates long intervals between the evaluation of our representatives. Moreover, consent built around the kinds of abstract, dogmatic disputes that characterize elections often create a governance vacuum that is filled in by "private" interests. Democratic theory appreciates that elected officials engage in consent-building between elections in order to improve their future electoral chances. But it does not acknowledge that public agencies also have a consent-building role. Public agencies can work to establish more detailed consent on an ongoing basis by encouraging deliberation, creating associations, and engaging in problem solving with both public and private groups.

A bottom-up perspective on consent building regards consent as growing from many small overlapping agreements, rather than from a single public will. This more organic view of consent parallels the idea of problem solving set out in chapter 4. Public agencies should be able to gradually build up broad-based consent from an overlapping series of focused problem-solving efforts. Strong consent is built up from small, local agreements into broader, more systemic agreements.[20] This organic model of consent fits Selznick's description of society as a "unity of unities."

One of the distinctive features of Mary Parker Follett's thought—in both her work on democracy and her work on management—is a focus on the idea of bottom-up consent.[21] She is quite negative about the idea of building democracy on the "consent of the people" understood as a unitary will (Follett 1924, 208), but she equally rejects the results-oriented consent advocated by the pluralists:

> The political pluralists say the state wins our loyalty by its achieve-ments. But it doesn't. Our loyalty is bound up in the interweaving relations between ourselves and the state. That interweaving is the dynamo which produces both power and loyalty. (1924, 221)[22]

In rejecting consent built strictly upon input (elections) or output (results-oriented), she is arguing for a more active conception of how citizens and stakeholders engage with the state: "But where we have stake, personal respon-sibility and vital interests, we make vigorous response. Here where our action tendencies are formed, democracy must begin" (1924, 223).[23] Follett's idea is consistent with Dewey's idea of the importance of publics.[24] Dewey's view, according to Smith, is "[t]hat which intervenes between the perceived problem and the governmental outcome is a *public*, a group of affected parties—aroused, engaged in conjoint activity, growing conscious of itself, organizing and seeking to influence officials" (1964, 602).

Yet Follett's view of consent misses something captured by Dewey's idea of publics. Follet's view of democracy is very localistic, based on the neighbor-hood as the unit of action (Follett 1919). But there are many state functions that we have an indirect or distant interest in or knowledge of, such as military affairs or international public health. These public functions can have a tre-mendous affect upon us, but the possible consequences are either so remote or randomly distributed that they are perceived as only indirectly important. Dewey's idea of "publics" captures this more diffuse interdependence. Yet publics often lack concrete agency and organization. The solution advocated here is that public agencies can not only foster the concrete engagement cham-pioned by Follett but also provide the organizational capacity to represent Dewey's diffuse publics.[25] In concrete terms, agencies can do this through pro-cesses of collaborative governance, which will be discussed in chapter 10, as well as by sponsoring "mini-publics" around concrete problem-solving (Fung 2002; Goodin and Dryzek 2006).[26]

Legislatures can play a similar role, but they lack the capacity and the hands-on experience to engage the public around concrete problem-solving activities.

If public agencies are institutionalized in particular ways, they can safeguard diffuse interests *and* engage in local problem-solving. This is not to suggest that public agencies should supplant legislatures. It only means that public agencies must be granted the latitude to engage in this kind of consent-building activity. The relationship between legislature and public agency is, as imagined here, analogous to the constitutional model of hierarchy described in chapter 6.

Of course, there is a possible tension between a view of public agencies as having autonomy built around competence and commitment to a particular mission (chapter 4) and a view of public agencies as actively building bottom-up consent. Autonomy based on competence and commitment can lead to an "expert" or "managerial" view of government. As Schlager writes in a review of common pool resource theory: "Numerous scholars and analysts have noted ... that public managers, trained as experts, come to view themselves as active problem solvers and to view citizens, at best, as incapable of helping themselves and, and at worst, as active and purposeful problem creators" (2004, 167). From a Pragmatist perspective, agency competence is invaluable, but it should be deployed in conjunction with wider deliberation and active public engagement rather than as a justification for making isolated expert decisions.[27]

Consent and Problem Solving

Chapter 5 described a Pragmatist strategy for public agencies to become more active and self-conscious problem-solvers. Problem solving was described primarily as a technique to improve agency performance. However, this chapter argues that problem solving is also a platform for building up consent. In fact, the role of agencies as (potential) problem-solvers places them in a critical position for building up more organic consent. Robert Reich makes this point nicely:

> Public Administrators may be in a better position than legislators to foster a national debate over certain value-laden issues simply because the administrators deal with specific application of general principles. Legislators, on the other hand, often have an incentive to keep their discussion to a fairly high level of generality; delving into knotty details will likely be seen as an invitation to controversy. (1985, 1638–1639)

From a Pragmatist perspective, consent is built not by agencies "solving" problems for the public (a results-oriented perspective) but by agencies engaging publics in the problem-solving process.[28] One of the reasons for the spiraling distrust of the state is that it must take on and arbitrate complex societal disputes. As clearly seen in regulatory disputes, opposing sides are rarely pleased with the outcomes produced by public agencies through top-down administrative procedures. Therefore, building consent requires that societal groups—including affected parties and more diffuse interests—be directly involved in problem solving. When done appropriately, problem solving that directly engages societal groups can produce more legitimate decisions. For example, Brown (2002) contrasts a more top-down "regional forest assessment" process in much of Australia, which at best engaged in public consultation designed to "overcome" conflict, with a more bottom-up process in South-East Queensland. In this region, timber interests and environmental groups (after significant early dispute) engaged in a bottom-up strategy of consensus building that was eventually enshrined in legislation. Brown argues that this created a much more meaningful framework for forest sustainability.

The Australian forest case, however, also points to a major limitation on any process of bottom-up problem-solving. Ultimately, the national government refused to recognize the South-East Queensland agreement, saying that it conflicted with national forest policy. This example shows that consent cannot be merely a matter of getting the stakeholders together or of achieving government consensus on a plan of action (e.g., the failed status quo strategy of the regional forest assessments in other parts of Australia). Problem solving requires a collaborative process that brings stakeholders and governments together in problem solving and consensus building.

Engaging stakeholders in problem solving potentially transforms their role from outside critics who may seek to subvert problem-solving strategies into parties who bear responsibility for the solution.[29] This can lead to more legitimate decision-making. Research on patterns of collaborative governance supports this finding. Lubell (2004), for example, finds that the collaborative U.S. National Estuary Program builds consensus for program goals. Weber, Lovrich, and Gaffney (2005) found a similar result in a study comparing endangered species regulation in two watersheds. They found that the watershed with a more community-based approach to problem solving created much more support for the endangered species act and more trust in federal and state agencies than did the watershed with a more agency-directed process.[30] In a study comparing "regulatory-negotiation" (negotiation with stakeholders) and conventional rule-making, Freeman and Langbein found that that regulatory negotiation creates a "legitimacy benefit" (2000, 110) that results from the satisfaction of stakeholders with the process itself and its outcomes. They find that negotiations reduce conflict.

These findings go beyond the United States. In the Netherlands, Glasbergen and Driessen investigated the Dutch version of collaborative governance—known as "interactive planning"—in four infrastructure projects (three highway projects and one dredging project). They found that interactive planning built consent: "Looking back at this project, there was a general feeling that relying on commonsense and a program of consultations created a broader basis for support than would have resulted from the application of a technical multicriteria analysis" (2005, 207). They found that citizen commitment to the project became stronger the more intensively they became involved in planning.

Consent arises not simply because stakeholders must take responsibility for their own problems but also because problem solving may be qualitatively superior when stakeholders are engaged in the process. In a case study of a chemical weapon disposal program, Futrell (2003) found that even in the context of a highly technical program, a collaborative decision-making strategy that engages citizens as "constructive critics" can generate better technical decisions by providing linkages between citizens' normative concerns and experts' technical concerns. For some classes of problems, like messy or wicked problems, stakeholder participation may be particularly important for finding effective solutions. As McCool and Guthrie point out: "Identifying the presence of linked subproblems often occurs only when those affected by proposed plans are directly involved in their development" (2001, 310).

Pragmatism suggests that stakeholders engaged in problem solving can be treated as a "community of inquiry."[31] It is difficult to imagine public opinion operating very effectively as a community of inquiry. However, if attention is focused on discrete and concrete problems, then it is much easier to imagine how authentic "communities of inquiry" can be constituted among groups of stakeholders. Using AIDS activism in the United States as an example of the democratization of expert inquiry, Bohman (1999) argues that to think of democracy as cooperative inquiry, we must move away from the focus on the primacy of expert authority. From a Pragmatist perspective, the democratization of expertise should also be understood as building the distributed competencies of stakeholders to engage effectively in problem solving.

Embeddedness

As described earlier, the Progressive model of organization implies a top-down model of accountability and a largely "closed system" model to guard against the temptations of corruption. This system has many admirable features, but it also creates some serious dilemmas—particularly for an operational organization, such as a police department, which must work in unstable, uncertain, and complex task environments. Notably, the heavy constraints placed on agency or field staff discretion make it difficult to craft collaborative and customized problem-solving strategies (Handler 1986; Noonan, Sabel, and Simon 2009). Pragmatism, by contrast, implies an open system model of organization, which encourages organizations to become "embedded" in their environments. Embeddedness implies not only openness to the environment, but also to strategies of working through the social structure of communities. We can find support for this idea in the "civic housekeeping" model developed by Jane Addams and other progressive settlement workers (Stivers 2002). This model suggests that organizations need a detailed understanding of and engagement with the environments in which they work. This logic of embeddedness can be understood as an extension of the logic of working with informal organization, as described in chapter 4.[32]

Yet embeddedness raises the specter of all the political difficulties—corruption and capture—that the Progressive model was designed to prevent.[33] Therefore, this section describes how embeddedness must be counterbalanced by organizational autonomy. Peter Evans (1995) has described how "embedded autonomy" has been an important ingredient of the successful developmental state in East Asia. He argued that the developmental state in East Asia cultivated two qualities. On the one hand, key public agencies (like finance) were deeply embedded in relationships to private firms and understood, in detailed terms, the factors that influenced their success.[34] On the other hand, to avoid capture by these organizations, a successful developmental state also had to maintain a strong degree of autonomy from these private firms. In other words, it had to be capable of imposing costs on the very firms with whom it had established close working relationships. It had to be able to pursue public values even while working closely with private interests.

As Selznick's cautionary tale of the cooptation of the Tennessee Valley Authority by private interests reminds us, embedding a public organization more fully in its environment represents a significant danger. As Nonet and Selznick (2001) put it in the context of their discussion of responsive law, this is a "high-risk strategy." In addition to cooptation by private interests, the risks may include wasted effort, internal politicization, and illegal action. To understand how these risks might be mitigated, we can first examine three examples where greater embeddedness led to, at best, partial failure and, at worst, egregious failure. The examples include a child welfare agency, a planning agency, and a police department. The next section will then examine what is common about the failure in all three cases and how failure might be prevented by building on the model of evolutionary learning.

Our first example—a child welfare agency—provides an illustration of how embeddedness is closely linked to broader organizational structure and process variables. John Hagedorn (1996) describes his attempts to reform a child welfare agency in Milwaukee in the late 1980s. The pre-reform organization was in many respects a classic Weberian hierarchy, which stressed the importance of internal specialization to achieve efficiency and a legal and punitive conception of child protection. Specialized caseworkers were notified, by referral, of potential child abuse and then spent much of their time preparing and pursuing court cases. Although this strategy—and its corresponding organizational structure—placed protection of children as its highest priority, it led to some unfortunate unintended consequences. For example, child welfare agencies like this often miss important clues that result in abusive situations, often resulting in the death of a child. In these cases, the agency is blamed for failing to remove a child in danger. In many other situations, however, the removal of a child can lead to a wrenching dislocation for both family and child. This punitive strategy also creates a stressful and adversarial relationship between case workers and families.

Hagedorn sought to reconstruct the organization around a different conception of child protection known as "family preservation." The central idea of family preservation is to intervene early where possible to reduce the kinds of psycho-social stresses that can lead to child abuse and therefore avoid the family dislocation that accompanies removal of a child. He acknowledged that this is not always possible and that children must be removed in certain situations. But the highest goal is family preservation. Such a strategy requires a very different type of relationship between the organization and its environment. To change this punitive relationship, Hagedorn sought to create neighborhood units that would integrate social services and act proactively to support a family preservation strategy. These neighborhood units were meant to be more proactive than reactive, which was possible because they sought to develop a less adversarial relationship with families and communities. In designing decentralized neighborhood-based pilot projects to deliver services, Hagedorn describes his hope: "Decentralized units would be far more likely to develop routines consistent with responsive and efficient client treatment than authorities removed from the scene" (1996, 131). This embeddedness in local communities could encourage a freer and more direct flow of information to the agency, preventing the kinds of decision errors that have plagued child welfare agencies. Ultimately, Hagedorn claimed his neighborhood demonstration projects were a success, but they remained marginal to the main operations of the child welfare agency and were never mainstreamed. Based on Hagedorn's account, political leaders and agency officials learned little from these experiments and as a result the experiment represented wasted effort.[35]

A second example—planning agencies—demonstrates how greater embeddedness can pose hazards for the internal functioning of agencies. Needleman and Needleman (1974) described the changing organization of planning agencies in the 1960s. The prototypical planning agency in the 1960s was also a classic Weberian bureaucracy. This agency regarded planning as a technical exercise. The professional planners that dominated these agencies regarded their job as devising plans that met high-level technical standards. In a sense, these planners approached their work as engineers might approach the development of the plan for a new building. The disadvantages of this approach are now well understood by the contemporary planning community. The urban renewal projects of the 1950s and 1960s were famous for ignoring the contextual details of neighborhoods (Jacobs 1961). Highways divided neighborhoods and killed off local businesses and street life, with little corresponding gain. The planners that criticized this earlier technical planning style in the 1960s and 1970s sought to develop a much more intimate relationship with local communities. Planning agencies were decentralized and planners were "embedded" in local communities so that they could develop close, intimate relationships with those communities.

Yet this strategy of greater embeddedness ultimately challenged the very cohesiveness and functioning of planning agencies. Locally embedded planners became spokespersons for their communities in their agencies, becoming what the Needlemans described as "guerillas in the bureaucracy." Whereas traditional planners clearly had little direct relationship with communities, some locally embedded planners came to regard themselves as advocates for their communities. Their loyalty to their communities often overrode their allegiance to their own agencies and they became active in organizing their communities against their own agency. This new advocacy role probably prevented the worst abuses of planners who approached planning as merely a technical exercise. However, it could also empty the planning process of any meaning other than to represent the competing interests of different communities.

The third example—the Rampart scandal in the Los Angeles Police Department—represents the most egregious failure of embeddedness. The Rampart Division was given extensive discretion to fight gangs in the Rampart Division of Los Angeles. This was an elite crime-fighting unit that was given a strong "results-oriented" message to fight crime. They developed an aggressive, street-savvy style that produced results and this ultimately gave them free rein to deal with gangs in an even more aggressive way. The deep involvement of the Rampart Division in the day-to-day world of gang life, however, led gradually to moral drift. Ends gradually came to justify even unlawful means of dealing with gangs, and from there, some officers drifted even further into unlawful behavior (Rampart Independent Review Panel 2000).

Each of these examples makes it clear that embeddedness is a risky strategy for public agencies but also suggests that there is much to be gained through greater embeddedness. Child welfare agencies may be able to utilize a less punitive style of governance; planning agencies may be able to be more sensitive to local needs and concerns; and police departments may be able to develop more effective strategies of crime control and improve their relationship with local communities (as some of the policing experiments described in earlier chapters suggest). So the question is how might a Pragmatist perspective help us to realize some of the advantages of greater embeddedness, while mitigating the risks that this might entail? The basic answer is that the more embedded a public agency, the more it must also have institutionalized strong processes to safeguard the public values it represents.

Embedded Autonomy

To be granted the discretion to adopt a strategy of greater embeddedness, an agency must have a number of the organizational and institutional elements in place that were set out in earlier discussions:

1. The agency must have a strongly institutionalized public mission with a well-developed "distinctive competence" for carrying out this mission. The basic idea builds on Selznick's conception of organization, as set out in chapter 4.
2. The agency must be strongly oriented toward problem solving, such that the interaction with the public is strongly motivated by concern for solving problems rather than for merely meeting public demands. As described in chapter 5, this problem-solving orientation must be generalized to the entire agency and not localized within specific units.
3. The agency must have a constitutional hierarchy in place, as described in chapter 6. The key feature of a constitutional hierarchy is that situationally specific problem-solving action is tightly linked to a "constitutional" process that upholds and refines the values inherent in the agency's public mission and distinctive competence. The agency must have a process in place to continually interrogate how concrete problem-solving efforts reflect and refine the agency's public mission and distinctive competence.
4. The agency must also have a process in place that encourages the development of personal and shared responsibility for both solving specific problems and for upholding the integrity of the agency mission. This process was outlined in chapter 7.

5. The agency has a strategy of engaging with the public in order to enhance
its public authority. To do this, it understands that its purpose is not to narrowly satisfy public demands, but to build broad-based democratic consent
for its public role. Although these two goals are not always distinct, the
latter is always value-based. The problem-solving activities of the agency
should enhance the general values that guide its subsequent actions. These
ideas were laid out earlier in this chapter.

These five processes are clearly reinforcing rather than separate processes.
A well-defined public mission and distinctive competence are necessary for
an organization to engage directly with the public in a responsible and
value-based way. Organizational structures and processes must support the
translation of the agency's mission and competence into concrete problem-
solving and public engagement, while also reinforcing the agencies' general
obligations and values. An agency that demonstrates the capacity to exercise these five processes can be both "embedded" and "autonomous" at the
same time.

The three failed examples described in the previous section can be analyzed
in light of this Pragmatist interpretation of embedded autonomy. In the case of
the child welfare agency, the experiment to develop a new and less punitive
relationship to communities was largely pushed by one policy entrepreneur,
with somewhat grudging support from higher-level agency leadership. As
Hagedorn's account makes very clear, the organizational innovations were
advanced *against* other groups in the agency who did not share Hagedorn's
belief in the value of these reforms. Beyond the appointed agency chief who
supported the initial experiment, Hagedorn had weak political and organizational support. The reforms were thus more of an insurgency against the existing organization than a deliberative problem-solving process.

In the case of the planning agency, the politicization of the agency and the
planning process reflected the weak intermediary links between the planning
organization and its embedded planners. Nor was there any process to support
the articulation of common planning values within which local concerns and
interests might be expressed and debated. However, the Needlemans do men-
tion one circumstance where the relationship between the agency and local
communities worked better. They describe how some embedded planners
sought to act as mediators between the community and the agency rather than
as community advocates. This mediated relationship created a two-way flow of
communication between the community and the agency that helped to align
the perspectives of both.[36] This flow of communication was roughly equivalent
to the face-to-face communication facilitated between precinct captains and
top brass through Compstat meetings.

In the LAPD case, the Rampart squad violated many legal and professional norms. What is also clear, however, is that they were not receiving clear messages from police leadership about fighting crime in a highly professional manner. Follow-up analysis revealed that LAPD leadership had little knowledge of what was occurring in the Rampart Division (Rampart Independent Review Panel 2000). The division was getting the message that "results matter," but there were few mechanisms in place to align top-level policy with field-level problem-solving. What was the top-level LAPD leadership doing if it wasn't paying attention to Rampart? They were probably focused on the administrative details of running a large police organization. Unfortunately, the Rampart case revealed that the LAPD had few institutional mechanisms to directly link public values, responsibility, and problem solving.

Although these examples are used to illustrate the potential pitfalls of greater embeddedness, there are also many examples that demonstrate possibilities for success. One of the most detailed examples is provided by Joel Handler (1986), who analyzed the success of Madison, Wisconsin, special education programs. Handler shows how the Madison school district developed a high-quality special education program by developing close cooperative relationships with parents. The program succeeded, in part, because it combined a strong commitment on the part of the school district to provide quality education for children with highly customized educational programs worked out between the school and parents. Handler argues that the system works because the school district starts by focusing on the specific problems and needs of children. It does this not by giving up on procedural values (due process), but rather by advancing these values within the context of the specific needs of each child and family. The Madison system has created a strong basis of trust between the school district and parents of special needs children.

A second success story concerns child welfare agencies. While Hagedorn's reforms were not successful, Noonan, Sabel, and Simon (2009) describe the success of the "Alabama-Utah model" of child protection. This model grants greater autonomy and discretion to child welfare agencies and their field staff, while articulating more general norms to guide practice.[37] As in Handler's special education case, the model emphasizes individualized problem-solving (customized strategies) crafted through collaborative partnerships with parents and other stakeholders. One of the key features of the Alabama-Utah model is the Quality Service Review (QSR). The QSR is a system for monitoring the quality of agency performance, which is a "collaborative process for specifying norms through analysis of cases" (Noonan, Sabel, and Simon 2009, 545). Therefore, in contrast to the failed experiments, the Alabama-Utah model creates a powerful mechanism for aligning general norms and values of child welfare with individual case management.

An important feature of both these more successful examples of embeddedness is that they operate in contexts where the demands for procedural safeguards and for hierarchical control are typically very high.

Conclusion

The idea of a "monistic" popular sovereignty reinforces a strategy of hierarchical accountability. A unitary public will is formed through elections, expressed through legislatures, and then hierarchically delegated, with the aid of strong formal controls, to public agencies. This idea of consent flowing from elections to agencies is one of the great achievements of liberal democracy, but it also sets up public agencies for a deeply troubled relationship with citizens. The business of government is complex and ever-changing, and private interests fill the vacuum created by the periodic nature of elections. This chapter has argued that the monistic conception of democratic consent must be complemented by a more immediate, bottom-up approach to consent. Building on the problem-solving strategy described in chapters 5 and 6, public agencies can become the center of this bottom-up consent-building. Agencies can directly engage affected stakeholders and the public in their problem-solving efforts. This engagement changes the relationship between the state and the public in a fundamental way. Instead of having public agencies attempt to "solve" public disputes, only to become the enemy of the disputants ("kill the messenger"), agencies can engage stakeholders more directly in problem solving and deliberation. The next chapter develops a distinctly Pragmatist approach to this strategy of collaborative governance.

CHAPTER 9

Collaborative Governance

◼

In the 1980s, the desert tortoise population in the Southwestern United States was declining at an alarming rate due to disease and loss of habitat (Beatley 1994). Environmental groups took the U.S. Fish and Wildlife Service (USFWS) to court to force them to list the desert tortoise as an endangered species. They won the case, and as a result, in 1989, the USFWS made an emergency listing of the desert tortoise on the endangered species list. While desert tortoise populations were declining, human populations were increasing. Located in the center of prime turtle habitat, Las Vegas had become one of the fastest-growing cities in the United States. The listing of the desert tortoise and the growth pressures on Las Vegas were like two trains running headlong toward each other on the same track. Local governments and developers took the USFWS to court to stop the listing of the desert tortoise. But they lost their case and the listing of the desert tortoise stood.

For developers and local governments, the implications were staggering. The Endangered Species Act (ESA) prevented the "taking" of any endangered species, which was interpreted broadly to mean that any alteration of desert tortoise habitat that could adversely affect the survival of the species was prohibited. The loss of the lawsuit and the magnitude of the opportunity costs to local governments and developers led them to search for alternatives. They found one in the process (section 10 under the ESA) that allows for "incidental take" (basically, exceptions to the strict prohibition against takings) if landowners develop "habitat conservation plans" to identify strategies to mitigate the impacts of takings. Clark County took the lead in sponsoring the development of the habitat conservation plan (HCP). They created a collaborative process to develop the plan that included all the affected stakeholders. The end result was an agreement among local governments, developers, environmentalists, and other stakeholders to protect the highest-quality desert tortoise habitat in the region, while allowing development to occur on less prime habitat (Beatley 1994; Reilly 1998; Hoben 2000; Wondolleck Yaffee 2000; Raymond 2006).

This chapter advances a Pragmatist approach to what has come to be called "collaborative governance," a governance strategy that challenges both adversarial and managerial visions of how public policy and regulation should operate (Cohen and Rogers 1983; Freeman 1997; Ansell and Gash 2008).[1] The Endangered Species Act's habitat conservation planning process is not always an ideal example of collaborative governance (Thomas 2003b), but the Clark County HCP is a good case of the potential for collaborative governance. It shows that even under conditions of bitter social conflict, collaborative governance can lead stakeholders to identify mutual gains.

How would a Pragmatist approach the topic of collaborative governance? In Dewey's most explicit book of political theory—*The Public and Its Problems*—he developed a model of the state and of the public that democratic theorists have come to extol as an inspiration for contemporary deliberative democracy. The book is notable for its development of a model of the state built around the notions of how publics manage their mutual interdependence. The book also cautions that modern technologies—both institutional and physical—had partially eclipsed the creation of a "public" that could develop a reasoned public response. A Pragmatist approach to governance might regard collaborative governance as a concrete strategy for fostering deliberation and learning about our mutual interdependence.

This chapter builds on the arguments of earlier chapters and on the spirit of Dewey's analysis of publics to develop a specifically Pragmatist interpretation of collaborative governance. Collaborative governance, as developed here, is a mode of governance in which public agencies engage with various stakeholders to jointly deliberate about public problems. Often contrasted to adversarial (Kelman 1992; Andranovich 1995) or managerial forms of governance, collaborative governance is now being used in many fields, including regulatory negotiations, school management, and community policing, and has become a benchmark of good practice in local and regional resource management (Wondolleck and Yaffee 2000; Ansell and Gash 2008).

There is now a sprawling literature on collaborative governance (Ansell and Gash 2008). This chapter organizes this literature around a distinctly "Pragmatist" analysis of collaborative governance.[2] Pragmatism would place particular attention on how collaborative governance binds stakeholders together into problem-solving "publics" that have the capacity for joint learning. Building on the model of Pragmatist learning set out in chapter 1 and elaborated in subsequent chapters, a Pragmatist might call out three interrelated dimensions of collaborative governance: (1) fruitful conflict through face-to-face communication; (2) creative and recursive problem-solving; and (3) the deepening

f stakeholders as both a prerequisite and a byproduct of col-
1apter draws selectively on the collaborative governance lit-
zero in on these three dimensions.

as Fruitful Conflict through Communication

What is the aim of binding stakeholders together into problem-solving publics that can engage in joint learning? It is important to clarify at the outset that the goal is not to produce consensus in order to minimize or eliminate conflict. We should not lose sight of Iris Marion Young's (2002) argument that pressures for consensus discourage the expression of difference. Attempts to minimize conflict are often disguised attempts to drive politics out of public life and are thus antithetical to Pragmatism's desire to enhance public deliberation.[4] Pragmatism neither ignores the centrality of conflict in social life nor places such a high value on social cooperation that it tries to paper over conflict. The goal of Pragmatism is not to minimize or eliminate conflict, but rather to encourage *fruitful conflict*. Fruitful conflict is conflict that in some manner enhances or advances knowledge, understanding, meaning, or capacity between different or opposing perspectives and interests.[5]

Nor would a Pragmatist interpretation of collaborative governance see it as merely a strategy for managing conflict. Many strategies of dispute resolution and mediation have the goal of *minimizing* conflict by focusing actors on what they share and bracketing areas of dispute. Such a strategy can be fruitful in the sense that it allows stakeholders to move beyond political stalemate or focus on possibilities for cooperation.[6] However, *fruitful conflict*, as understood here, often requires stakeholders to expand (rather than narrow) the field of conflict, often critically scrutinizing stakeholders' basic beliefs and values.

The concept of fruitful conflict can be closely linked to the Pragmatist emphasis on problem solving. Conflict is made more constructive by focusing it around concrete problem-solving rather than around the expression or defense of specific values or positions. When applied to mediation, this problem-solving perspective has been criticized by Bush and Folger (1994). They argue that a problem-solving approach ultimately leads to a "satisfaction" view of mediation, in which mediators seek to "satisfy" parties that their problem has been solved (1994, 56). A satisfaction approach leads mediators to selectively frame problems in narrow ways that permit short-term resolution but ultimately undermines the satisfaction of parties. They argue that mediation should not be thought of in problem-solving terms but rather in terms of "opportunities for moral growth and transformation" (1994, 81).[7]

Bush and Folger's argument is well taken, but it is somewhat misleading if we adopt a Pragmatist perspective on problem solving. For Bush, Baruch, and Folger, the limitation of a problem-solving approach is that it treats conflict *as* the problem. The Pragmatist stance, however, is that a focus on the "problem" redirects attention away from the symptoms of conflict per se (e.g., dislike or distrust of rival parties) toward its deeper causes. Moreover, Pragmatism understands problems as opportunities for growth. In this sense, Pragmatist problem-solving is consistent with their "transformational" approach to mediation.

Starting from these perspectives on fruitful conflict, the drawback of adversarial strategies of governance is not that they are conflictual per se but that the conflict yields so little in terms of knowledge, understanding, meaning, or capacity. In fact, a powerful implication of this Pragmatist interpretation is that *increased* conflict is often desirable to the extent that it can be structured in a productive fashion. By contrast, so-called adversarial models encourage unilateral strategies of decision making that allow stakeholders to pursue their goals without entering into *direct* conflict with opposing stakeholders. In this sense, adversarial models of governance avoid conflict. From a Pragmatist perspective, collaborative governance is not a technique for reducing or eliminating political conflict. It is a technique for structuring conflict in such a way that it is productive rather than merely antagonistic (McNary and Gitlow 2002, 582).[8]

The Clark County desert tortoise case leaves no doubt that collaborative governance cannot easily sweep political conflict under the proverbial rug. Early planning meetings were described as "violent" and a weapons check was necessary for the first two years (Hoben 2000, 4). It is clear that the stakeholders in this case had very different values and interests and these could never be papered over by appealing to some larger set of values or perspective. On the other hand, this case suggests that even venomous conflict can be channeled in a more fruitful direction. Pragmatist collaborative governance does expect people to cultivate an open attitude toward engagement with others, but it does not require them to renounce or compromise their own interests or beliefs (Shields 2003).

Pragmatist collaborative governance is therefore a deliberative approach and, at a minimum, requires an exchange of perspectives. As Oberg writes in a study of corporatist deliberation: "A precondition for deliberation is that the parties meet in some sort of arena in which they have to listen and respond to each other's arguments" (2002, 469). Furthermore, deliberation depends on the ability of stakeholders to be able to authentically reflect upon the perspectives of opposing stakeholders. Thus, a Pragmatist model of collaborative governance will stress the importance of meaningful dialogue, which requires people to engage concretely in the details of their conflict rather than in stylized or sound-bite conflict.[9] This is a central point. Fruitful conflict is conflict that seeks to transcend the us-versus-them dynamics so familiar in our present democratic politics. Deliberation, therefore, typically works best in face-to-face settings, where people can break down us-versus-them stereotypes (Kelman 1992).[10]

From a Pragmatist perspective, fruitful conflict requires "face-to-face communication."[11] As Ansell and Gash write:

> Face-to-face dialogue is more than merely the medium of negotiation. It is at the core of breaking down stereotypes and other barriers to communication that prevent exploration of mutual gains in the first place.... It is at the heart of a process of building trust, mutual respect, shared understanding, and commitment to the process. (2008, 558).[12]

Effective communication requires some recognition of the perspective of your counterpart, or what Jane Addams called "sympathetic understanding" (Shields 2006). In the desert tortoise case, the early stages of the process were described as "like being at a high school dance, with all the beards and long hairs on one side and all the suits and boots on the other" (Hoben 2000, 4). But as a byproduct of long meetings and meals together, as well as taking several common field trips to investigate habitat conditions, these two social groups gradually were able to communicate in a fruitful way. As one stakeholder noted, once the participants had come to understand each other's bottom line, "subsequent discussion . . . became less contentious and more productive" (Hoben 2000).

FRUITFUL CONFLICT CAN TRANSFORM SITUATIONS AND STAKEHOLDERS

A Pragmatist perspective suggests that conflict may be made more fruitful by simultaneously focusing and widening the scope of conflict. A strategy of focusing conflict on specific issues can prevent conflict from getting bogged down in peripheral issues. Focusing the conflict allows the parties to concentrate and align their conversation on key disputes that are necessary to resolve before a deepening of discussion is possible. However, a Pragmatist perspective suggests that conflict may also be made more fruitful by widening the perspective on conflict to reveal the character of interdependence between parties or the dimensions upon which they agree. Putnam (2004) describes how bargaining "transformations" can occur by shifting the level of abstraction of disputes: from the specific to the general, from the concrete to the abstract, from part to whole, from individual to system level, and from literal to symbolic (or vice versa).[13] For example, in a polarized conflict over the expansion of Schiphol airport in the Netherlands, a richer set of alternatives was identified in order to make the conflict more tractable (Van Eeten 2001).

In Pragmatist terms, fruitful conflict can be *transformative*, transforming either the definition of the situation or the stakeholders themselves.[14] Situations are transformed when a meaningful exchange of perspectives with other stakeholders leads them to reflect back on—and revise—their understanding of their own position or the position of their opponents. Putnam describes a transformation as follows:

> Transformation refers to moments in the conflict process in which parties reach new understandings of their situation, ones that redefine the nature of the conflict, the relationship among the parties, or the problems they face. New understandings are marked by different meanings or interpretations of events. The parties involved have a fundamentally different view of what is happening than they did when they entered the negotiations. (2004, 276)

Disputes may be intractable—that is, "resistant to resolution" (Campbell 2003, 363). In this case, reframing to reveal new or different dimensions of a situation is often a useful strategy (Schön and Rein 1995; Putnam, Burgess, and Royer 2003).[15] Pragmatist collaboration does not assume that transformation *will* occur; rather, it seeks to foster the conditions under which transformation *can* occur.

It is interesting that a scholar with strong Pragmatist instincts set out a similar understanding of collaboration in the 1920s. Mary Parker Follett argued for a model of organizational collaboration that distinguished coercion and compromise from what she termed "integration." Integration was not merely an adjustment of one's interests to the interests of others but a creative search for new positions that transcended (transformed) the different perspectives and interests of different parties. As Follett pointed out, integration is different from negotiation and compromise. Although integration comes close to what the bargaining literature calls a win-win perspective, there is an important difference. Her idea was that value is created when the meanings participants bring to the bargaining table are enriched, expanded, and deepened through the exchange of perspectives. The idea is nicely expressed by Robert Reich, who argues that public deliberation "allows people to discover latent public values that they have in common with others, and in the process to create new public values" (1985, 1636). Collaboration is successful, on this count, when participants' own purposes have been deepened and enhanced through the recognition of the perspectives of others. Compromise without change in perspectives may lead to successful management of conflict, but not to "fruitful conflict."

Collaboration as Creative Problem-Solving and Recursive Learning

Pragmatism would envision collaborative governance as a strategy of problem solving, a position already well established in the literature (McCann 1983; Logsdon 1991; Hood, Logsdon, and Thompson 1993; Lasker and Weiss 2003; Bryan 2004). Bryan (2004) argues that collaborative governance does a good job of confronting public problems, because it creates "shared ownership" of those problems. Since stakeholders bring different perspectives and interests to the table, however, it is frequently the case that they do not share a common understanding of "what the problem is." Therefore, the first task of collaborative governance is typically to engage stakeholders in a process of joint problem definition. Collaborative governance, as Kelman (1996) puts it, seeks to transform adversarial relationships into a "shared problem."

The literature on collaborative governance strongly supports this perspective and finds that the problem-definition phase of collaboration is a critical step toward deeper collaboration. In a study of watershed planning, for instance, Bentrup (2001) found that problem definition was essential for fruitful conflict. The key transformative step was not in the mere acknowledgement of how other people understood the problem but rather in the joint redefinition of the problem itself. As Putnam writes: "They are not simply defining the problem in a way acceptable to both sides; they reconstitute the building blocks on which the problem resides" (2004, 290).[16] Approaching conflict as an issue of "problem-solving," according to Kelman, requires addressing "underlying causes of the conflict" (1996, 100).[17]

Thus, the problem-definition phase assumes joint inquiry into the character of problems followed by a joint reconstruction of each stakeholder's conception of the problem.[18] Reich provides a good description of the provisional and probative character of problem definition:

> During the course of deliberation, people may discover new information and new perspectives about what is at stake in the decision before them. This may lead individuals not only to modify their choice of means for achieving their ends, but perhaps to reconsider those ends. (1985, 1635)[19]

In Pragmatist terms, problem definition is reflexive. Stakeholders enter the process with their own goals and perspectives, but these may be malleable and open to reframing through deliberative interaction with others.[20] In a collaborative process, joint deliberation about problem definition can lead stakeholders to scrutinize their own priorities and commitments from the perspective of opposing stakeholders. This is what Sabel and Zeitlin (2008) call "learning from difference."

This joint action can be thought of as a creative process in the sense that it requires a process of discovery of positions that will allow stakeholders to define issues as "shared problems."[21] Follett saw this creative search for what she called "integration" as the heart of collaboration. In *Creative Experience*, she writes: "But the process is not that I integrate my desires, you yourself, and then we together unite the results; I often make my own integration through and by means of my integration with you" (1924, 177).

Problem definition and reconstruction is also recursive—that is, it arises through a circulation of perspectives. Putnam's analysis of collaborative transformation is, in fact, implicitly described as a recursive process that moves between perspectives, starting with

> a jump in which one party lays out the parameters of an agreement followed by a detail phase in which specific issues are packaged and exact settlement is constructed. . . . The agreement is then crafted from a metalevel or framework that works from the whole down to the parts. The critical moment occurs when both parties develop this framework to shift the nature of the negotiation away from small-scale concessions and compromises. (2004, 281)

In this example, transformation is produced through a process of shifting back and forth between attention to paradigmatic reframing and attention to concrete details.[22] We see in this description both the cosmopolitan localism and the analytical holism characteristic of Pragmatist learning.

Having argued that a Pragmatist model of collaborative governance is a process of reflexive, creative, and recursive problem-definition, it is but a short step to describe collaboration as a social learning process. A learning perspective is well represented in the collaborative governance literature (Reich 1985; Sabel 1994; Saarikoski 2000; Daniels and Walker 2001; Margerum 2002; Bouwen and Taillieu 2004; Berk and Schneiberg 2005; Sabel and Zeitlin 2008); and a number of studies have found that enhanced stakeholder knowledge is an important byproduct of collaborative governance.[23] A Pragmatist approach might go further and suggest that stakeholders can also learn more about their own perspective and the perspectives of other stakeholders through collaboration. This is the "social" aspect of social learning. In one of the few studies to quantify this aspect of social learning, Pahl-Wostl and Hare (2004) report that half of the actors involved in a Swiss experiment in collaboration reported that they had learnt more about their own perspectives and had improved their understanding of the role of the other actors.

A Pragmatist learning model suggests that the key intermediate step between problem definition and problem solving is collaborative structuring of further inquiry and experimentation. Once stakeholders agree on a workable definition of the problem, they must then agree to set out the subsequent problem-solving strategies as opportunities for learning. As the literature on democratic experimentalism stresses, to do this, stakeholders must establish metrics or benchmarks that will allow them to collectively judge the success of problem-solving interventions (Dorf and Sabel 1998; Schneiberg 2005; Sabel and Zeitlin 2008). As in the problem-definition phase, this problem-solving phase requires joint definition of metrics and benchmarks for evaluating interventions.

The experimental stance is not simply a product of collaboration; nor is it simply justified because it is a "scientific" approach to problem solving. More importantly, an inquiring and experimental attitude helps to hold collaboration between different stakeholders together in the first place. When successful, it does this by reframing the basic relationship among stakeholders away from a contest of rival goals and preferences toward a position of shared uncertainty. Where stakeholders can find a ground of shared uncertainty, they will discover common ground for a provisional stance toward problem solving. Exploring this zone of uncertainty, problem solving begins as a probative search for strategies, metrics, and benchmarks that all stakeholders can agree will provide subsequent opportunities for learning.[24]

When stakeholders are fundamentally opposed to one another, this zone of shared uncertainty may be quite small or it may seem to lie at the margins of real reform. Pragmatism, however, emphasizes that learning is an iterative process. By building trust or shared knowledge, the results of a small experiment can provide support for more far-reaching inquiries and experiments in the future.

LEARNING TO COLLABORATE

The idea that "small wins" can scaffold larger gains supports a strategy of building up the capacity to collaborate.[25] Sullivan and Skelcher (2002) and Sullivan, Barnes, and Matka (2006) have identified a range of important collaborative capacities. In a study of local health partnerships in the United Kingdom, Sullivan, Barnes, and Matka found that one particular collaborative strategy "was a product of the levels of pre-existing capacity between stakeholders. The shape and foci of that strategy in turn influenced how and where collaborative capacity was targeted and further capacity generated" (2006, 307). Collaborative capacity may depend on the "empowerment" of some stakeholders, which is necessary when one stakeholder is markedly weaker than others (Handler 1996).

Some aspects of collaborative capacity are learned. Although Raymond (2006) argues that trust was not necessary for collective action in the desert tortoise case, most scholars of collaborative governance regard trust as a necessary scaffold for collaboration (Ansell and Gash 2008). Trust in particular persons and institutions can be developed in many ways, but often it must be learned in the process of collaboration. If trust is successfully built up during early rounds of collaboration, it can then serve as a capacity for more ambitious collaborative agendas.[26] Learning to trust stakeholders with opposed goals and preferences is rarely an easy process, but the literature on collaborative governance finds that trust can be fostered even in high-conflict situations. To provide just one example, Moore, Parker, and Weaver (2008) describe a situation of high distrust between local Ohio farmers and the Environmental Protection Agency (EPA) and a high degree of resistance to the EPA's water quality remediation strategies. Through a participatory process, farmers were converted into local "experts" who conducted additional investigations into the level and sources of pollution. Through this process, they came to accept the EPA's evaluations of local water quality while also devising local solutions to water quality programs. Expanded trust in the EPA provided a basis for consent and scaffolding for creative problem-solving.

Trust, as used here, is the expectation that others will honor their commitments and will not behave in an underhanded manner. It is not the same thing as friendship or consensus. Stakeholders may come to trust opposing stakeholders without liking or agreeing with them. Margerum provides a good example in his description of a watershed planning collaboration in Wisconsin: "At the first meeting of the Johnstone River case, one farmer leaned over to the environmental representatives and said, 'I don't like greenies'" (2002, 249). However, within a few months, the committee agreed to several common concerns, and although the two protagonists did not agree on all aspects, they worked closely on several initiatives. One critical ingredient of trust building is face-to-face dialogue.[27] Another is joint inquiry, which can have a leveling effect that helps to promote trust. As Bohman argues: "The more deliberation is like inquiry the more thoroughly everyone is dependent on everyone else both for their cooperation and for their contribution to the collective organization of knowledge" (1999, 594). In a study of watershed partnerships, Leach and Sabatier (2005) suggest that "joint fact finding" is a useful step toward building trust in conflictual stakeholder groups.

A Transactional Model: Interdependence, Emergence, Feedback

For Dewey, a public is ultimately based on the interdependence of its members. If collaborative governance binds stakeholders together into problem-solving publics, then fruitful conflict, creative problem-solving, and recursive social learning can be seen as processes that enable stakeholders to explore the character and meaning of their interdependence. In Dewey's logic of "transactions," however, interdependence is not simply a preexisting condition. Instead, the parties to the transaction are understood to be part of a larger field of action and their interdependence can be deepened or elaborated through engagement.[28] The value of this transactional logic is that it points in a general way to how the collaborative process can support the development of more ambitious collaborative problem-solving.[29]

An example from the field of water management indicates how agencies and stakeholders can learn about and deepen their interdependence. Lach, Rayner, and Ingram (2005) describe three different styles of water management. In the traditional approach, water agencies minimize their interaction with external stakeholders. Instead, they focus on developing infrastructure-intensive strategies (building dams and water conveyance infrastructure) that enable them to establish their sovereignty over water resources. As water scarcity increases, however, water agencies discover that this sovereignty logic can be counterproductive. In their attempt to adapt, they often try to develop specific interagency agreements that will allow them to "spread the risk" of water management. This adaptation requires agencies to cooperate with other agencies, but it is largely a defensive attempt to shore up sovereign control over resources. If this defensive approach fails, some water agencies move toward a third strategy of engaging in even deeper and more intense collaboration with other stakeholders. This strategy can lead to more creative and ambitious efforts to jointly address the "wicked problems" of local water management.

This example illustrates how the creativity and ambition of collaborative problem-solving can be a function of the interdependence of stakeholders. To clarify this point, it is useful to distinguish two different types of interdependence at work in this example. The first type of interdependence is externally defined (exogenous). For instance, water agencies and stakeholders are interdependent in the first place because of the background condition of water scarcity. The second type of interdependence depends on choices made by the water agencies and stakeholders. When they engage in joint programs or projects together, they voluntarily enter into a more interdependent relationship with each other. As Lach, Rayner, and Ingram's description of three stages of water management suggests, creative and ambitious problem-solving only becomes possible when stakeholders willingly engage in this type of "enacted interdependence."[30]

Scholars of collaborative governance have pointed to the importance of both types of interdependence (Logsdon 1991; Hood, Logsdon, and Thompson 1993; Wondolleck and Yaffee 2000; Bouwen and Taillieu 2004). Some scholars emphasize the first type. Logsdon (1991), for instance, views interdependence as an exogenous condition that helps to explain whether actors will engage in collaborative governance. Other scholars emphasize enacted inter-dependence. Margerum, for example, observes that collaboration implies that "the parties must in some ways become dependent on each other" (2002, 250).

In fact, collaborative governance facilitates the exploration and linkage of both types of interdependence. Stakeholders must first perceive and acknowl-edge their existing interdependence before they will voluntarily commit them-selves to becoming more deeply interdependent with other stakeholders (Selin, Schuett, and Carr 2000).[31] Brown, for example, offers a telling description of the Australian timber industry's eventual acknowledgement of its interdependence with opposing stakeholders: "The Queensland Timber Board accepted that public opposition was not simply a political impediment fixable through gov-ernment or public relations, but an issue of business practice that industry had to internalize and confront" (2002, 28). As this example suggests, a significant cognitive shift is often necessary before stakeholders will willingly consider a voluntary deepening of interdependence. The water agencies described by Lach, Rayner, and Ingram initially adopted defensive management strategies that sought to minimize interdependence on other stakeholders. The cognitive shift came only when water agencies and stakeholders more fully recognized their shared fate, and thus recognized a need to enact deeper interdependence.[32]

Collaborative governance requires stakeholders to bind themselves to a process where they jointly determine strategy with other stakeholders (Thomp-son and Perry 2006). To do this, stakeholders must forsake some of their au-tonomy. As resource-dependency theory suggests, however, people and groups often avoid dependence on others (Pfeffer and Salancik 1978). When and how then do people and groups voluntarily forsake some measure of their freedom of movement to engage in more interdependent relationships with others? While acknowledging that external conditions (like water scarcity) set the basic parameters of interdependence, the collaborative governance literature suggests that a number of cognitive thresholds must be crossed before stake-holders will successfully engage with each other. A first critical threshold is for stakeholders to achieve "mutual recognition" (Saarikoski 2000) or "joint ap-preciation" (Gray 1989; Plummer and Fitzgibbon 2004). This means that stake-holders must acknowledge one another as legitimate interlocutors. This may be easy or difficult to achieve, depending on the character of a dispute or the his-tory of conflict between stakeholders.

A second threshold that must be achieved is commitment to the collabora-tive process itself. Stakeholders must not simply acknowledge each other as legitimate interlocutors but must also become committed to working together in a collaborative way. Although the terminology used varies rather widely in the literature, case studies suggest that stakeholders' level of commitment to collaboration is a critical variable in explaining collaborative success or failure

(Alexander, Comfort, and Weiner 1998; Margerum 2001; Gilliam et al. 2002; Gunton and Day 2003; Tett, Crowther, and O'Hara 2003).[33]

Finally, a third process threshold is achieved when stakeholders develop a sense of "joint ownership" over the collaborative process (Weech-Maldonado and Merrill 2000; El Ansari 2003). This means that stakeholders must develop an understanding that they are collectively responsible for the development and success of the collaborative venture.

These cognitive thresholds of recognition, commitment, and ownership provide a necessary platform for the exploration and deepening of stakeholder interdependence. These thresholds were clearly met in the desert tortoise case. As one participant reported: "The most important achievement I saw was that a group of people walked into the room hating each others' guts and ready to slit each others' throats . . . and now if you were to come visit those meetings and say something against the plan, you're apt to get eaten by both sides" (Hoben 2000, 6).

To summarize this section, collaborative governance is a process for exploring and enacting interdependence among stakeholders. To voluntarily engage in collaboration, stakeholders must first acknowledge and appreciate their existing interdependence. They must then be willing to further deepen their interdependence with one another. To do this, stakeholders must acknowledge each other as legitimate interlocutors; they must commit themselves to a process of addressing this interdependence through collaboration; and they must establish a joint sense of ownership over this collaborative process. When these cognitive thresholds have been achieved, a "problem-solving public" has been created.

Collaborative Governance as Emergence and Feedback

Pragmatism would not make light of the difficulty of creating even small publics. Getting stakeholders to engage in meaningful discourse is an important step toward achieving mutual recognition, commitment, and ownership (Lasker and Weiss 2003). But there is a Catch-22 inherent in the process of creating "buy-in." Meaningful discourse is itself a function of mutual recognition, commitment, and ownership; stakeholders engage in serious discussion only when they feel vested in the collaborative process. Superficial discourse, however, can easily erode this sense of investment. Dialogue is thus a necessary, though not sufficient, condition for getting adversaries to engage in deeper interdependence.

To escape this Catch-22, it is useful to analyze collaboration as an emergent process.[34] A basic commitment of all process ontologies is that outcomes cannot be easily read off starting conditions. Outcomes are explained by something that *emerges* out of interaction, which may be positive or negative. To produce a virtuous cycle of collaboration, it is necessary to understand how collaboration can produce emergent outcomes that stimulate deeper subsequent interaction, as exemplified by this description of a local resource management case: "The meetings to draft the CCMP initially stimulated broader, more frequent contacts among stakeholders and generated increasing momentum to continue interactions" (Schneider et al. 2003, 145). Emergent phenomena are subtle and not always easily observable. Yet they are critical for understanding collaborative outcomes.

The key to understanding collaboration as an emergent process is to appreciate that something new is created as the product of collaboration—an institutional framework, a joint appreciation, a small triumph, new knowledge or ideas, greater trust, or shared attention to a boundary object. In a British Columbia land use planning case, for example, "Two-thirds of respondents agreed that the LRMP process had second-order effects including changes in behaviors and actions, spin-off partnerships, umbrella groups, collaborative activities, new practices or new institutions" (Frame, Gunton, and Day 2004, 71). Emergent outcomes like this may be negative or positive, but positive feedback can provide structure for supporting deeper collaboration. This positive feedback between process and structure is what chapter 1 referred to as the principle of processual structuralism.

Weber (2009) describes a case of successful collaborative governance in the Blackfoot watershed in Montana. Watershed stakeholders, he observes, had incentives to collaborate, but they lacked the community capacity to effectively work together on watershed problems. He argues that the key to their success was the development of a new set of ideas related to the character of the watershed as a place and to the relationship of stakeholders and their problems to one another. Despite high levels of conflict and institutional fragmentation in the watershed, these new ideas provided a basis for productive negotiations and actions. The Blackfoot watershed community subsequently developed a successful and sustainable collaboration.

One clue to producing successful emergent outcomes lies in the creative character of joint problem definition, inquiry, and experimentation, as described in earlier sections. Lasker and Weiss describe this in terms of creating synergy between stakeholders:

> Rather than agreeing to a position or solution that a person, organization, or interest group advocated at the start, a group of people who create synergy develops consensus around ideas and strategy they generate together. In this kind of process, consensus does not require

anyone to "give in" or "give up." Instead, participants contribute to the development of something new and feasible that many people can support. When a broad group of participants develop and "own" a solution that makes sense to them, implementation is more likely to go smoothly and is more likely to be sustained. (2003, 26)[35]

If we take emergent phenomena seriously, we become attentive to how the outputs of each round of interaction produce virtuous cycles of interaction. As Imperial observes: "When viewed over time, collaborative activities also tended to reflect a trial and error process with practitioners becoming engaged in an expanded set of activities once they learned how to work together" (Imperial 2005, 287). Heikkila and Gerlak (2005) describe the development of an Everglades conservation program as occurring in an "incremental and piecemeal" fashion, but this process still led to accumulated experience in working together productively.

As both Imperial and Heikkila and Gerlak point out, there can be an incremental, trial-and-error quality to collaboration, yet positive feedback can lead to more extensive and systematic cooperation. Feedback from emergent outcomes can incrementally deepen understanding or appreciation of interdependence and expand the sense of ownership and responsibility. When the feedbacks are positive and cumulative, they can lead to opportunities for deeper collaboration. For example, after the desert tortoise planning process had successfully created a single species habitat conservation plan for the desert tortoise, the same group went on to establish a governance framework for an additional 200 species.

By conceiving of collaborative governance as an emergent process that produces positive or negative feedbacks, stakeholders become attentive to how the products and byproducts of early collaboration can scaffold more ambitious problem-solving. One way to think about these positive feedback effects is in terms of what have been called "small wins"—achievements of limited scope and ambition. In his article on small wins, Karl Weick (1984) has provided a good model for thinking about the developmental possibilities of collaborative governance. Small wins are important, he argues, because they allow stakeholders to manage emotions in a positive way; a virtuous cycle of small wins, he argues, can produce much more significant problem-solving than initially more ambitious efforts. The importance of small wins has been recognized as especially valuable for so-called intractable conflicts, where opposed stakeholders see no way forward. Putnam, Burgess, and Royer (2003) argue that intractable conflicts can be moved toward more tractable conflicts through incremental improvements in the situations of the negotiating parties.[36]

A Pragmatist model of collaborative governance is there: the sense that it looks for even small opportunities to ad flict.[37] On the other hand, this pragmatism ultimately aims f mental improvements at the margins of disputes. Therefor do not feedback positively to deepen subsequent collaborat status from this perspective. In the Pragmatist model of eme new has to be created.

Conclusion

A Pragmatist perspective can understand collaborative governance as a process that binds problem-solving publics together so that they can engage in *fruitful conflict*. The purpose of Pragmatist collaboration is not to minimize conflict or produce consensus, but to use the interplay of different perspectives to generate mutual learning. A public is bound together, first and foremost, by face-to-face communication, which is necessary to break down barriers to mutual learning. Most political disputes avoid direct conflict, so stakeholders build up defenses against recognizing or appreciating the perspectives of their opponents. To be bound together as a problem-solving public, it is not necessary that stakeholders like or agree with each other. However, there does have to be some modicum of mutual recognition between stakeholders that they are part of a collaborative process. While there is no assumption that stakeholders must ultimately compromise their beliefs or find a consensus position, stakeholders must become committed to deliberating with other stakeholders to define and solve problems. Stakeholders become fully bound together as problem-solving publics only when they jointly take ownership of the collaborative process— that is, when different stakeholders become invested in and take responsibility for the outcomes produced by their attempt to define and solve problems.

In many political situations, even these relatively minimal conditions for creating problem-solving publics may be difficult to achieve. A Pragmatist model of collaborative governance, however, calls attention to a number of possibilities for facilitating fruitful conflict. The first strategy is to focus stakeholders on concrete problems and to shift their attention and energies away from doctrinaire position-taking. This does not mean that stakeholders will naturally share an understanding of the problem. Typically, they will not. Pragmatism would therefore emphasize the importance of a preliminary phase of joint problem definition. Stakeholders are likely to have greater conflict over the causes or solutions to problems than over the definition of the problem itself. Again, it may be more important that stakeholders develop a mutually intelligible way of describing problems than a consensual agreement on problem definition.

third strategy for facilitating fruitful conflict is to move stakeholders beyond a typical negotiation stance. It is possible to do this by focusing on the zone of uncertainty that stakeholders may share and thus to transform the negotiation into an inquiry. In an inquiry, stakeholders must approach problem definition and problem solving as an opportunity for joint learning. Such an approach gives interactions a future orientation that can destabilize past disputes. In defining problem-solving interventions, stakeholders should try to jointly define metrics or benchmarks to evaluate these interventions. In other words, they should treat these interventions as experiments.

A fourth strategy for facilitating fruitful conflict is to shift perspectives in order to reconstruct and reframe the terms of debate. This may mean shifting to a more abstract level of deliberation or it may mean focusing on particulars. Ultimately, fruitful conflict is facilitated by moving back and forth between different perspectives. The goal is not to force stakeholders to discard or change their assumptions per se but to get them to critically scrutinize their assumptions in light of different perspectives.

Despite these Pragmatist strategies for facilitating fruitful conflict, collaborative relationships often begin on an antagonistic and distrustful note. A Pragmatist perspective on collaborative governance is developmental. It says that stakeholders can learn to collaborate. Trust building is one important feature of learning to collaborate. To communicate authentically, to acknowledge the legitimacy of competing perspectives, to commit to collaboration, and, ultimately, to take ownership and responsibility for the collaborative process, stakeholders must develop a measure of trust in each other. Again, affection or agreement is less important than the expectation that other stakeholders will deal with them honestly and straightforwardly. Trust can be built through successful face-to-face communication and interaction.

To break out of a vicious cycle of distrust and negative communication, Pragmatism would focus on how outcomes from early rounds of collaboration can feedback positively into subsequent collaboration. How do the "emergent outputs" from one round of deliberation scaffold deeper collaboration in the next round? These "emergent outputs" may range from an increased understanding of the positions of opposing stakeholders, to shared knowledge produced by joint fact-finding, to a successful problem-solving experiment. Often it is difficult to predict what specific kinds of outputs will shift relations from a vicious to a virtuous cycle. However, we can note two general features. The first is recognition of interdependence. Stakeholders become motivated to transform negative relationships as they come to appreciate their shared fate with opposing stakeholders. Early rounds of problem definition and problem inquiry may help stakeholders to better understand this shared fate. The other general feature is the importance of "small wins." Small, tangible achievements are very valuable for demonstrating to stakeholders that a more virtuous rei. tionship is possible. Early in the collaborative process, ambitions should be measured and strategic in order to increase the likelihood of tangible success. These gains will build mutual recognition, commitment, ownership, and, ultimately, trust. These small wins can provide scaffolding for more ambitious strategies.

Fruitful conflict is gradually transformative. Creative discovery of jointly constructed problem definitions and future-oriented inquiry and experimentation can lead stakeholders to change their own perspectives about public problems and also about other stakeholders. Recognition of interdependence and small wins can reinforce these new views and begin to reveal new possibilities for collaborative problem-solving. Deeper trust can enhance mutual recognition, commitment to collaboration, and joint ownership of the process, producing more far-reaching and critical deliberation.

This idea of collaborative governance can be applied to any sphere of life, from workplace relations to international negotiations. However, this book has focused on how public agencies can foster collaborative governance, helping to bind problem-solving publics together and providing the leadership to foster virtuous cycles of mutual learning among stakeholders. Indeed, public agencies are almost uniquely positioned to play this role, because they are the designated leads for concrete problem-solving. Public agencies can engage stakeholders in focused problem-solving efforts and they can empower stakeholders to deliberate about these focused problems.

Public agencies, however, are often the main barrier to a fuller development of collaboration. It is a common story in the literature on collaborative governance that agencies, guarding their traditional prerogatives and procedures, will prevent effective collaboration or turn it into ritual (Flyvberg 1998; Yaffee and Wondolleck 2003; Thomas 2003a; Ebrahim 2004; Edelenbos 2005). The success of collaborative governance therefore depends on a broader transformation of the role of public agencies in democracy. Developing collaborative relationships with stakeholders is one part of that broader transformation, but successful collaborative governance also requires a specific kind of public agency—one that embodies the autonomous, responsive, problem-solving qualities described in earlier chapters. The concluding chapter draws these ideas together to describe the mutually reinforcing conditions that can help realize the promise of collaborative governance.

10

Problem-Solving Democracy

A true public philosophy is problem-centered.
—Philip Selznick, *The Communitarian Persuasion*

Public philosophy is a bridge between the past, the present, and the future. From the past, it builds on a living tradition of thought characterized by certain themes and values. In the present, a public philosophy addresses contemporary public problems of political and social life, providing a guide to analysis and suggesting strategies for addressing these problems. Looking ahead, a public philosophy helps us to imagine different possible futures. The central goal of this book has been to show how Pragmatism, as a public philosophy, provides an intellectual tradition of analyzing public affairs, a guide to tackling contemporary problems, and a framework for reimaging institutions, governance, and democracy.

A public philosophy is not a description of the world as it is. It is an intellectual resource for common deliberation, critical analysis, and imagination. The test of a public philosophy therefore cannot, strictly speaking, be its empirical veracity, though its empirical claims may be so judged. Nevertheless, it is possible to judge a political philosophy in terms of whether it is realistic, relevant to contemporary concerns, and conceptually coherent. This book has sought to demonstrate that Pragmatism meets all three criteria for a successful public philosophy. To be realistic means that Pragmatism suggests courses of action within the realm of possibility. This book therefore has sought to provide examples—from policing, education, environmental protection, and other policy arenas—to demonstrate that real-life manifestations of Pragmatist institutions, governance, and democracy already exist. To be relevant to contemporary problems means that Pragmatism has something to say about important issues and dilemmas of our day. To demonstrate this relevance, the book has tackled the very important dilemma of distrust in democratic institutions and, in particular, the embattled role of public agencies. Conceptual coherence means that Pragmatist ideas hang together in a reinforcing way and can be specified with some degree of clarity. To demonstrate this coherence, the book is organized around the central idea of evolutionary learning, showing how it could be consistently used to address a wide range of issues.

A public philosophy distills a philosophical perspective in such a way that it is useful for public affairs. Most philosophies have implications for public affairs, but they are cast at too high a level of abstraction, generality, or obtuseness to be generally useful for practical matters. While Pragmatism prides itself on being one of the most practical of philosophies, the practical implications of many of its most intriguing ideas are not obvious. This book has sought to explore the application of Pragmatist ideas to concrete matters while staying true to the broader outlines of the philosophy. For the most part, these arguments have been guided by classical perspectives on Pragmatism, working primarily with the ideas expressed by the founding generation of Pragmatist philosophers—Charles Peirce, William James, John Dewey, and George Herbert Mead. These four philosophers do not encompass the entire tradition of Pragmatism, but focusing on them has made the central task more manageable.

While a public philosophy has to be more applied than general philosophy, it often appears abstract from the perspective of "real world" matters. Although a public philosophy is a guide to how to engage in public affairs, it can rarely provide a detailed recipe for action. In any case, from a Pragmatist perspective, it is important to tackle problems in a contextual fashion, engaging in inquiry about the character of problems and their solutions. Consequently, the goal is not to create a formulaic approach to contemporary issues. As a resource for deliberation, critical analysis, and imagination, however, a public philosophy can and should distill key values and ideas that can guide practice. Practitioners may inadvertently create Pragmatist-like innovations without the benefit of philosophical reflection, but only by distilling these guiding values and ideas can we deepen, refine, and share them.

Since public philosophy tries to distill values and ideas at a middle range of abstraction and because Pragmatism strongly supports the value of inquiry, it forms a natural alliance with the social sciences. One of the goals of this book, therefore, has been to resurrect and reinforce a Pragmatist social science. The two chapters on institutions described a Pragmatist tradition of institutionalism, and the chapter on organization does the same thing for organization theory. A Pragmatist approach to problem solving was described through an examination of social scientific studies of public problems. Later chapters set out broad frameworks in which to understand key social scientific concepts like power, authority, and collaborative governance. While the core purpose is always to distill Pragmatist ideas, this work has been committed to grounding these ideas in broader social-scientific understandings.

Pragmatism suggests that we make progress by working back and forth between general values and ideas and concrete problem-solving. That model has been followed here. The book progresses by working back and forth between articulating the general logic of evolutionary learning as it might apply to institutions, governance, and democracy and then working out how these ideas might apply to the problematic role of public agencies in contemporary democracy. We can follow this same strategy in summarizing some of the core themes of the book.

Evolutionary Learning

As set out in chapter 1, the founding Pragmatists sought to overcome the dualisms that they regarded as problematic in continental philosophical traditions—dualisms like subject versus object, theory versus practice, mind versus body, and so forth. To overcome these dualisms, the Pragmatists made several intellectual moves. First, they adopted a triadic logic, introducing a third category to mediate between the poles of a dualism. Second, to avoid the reification of either pole, Pragmatism coupled meaning tightly to action, as stressed by Peirce's and James's ideas about "fixing" the meaning of ideas by evaluating their consequences or by Dewey's emphasis on experience and problem solving. Third, as expressed by Dewey's transactionalism, Pragmatism emphasizes the continuous and interactive relationship between the poles of a dichotomy. One of the core ideas of a Pragmatist public philosophy is to look for ways that dualisms prevalent in public life can be overcome.

The discussion here has built explicitly on this antidualism. Institutions are defined as "grounded concepts"—conceptual objects grounded in subjective experience—in order to overcome the subject–object tension inherent in much of contemporary institutionalism. We examined how Selznick's approach to organization theory overcomes the Weberian dualisms of impersonal versus personal and formal versus informal and also how Selznick's and Follett's analysis of relational authority overcomes the dualism of centralization versus decentralization. As illustrated by the Compstat example, the book argued that organizations can engage in high-performance problem-solving by addressing the gulf between headquarters-level planning versus field-level operations. The dualism of public versus private was attacked by developing the ideas of pluralist consent and embedded autonomy. Dewey's transactionalism was used to think through a number of basic issues, including institutional change, power, responsibility, authority, and collaboration.

Antidualism led Pragmatists to evolutionary learning. For Pragmatism, people and institutions learn when they focus their attention on concrete problems that link meaning tightly to action. Given that we have so many public problems, it may seem strange to emphasize the importance of focusing on problems. They bombard us constantly. In practice, however, public debates, political conflicts, and institutions tend to structure political life in a way that removes us from a shared focus on problems and problem solving. One of the general lessons of Pragmatism's evolutionary learning approach is that it would try to organize political life as much as possible so that different stakeholder groups—public and private—can engage in fruitful conflict focused around problem solving. Several chapters, but notably the chapter on problem solving and collaborative governance, provide ideas for how political life can be structured in this way.

People and institutions also learn when they are able to reflect, in a critical way, on their own beliefs and practices. This means that when people and institutions approach problems, they engage in inquiry about the nature of those problems and treat problem-solving as an opportunity for learning (e.g., experimentation). This may be obvious for some people and institutions, but it is much harder for others. It becomes particularly difficult when political life is bureaucratized or adversarial. In such cases, institutionalized patterns of behavior and ritualized conflict can make beliefs and practices very resistant to change. It is also much easier for individuals to reflect critically on their beliefs and practices than it is for groups. Several chapters—notably the chapter on problem solving, recursiveness, and collaborative governance—provide ideas about how inquiry can be collectively structured.

A third important feature of evolutionary learning is deliberation. Pragmatism places communication at the center of its philosophy and particularly values direct face-to-face communication. Joint deliberation about problems and about the nature of knowledge is critical for learning. In groups, direct face-to-face communication is the basis of fruitful conflict. In organizations, it is the basis for creating relational authority and developing shared responsibility. In political publics, deliberation is the basis for "civilizing" power and building consent. All the chapters emphasize this important function of face-to-face communication and joint deliberation.

Antidualism also motivates four additional principles of evolutionary learning introduced in chapter 1: cosmopolitan localism, analytical holism, progressive conservatism, and processual structuralism. These were less explicitly flagged in the chapters, but they fundamentally shaped how problem solving, reflexivity, and deliberation were conceived in different institutional, organizational, and political settings.

COSMOPOLITAN LOCALISM

As described in chapter 1, evolutionary learning sets up a creative tension between context-dependent local action and more cosmopolitan action. Learning grounded in local context prevents reification of more cosmopolitan ideas, while cosmopolitan perspectives discourage the parochialism of local problem-solving.

This cosmopolitan localism has been expressed throughout the book. Chapter 3 argued that a "constitutional process" of institutional change can develop out of the interaction between "grounded concepts" and "meta-con-cepts." The chapter on recursiveness showed how the headquarters level of a metropolitan police organization could be linked to concrete precinct-level problem-solving through the intermediation of Compstat meetings. The concept of a "constitutional hierarchy" developed in that chapter entailed a semi-autonomous but intensely interactive relationship between cosmopolitan policymakers and street-level bureaucrats. Building on Norbert Elias's analysis of "civilizing" processes, chapter 7 argued that the Pragmatist understanding of power and responsibility embodies this idea of cosmopolitan localism: self-restraining power (responsibility) develops with more cosmopolitan interdependence. Chapter 8 suggested that consent can be built up through localized problem-solving with affected stakeholders while working toward a wider base of consent based on overlapping problem-solving publics.

ANALYTICAL HOLISM

Analytical strategies gain traction by decomposing problems into simpler, more tractable issues, while synthetic strategies produce knowledge through integration and by treating the world more holistically. Pragmatist learning moves back and forth from analysis to synthesis.

The chapter on problem solving discussed Herbert Simon's analytical model of problem decomposition. Simon argued that decomposition allows decision makers to simplify complex problems to make them more tractable. But the "wicked problems" literature argues that many problems are not so easily decomposable and that neglecting this interdependence can be self-defeating. A Pragmatist problem-solving strategy would move back and forth from analysis to synthesis. Gaining traction on problems requires highly focused strategies. The Boston Gun Project was successful because it focused narrowly on the homicide problem rather than on the more "wicked" gang problem. After analytically isolating the homicide problem, however, the Boston Gun Project approached it in a very holistic fashion, integrating the resources and authority of many public agencies. An analytically holistic strategy to problem solving might also treat the successful reduction of homicides as a first step toward a more "synthetic" approach to the wicked problem of youth gangs.

Simon also applied his analytical model to organizational structure, arguing that we can think of organizations as "nearly decomposable" systems. These systems are modular, maximizing interdependence within modules and minimizing interdependence across modules. Like problems, however, organizational activities are not always readily decomposable into semi-independent units. The chapter on recursiveness described the possibility of a productive coexistence between analytically decomposable "hierarchy" and more synthetic "heterarchy." Dynamically, hierarchy and heterarchy can be brought together through a recursive looping of perspectives. As described in the case of the Compstat system, precinct units of the NYPD took the lead on local problem-solving (analytical decomposition); however, these units were geographically based and therefore treated local problems in a more holistic fashion than did the functionally based units they supplanted. The precincts became the point of (holistic) integration of functional units. Likert's model of a "linking pin" organization was presented as a structural model for unifying hierarchy and heterarchy.

PROGRESSIVE CONSERVATIVISM

Meaning accumulates over time in a conservative fashion, but it can be progressively and nonincrementally revised and reconstructed in the face of new challenges.

Much of the book has drawn on this theme of progressive conservatism. The chapters on institutions and institutional change, for example, contrasted institutions as "congealed taste," which understands them to be resistant to change (conservatism), with a view of institutions as subject to "rational design" (progressivism). A Pragmatist institutionalism joins these two images together. Experiences and meanings can accumulate around institutional concepts (sedimentation), but institutional change can be steered toward more rational design. The chapter on large-scale institutional change suggested "meta-concepts" can steer this evolutionary learning process on a grand scale. The chapter examined sustainable development as an example of how a new meta-concept can produce large-scale institutional change.

Progressive conservativism is at the heart of evolutionary learning. Successful evolutionary learning requires retention of past successes, while exposing this knowledge and practice to continuous challenge. The ideas about institutional change, problem solving, recursiveness, responsibility, consent building, and collaboration all embody this idea.

PROCESSUAL STRUCTURALISM

Pragmatism encourages us to see the world in dynamic and emergent terms. But this is not a world in pure flux. Processes are always contingently supported by structures.

The book has argued that a distinctive aspect of the Pragmatist model of learning is its attention to how learning processes are structurally scaffolded. As most directly expressed in Dewey's discussion of habit, higher-order learning must be built upon solid foundations. Although this point is hardly controversial or novel in the field of education or psychology, its wider application in the social sciences typically goes unappreciated. As developed in the chapters on institutions, institutional design assumptions often overlook the institutional scaffolds that support or discourage successful institutional reform. Likewise, chapter 3 suggested that we think of basic "competences" as a fundamental scaffolding for high-performing organizations; and chapter 4 argued that more holistic problem-solving has to be built upon the scaffolding of more focused problem-solving efforts. The chapter on collaborative governance argued that ambitious efforts at collaboration must be scaffolded upon a series of "small wins" and upon the establishment of trust and recognition among opposing stakeholders.

When applied to ethics, problem solving, or collaboration, evolutionary learning is not a natural condition of the world. Much of the time, we fail to learn. But sometimes people become more ethically responsible, organizations learn to solve difficult problems, and stakeholders come to acknowledge and trust one another. The evolutionary learning model suggests an agenda for a Pragmatist social science: to understand the conditions in which evolutionary learning becomes possible.

Public Agencies as the "Linchpin" of Problem-Solving Democracy

Chapter 1 described some of the strains in contemporary democracy that can create counterproductive cycles of public distrust and increased demands for accountability. Public agencies are often at the epicenter of these tectonic strains because they have a highly ambivalent role in contemporary democracy. These agencies are often seen as both essential to and at odds with democracy. Public programs and purposes are complex. Public health, education, market regulation, and environmental protection are all widely shared public purposes that require complex administrative programs staffed with technical experts. But we also fear that these complex administrative programs give power to experts or interest groups who use it to supplant the "popular will" of the people.

These are old debates, but they are sharpened by the increasing complexity of the economy, by new patterns of political mobilization, and by a slew of challenges to public bureaucracies. Fiscal crises beginning in the 1970s sharpened the conflicts with the "bureaucratic" state, which was seen as bloated and unresponsive. A rising challenge to planning and to bureaucratic intervention in daily life arose in the 1960s and was symbolically capped by the failure of the Soviet Union's "planned economy." Globalization and neoliberal triumphs ushered in the apparent triumph of the market. New Public Management (NPM) celebrated "management by results" and the importance of importing private business models into the operation of the state. Technological change, rising expectations, and the expansion of the advocacy sector all created new demands on the state, while fiscal problems and new demands for accountability placed greater constraints on the state's capacity to meet these demands. All these developments, taken together, have accentuated the ambivalent role of the administrative state within the democratic order.

At the heart of this ambivalent role of the administrative state are twin challenges. One of these challenges is to stem the increasing public negativity toward bureaucracy. Whereas Max Weber saw bureaucracy as a highly efficient form of organization, our contemporary world regards bureaucracy as hopelessly inefficient. The other challenge is democratic. While Weber saw bureaucracy as developing in tandem with the rising egalitarian and democratic trends of his time, our contemporary world tends to see large-scale bureaucracy as a self-serving juggernaut that runs roughshod over popular democracy. As a public philosophy, Pragmatism does not resolve these tensions. No public philosophy could. But Pragmatism does open up some new perspectives on bureaucracy and democracy, suggesting a more productive interpretation of the democratic role of public agencies.

This book has drawn on Pragmatism to reimagine the democratic role of public agencies. Our traditional model of democracy views public agencies as the culmination of a long chain of representation that starts with the voters, passes through elected representatives, and ends with public agencies. An alternative model of democracy starts with the concrete problems of affected stakeholders and builds up consent for public action through collaborative governance. Public agencies are the focal point for this model of collaborative problem-solving. From a Pragmatist perspective, this alternative model of consent building should complement rather than replace the traditional model of representative democracy. Elections constitute the public will in a diffuse and cosmopolitan sense. *Problem-solving democracy* builds consent with smaller publics focused on specific problems.

An important implication of this argument is that public agencies become the linchpins of this more compound democracy. They link together the delegated authority that flows from people to legislatures to public agencies with the problem-solving authority that emerges from their bottom-up facilitation of collaborative problem-solving. To serve this linchpin role, public agencies require a significant level of discretion and trust. To earn this discretion and trust, agencies have to demonstrate their competence at creatively aligning the public values expressed through representative democracy with public values expressed through collaborative problem-solving. To do this, they need to be organized in a different way than they currently are. Much of the book has focused on specifying a Pragmatist view of organization that might support this linchpin role.

Pragmatist Organization

"Pragmatist organization" can be contrasted with two alternative conceptions. Over a century ago, Max Weber advanced our traditional conception of organization—the formal, impersonal, rule-oriented, hierarchical "bureaucracy." Viewing this Weberian bureaucracy as rigid and inefficient, a more recent conception seeks to create a leaner and more responsive organization by replacing management-by-rules and command-and-control with management-by-results and performance measurement. A Pragmatist model of organization shares this concern with the pathologies of excessive management-by-rule and applauds, to some degree, the shift toward more flexible and entrepreneurial organization. Yet it is far less sanguine about a wholesale transition from rules to results.

It was not necessary to look too far to elucidate an alternative Pragmatist conception of organization. It has long been with us, though mostly hidden from view in contemporary debates about institutionalism and bureaucratic management. Chapter 4 argued that Philip Selznick and Mary Parker Follett offer an important "Pragmatist" alternative to Weberian views of organization, which has been extended in recent years by the work of Donald Chisholm (1995, 2001), Arjen Boin (2001), Charles Sabel (2006), and Michael Cohen (2007).

The book's focus on Selznick, in particular, can be explained in at least four ways. First, Selznick can anchor a tradition of Pragmatist organization theory, which is in turn rooted in the tradition of Pragmatist institutionalism. Second, if we weave together the different ideas inherent in his work—the politics of organization, administrative leadership, organizations as self-regulating polities, and responsive law—we arrive at quite a global view of Pragmatist organization. Third, Selznick's work is rather uniquely attentive to the role of meaning in organizational life, while showing how it is closely connected to action. Finally, Selznick's emphasis on organizational competences provides an important framework for thinking about organizational performance. One of the important goals of this book, therefore, has been to illuminate this Pragmatist interpretation of Selznick's work.

In chapter 2, Selznick's approach to organization is contrasted with Max Weber's. Distinguishing modern rational-legal bureaucracy from a patrimonial bureaucracy built around personal loyalties, Weber saw the modern world as substituting the cold, impersonal rationality of impartial bureaucratic rules for the inherent inefficiencies of personal loyalty. Weber feared this hegemony of impersonalism, concerned that it would empty the modern world of meaning and meaningful relationships. He interpreted bureaucracy as representing a sharp tradeoff between efficiency and meaningfulness.

Guided by Pragmatist assumptions and building on the work of the human relations school and Chester Barnard, Selznick refused this sharp dichotomy between the personal and the impersonal. Although criticized by Gouldner for his early pessimism about organization, Selznick ultimately developed a much more positive view of large-scale modern organization than did Weber. At the heart of this more positive view was Selznick's argument that formal and informal organization could be harnessed together and that work in large-scale organizations could be meaningful. Selznick stressed the role of leadership in harnessing the informal with the formal and the importance of mission for making work meaningful. Boin's (2001) analysis of the development of the U.S. Federal Bureau of Prisons provides a good description of how Selznick's ideas can work in practice. Creating large-scale public organizations that are effective and meaningful to work in is not easy, but it is not impossible either.

Selznick's model of organization also differs quite fundamentally from New Public Management models that emphasize the importance of external incentives for motivating work in organizations. While external incentives are important, they are blunt instruments for guiding action. Instead, Selznick argues that organization must be integrated around core meanings and values and that development of an organization's "distinctive competence" is ultimately a more powerful factor for shaping performance than rules or incentives.

Ultimately, Selznick's model of organization emphasizes the importance of cultivating individual and organizational competence. This competence-based approach differs from both the more structurally based approach of Weberian bureaucracy and the incentive-based approach of New Public Management (NPM). Schools provide a straightforward example of the contrast. A Weberian approach would try to improve educational performance by manipulating structure, policy, and oversight. New Public Management, by contrast, would stress performance management, which in the case of schools would mean the extensive use of testing to reward and punish schools and teachers. A competence-based approach would not place a stress on structure, policy, oversight, or performance management. Instead, it would focus on upgrading the competences of teachers and the capacity of schools. Rules, incentives, and competences, of course, are not stark alternatives. Yet, as recent experience with school reforms in the United States shows, emphasis matters.

At the core of the traditional Weberian model of hierarchy is a command relationship that extends vertically from the top to the bottom of the organization. This hierarchy emphasizes the authority of superordinates in the organization over their subordinates. Although Weber emphasized that authority rests on legitimacy—on an acceptance of the rightful exercise of that power— he regarded the modern form of authority as distinctly impersonal and resting on its "rational-legal" quality. Thus, either science or law must become the legitimate basis for authority. As with Weber's point about the sharp separation of the formal and the informal, this rational-legal model supports the notion of formal, impersonal command. By contrast, Selznick builds on Follett's and Barnard's relational model of authority in which authority is built up (or drawn down) through ongoing interaction between subordinates and subordinates. Thus, the Pragmatist model of organization does not reject hierarchical command or authority but rather places them within the context of a circular flow of interaction.

Chapter 6 proposed a model of "constitutional hierarchy" as an alternative to a hierarchy constructed around tight chains of command. A constitutional hierarchy would increase the relative autonomy of hierarchical levels, allowing the constitutional level to focus attention on safeguarding and refining the public values inherent in the organization's public missions and on wider problem-solving strategies. Instead of a tight command structure promulgating detailed operational rules, a constitutional hierarchy rests on fewer and more general rules. Rules proliferate in many contemporary bureaucracies, while being ignored or worked around. In a constitutional hierarchy, rules ought to be kept to a minimum, but they also ought to really count. This system can only work if there is a very close meshing between constitutional rule-making and operational practices. Policy must inform practice and practice must inform policy in a recursive cycle. Structurally, the levels of a constitutional hierarchy are loosely coupled; in action, they must be far more closely linked than in the typical hierarchical organization.

This circular flow of interaction is a recursive process. As developed in chapter 6, recursiveness implies the possibility of temporary inversions in the hierarchical relationship between superordinate and subordinate. Structurally, the organization remains nominally hierarchical. But, behaviorally, recursive systems are more heterarchical than hierarchical. They are often nested systems with strong elements of modularity, though not necessarily easily decomposable. From the perspective of New Public Management, the NYPD's Compstat strategy appears to be a system for achieving top-down accountability over field agents and for creating a results-based management system. From the Pragmatist perspective, what is critical about CompStat is the way it enables face-to-face communication between top-level executives and field officers, allowing them to engage in joint inquiry and shared responsibility across hierarchical levels. Although incentives are built into the CompStat process, it is this intensive communication around problem solving that facilitates a shared responsibility between top-level executives and street-level bureaucrats.

A focus on problem solving is a critical aspect of the Pragmatist method, a way to overcome dogmatic conflict and focus people on productive action. This idea can be applied in many ways to organizations and public agencies. Individuals and organizations routinely encounter problems, but few organizations are oriented toward problem solving in any serious and sustained way. Pragmatism asks organizations to adopt a more self-conscious approach toward problem solving, one that attacks problems in a focused, holistic, and proactive fashion. Such a strategy requires special skills and knowledge and naturally complements a competency-based approach to organization.

A Weberian hierarchy—with its framework of command-and-control and management by rules—depends on a closed organizational system to work well. Administratively, this is highly problematic because it discourages organizational responsiveness to changing external demands. Anyone who thinks this is merely a theoretical nicety should read the literature on police agencies, who struggle with this dilemma in their daily work. To be effective problem-solvers, Pragmatism suggests that public agencies must be more open to their environments. However, this openness can threaten the integrity of the organization and public values. Chapter 8 proposed a model of embedded autonomy that allows organizations to engage more actively and responsively with the public. A strong constitutional system articulating general, meaningful rules; a strong problem-solving community that values competency and responsibility; and a strong buy-in to the broad public mission of the organization are the best guarantees against the perils of embeddedness. The Pragmatist model is probably easier to realize when the work of a public agency is widely perceived as valuable and important, where external constituencies are not actively seeking to colonize the agency for their own purposes, and where bureaucrats do not face attractive opportunities for rent-seeking. Yet the Weberian and NPM models suffer under these same conditions.

Final Words

This book has argued that Pragmatism's model of evolutionary learning provides a useful resource for imagining a more constructive relationship between public institutions, the governance of public problems, and democratic consent. The book has focused on applying this model to the beleaguered role of public agencies in contemporary democracy. The result has led to a description of a distinctive style of democracy where public agencies—when organized in particular ways—can play a key role in building democratic consent through focused problem-solving collaboration with the public. These ideas hardly exhaust the potential insights of Pragmatism, which can be and have been applied to many other dimensions of public affairs, including environmental ethics, legal reasoning, and civic education. Hopefully, however, they provide a resource that will help others continue to refine Pragmatism as a public philosophy.

NOTES

Chapter 1

1. On spirals of distrust, see Djelic and Sahlins-Andersson (2006, 380). Declining trust in government is a complicated issue (Bovens and Wille 2008), but the best cross-national research finds that erosion of trust results from rising expectations (Dalton 2004). For a broad discussion of trust in government agencies, see Thomas (1998).

2. A classic debate between Carl Friedrich and Herman Finer elaborated many of these themes (McSwite 1997).

3. Throughout the text, Pragmatism, the philosophy, will be capitalized to distinguish it from pragmatism, a practical or commonsensical way of behaving.

4. The literature is extensive. Important overviews of the Pragmatist tradition include Thayer (1981), West (1989), Diggins (1994), Menand (2001), and Westbrook (2005). For recent studies of Peirce, see Hookway (1985, 2000) and Colapietro (1989); on James, see Simon (1998); on Mead, see Baldwin (1986), Cook (1993), Wiley (1993), and Joas (1997); on Dewey, see Westbrook (1991), Campbell (1995), and Ryan (1995).

5. Not everything about CAPS, of course, has been a success. District Advisory Committees established to consult regularly with the Chicago police have not functioned well. Participants at beat meetings are not always representative of their communities and Latinos have seen deterioration in their neighborhood conditions. Surveys and subsequent analysis also find a decline over time in citizens' perceptions of the link between issues discussed at beat meetings and the problem-solving strategies subsequently adopted by the police.

6. Arguably, we might also add postmodernism, utilitarianism, and social democracy.

7. This alliance has historical roots, but has not always been harmonious (Ross 1992; Smith 1994). As Smith shows, social scientists influenced by Pragmatism polarized into two rival camps, "objectivists" and "purposivists." Lindblom and Cohen's (1979) statement about "usable knowledge" provides a more contemporary account of social science practice consistent with a Pragmatist perspective.

8. In other words, the point is not that public philosophy sets out the "values" of inquiry while social science establishes the "facts."

9. Evolution signifies a process of continuous adaptation to natural and social environments. Learning signifies the acquisition or revision of meanings or competencies that aid that adaptation. The amalgam of the two was inspired by Darwin, but historically rooted in the "reformed liberalism" and "transcendentalism" of Emersonian New England (West 1989; Greenstone 1993; Menand 2001).

10. Peirce sought to develop an evolutionary model that balanced chance against determinism. His essay "Evolutionary Love" distinguishes his understanding of evolution as growth (agapastic evolution) from evolution by "fortuitous variation" and by "mechanical necessity." Hausman summarizes: "Agape, which Peirce called evolutionary love, is more generally to be open to letting unexpected occurrences and ideas take their own course" (2008, 218).

11. See Hodgson and Knudsen (2006), however, for a detailed discussion of this point. They reject the Lamarckian label for socioeconomic evolution. Sementelli (2007) argues that Veblen's and Commons's models of evolution, while emphasizing habit, were not Lamarckian.

12. James Mark Baldwin, a psychologist and contemporary of the classical Pragmatists, argued that "organic" evolution was characterized by feedbacks from adaptation to selection. Popp (2007) describes Dewey's theory of democracy as creating social conditions for growth; he talks about democracy as producing a kind of Baldwin effect (to select good ideas). On cumulative effects, Garrison quotes Dewey: "The connection of means-consequences is never one of bare succession in time. . . . There is a deposit at each stage and point entering cumulatively and constitutively into the outcome" (cited in Later Works, 1:276). Hall and Whybrow (2008) argue that Veblen derived his concept of cumulative causation from Peirce (cf. Foresti [2004] who argues that it was derived from "cues" from Kant and Darwin). They quote Veblen as describing cumulative causation as "changes cumulatively going forward in the institutional fabric of habitual elements that govern the scheme of life."

13. The master code of pragmatism is a rejection of the dualisms typically associated with Cartesian modernism. As Hans Joas puts it: "Antidualism was one of the leitmotifs of pragmatism" (1993, 72). On Dewey's and Mead's antidualism, see Baldwin (1986, 29–35) and Joas (1997, 61). On Peirce's anti-Cartesian approach, see Mills (1966, chap. 7). The Pragmatist instinct to balance dualisms can be seen as structuring a whole complex and interrelated field of modernist dichotomies. Anselm Strauss sums this up nicely: "In the writings of the Pragmatists we can see a constant battle against the separating, dichotomizing, or opposition of what Pragmatists argued should be joined together: knowledge and practice, environment and actor, biology and culture, means and ends, body and mind, matter and mind, object and subject, logic and inquiry, lay thought and scientific thought, necessity and chance, cognitive and non cognitive, art and science, values and action" (1993, 45).

14. Peirce rediscovered the idea of continuousness in Greek philosophy and he referred to it as "synechism." Dewey later emphasized the continuous transaction between actors and their environments.

15. Peirce's most important use of this triadic logic may have been the relationship he proposes between mind, nature, and society. Nature represents the external objective world; mind grasps this objective world through a system of signs. Unlike Kant, however, who saw mental conceptual structures as transcendental, Peirce argued that the meaning of mental signs was fixed by reference to society. He argued in favor of a provisional truth fixed by the "community of inquiry."

16. Mead, for example, articulated a developmental model of the "social self." He argued that a "social" self develops when the self becomes capable of reflecting upon itself from the perspective of society. Individuals are capable of "role-taking," which is a fundamental Pragmatist mechanism of developing shared understanding through dialogue. Conceptually, he distinguishes a triadic relationship between the I, the me, and the generalized other. The I is the source of spontaneous impulse. The me is the self that develops a relationship with the I, which means that the conscious me develops an awareness of the I as an object. In temporal terms, the I is always apprehended as the immediate past. Only the me is accessible in the present. So far, the conceptual logic is dyadic, positing a relationship between the I and the me. The developmental sequence

only appears when the conceptual logic becomes triadic. Mead argues that for the me to more fully take the I as an object, it requires a degree of autonomy from spontaneous impulse. The source of this autonomy is a third term of reference—a point of perspective with which to regard the I as an object. For Mead, this third term is the generalized other, the perspective of society at large. From this larger perspective, the me is able to adopt different roles vis-à-vis the I.

17. With Pragmatism, we have to always be careful to not prioritize one end of a dualistic opposition. While stressing "learning by doing," Pragmatism does not prioritize practice over theory. Learning arises from direct experience with the world, but this experience is symbolically mediated. Symbols are tools to probe and understand this world, while experience can lead to the refinement and revision of these symbolic tools. Learning depends on the interaction between abstraction inherent in symbols and the situated logic of experience with concrete problems. Theories are useful, but they have to be grounded in practice. This point is also important to make because the term "pragmatism" is often used colloquially to refer to practical action devoid of principle. Pragmatism, the philosophy, adopts fallibilism, but it by no means rejects principled action. Knowledge, principles, and values, however, are treated as provisional and subjected to continuous testing and revision.

18. Joas (1997) describes how a Pragmatist model of action emphasizes the creativity of action.

19. Pragmatism's emphasis on continuous revision leads to a rejection of the sharp separation of means and ends. Dewey describes the separation of instrumental and final (consummatory) ends as a "great evil" (1929, 169). Not only are "ends" partly emergent from action (which economists label "endogenous preferences"), but they are shaped by our choice of "means." See Whitford (2002) for a good discussion on this point.

20. Marc Tool has summarized Pragmatism's social valuation principle as follows: "Maximize opportunities for effective social and individual non-invidious development" (1977, 832). This developmental ethic is not teleological. Pragmatism tries to identify the possibilities for growth and progress without assuming these possibilities will be realized (Marcel 1974). Nor is it utopian. Pragmatism remains hopeful for human growth, but harbors no illusion of human perfectability (Rorty 2000; Westbrook 2005).

21. In *Education and Experience*, Dewey writes: "The criterion of the value of school education is the extent to which it creates a desire for continued growth and supplies means for making the desire effective in fact" (1938, 58). Writing about Dewey on education and democracy, Popp (2007) argues: "All such reorganizations or reconstructions are subjected to the standard of growth in that the test for such reorganizations is whether they open the way for subsequent achievements of greater meaning and autonomy." Cunningham argues that [moral] growth for Dewey is the "broadening and deepening of the agent's capacity to take all the interests inherent within the situation into account" (1994, 353). See Festenstein (1997, chaps. 2 and 3) for a general discussion of Dewey's view of growth. For discussions of the Pragmatist view of progress, see Marcell (1974), Sheppard (2003), Koopman (2006), and McGowan (2008).

22. On the idea of incommensurability in the Pragmatist tradition, see Russill (2005). For Pragmatism, reflexive inquiry produces dialogue between different perspectives. Mead, for example, argued that individual growth occurs when people engage in an internal dialogue with a "generalized other" (Wiley 1994).

23. As conceived by Campbell, social experimentation is a constrained version of a random controlled experiment (a quasi-experiment), as developed in psychology. For a discussion placing this understanding of "experiment" in historical context, see Dehue (2001). It is worth noting that Rortyian neo-Pragmatism is not sanguine about Dewey's "experimentalism." For a good discussion of Rorty's "post-experimentalism" and what it misses about Deweyian Pragmatism, see Waks (1997). Talisse nicely summarizes the classical Pragmatist stance toward the metaphor of scientific inquiry in general: "Pragmatists

often articulate their vision of democratic practice by means of an analogy with scientific inquiry. Although this practice is sometimes misunderstood as a quasi-positivist insistence that all real questions are scientific questions, the pragmatist sees science not as a privileged tribunal, but as an especially well-refined instance of those intellectual processes we engage in when confronted with a problem of any sort" (2005, 107).

24. The classic statement is Dewey's (1928) *Quest for Certainty.*

25. In *Art and Experience,* Dewey nicely captures the conservative aspect of meaning: "Between the poles of aimlessness and mechanical efficiency, there lie those courses of action in which through successive deeds there runs a sense of growing meaning conserved and accumulating toward an end that is felt as accomplishment of process" (1980, 39).

26. In fact, Dewey's definition of inquiry is: "turning elements into unified whole" (1980, 104–105). On Dewey's holism, see McDonald (2004, 119). For a broader discussion of holism in Pragmatism, see Misak (1999) and White (2005).

27. This processual structuralism is rooted in Pragmatism's relational and processual ontology. A relational ontology is one in which social entities are to be understood in terms of their relationships rather than in terms of their inherent (essentialist) characteristics. James announces this relational perspective in his essays on radical empiricism, alongside a discussion of the continuous nature of social life. Drawing on Pragmatism, Emirbayer (1997) elaborates on relational arguments in his "Relational Manifesto for the Social Sciences." A processual ontology emphasizes the importance of ongoing social interaction to the construction and negotiation of social order and meaning. On "processual" philosophy, see Rescher (2000).

28. In a very broad sense, it might be fair to say that much of organization theory and public administration is about problem solving. Nevertheless, it is difficult to find explicit treatments of problem solving. See chapter 5 for important exceptions.

29. In studies of private firms, this is called a "competency" view of the firm.

30. The Pragmatist tradition is still recognized in contemporary studies of cognition (on Jerome Bruner, see Stone 2006) and social psychology (Fiske 1992, 1993; on political psychology, see Rosenberg 2003). Among current disciplines of psychology, Pragmatism has very strong affinities with the ecological psychology of Gibson (Good 2007; Noble 2007) and with cognitive linguistics (Johnson 2006). On influences within psychiatry, see Brendel (2006).

31. Dewey and Mead shaped the Chicago School of Sociology through their influence on Robert Park (Matthews 1977), Florian Znaniecki (Wiley 2007), and Everett Hughes (Helmes-Hayes 1998). James had a strong influence on Charles Cooley at the University of Michigan (Herranz 2003) and on W. E. B. Du Bois (Taylor 2004). These influences, in turn, later shaped the development of symbolic interactionism (Shalin 1986), especially the work of Herbert Blumer (Tucker 1988), Anselm Strauss (Strauss 1993), Norman Denzin, David Maines (Maines 2001), and Tomatsu Shibutani (Baldwin 2006).

32. The Pragmatist roots of institutional economics live on in the work of Geoffrey Hodgson (Hodgson 2004, 2006, 2007) and Daniel Bromley (2006). Jens Beckert (2003) has developed Pragmatist ideas in the related field of economic sociology.

33. See Anderson (1994), Johnson and Knight (Knight and Johnson 1996, 2007), Bohman (1999, 2002), Caspary (2000), Festenstein (2001), Dryzek (2004), and Fung (2007).

34. One of the founders of policy studies, Harold Lasswell was influenced by Pragmatism in his attempt to establish the policy sciences as a "problem-oriented" discipline (Ascher and Hirschfelder-Ascher 2004; but see Kaufman-Osborne 1985 for a critique). More recent attempts to link public policy and Pragmatism include Buchholz and Rosenthal (1995). Planning draws even more substantially on Pragmatism (Hoch 1984a, 1984b; Forester 1993, 1999; Blanco 1994; Lawrence 2000; Holden 2008). In environmental planning, two legendary figures, Aldo Leopold and Benton MacKaye,

were influenced by Pragmatism (Minteer 2001). For influences on geography, see Allen (2008), Hepple (2008), and Cutchin (1999); for the Pragmatist influences on Gilbert White's geography, see Wescoat (1992). Social work has also been influenced by Pragmatism through the work of Jane Addams (Seigfried 1999; Shields 2003, 2006, 2008; Whipps 2004).

35. Among contemporary legal theorists, Posner (2003) has advanced the importance of legal pragmatism, though his pragmatism is not rooted strongly in Pragmatist philosophy.

36. In the related fields of organization and management theory, Mary Parker Follett (Ansell 2009), Ordway Tead (O'Connor 2001), Herbert Simon (Kerr 2007), and W. A. Shewhart (the founder of quality management; Sliwa and Wilcox 2008) drew on Pragmatism in their work. More contemporary authors influenced by Pragmatism include Philip Selznick (1966, 1984), Donald Schön (Schön 1983), Donald Chisholm (2001), and Michael Cohen (Cohen 2007). Pragmatism has also influenced the more specialized fields of organizational learning (Elkjaer 2004) and knowledge management (Cavaleri 2004). In systems theory and operations research, Pragmatism influenced Fred Emery (Barton and Selsky 2000), C. West Churchland (Matthews 2006), and Russell Ackoff (Ormerod 2006).

37. Shields (2008) provides a recent overview of this discussion.

38. There has also been considerable debate about whether pragmatism provides a good philosophical foundation for public administration (Stever 2000; Zanetti and Carr 2000) and a lively debate about whether the "classical" pragmatism of Dewey or the "neo-Pragmatism" of Rorty offer the best "foundations" for public administration (Stever 2000; Miller 2004, 2005; Shields 2004, 2005, 2008; Stolcis 2004; Webb 2004; Evans 2005; Hildebrand 2005; Snider 2005; Hoch 2006).

39. There is also much important work in the contemporary social sciences with strong affinities with Pragmatism, even if it is not directly influenced by it. This includes Mannheim's sociology of knowledge (Nelson 1995), Bateson's work on social ecologies (Harries-Jones 2002), Vygotsky's historical-cultural activity theory (Miettinen 2001), work on situated action and communities of practice (Suchman 1987; Lave and Wenger 1991; Brown and Duguid 2000), Bandura's work on social learning (Holden 2008), Elias's figurational sociology (Zimmerman 2006), Giddens's structuration theory (Giddens 1984), and Bourdieu's concepts of practice and habitus (Colapietro 2004).

40. The critique from the left, mounted by Randolph Bourne, Lewis Mumford, and later by C. Wright Mills, was either that Dewey (in particular) was stuck in a lost agricultural world of small communities and had no response to the rising political power of the modern corporation or that the "scientific" approach of Pragmatism was the handmaiden of capitalism (Lustig 1983) or of social engineering and technocratic planning (Jordan 1994). For a direct critique of the "social engineering" criticism, see Kaufman-Osborne (1985).

Chapter 2

1. For a view of Dewey's thinking about technology, see Hickman (1992).

2. In fact, this has been a major point of divergence in the burgeoning institutionalism literature. Sociological institutionalists typically stress either the normative or cognitive aspects of institutions, while rational choice institutionalists emphasize how institutions are deployed instrumentally.

3. For the influence of Pragmatism on institutional economics, see Ayres (1951), Mirowski (1987), Pickens (1987), Bush (1989), Liebhafsky (1993), Albert and Ramstad (1997, 1998), Twomey (1998), Webb (2002), Bromley (2006), and Hall and Whybrow (2008), The Chicago School of Sociology and symbolic interactionism were strongly influenced by Dewey and Mead (Blumer 1969; Shalin 1986; Maines 2001). For the influence of Pragmatism on Follett, see Stever (1986), Mattson (1998), and Ansell (2009). On Selznick, see Selznick (1973).

4. Arguably, there is also a political science tradition of institutionalism that could be associated with Charles Merriam and the "Chicago School" of political science, which strongly influenced Herbert Simon. A case might also be made for a pluralist institutionalism associated with Arthur Bentley, who co-authored *Knowing and the Known* with Dewey.

5. See Twomey (1998) and Kilpinen (2004) on Veblen's social psychology; see Albert and Ramstad (1997, 1998) on Commons's relationship to Dewey's and Mead's social psychologies. See Kilpinen (2003) for a more general discussion of Pragmatist psychology and institutionalism.

6. See Twomey (1998) on Veblen and Herranz (2003) on Cooley.

7. A habit, for Peirce, was a tendency to act in a repeatable way and was related to his larger search for a middle ground between chance and determinism (Hausman 2008). Habit is also connected to his idea of synechism, or continuity. As Miller describes Peirce's view of habits as follows: "Habits are rooted in other habits, imply further habits, and are ramified in their interconnections (1996, 71)." For James, habit had the distinctive feature of being plastic and hence moldable (see his chapter on habit in *Principles of Psychology*). For Dewey, the distinctiveness of habit was its disposition to action and the connection it made between mind and body (see especially his *Human Nature and Conduct*). Building on Pragmatist and Veblenian traditions, Hodgson has recently defined habit as "a disposition to engage in previously adopted or acquired behavior or thoughts, triggered by an appropriate stimulus or context" (2006, 6).

8. The Chicago School of Sociology actually had a rather ambivalent stance toward the concept of habit and symbolic interactionism largely dropped the idea of habit altogether (Camic 1986; Baldwin 1988). For a broad overview of the use of "habit" in sociology, see Camic (1986).

9. Webb writes that: "Ayres' favorite analogy made the choice of the appropriate wrench by a skilled mechanic analogous to the instrumental choice of a public policy to deal with a social problem" (2002, 991).

10. Murray Murphey, in his introduction to Veblen's *Instinct of Workmanship*, writes: "A habit, of course, characterizes an individual at a particular time, but when habits are widely shared and become established within a group, Veblen called them institutions. Thus for Veblen institutions were not organizations or objects but habits or complexes of habits. For example, when Veblen said that private property was an institution, he referred not to the objects owned, but to the set of established beliefs constituting prescriptive rights and duties, by which the objects are made to be property. Institutions then are shared established beliefs, and as beliefs change so institutions change" (xxxiii). Murphey goes on to distinguish Veblen from James and Dewey: "It is at this point that one can see how radically Veblen differed from writers such as James and Dewey. In Veblen's view it was the group—the community—that was important in understanding sociocultural change, not the individual. It was the group that carried the gene pool which determined the instincts or motives of its members, and it was the group that created and transmitted the habits that provided the means for their fulfillment. Individuals are just particular combinations of instincts and habits, and their behavior is explained by their twin heritage" (xl). It is true that James did have a more individualist psychology, but Murphey's argument is less appropriate for Dewey, who largely subscribed to Mead's view of socialization (Whipple 2005).

11. Bromley (2006) builds his institutionalist model of "volitional pragmatism" on Peirce's model of abduction. Institutions, he argues, are built on "settled belief." But he argues that institutional change operates abductively.

12. This brings the idea of abduction close to the idea of intuition, tacit knowledge, and sense making. Paavola (2005) argues that abduction is more deliberate than intuition: "A paradigmatic example of abductive reasoning is a detective's reasoning . . . where various, and minute clues help to delimit and instigate the search for hypotheses, and

where the goal is to find such a pattern to which all the relevant information and clues can be fitted." See Miller (2008) for a discussion of the Pragmatist affinities of Polanyi's work on tacit knowledge and a comparison with Herbert Simon's work.

13. Note, however, that Helmes-Hayes (1998) regards this situational perspective as distinguishing Hughes from the symbolic interactionists.

14. As Webb notes: "Dewey's instrumental analysis of ethical problems could hardly be further from straight-line instrumentalism. In attempting to fashion solutions to practical social problems, conflicting ends are present from the beginning, and new ends emerge and old ends are modified in the process of inquiry. In Dewey's view, means and ends interpenetrate and reshape each other. Neither is seen as 'outside' or fixed or beyond criticism" (2002, 993).

15. See Whitford (2002) for a good discussion of the importance of the continuous interaction of means and ends to Dewey's philosophy.

16. This view of institutions leads to a focus on conditions that allow persistence through time. Paralleling Max Weber's work on bureaucracy, Hughes focused on the role of functionaries in the organization. Abbot notes that although Hughes is largely forgotten as an institutional theorist, he continues to be remembered and used for his work on occupations and careers (Abbott 1992). And in his defense of the "old" institutionalism, Stinchcombe (1997) points to the value of seeing institutions as "staffed."

17. Stinchcombe describes this link between character and distinctive competence as one of the most valuable features of the "old institutionalism." In describing Coase's "old institutionalist" notion of transaction costs, he provides the following example: "Similarly, a university contracts out its janitoring and waste removal tasks, but keeps it research and teaching in-house, because it has a believable commitment to scholarship, and no noticeable commitment to clean buildings" (1997, 12).

18. Barzelay and Gallego have recently described an "institutional processualism" consistent with a Pragmatist perspective: "Like both processualism and institutionalism, institutional processualism takes a strong interest in how situated interaction (and, in this way, human agency) can feed back upon context" (2006, 538).

19. The broader intellectual influences that support an ecological perspective certainly include Darwin, but they also include James's defense of relational thinking in his "Essays on Radical Empiricism."

20. According to Stinchcombe, Commons shared this ecological perspective: "What Commons (especially when combined with Schumpeter) managed to do, then, was to jump over the institutionalism of organizational ecology of one population (developed especially by Adam Smith for firms, and theorized differently by Hannan & Freeman) directly to the establishment of an evolutionary ecology of multiple competing species (defined by their working rules and by the opportunities—or niches—those exploit)" (1997, 14).

21. Dewey saw character as the interpenetration of habit. This is an ecological conception at the individual level.

22. As a model of institutional evolution, this Pragmatist view has some clear affinities with Nelson and Winter's (1985) model of evolutionary learning in organizations. Building on Herbert Simon's model of organizations as a bundle of routines, they view institutional evolution as the process of natural selection of routines.

23. Hall and Whybrow (2008) have argued that Veblen's theory of institutional evolution was derived from Peirce's idea of continuousness.

24. To stress the artifactual character of institutions is to draw a connection with the work of Vygotsky and activity theory. For a good discussion, see Miettinen and Virkkunen (2005).

25. The approach here is similar to that elaborated by Mead in his critique of Cooley's "mentalistic" view of social action, though Schubert (2006) argues that Mead misinterpreted Cooley.

26. As Garrison writes: "An event has no antecedent fixed meaning or essence; instead, meaning and essence emerge as a consequence of transactional processes" (2001, 286). He also points out that Dewey and Bentley have a specific transactional understanding of situation: "Thinking about 'situation' transactionally reminds us that environment and organism, or context and actor, are methodological distinctions within a single, unified, ever-evolving subject matter" (2001, 288).

27. Nonaka (1994) summarizes Bateson's argument about how abduction is related to concept formation: "According to Bateson, concepts are created through deduction, induction, and abduction. Abduction has a particular importance in the conceptualization process. While deduction and induction are vertically-oriented reasoning processes, abduction is a lateral extension of the reasoning process which centers on the use of metaphors. Deduction and induction are generally used when a thought or image involves the revision of a preexisting concept or the assigning of a new meaning to a concept. When there is no adequate expression of an image it is necessary to create completely new concepts" (1994, 25). Carr et al. rely on Boje's description of abduction: deduction verifies a priori theory; induction generates theory from observations; and abduction relies upon intuition and ongoing inquiry where researchers "have a more spontaneous creative insight they speculate may be tied to their data." (2004, 84).

28. The Pragmatist notion of community, however, is transactional rather than essentialist. As Seigfried writes: "If communities exist in virtue of what their members have in common—preeminently aims, beliefs, aspirations, and knowledge—then there are few intact communities in contemporary postindustrial societies. Dewey recognizes that only through communication can a common understanding in the sense of similar emotional and intellectual dispositions be reached" (1999, 208). See Follett's essay "Community as Process" for additional thoughts along this line (Follett 1919).

29. I see this point as consistent with Dorothy Smith's idea of "institutional ethnography."

30. Of course, this point has been emphatically made by some scholars (Rudolph and Rudolph 1984).

31. For example, recall Burke's critique of the French revolution. Congealed taste is equivalent to the idea of sedimentation described by Berger and Luckmann (1967).

32. For a Pragmatist, envisioning the end point in a sequence of institution-building moves is a powerful way to prevent directionless drift or the reinforcement of the status quo inherent in incremental moves. As best described by Dewey, however, ends and means are in an endless cycle of coevolution. The envisioned plan—which Dewey called the "ends-in-view"—must also be adapted to these incremental adaptations. Like incrementalists, a Pragmatist does not regard it as simple and straightforward to predict the changes that will arise from design interventions. Therefore design strategies need to be revised as the institutional scaffolding for change is built.

33. To focus on concepts is not to assume that they necessarily work as imagined by classical logic. They often operate more like Wittgenstein described them in his idea of language games. Concepts are polythetic (Needham 1975)—people may attribute many, often contradictory, meanings to a concept (as suggested by the definition of "institution"!). The idea of concept that comes closest here is that suggested by the work by Rosch, Lakoff, and Johnson on the relational and embodied character of concepts. (See Johnson [2006] for a discussion of the affinities between this embodied view of mind and the Pragmatist view of mind.) This polythetic, embodied view of conceptual meaning allows us to appreciate the metaphorical quality of institutional action. For a discussion of the relationship between metaphor and concept formation in Peirce's semiotics, see Sorenson and Thellefsen (2006).

34. In attempting to revive a Pragmatist institutional economics, Bromley (2006) and Hodgson (2006) both equate institutions with rules. As Hodgson writes: "Hence an institution is a special type of social structure that involves potentially codifiable and (evidently or immanently) normative rules of interpretation and behavior" (2006, 4).

While sympathetic to their larger project, this focus on rules is too narrow. A number of Bromley's examples actually illustrate the more foundational role of concepts. For example, he uses the following illustration: "Official categories define who we are and what we may do. The terms husband and wife are legal concepts, and so the state sets the minimum age (even the gender) for which individuals may acquire those appellations" (2006, 37). And elsewhere, he provides the following example: "We see, therefore, that the concept of income (and of profit) is itself a social construct. If this is doubted, engage an accountant with good knowledge of American and European accounting protocols in a conversation. You will quickly learn how the concepts of profit and loss differ under two distinct social, economic, and political settings" (2006, 42).

35. But this is true not just of Selznick but also of the Durkheimian tradition of institutional analysis, which sees conceptual distinctions as developing sacred meaning. Yet the advantage of a Pragmatist theory of institutions over a Durkheimian approach is that Pragmatism rejects any strong distinction between psychology and sociology.

36. See Mary Douglas's *How Institutions Think* (1986) for a powerful reflection on how institutions enter into our thought processes.

37. "Experience" was arguably the most central concept in Dewey's philosophical work and he wrote three major books exploring the idea: *Education and Experience, Experience and Nature*, and *Art as Experience*. These works built on James's pathbreaking work on experience in *Varieties of Religious Experience* and *Essays in Radical Empiricism*. Although the term "experience" may have been less central to Mead's work, *Mind, Self and Society* can be interpreted as specifying the social and communicational basis of experience.

38. This emphasis on "disposition" is quite consistent with the meaning Peirce gave to habit. Peirce sought to find a middle way between "chance" and "determinism" and his emphasis on habit reflected this middle path.

39. This idea builds on Peirce's triadic analysis of semiotics. As in his model of semiotics, context may be other concepts or dispositions.

40. D'Adderio's (2008) discussion of the continuous interaction between formal rules and SOPs and behavioral routines develops a very similar argument.

41. Miettinen (2001) discusses the meaning of practical reason for new sociological institutionalism, which draws on Garfinkel's notion: "Ethnomethodology studied the preconscious 'practical reason' (knowledge without concepts) governed by rules that are recognized only when they are breached."

42. For a good discussion of this point, see Miettinen (2001). The parallel being drawn here is between institutions as grounded concepts and Dewey's discussion of reflexivity and habit. Concepts are analogous here to reflexivity. Concepts, while grounded in context, always have a decontextualized aspect. They are, in Peircean terms, "generals." By contrast, my discussion of the grounding or funding of concepts in experience is parallel to Dewey's idea of habit. The institutional process is therefore, following Dewey, a continuous interchange between the grounding of concepts in experience and the reflexive use of concepts to reconstruct experience. (Note the discussion by Morris [1999] on the way that Pragmatism is "theory centric," which focuses on how theories are used to reconstruct empirical understanding).

43. "Ecology" is also a close cousin of the term "system." Both terms tend to imply some interdependence between parts that make up a larger whole. However, the term "system" implies that the parts play some specific functional role in the maintenance of the whole. This may be true, but often is not. The term "ecology" assumes interdependence and interconnection but does not assume functional relationships. Ecological relationships are as likely to be competitive and conflictual as they are functional. The term "system" also implies that the broader institutional logic of interdependence is somehow independent of how people use and create this interdependence. By contrast, the term "ecology" signals the environmental groundedness of institutions and

suggests that patterns of relationships are created by social interaction and by the use of institutions.

44. For a good empirical example, see Mohr and Duquenne (1997). On the idea that concepts often hang together as systems see Dewey (1910, 180).

Chapter 3

1. The analogy between natural and social evolution breaks down because there is often no clear separation between "organism" and "environment" in the social world. In the place of a distinct environment that exerts selection pressures on institutions, other institutions are often their primary environment.

2. Institutional theorists have begun to give a great deal of attention to the problem of understanding institutional change (Schickler 2001; Greif and Laitin 2004; Pierson 2004; Thelen 2004; Berk and Galvan 2009).

3. Described in this way, we can see how symbolic interactionism and the institutional economics of John Commons might be more closely related than they appear to be at first glance. Commons understood institutions as a going concern in which there was a continuous revision of the working rules of the enterprise, just as the symbolic interactionists see institutions as arenas where there is an ongoing negotiation of the social order. Both perspectives assume publics engage in debate about the fate of their collective enterprises.

4. Although we tend to think of constitutional processes as "macro" phenomena that govern nations, these processes can operate even at very "micro" levels. Consider the formation of a friendship. When two people form a friendship, they are establishing a sense that their relationship is a "going concern." Forming a friendship means forming a primitive, informal, and unwritten constitution—a sense of the meanings, values, and norms of behavior that orient and govern the relationship. Meso-level activities also have constitutional processes. For example, restaurant kitchens have a similar kind of "constitution"—a mostly unwritten code—that is continuously negotiated about the appropriateness of behaviors (Fine 1996). Symbolic interactionists call this constitutional process a "negotiated order."

5. Charles Anderson (1994) has argued that this emphasis on the development of internal self-government is a key feature of Pragmatist liberalism.

6. In *Human Nature and Conduct*, Dewey discusses "Metanorms that emerge to flexibly govern specific situations" (1957, 169).

7. As Star and Griesemer (1989) argue: "Consensus is not necessary for cooperation nor for the successful conduct of work" (388). In a similar discussion, Lanzara and Patriotta talk about the generative character of an institutional "template"—a "master model or pattern by which other similar things can be made" (2007, 638).

8. Sapsed and Salter observe: "It is also the case that some boundary objects are more prone to neglect than others, because they are more 'charged' with meaningful action and less ambiguous" (2004, 1530).

9. Mead may have been getting at a similar point in his discussion of "teleological objects" (essay 17 in *The Philosophy of the Act*) where he argues, "A teleological object is one that defines other things in terms of itself."

10. Festenstein (1995) sees Dewey's model of growth as teleological. MacGilvray (1999) describes the Pragmatist model of intelligence as teleological. However, as Cunningham notes: "Dewey's 'natural teleology' . . . is provisional and contextual, rather than eternal" (1994, 349).

11. Kidd (1992) argues that the current concept of sustainability builds on six distinct but overlapping strands of thought. All six strands of thought examined the capacity and limits of growth. See also Mebratu (1998) and Robinson (2004) on the history of sustainable development prior to 1987. Pumar (2005) describes the emergence of sustainable development as a concept in terms of the specific intellectual networks.

12. Pumar (2005) challenges the idea that the Brundtland Commission was the takeoff point for sustainable development, though he admits that this was an important watershed.

13. Goodland writes: "Part of the success of the Brundtland Commission's definition stems from its opacity" (1995, 4).

14. Robinson writes that "the power of the concept of sustainability, then, lies precisely in the degree to which it brings to the surface these contradictions and provides a kind of discursive playing field in which they can be debated" (2004, 382).

15. As Kemp, Parto, and Gibson note: "Over more than two decades since the publication of Our Common Future, the idea of sustainable development has been widely, if ambiguously, embraced by a great variety of institutions around the world. There has been much dispute about the meaning and implications of the concept and much criticism of the actual behavior of bodies that have claimed devotion to it" (2005, 14).

16. As Vogler writes: "The Rio Declaration on Environment and Development also mentions the achievement of sustainable development in ten of its 27 clauses. What had been intended as a visionary, brief and inspiring Earth Charter was . . . turned into an example of how the sustainability concept can be transformed by international politics into a portmanteau of special interests, contradictory approaches and inoffensive platitudes" (2007).

17. Boehmer-Christiansen argues that bureaucracies were attracted to the concept because: "It increased their own political space as well as allowing them to bring new allies in the process of governing. Sustainability became a tool for intra-governmental turf battles advancing capacities and roles in old contests over interests and values, including access to knowledge, resources, and jobs not only outside, but also inside government" (2002, 355). She uses the expansion of the concept within the United Kingdom, the World Bank, and the European Union as an example.

18. As Mebratu writes: "In the 1980s, some proclaimed that sustainable development was no more than a catch phrase that eventually would wither out as the concept of appropriate technology of the 1970s did" (1999, 494). However, it did not suffer the same fate as appropriate technology and instead diffused rapidly across many different policy communities. Sustainable development and sustainability, he writes, became "core elements of the policy documents of governments, international agencies, and business organizations" (1999, 494).

19. Aquirre observes: "The use of the concept in its new rhetorical sense may be long lived because of the ongoing process of institutionalization and its attendant economic, cultural, and social arrangements. This process of institutionalization is quite advanced and multidimensional, ranging from the establishment of professional journals to bureaucracies, training programs, and international treaties" (2002, 107).

20. For a more general discussion of the role of sustainable development experiments, see Berkhout et al. (2010).

21. A 2001 survey by the International Council of Local Environmental Initiatives (ICLEI) found that around 6,400 local authorities in 113 countries were undertaking LA 21 planning processes. In Japan, for instance, 13% of local governments had created LA 21 plans by 1999 (Barrett and Mikoto 2002). In Europe, where the process has been the strongest, there was considerable variation in participation by local governments in different European nations (Voisey et al. 1996; Echebarria, Barrutia, and Aguado 2004, 2008). In Germany, where support was eventually quite strong, LA 21 spread to local authorities near "pioneering cities" and where they had financial support from state governments (Kern, Koll, and Schophaus 2007).

22. The difference between the development of LA 21 in Europe and the United States illustrates the interactive affects of top-down and bottom-up activities. Shortly after Rio, European local governments met in the Danish city of Aalborg and signed a charter for advancing sustainable development at the local level. European national governments (on the whole) and the European Union also provided significant support for LA 21. In

the United States, a President's Council on Sustainable Development was created in 1993, and charged with creating a national sustainable development plan. But this council was defunct by 1999. Smardon (2008) suggests that the concept "smart growth" rather than "sustainable development" has dominated conversations at the local level in the United States.

23. Not surprisingly, local processes have varied a good deal in terms of their success in mobilizing new sets of stakeholders into the planning process (Freeman 1996; Selman 1998; Barrett and Mikoto 2002; Feichtinger and Pregernig 2005).

24. Kates, Parris, and Leiserowitz (2005) describe a broad range of efforts to define specific indicators of sustainable development at the national and global levels.

25. For example, the creation of sustainability indicators on the Island of Guernsey expanded participation in sustainable development by generating interest. McAlpine and Birnie write: "In 2002, the Policy and Research Unit was only able to collect 34 (66%) out of the total 51 proposed strategic indicators due to a lack of available data. In 2003, they established 47 (86%) of the proposed indicators thanks to extra data provided by a wider group of stakeholders who had become engaged over the previous year. By 2004 the third Sustainable Guernsey report introduced four new strategic indicators and contained data supporting all of the 55 indictors; in other words; 100% of the data required to monitor the Island's sustainability had been actively collected" (2005, 251).

26. The evidence for the importance of networks comes from an expanding number of case studies on particular networks. See Selman (1998); Barrett and Mikoto (2002); Kern and Lofflesend (2004), Barrutia, Aguado, and Echebarria (2007); Echebarria, Barrutia, and Aguado (2008): Fidélis, Teresa, and Pires (2009); and Happaerts et al. (2010).

27. In a study of sustainable municipal water management in Australia, Brown (2008) distinguishes five different "phases" of mobilization to explain different levels of implementation of sustainable development. In the less successful phases, environmental perspectives were marginalized or balkanized. In the more successful phases, environmental champions were able to forge crosscutting connections across departments with engineering, operational, or maintenance functions and interdepartmental relationships were supported by new external relationships with external groups.

28. In a survey of Italian municipalities, Sancassiani found "an increasing emphasis on interlinking the three dimensions of sustainability (environmental, social, and economic) and also greater "interdepartmental collaboration in implementing LA21, involving more than the Environmental and Territorial Departments, and this is seen to contribute to improving the capacity of local authority officers in this area" (2005, 194).

29. Yanarella and Bartilow (2000) argue that LA 21 is caught between international "environmental moralism" and local "policy incrementalism." They argue that the "vagueness" of Agenda 21 undermines local sustainability programs. Steurer and Martinuzzi (2005), however, argue that sustainable development planning must be recognized as differing from either traditional policy planning or incrementalism. Instead, plans are conceived of as an "adaptive system that can continuously improve." While noting limitations to the process, they find signs of transition toward this more flexible strategic process. Similarly, Meadowcroft argues that "[sustainable development] strategy is understood not as a fixed output, but as an iterative process" (2007, 154). See Sheppard (2003) on the value of using Dewey and James's melioristic model of progress to advance an urban sustainability agenda.

Chapter 4

1. Sometimes we talk about organizations as associations, while at other times we use the term to refer to the set of institutional features by which associations operate. Both aspects are essential. Trade unions, political parties, private corporations, public agencies, and sports teams are all organizations because they are associations that have

developed specific institutions to allow them to act collectively. Electoral systems, driving rules, and operettas, by contrast, all facilitate collective action, but they are not themselves associations. A crowd, a dinner party, or a line to buy theater tickets may be associations, but they lack well-developed institutions that allow them to act in a concerted fashion. Finally, tribes, cities, and nations are associations with institutions that may allow them to act in a collective and goal-oriented way, but they are encompassing and general-purpose rather than special-purpose associations.

2. Whipple argues that "Dewey failed to place his theoretical democratic ideal directly within the context of the growth of large-scale organizations, the lack of a sustained engagement with which is particularly conspicuous in Dewey's classic work in political theory, The Public and Its Problems" (2005, 164). For an argument that Dewey did have an understanding of large-scale organization, see Stever (1993, 2000a).

3. The "New" Sociological Institutionalism took Selznick as the archetype of the "Old" Institutionalism (Powell and DiMaggio 1991). They associated his work with Parson's structural-functionalism and their distinction between Selznick's value-oriented institutionalism and their own cognitive and phenomenological institutionalism is a founding assumption of New Sociological Institutionalism. Yet if we understand Selznick as a Pragmatist, influenced by Dewey's social psychology, and not as a Parsonian structural-functionalist, then the dividing line between old and new institutionalism is more complicated. See Selznick (1996) for his own gentle response to this demarcation between an "old" and a "new" institutionalism.

4. Kant also separated reason and emotion. As MacKinnon writes: "Instead of feelings, 'the pure moral motive' is the foundation of character—the consistent and practical habit of mind set by reason itself" (2001, 342).

5. Kallinkos (2004) argues that the distinctive "modernist" characteristic of bureaucracy is not hierarchy or rule-bound behaviors but rather the "non-inclusive" character of the relationship between roles and persons. Bureaucracy does this by separating role from personality, incorporating persons in a noninclusive way—e.g., noninclusive of their entire personality. Consequently, role, not person, is the fundamental building block of the bureaucratic order. Drawing on this distinction, Maravelias (2003) argues that the key feature of post-bureaucracy is that it moves the responsibility for demarcating the boundary between professional and nonprofessional aspects of life from the organization to the individual. Höpfl (2006) has argued that Weber's theory of bureaucracy is more like a list of attributes and less like a systematic conception. He argues that in taking Weber as the definitive statement of "bureaucracy," those in the "post-bureaucracy" lineage are reconstructing a more systematic Weber than actually existed.

6. Weber's conceptualization of history saw modernization as a transformation from personalistic to impersonal authority via the transition from traditional or charismatic authority to rational-legal authority. It is easy to understand bureaucratization—the separation of person from office—as a variable in Weber's scheme. After all, this was his key argument about history. Yet it is less easy to see authority and legitimacy as variable. Organizational change, in Weber's scheme, shifts from one type of authority, and hence legitimacy, to another type.

7. Follett's model of organization also suggests that "obedience" and "liberty" can be reconciled (Follett 1941, 64–65).

8. In Weberian terms, this is sometimes referred to as the "institutionalization of charisma" in order to differentiate it from the "routinization of charisma." Weber recognized the possibility of this institutional path, though his theory of bureaucratization did not.

9. Schubert observes that "Cooley's conception of continuity between personal identity, primary group (or community) and social organization (or society) is altogether unprecedented. Ferdinand Tonnies, whose term *Gemeinshaft* (community or primary group) provided a focus of orientation for Max Weber and Emile Durkheim, differentiated

in a dualistic way between *Gemeinshaft* (group) and *Gesellschaft* (society). He defines *Geminshaften* as thick, organic unities, characterized by hierarchies, habits, moral orientations and emotions. *Gesellschaft* is, in every sense, just the opposite of *Gemeinshaft*: *Gesellschaften* are controlled by conventions, laws and public opinion. It is not possible to subsume Cooley's ideas within this European scheme" (2006, 54).

10. Chester Barnard argued that rule was based on informal organization and that executive leaders confer identity on employees (Stever 2000a, 112). In developing a model of knowledge and learning, Barnard drew on Dewey's model of experience (Novicevic, Hench, and Wren 2002).

11. Dewey's focus on face-to-face relations in *Freedom and Culture* distinguishes between association and community (1989, 122). A community adds to association the function of communication, in which emotions are shared as well as joint undertakings engaged in. Note the parallel with Selznick's distinction between organizations as instruments or institutions.

12. In his *Theory of Valuation*, Dewey writes that: "Value-propositions . . . exist whenever things are appraised as to their suitability and serviceability as means" (1939, 51). "Ends," he writes, "are determinable only on the ground of the means that are involved in bringing them about" (ibid., 53).

13. She argues that the goal is "fact-control" rather than "man-control" (1941, 295).

14. Follett also suggests that people can develop the "habit" (the attitude) for joint study of the situation and for obeying the law of the situation. She is clear, however, that training is not to be used to produce the attitude to accept orders; rather, training is used to produce the habit of joint study of the situation (Follett 1941, 61). The key to authority and consent is, therefore, to stress the "jointness" of the activity of managers and employees rather than the vertical status ordering of one over the other. Although Follett's view of the law of situation emphasizes the importance of employees having discretion, she emphasizes that she is not advocating the independence of workers in decision making. She is not rejecting the idea that some form of structural hierarchy is necessary for complex coordination. Rather, she suggests a transformation of the way those vertical positions fundamentally relate to one another.

15. Follett argues that authority and responsibility are derived from tasks (function) and not from position in the hierarchy (1941, 147). Authority should follow knowledge and experience. She argues against a principal-agent model of authority in which "the President delegates authority and responsibility" (ibid., 148). Instead, she insists that "legitimate authority flows from co-ordination, not co-ordination from authority" (ibid., 150).

16. She stresses the role of leaders in helping to achieve integration in the organization, or as she puts it, the role of the leaders is to "organize experience" (Follett 1941, 258). The leader does this through articulating the common purpose of the enterprise, thus helping the various moving parts of the organization to know how they fit together. This argument anticipates Selznick's more elaborate argument about the role of leaders in shaping organizational missions (Selznick 1957). "The great leader," she writes, "is he who so relates all the complex outer forces and all the complex inner forces that they work together effectively" (Follett 1941, 265).

17. For example, she writes, "One of the tests of conference or committee should be: are we developing genuine power or is someone trying unduly to influence the others?" (1941, 103).

18. "Four fundamental principles of organization are: coordination by direct contact of the responsible people concerned; coordination in the early stages; coordination as the reciprocal relating of all the factors in a situation; coordination as a continuing process" (Follett 1941, 297).

19. Essentially, she is expressing here the idea later called "simultaneous engineering" or what Sabel (2006) calls "concurrency."

20. "The aim of organization engineering," she writes, "is control through effective unity" (Follett 1941, 184).

21. Parker identifies both "behavioral" and "holistic" models of control in Follett's work but stresses the importance of "self-control" in both models. "[T]he synthesis of individualism and collective control," Follett writes, "is collective self-control" (1941, 308). Yet it is not simply self-control at work in integrative groups. She also writes that "central control is coming more and more to mean correlation of many controls rather than a superimposed control" (ibid., 295). Follett writes that the "correlation of many controls" means the "gathering up of many authorities found at different points in the organization" (ibid., 296). She talks about planning as a "horizontal" rather than a "vertical" process (ibid., 301). Nor are planning and operations separate processes: "Thus planning remains an integral part of the management of the self-governing units" (ibid., 205). In making this argument, she draws on an organic view of the organization as an integrated whole (ibid., 185).

22. Follett's concern with the capacity of employees to assume responsibility makes her a very relevant figure to contemporary empowerment research. As Follett wrote: "The manager cannot share his power with division superintendent or foreman or workmen, but he can give them opportunities for developing their power" (1941, 113). Boje and Rosile (2001) argue that Follett transcends the debate between empowerment and disempowerment perspectives. In distinguishing delegation from power, Follett argues that power is a capacity and therefore cannot be delegated. With respect to employees, they are not "delegated" power but rather have to have the opportunity to develop their own capacity. Eylon argues that "the paradox of empowerment is that the very existence of circumstances that place one group in a position to "provide" another group with power implies that power is a finite commodity controlled by a sub-set within the organization" (1998, 21). Eylon suggests that Follett's concept of building up "co-active" power (power-with) helps to address the limitations of conceiving of empowerment as "sharing" power. The important thing is not how to divide power, but how to organize joint power.

23. For empirical support for this relational model of authority, see Tyler (1997).

24. Selznick's relational model of authority explores the middle reaches of organizational life, between the authority inscribed in formal organizational charts and the day-to-day negotiations of organizational life. In this world, authority is not preordained and legitimacy must be earned. Yet legitimacy is not earned simply by producing immediate goods desired by followers. From a Pragmatist perspective, the relational model of authority should be a legitimacy-enhancing model. Leaders achieve authority when they cultivate general purposes and principles of rule. There are several important consequences of this perspective. First, authority is not narrowly attributed to formal office; it is also partly a property of specific leaders who "earn" it. Second, authority and legitimacy are achieved through a larger process of interaction and then diffused throughout the broader organizational culture. Culture "authorizes" leaders to act. But authority is also linked to the emergent purpose of organization and that is what the cultivation of mission is all about. Authority and legitimacy depend on making organizational purposes appeal to higher principles.

25. The term "goal displacement" was coined by Robert Merton.

26. In *The Moral Commonwealth* (1994), Selznick puts Michels's iron law of oligarchy in context, describing the conditions that will lead to oligarchy.

27. The TVA book reflects Selznick's broader analysis of institutionalization as an infusion of value. The concept of grassroots planning was gradually emptied of much of its original meaning, but it still became the basis of an infusion of value in the TVA. Grassroots planning became part of the founding myth around which the TVA community crystallized. Selznick's marriage of Weber, Michels, and Dewey is useful because it points to how Pragmatism might explain negative as well as positive outcomes.

28. This notion that institutionalization is a process of vesting of interests was an important aspect of Pragmatist-inspired institutional analysis: John Commons made this a key

aspect of his institutional economics, emphasizing that an organization is institutionalized when it becomes a "going concern." Selznick also talks about institutions as "going concerns" (1969, 44–45).

29. The distinction between Weber and Selznick in terms of authority and legitimacy can be seen in this distinction between autonomous and responsive law. As Nonet and Selznick write: "Legitimation not competence is the central concern of autonomous law" (2001, 104). Any move away from a focus on legitimation is risky, they observe, not only because it can erode the gains of autonomous law by becoming politicized, but also because responsive law can degenerate into incrementalism (2001, 84–85n).

30. For an important discussion of networks that invokes Selznick's analysis of cooptation, see O'Toole and Meier (2004).

31. In the Weberian tradition, institutionalization is often associated with the consolidation of corporate groups and their development of autonomy from the biographical individuals that create them and from their external environments. Although useful and insightful for understanding institutionalization, the Weberian approach sets a standard that makes all departures from consolidation (e.g., from bureaucracy to networks) or autonomy (e.g., from closed to open systems) appear as steps toward deinstitutionalization. Again, it is formality and impersonalism that do the work of preserving the consolidated and autonomous character of the organization in the Weberian tradition. By contrast, Selznick's interpretation of institutionalization offers a different standard of evaluation. Institutionalization depends on the degree to which an organizational community has been created around a distinctive public mission and the degree to which a strong "organizational character" has been molded around this public mission. Just as Selznick's model suggests how to combine centralization and decentralization, his approach also provides a framework for thinking about how institutions can be open while preserving integrity. Civil servants socialized into the mission and principles of a public agency can both be granted greater discretion and responsibility (decentralization) and be trusted to engage flexibly with external stakeholders. As Nonet and Selznick write: "All institutions experience a conflict between integrity and openness. Integrity is protected when an institution is strongly committed to distinctive mission or can be held accountable to that mission by external controls" (2001, 76). In Nonet and Selznick's notion of responsive law, judges, agencies, or beat officers can be granted the discretion to become flexible "problem-solvers" to the extent that their behavior upholds the integrity of public purposes.

32. We see again that freedom and constraint develop together. Emery and Trist (1972) argued that adaptation to turbulent fields required the development of "ideal seeking systems"—a focus on the elaboration of values that orient, in a general way, complex adaptations. Unfortunately, they do not elaborate this idea.

33. In *The Moral Commonwealth*, Selznick writes: "The hallmarks of character are special competence and disability. 'Character' refers to the commitments that help to determine the kinds of tasks an organization takes on, the opportunities it creates or closes off, the priorities it sets, and the abuses to which it is prone" (1992, 321).

34. One can immediately sense some affinities between a Pragmatist institutionalism and "learning organizations" (Senge 2006) or "communities of practice" (Lave and Wenger 1991). Wilson (1989) hints at "competency-based" government when he suggests that programs should not be assigned to agencies whose missions conflict with program implementation.

35. The Pragmatist model is action-oriented and tries to simultaneously refine the values by which we act in the world; but action is also a capacity. This is Dewey's point about moral development.

36. As Stinchcombe observes, "Selznick was primarily developing a theory of the 'distinctive competence' of an organization, its ability to realize values in a way that no other organization could" (1997, 12).

37. Later chapters will confront the problem of how to square this idea of a distinctive competence with the idea of democratic control of public agencies.

38. In the human resources field, there already exists the idea of competency management. This approach typically focuses on identifying task competencies in order to use this knowledge to select or train competent employees (see Young and Dulewicz on the United Kingdom's Royal Navy; 2005).

39. Unlike monasteries, public agencies are open organizations intended to serve a mission that provides valuable goods and services to the public.

40. Again, Dewey's discussion of the interaction of ends and means is relevant. A competency is both an end-in-itself and a means-to-an-end.

41. NASA's recent experience with "better, faster, cheaper" provides another telling example of this point.

42. The description suggests another distinction that needs to be made. It is common in the last decade to focus on "benchmarking" as an important strategy for achieving organizational performance. Benchmarking and competence-building are overlapping, but conceptually distinct activities. Benchmarking refers to a strategy of searching for and implementing best practices; competence-building refers to a strategy of continuous skill development.

43. Note that the literature on "dynamic capabilities" traces its roots back to Selznick's work (see Zollo and Winter 2003).

44. The idea of core competency comes from Prahalad and Hamel (1990).

45. Bryson, Ackerman, and Eden (2007) develop a resource-based view of public organizations that identifies and analyzes an organization's core competencies.

46. For one example, see Hagedorn's (1996) study of the Milwaukee child welfare agency.

47. Durant's (1992) study of the Bureau of Land Management provides a good example.

Chapter 5

1. In Dewey's *Logic: The Theory of Inquiry,* he argues that inquiry begins with an uncertain situation, which becomes a problematic situation when subject to inquiry (1980, 106–107). Inquiry defines the problem and advances a preliminary solution. This solution is an "idea" that takes account of anticipated consequences (1980, 108–109).

2. A number of other sources also provide important insights on problem solving. For a problem-oriented view of the firm, see Tyre and von Hippel (1997), Marengo et al. (2000), Nickerson and Zenger (2004), Marengo and Dosi (2005), and Mathur (2007). For insights on public agencies, see Landau and Stout (1979), Chisholm (1992), and Kettl (2005, 30). For a problem-oriented approach to planning, see Blanco (1994). For additional insights into problem-solving courts, see Corrigan and Becker (2003).

3. For other approaches, see Hisschemöller and Gupta's (1999) typology of policy problems based on whether there is certainty about relevant knowledge and consensus on value. Gormley (1986) characterizes problems according to their complexity and saliency. Peters (2005) distinguishes chronic problems, which are marked by (1) value dissensus; (2) technological change; and (3) external problems that constantly change and remain outside control. Beamish (2002) describes "crescive" problems that develop slowly, often going undetected.

4. Reiter-Palmon and Illies (2004) also argue that weakly structured problems often require creative problem-solving.

5. Pragmatism is consistent with a social constructivist approach to public problems, which recognizes problems as symbolic, discursive, and rooted in meaning. Ultimately, this view suggests both opportunities and constraints on problem solving. On the one hand, problem framing is clearly a political act and publics are subject to manipulation

(Weiss 1989). The agenda-setting literature, for instance, suggests that powerful actors can skillfully place problems on the agenda. Problem framing is designed to capture support and to get issues on the public agenda. Problems may therefore be socially constructed in a way that generates a sense of fear (Goode and Ben-Yehuda 1994), demonization (Kersh and Morone 2002), and moral drama (Gusfield 1984). Competitive framing can ensure that relevant information is brought up, but it is also likely to polarize debates between dichotomous alternatives. Linder argues that competitive framing produces "morality plays" that dispel ambiguity and impose "Manichean" order on actors and events (1995, 219). Saguy and Riley (2005) argue that competitive framing leads to exaggerated alarmist claims, which can undermine the possibility of synthesis or integration. On the other hand, social constructivism allows us to understand how apparently fixed interests are actually malleable and subject to reconstruction. The literature on "framing" suggests that problem definitions can be constructed in a fashion that allows innovative solutions and fruitful conflict (Schön and Rein 1994). Bryson, Cunningham, and Lokkesmoe (2002), for example, suggest that problem framing is critical for solving wicked problems.

6. See also Ulrich (1988) and Peters (2005)

7. For Simon, problem solving requires "heuristic search," which entails using various rules of thumb to simplify the search process. Simon also argued that different individuals (e.g., experts versus novices) will solve problems in different ways and that these ways may be group-specific (e.g., professional; national) (see Fernandez and Simon 1999). These points are quite compatible with a Pragmatist model of practical reason. However, see Mousavi and Garrison (2003) for a critique of Simon's view of rationality, which they contrast with a Deweyian transactional model. A number of authors have pointed to Simon's positivism as the source of divergence between a Deweyian and Simonian account of rationality. Harmon and White, for example, write that: "Simon's account of administrative decision making is descriptively and normatively underwritten by the logical positivists' radical, epistemological separation of value and action. Briefly stated, values provide the bases on which the proper ends of action are decided, while facts are relevant to calculating the effective means for their attainment" (1989, 145).

8. In fact, ecologists of natural ecosystems have embraced Simon's view of hierarchy and made it their own (O'Neill et al. 1986; Holling, Gunderson, and Peterson, 2002). It is used to describe the hierarchical character of ecosystems. It is interesting to point out that by inspiring ecologists to think of ecosystems in nested, hierarchical terms, Simon's theory of hierarchy led them to shift from a "small-scale view" of biological ecology to a "multiscale and landscape view" (Holling, Gunderson, and Peterson, 2002, 72).

9. Note that Chisholm's ecology is a set of parallel, not nested subsystems. It is a set of what ecologists currently call "patches." For an intriguing discussion of how natural ecologists see the relationship between patches and hierarchies, see Wu and Loucks (1995).

10. Peters (2005) echoes Schulman. Gerson (2009) contrasts decomposable and compound problems, arguing that the latter requires "collaborative complexity."

11. Brusoni (2005) uses a case study of the chemical industry to show that integration must counterbalance modularity. Additional modeling by Brusoni et al. (2007) finds that modular approaches do not outcompete more integrated strategies in the long term. Marengo and Dosi (2005) argue that strictly modular solutions can lead to suboptimal local solutions.

12. As Mitroff suggests, a sophisticated system is one in which the parts change in relationship to changes in other parts of the system (1998, 82).

13. See Puntambekar and Hubscher (2005) for a good discussion of the literature on scaffolding.

14. Follett, for example, used her "law of the situation" to rethink the character of authority relations. In authority relations, she argued, both manager and employee should be bound by the "law of the situation." For Follett, this situation-based approach depersonalized authority, undermining the degrading element of personal control inherent in command-and-control relationships. However, situationally focused authority also repersonalizes relationships, as people are joined together around concrete problem-solving (1941, 58–60).

15. In describing governance strategies for resource management, for example, Weber notes that "abstraction equals death for partnership, but once you talk about a definable piece of land, you get beyond philosophy . . . you can agree on what is acceptable and what is not" (2003, 74).

16. For a critique of the problem-oriented policing movement as myth and ceremony, see Manning (2005).

17. Examples like Bratton's are legion in police work. Here is a nearly identical example by Sparrow: "In Philadelphia in 1987–88 police received and answered 505 virtually identical calls in the space of six months. They were all complaints of excessive noise or disturbance at a particular bar. The female complainant, a neighbor to the bar, always asked not to be disturbed and police officers attending always found things 'quiet on arrival.' They always disposed of the incident 'no further action necessary.' They never looked into the cause, because they were not obligated nor expected to. It was not their job; their job was to deal with the call and move on to the next. A sergeant who had been introduced to the concept of 'problem-solving policing' moved into the district, noticed the pattern, and decided to look into it. The next time the woman was called she was asked her name and address (which was normally not recorded for a call of this type), and visited. The problem was noise, and particularly vibration, from juke-box speakers which are fixed to a common wall. Arrangements were made for the lady to meet the proprietors, and the speakers were moved to an interior wall. The complainant was happy, and the rash of calls stopped" (Sparrow 2000, 225).

18. In her discussion of the "law of situations," Follet discusses the importance of the "joint study of the problem" (60).

19. Dorf and Sabel make a similar point in their analysis of drug treatment courts: "From the perspective taken by treatment courts, addiction is like many other contemporary problems in that an effective response requires contextualized or situation-specific coordination of many different kinds of changing services" (2000, 839).

20. Haas writes that: "Policies are themselves experiments that participants monitor and about which they reflect in order to improve them over time" (2004, 575). Ostrom also has a discussion of "policies as experiments" (1999, 519).

21. Cordner and Biebel found that the San Diego police did not use problem-solving techniques very systematically: "The scope of their problem-solving efforts tended to be small—typically one person, one address, one building, one parking lot, or one intersection. As this picture indicates, most everyday POP [problem-oriented policing] in San Diego fit a narrow approach to 'soft' problems, rather than the more wide-ranging approach to all kinds of substantive community problems, including serious crime, envisioned by the ideal POP model" (2005, 175–176).

22. Problems are linked and interdependent, sometimes in complex ways. Rodriguez-Garavito provides a good example related to the problem of regulating sweatshops in Central America: "There are no magic solutions or shortcuts. You could say, 'Well, what we have to do is improve labor courts.' Perfect. Let's create twenty more courts. Great. But where are the judges" (2005, 213). Silverman offers another vivid example in his description of the New York Police Department's campaign to rid the Bayside community of crime: The police and the attorneys analyzed the problems—they were all intertwined. Bell Boulevard's bars fueled Francis Lewis Boulevard's drunken drag racers and spectators. Upon leaving the bars, patrons headed to Francis Lewis and lined the

boulevard. Limit the drinking, CEI advocates came to believe, and you curtail the racing (Silverman 1999, 133–134). As Silverman notes of police problem-solving in the Bayside Community: "The comprehensive assault on Bayside's problems is a premier example of the NYPD's creative problem solving. When the Queens borough commander reviewed the tactical blueprint, he remarked, 'MacArthur did not make this much effort in planning his invasion'" (Silverman 1999, 135).

23. In a discussion of C. West Churchman's concept of "sweeping in," Ulrich (1988) argues that we should not commit the error of seeing everything as incorporated into a systemic framework. He argues that a systems approach must be seen as making critical boundary judgments (both normative and empirical) based on the "purpose" of the system. Churchman, who was primarily using systems theory to address large-scale social problems, developed the idea of "sweeping in" to capture the idea of the systemic interdependence of problems. Ulrich, Churchman's student, also describes Churchman's concept of "unfolding," which provides a kind of stopping rule for systems. Both Ulrich and Churchman emphasized critical reflection on system boundaries. Matthews (2006) demonstrates the genealogy of C. West Churchman's systems theory in pragmatist philosophy.

24. Or as Tainter (2000) argues, problem solving is a response to complexity, but it also generates additional complexity. Lach, Rayner, and Ingram discuss the way that solutions created by one party create problems for others (2005, 7).

25. One generic problem of governing is that the State must typically deal with the "output" of problems; hence it is always battling after the fact when problems are at their most intractable. But there is also a governing dilemma associated with trying to handle problems preventatively: the State faces a more difficult justification or rationale for intruding upon affairs where problems are not yet manifest. Planning is the quintessential "proactive" problem-solving strategy and often faces this dilemma of proactive intervention. See Hoch (2002) on the difference between rational and pragmatic planning.

26. For an example of early intervention with families with troubled children, see Eckholm (2008); see also Eckholm (2009) on Florida's shift toward emphasizing family preservation.

27. Lei, Hitt, and Bettis observe that "firms capable of developing highly successful products actively inculcate a proactive, examination of problems from numerous technical and design viewpoints. Moreover, the firms also encourage customer input to help experiment with new concepts before full-scale introduction" (1996, 558).

28. Preventive and reactive strategies are sometimes counterpoised as sharply different alternatives. For example, in child protective services, "family preservation" and "child protection" are often counterpoised as competing ideologies (Hagedorn 1995). But this is not necessarily the case.

29. Sparrow has this point in mind when he distinguishes preventive from proactive (2000, 191–192).

30. Brightman uses a "Dewey-Bentley" mode of inquiry to analyze how managers deal with ill-structured problems. He argues that "the creative formation of conjectures in the absence of data is not the key to successful inquiry. Rather the interweaving of observation, conjecture, verification, and additional observation are the key ingredients of successful problem solving" (1978, 5). He argues that the Dewey-Bentley model is more relevant for operational than strategic problem-solving.

31. Recent work in public health has found that a "systems" approach to problem solving can improve upon traditional "compliance-based" regulation. The systems approach attempts to get beyond problem symptoms or identification of noncompliance to identify more fundamental causes of problems (Cassady et al. 2006). Tucker, Edmondson, and Spear (2002) find that nurses often engage in "first-order" problem-solving—e.g., solving the problem without engaging in deeper root cause analysis.

32. On "knowledge-intensive firms," see Starbuck (1992).
33. A literature on knowledge and learning in recent years has challenged the notion of knowledge as "encoded." See Blackler (1995) for an overview of this literature.
34. Sparrow argues problem solving is a skill to be learned (2000, 141).
35. On the need to build the capacity of local groups—especially disenfranchised groups—to participate in local environmental problem-solving, see Stone (2001, 2005), Elliot and Kaufman (2003), and Briggs (2008).
36. Thanks to Satoshi Miura for reminding me that Pragmatist problem-solving is also empowering.
37. This is one answer to Hoch's criticism of Pragmatist problem-solving. Hoch argues that there is a tension—even a contradiction—in the Pragmatist stance toward problem-solving: "By characterizing social problems as part of an objective situation within human experience, Dewey treats instrumental inquiry, rather than any specific social accommodations reached among individuals or groups, as the source of value. . . . Ironically, this pragmatic confidence in the efficacy of instrumental mastery over the problems of the physical and social environment alike contradicts pragmatism's reliance on a community of inquirers who already agree about what counts as successful inquiry" (1984b, 341).
38. Peters argues that as you get wider involvement in policymaking, problem solving gets more difficult (2005, 358). Bryson, Crosby, and Stone describe the challenges for cross-sectoral problem-solving and conclude their review of the literature by arguing that "the normal expectation ought to be that success will be very difficult to achieve in cross-sector collaborations" (2006, 52).
39. In the very different context of water management projects, Pahl-Wostl arrives at a similar conclusion: "It is argued here that in a first phase the formation of information networks, processes of negotiation, and coordination among stakeholder groups are of major importance" (2005, 460).
40. As Nonet and Selznick observe: "Any theory that makes problem-solving a central function of law readily appreciates that the barriers by which, institutions are separated, spheres of competence defined, and bureaucratic turfs enclosed hinder the deployment of resources necessary for effective action" (2001, 110). This compartmentalization has been particularly frustrating in environmental problem-solving. Durant describes how environmental problems have traditionally been dealt with one at a time and then institutionalized that way, which led to centralized expert decision making, resulted in administrative fragmentation, and made them difficult for citizens to understand (2004, 178). See Kanter's (1984) description of "segmentalism" for a classic organization theory discussion of this phenomenon. See also Caspary on Dewey's view about overcoming compartmentalization (2000, 159).
41. See also Virkkunen and Kuutti (2000) on this case.
42. For a discussion of experiments with "Pragmatic localism" in British government, see Coaffee and Headlam (2008).
43. See Garrison (1999) on Dewey's view of "practical reason," which builds on Aristotle and Peirce but also departs from their treatments in some important respects.
44. Knight and Johnson (2007) view Pragmatism's consequentialism as compatible with a rational choice model. They are right on this point, as far as it goes. But their argument misses the other ways in which Pragmatism departs from rational choice.
45. Toulmin distinguishes between rationality and reasonableness. Reasonableness means "practical reason" (2001, 110). As an example of reasonableness in contemporary life, Toulmin uses the example of a clinical approach as it might be applied by a contemporary medical doctor. "Using a 'clinical' approach does not mean giving up hope of establishing general truths" (Toulmin 2001, 111). It simply implies that findings hold generally, but not invariably. Posner (2003) also uses reasonableness as a criterion for judicial decision making.

46. On "situated rationality," see Mannheim (1940), Manning (1988, 266), Weick (1993), and Linder and Peters (1995). For a Deweyian approach to "situated cognition," see Garrison (1995). Manning describes "situational propriety" (a theme in Erving Goffman's work) as the idea that "the meaning of our actions is linked to the context in which they arose, and that we can rarely understand behavior without knowledge of the situation in which it occurred" (Manning 1992, 10–11). Garfinkel (1967), Knorr-Cetina (1981), and Suchman (1987) draw on Peirce's idea of "indexical" meaning to describe the operation of practical reason in context. Note, however, that a Pragmatist approach also suggests that decision making has a "trans-situational" aspect: a decision in the present links past experience to an ("imagined") future.

47. Majone (1989) and Forester (1999) advocate a model of practical reason for policy studies and public planning, respectively. Garrison (1999) links a Pragmatist practical reason to public administration. Bourdieu's model of praxis bears a number of similarities to the idea of practical reason.

48. From the perspective of the Dreyfus and Dreyfus model, "analytical rationality is a limited rationality: it is appropriate to the lower levels in the performance of a skill, but not to high-level performance" (1986, 21). Fiske and Taylor develop a "motivated tactician" model of social psychology influenced by Pragmatist psychology, which they describe as follows: "the motivated tactician is viewed as having multiple information-processing strategies available, selecting among them on the basis of goals, motives, needs, and forces in the environment" (Taylor 1998, 75). Fiske (1993) provides an overview of a Pragmatist tradition of studying social cognition and perception.

49. For a model of social action emphasizing skill, see Leifer (1991) and Fligstein (1997). Majone describes skill in terms of craftsmanship: "Craft knowledge—less general and explicit than theoretical knowledge, but not as idiosyncratic as pure intuition—is essential in any kind of disciplined intellectual inquiry or professional activity" (1989, 44). See Polanyi (1958), Schön (1983), and Manning (1988, 212–215) on tacit knowledge.

50. Flyvbjerg provides a useful summary: "Phronesis goes beyond both analytical, scientific knowledge (episteme) and technical knowledge or know-how (*techne*) and involves judgments and decisions made in the manner of a virtuoso social and political actor" (2001, 2). He also writes: "Phronesis is that intellectual activity most relevant to praxis. It focuses on what is variable, on that which cannot be encapsulated by universal rules, on specific cases. Phronesis requires an interaction between the general and the concrete; it requires consideration, judgment and choice. More than anything else, phronesis requires experience" (2001, 57).

51. For an elaboration of this point, see Berk and Galvan's (2009) model of "creative syncretism."

52. As Klein observes: "Intuition depends on the use of experience to recognize key patterns that indicate the dynamics of the situation. Because patterns can be subtle, people often cannot describe what they noticed, or how they judged a situation as typical or atypical" (1999, 31).

53. Klein, like Flyvbjerg, draws inspiration from the work of Hubert Dreyfus (Klein 1999, 1).

54. Building on pragmatist psychology, Rosenberg describes three different modes of cognitive reasoning: sequential, linear, and systematic (Rosenberg 2002). The combination of selective attention and gestalt schema corresponds rather well to Weick's "sensemaking" approach to organizational analysis (Weick 1996).

55. Kosslyn notes that "imagery played a major role in theories of mental events up until psychology and philosophy parted ways; indeed, it held sway during the infancy of scientific psychology, when both Wilhelm Wundt and William James devoted much energy toward understanding it" (1994, 1). Sadoski and Paivio (2001) observe: "The centrality of imagery and the imagined event in cognition found its most fundamental place in Mead's philosophy. Like other pragmatists, Mead centered on the act. He held that we exist in an action-oriented, ongoing present with an eye to the past and eye to

the future. Mental images remembered from the past and mental images projected into the future were a vehicle for the transaction of reality. Mead's positions on imagery have been reviewed and found to be consistent with the role of images in current cognitive psychology."

56. Sadoski and Paivio (2001) similarly argue that images play a critical role in memory and in processes of mental imagination, and they develop a dual coding theory to describe the use of both images and propositional language in information processing: "The most basic assumption of DCT [Dual Coding Theory] is that cognition in reading and writing consists of the activity of two separate coding systems of mental representation, one system specialized for language and one system specialized for dealing with non-verbal objects and events." This dual processing view is close to Gregory Bateson's view of mind as operating according to both digital and analogue information processing. He showed how this had important consequences for social communication.

57. Klein (1999) provides some good examples of how images are used to imagine future scenarios in everyday decision making. For a general statement on the role of image in social and political life, see Boulding (1960).

58. Majone argues that "restricting the role of reason to discovering appropriate means to given ends, instrumental rationality relegates values, criteria, judgments, and opinions to the domain of the irrational or purely subjective" (1989, 23).

59. For Pragmatist-inspired theories of emotion, see Denzin (1984) and MacKinnon (1994).

60. De Sousa (1987) and Nussbaum (2003) have developed similar arguments from cognitive and philosophical perspectives, respectively.

61. Although incrementalism has been accused of being conservative, it takes on a more progressive tincture in light of Dewey's experimentalism, which values ongoing and continuous revision of existing practice.

62. Perhaps Etzioni's (1968) concept of "mixed scanning," which seeks to take the best of both the incrementalist and rationalist perspectives, is closer to Peirce's abductive iteration between observation and imagination. See Blanco (1994) for a comparison between Dewey's ideas of the means–ends continuum and Lindblom's pragmatism and Etzioni's mixed scanning.

63. Hargadon and Betchky (2006) describe creative problem-solving as the recombination of existing ideas. They also argue that "reframing" is the core process of creative problem-solving and that collective interaction is often necessary to aid individuals to engage in reframing.

Chapter 6

1. Mead's analysis of recursiveness can be seen as a cycle between three perspectives: I, me, and generalized other. Peirce's "unlimited semiosis" is a continuous cycle between sign, object, and interpretant. James suggests that we understand experience as a continuous shift in perspective from "flights" (process) to "perchings" (structure).

2. Note that the term "recursiveness" may have different meanings in different fields. For example, the term has distinctive meanings in mathematics, computer science, and linguistics.

3. Bateson thinks recursiveness is triggered by difference (by something making a difference), which is similar to Peirce's view of the "fixation of belief" (meaning as built on what difference something is making). Bateson was influenced by Maturan and Varela's "autopoietic" concept of recursion. Clark writes: "Recursiveness means the socially accomplished reproduction of sequences of activity and action because actors involved possess a negotiated sense that one template from their repertoire will address a new situation. The sequences are activated and unfold in accordance with the socially constructed durational time based on events within processes. . . . Recursivness is always

improvised, even when the new cycle seems to replicate the old cycle and even when those seeking to impose reproduction are in agreement. . . . Recursiveness in social systems tends towards the autopoietic and is a form of self-organising complexity subject to dislocation" (1999, 67).

4. This tension between nesting and heterarchy is implied by Hofstadter's treatment but not clearly stated.

5. Hofstadter also uses Russian dolls as an example of nesting (1979, 127).

6. Koestler (1967) suggested the concept "holon" to describe nested entities that are both wholes and parts.

7. In Pragmatism, there is no single privileged perspective from which to develop knowledge or make truth claims. Knowledge develops according to one's perspective. Yet Pragmatism also argues that different perspectives are actually quite useful for the collective generation of knowledge. In fact, it is precisely this tension between competing perspectives through which progress is achieved.

8. Inversion is similar to switching back and forth between figure and ground. See Hofstadter (1979), chap. 3.

9. Karmen (2000) develops a skeptical analysis of the more vaunted claims of Compstat advocates. He argues that crime in New York "crashed" because of a "fortuitous confluence" of factors, many of them unrelated to the NYPD. However, he acknowledges that Compstat was one of these fortuitous factors. When comparing the reduction of homicides in New York to similar reductions in other cities, Rosenfeld, Fornango, and Baumer (2005) do not find that Compstat reduced homicides. Berk (2005), however, criticizes their statistical analysis.

10. Precinct commanders were given much more discretion over the assignment and deployment of precinct personnel (Silverman, 1999, 211–212). "In keeping with the theme of empowerment, local commanders were given broad discretion in how they investigated the complaints and what kind of discipline they imposed and they were not required to report back to IAB with the results of their investigation" (Silverman 1999, 215). Silverman describes this greater discretion as follows: "By increasing the authority and responsibility of precinct commanders, the NYPD freed them from having to forward information along the chain of command simply to receive high-level confirmation or assurance" (1999, 183).

11. Maple argues against seeing Compstat as a technological fix: "Outsiders often assume technology drove many of the changes in policing that we modeled in the NYPD. What a joke. A faith in timeless ideas like mapping came first, and we worked our way around or over the technological hurdles because we knew the results would be worth the trouble" (1999, 104–105).

12. See Silverman's discussion of the "myths" about Compstat, most of which describe Compstat from a single point of view (statistics, technology, strategy meeting, accountability, etc.) (1999, 189–192). Scholars have often had a hard time classifying Compstat as a model. Weisburd et al. (2003) argue that one of the reasons Compstat has diffused rapidly is that it reinforces a hierarchical style of policing that was under pressure from community policing advocates. Some see it as a variant of the "rational legal-bureaucratic model" and in opposition to a "community policing model" (see Walsh and Vito 2004). Magers (2004) argues that Compstat combines the rational-bureaucratic and community policing models. Walsh and Vito distinguish three policing models: the rational-legal bureaucratic model, the community policing model, and the strategic management model. They argue that Compstat is an attempt to "synthesize the elements of the rational-legal bureaucratic and community problem-solving paradigms with strategic management concepts taken from the business world" (2004, 66).

13. Firman argues that Compstat helps to overcome the tension between creativity and control in police work by "making sure things are 'under control' while maintaining support for local (district) initiatives to meet demands" (2003, 458).

14. Weisburd et al. argue that Compstat has six key elements: "mission clarification, internal accountability, geographic organization of command, organizational flexibility, data-driven problem identification and assessment, and innovative problem solving" (2003, 427).

15. As Maple notes: "In the NYPD of early 1994, not many detectives had access to all nineteen data systems, due in part to concerns that corrupt cops might sell information back to criminals, but mostly because catching crooks was not the department's top priority" (1999, 88).

16. Silverman provides a good description of the evolution of Compstat (1999, chap. 5).

17. According to Silverman: "Traditionally, NYPD headquarters was perceived as the nerve center of the department's decision-making apparatus. Changes in operational police tactics were conceived, formulated, and issued from headquarters, primarily on a citywide basis, and often with very little input from field commands. The post-1993 restructuring and crime-control strategies provided field commanders with far more leverage over their own troops" (1999, 183).

18. Willis, Mastrofski, and Weisburd (2004) studied the implementation of Compstat in the Lowell, Massachusetts, police department and found that it did not increase innovative problem-solving. They found that it did not encourage innovative problem-solving because Compstat was largely used to reinforce hierarchy and accountability. Willis, Mastrofski, and Weisburd (2003) report similar findings for the use of Compstat in Minneapolis and Newark.

19. Later, Maple writes: "If you asked the detectives if they talked to Narcotics about these cases, they'd stroke you by saying, 'We work very, very closely together.' In reality, they only work together on what they perceive to be 'big cases,' and not many of their 'big cases' involved small players in the narcotics business" (1999, 103).

20. Moore observes that Compstat was a "shift in responsibility and status from those who led special functional units to those who led the geographically defined, patrol-dominated precincts" (Moore 2003, 472).

21. Silverman notes that Compstat personnel "developed the idea of a pattern identification module (PIM), or unit, for each borough. A PIM is composed of representatives of the housing, transit, patrol, detective, and organized crime control bureaus, and the robbery squad" (1999, 119).

22. The Compstat system has many of the features Sabel (1994) describes as "learning-by-monitoring."

23. As Moore observes: "If the system operates as a strict liability system, never pays much attention to what the managers are trying to do to deal with crime, or rewards them only when they do the conventional things to deal with particular crime problems, then the system will not do much to encourage organizational learning. . . . If, on the other hand, the system is interested in how managers are thinking about dealing with particular crime problems, and exposes that issue in collaborative discussion about what could be tried to reverse a problematic crime trend, then COMPSTAT can very well serve as a device for increasing the innovativeness and learning of the organization in dealing with selected crime issues" (2003, 485–486).

24. Weisburd et al. (2003), however, argue that police departments who have adopted Compstat have emphasized control over empowerment.

25. Another model that tries to combine the values of hierarchy and teams is Nonaka's "hypertext" model of organizational knowledge creation: "The core feature of the hypertext organization is the ability to switch between the various 'contexts' of knowledge creation to accommodate changing requirements from situations both inside and outside the organization" (Nonaka 1994, 32). His hypertext model combines heterarchy and hierarchy: "Non-hierarchical, or 'heterarchical' self-organizing activities of teams are indispensable to generate new knowledge as well as to acquire 'deep' knowledge through intensive, focused search. On the other hand, a hierarchical division of

labor is more efficient and effective for implementation, exploitation, and accumulation of new knowledge as well as acquisition of information through extensive, unfocused search" (Nonaka 1994, 32).

26. Cavaleri (2008) argues that the roots of the idea of a learning organization are derived from Pragmatism; and Elkjaer (2004) suggests a model of organizational learning inspired by Dewey's model of experience. Cavaleri also argues that the intellectual genealogy of Deming's Total Quality Management (the forerunner of contemporary continuous process improvement models) can be traced back to the Pragmatist philosopher C. I. Lewis's *Mind and the World Order*. Emison (2004) has also argued that Pragmatism provides a philosophical framework for Total Quality Management, and Silwa and Wilcox (2008) show that pragmatism inspired the work of W. A. Shewhart, one of the founders of quality management (which was one of the foundations for Deming's work).

27. Following Peirce, they see emergent strategy as an abductive process, which is built from the "middle levels of the organization" (2004, 84).

28. There is now a considerable literature on "post-bureaucracy." Part of the controversy around this literature is its epochal prediction—its argument that the era of bureaucracy is coming to an end and the era of "post-bureaucracy" is beginning (McSweeney 2006). McSweeney, by contrast, argues that in the United Kingdom there has been an intensification of bureaucracy. The post-bureaucracy model paralleled a similar discussion about the development of postindustrialism (Emery and Trist 1972).

29. Nonaka proposes a "middle-up-down management" that he contrasts with a "top-down" or "bottom-up" model (1994).

30. Sabel (1999) describes a similar "constitutional" organization.

31. Adler and Borys argue that enabling rules can be designed to allow discretion, capture lessons from experience, and promote integration of perspectives across the organization. "In an enabling approach to procedure design . . . employees are provided with a wide range of contextual information designed to help them interact creatively with the broader organization and environment. Procedures are therefore designed to afford them an understanding of how their own tasks fit into the whole" (1996, 73). They also argue that enabling procedures must be open to flexible readjustment (Adler and Borys point to Blau's 1955 discussion of "adjustive development," where practices develop in the course of working out operational problems.)

32. Maines argues that Blumer developed a recursive theory of social structure and social action that built on Mead and Dewey's view of the "inextricably interrelated" of the knowing and the known (Maines 2001, 62–63). Trueit (2004) points out that Peirce's mode of inquiry is "ongoing and recursive." She links this idea of inquiry to Churchland's inquiring systems and to contemporary models of learning organization. On "recursive constructivisim" in cognitive psychology, see Bickhart (2005), who links this approach back to Pragmatism and to the idea of scaffolding.

33. This reading of *Human Nature and Conduct* is indebted to a small conference, "Rereading Dewey: Implications for Organizational Studies," organized by Michael Cohen, Karl Weick, and myself at the University of Michigan. It was Michael Cohen's inspired idea to have all the participants of the conference read HNC. My analysis here has been influenced by Cohen's argument that Dewey's analysis of habit offers a way to reinvigorate organization theory's concept of routine (Cohen 2007).

Chapter 7

1. MacGilvray argues that this "democratization" of power raises its own problems: "Such a concept of the political tends at once toward a frustrating vagueness about the limits of public power and a disconcerting lack of concern about its abuse. This raises an obvious objection on liberal grounds: Lacking a principled means of limiting public

power, it seems that pragmatic politics is in constant danger of collapsing into a tyranny of the majority" (1999, 553).

2. This relational view led Jane Addams to view power as a "distortion" of human relationships (Whipps 2004).

3. Of course, Foucault has expressed the darker side of this "power-knowledge" relationship and sees it as the basis of modern forms of power.

4. An extension of this view of iconic power might be what French and Raven (1959) called "referent power." A has power over B when B "identifies" with A.

5. "The dependence of actor A upon actor B is (1) directly proportional to A's motivational investment in goals mediated by B and (2) inversely proportional to the availability of those goals to A outside of the A-B relation" (Emerson 1962, 32).

6. Again, Foucault's idea about surveillance as a form of modern power and his view of the knowledge professions as critical arbiters of power express the dark side of triadic power.

7. Risse (2004, 297) distinguishes bargaining and arguing in terms of a dyadic versus a triadic logic. He argues that the creation of publics transforms strategic bargaining into argumentative action.

8. Allen argues for building a Pragmatist approach to power on "its expedient, anti-foundational view of power, one that is grounded in our shared experience of it as a dynamic relationship. If this interpretation is accepted, it sets apart a pragmatist reading from the more conventional view of power as an inscribed capacity waiting to be deployed, and the all too easy assumption that size matters and that more resources equals greater power" (2008, 1622). See also Dennis and Martin (2005) for a related discussion of how symbolic interactionists have approached power. Luckenbill, however, argues that symbolic interactionism does not have a coherently formulated view of power and develops a symbolic interactionist view of power as a "collective transaction." Power is a relationship between a "target" and a "source" (and explicitly not an attribute of the target) and resides in the "joint action" of the target and the source (1979, 107).

9. Abowitz (2000) describes how Dewey's transactional logic can be used to understand power dynamics within public schools. She uses a transactional approach to understand the relationship between school authorities and groups that engage in "resistance" to school authority.

10. There are many affinities between Elias's work and Pragmatism. An antidualist project runs throughout Elias's work and he embraces a process-oriented perspective that emphasizes the possibility of emergence (Quilley and Loyal 2005).

11. See Newton (1999) for a comparison of Elias's and Foucault's views of power

12. Market-oriented utilitarians, in fact, envision an even more radical decentralization of accountability in the form of markets. Rather than trying to hold managers accountable with detailed rules, managers can be indirectly held accountable through competition with other managers or more directly by consumers or clients demanding improved service. This logic leads directly to ideas like voucher systems for schools (Chubb and Moe 1990).

13. There is considerable sympathy for this point in the public administration literature, as nicely summarized by Sowa and Selden: "In the evolution of public administration theory and practice, a general consensus has been reached that the investment of discretionary power in administrative agencies is a fact of life" (2003, 700).

14. See Huber and Shipan (2002) for an analysis of the conditions under which legislatures will grant public agencies greater autonomy.

15. Power (1997), Hood et al. (1999), and Moran (2002) suggest that expanded monitoring and auditing activities are associated with a decline of trust.

16. The continental European Rechstaat tradition grants agencies an important degree of autonomy. In this tradition, state employees claim a degree of autonomy because, by definition, they serve the public interest. A similar claim is made by the American Progressive tradition for experts: they can claim a degree of autonomy because they

represent the public interest. Both claims draw on the Weberian notion that public servants and experts embody neutral competence. The autonomy envisioned by both traditions is of the variety described as "autonomous law" by Nonet and Selznick (2001).

17. Behn (2001, 31) notes that the "let the managers manage" adage of NPM accepts the failure of the politics/administrative dichotomy and empowers managers for "problem-solving." But he contrasts the "make the managers manage" approach of NPM, which he says assumes the politics/administration dichotomy.

18. Anechiarico and Jacobs (1998) describe the counterproductive effects of corruption control in police departments. Romzek and Dubnick (1987) describe negative consequences of strong external accountability on NASA.

19. The responsibility-accountability debate is an old one in public administration. For a recent discussion, see Dunn and Legge (2000) and McSwite (1997).

20. In a book exploring the implications of Dewey's work for environmental ethics, McDonald writes that for Dewey "both valuation and moral reflection arise in problematic situations" (McDonald 2004, 110; see also Eames 1961). For Dewey, values are not desires or preferences. Although they have an "immediate" quality, values become "intermediate" through cultivation and reflection. See Joas (2000) for a discussion of Pragmatist perspectives on the genesis of value.

21. Mark Moore (1995) has articulated a value-creating model of public administration compatible with a Pragmatist approach. His book, *Creating Public Value*, does not suggest that public managers substitute their own values for those of a larger democratic public. Rather, he suggests that public agencies often play a central leadership role in shaping and defining public values. Good leadership, according to Moore, is about creating value by building a broad base of societal consent. Although Moore's argument goes beyond Selznick in its emphasis on how public agencies might interact with the broader public to shape value, his idea of value creation is consistent with Selznick's model of leadership and institutionalization as value infusion. On linking problem-solving and value-creation, see Sparrow (2000, 245).

22. For an extensive Pragmatist interpretation of the issue of moral responsibility, see Smiley (1992).

23. Many conservatives who do not embrace an individualist ethic might also support this position. For a discussion of William James's approach to "self-regulation," see Fox and Riconscente (2008).

24. In *The Communitarian Persuasion*, Selznick observes that enhancing personal and social responsibility is a theme of communitarianism (2001, 7). Communitarianism, he observes, is about compassion but also about meeting obligations to others. He notes that liberalism lacks an ethic of responsibility (2001, 10).

25. There is, of course, the traditional republican idea that "you get the government you deserve" and that the efficacy of the government is directly related to the virtue of its citizens.

26. An ethos transcends personal-impersonal, individual-social, and public-private distinctions. Ethos is linked to what Selznick called "character" and ultimately to ethics. A Pragmatist ethos of responsibility is not a fixed set of ethical standards but an active set of skills. As McDonald notes, Dewey rejected an ethics of perfection of character (virtue ethics), which was built on foundationalism, and instead understood character as active habits: "character is revealed in action, that is habits of action" (2003, 120). In *The Cosmopolitan Self*, Abolofia (2001) analyzes Mead's theory of how an individual develops into an ethical self.

27. Weber believed that bureaucracy promoted a particular kind of responsibility: a responsibility to follow the commands of superiors (see du Gay 2000, 46). The chief feature of the bureaucratic ethos is "the capacity to set aside one's private political, moral, regional and other commitments" (du Gay 2000, 76). Clearly, this bureaucratic ethos does not depend on deliberation about responsibility.

28. By obscuring the connection between responsibility and actual problems (as opposed to jurisdictional claims and spheres of authority), external accountability systems can also encourage civil servants to see problems in fragmented terms. A standard mantra in large organizations is "that's not my problem." The Pearl Harbor Commission noted this about the relationship between problems and responsibility: "Surprise when it happens is likely to be a complicated, diffuse, bureaucratic thing. It includes neglect of responsibility but also responsibility so poorly defined or so ambiguously delegated that action gets lost" (cited in National Commission on Terrorist Attacks upon the United States (2004, 406).

29. Caspary (2000, 70) suggests the importance of responsibility in Dewey's thought. Dewey, he notes, acknowledges that responsibility brings with it anxiety of uncertain outcomes (2000, 158, 172).

30. A related point is that those that oversee the work of public agencies must have a certain tolerance for unforeseen error. Holding public officials accountable to a standard of omniscience will erode the willingness of people to take responsibility for a problem in the first place.

31. As William Bratton writes: "Once I was satisfied they could handle the responsibility, I decentralized power to the ten district commanders . . . I gave them authority and responsibility but held them accountable" (1998, 160). Another example is provided by Admiral Rickover's successful submarine corps. Rickover emphasized pushing responsibility down to the operator level; he insisted on "the individual's ownership of the task" (Bierly and Spender 1995, 651).

32. See Rees (2008) on how a hospital developed a concept of responsibility that led to a form of self-regulation. He argues that this was inspired by the Pragmatist tradition and that a central theme of pragmatism is that "meaningful institutional reform depends on a corresponding change in moral sensibilities" (2008, 20).

33. As a model of institutional design, the tensions between power-dividing and power-sharing models have recently been explored by Roeder and Rothchild (2005), who argue in favor of the power-dividing model.

34. As Lijphart (1999) has shown, federal countries tend to have relatively independent judiciaries that safeguard and interpret the constitutional powers of different levels of government.

35. As Beer elaborates: "Governing himself through two different governments, the voter views the political world from two perspectives, one shaped by the social pluralism of the general government [e.g., the idea that the pluralism of a large republic would undercut a faction], the other shaped by the territorial pluralism of state government. In his political life, as a member of one nation, he does not separate from one another the two perspectives and the interests each elicits in him. His state perspective affects his choices and decisions in federal politics as his federal perspective affects his choices and decisions in state politics. One may call this process "representational federalism" because it gives representation in the general government to the territorial pluralism of the states and representation in the state governments to the social pluralism of the general government" (1993, 14).

36. One way to think about recursiveness is in terms of a cyclical whole-part relationship, where the parts are in the whole and whole is in the parts. In terms of federalism, this could be conceived as merely a bilateral form of interpenetration. The parts (states) are represented in the whole (the federal government) through their representation in a legislative chamber that represents the states (in the United States, the Senate; in Germany, the Bundesrat). As Swenden observes: "German regional political leaders accepted centralization more easily because they were being offered a strong say in federal law-making in return (via the Bundesrat)" (2004, 385). It is less obvious to see how the whole is in the parts. The U.S. framers did consider a federal veto of state legislation, but this failed to be adopted. However, you might say that the federal government's right to administer federal programs within the sovereign territory of the states is akin to the whole-in-the-parts.

Chapter 8

1. On the "monistic" view of the state, see Laski (1917).
2. Seigfried provides a useful summary: "The problem with the liberal model of democracy, especially as practiced in conservative politics, is that it claims to guarantee an equal voice to all while actually protecting privilege. It assumes that political outcomes produced by the merely additive deliberative process of one person, one vote are a just expression of the public good. To reach this conclusion, it also assumes that each person is equally positioned, that no person is any better situated or more powerful than another, and that persons do not aggregate into powerful coalitions that can only diminish the input of those less well situated but can deliberately isolate them and encourage antagonistic behavior preventing a counterbalancing coalition" (1999, 210).
3. On Dewey's critique of majority voting, see Bohman (1999).
4. For an important discussion of "extra-formal" democracy and its links to the Pragmatist tradition, see Bogason, Kensen, and Miller (2004).
5. Da Silva (2008) explores the interaction between Dewey and Laski. Laski saw Aristotle as providing the original pragmatist model of the state, with his idea of the mixed constitution (Laski 1917, 15; Da Silva 2008). In tracing the history of pluralism in American political science, Gunnell (1996) argues that the major critique of Laski was William Elliot's *The Pragmatic Revolt against Politics* (1928).
6. Da Silva argues that Dewey's approach was far more pluralistic than contemporary communitarian theory: "While Dewey underlines the importance of communication between different individual and collective actors as a way of guaranteeing the coexistence of a plurality of ways of life and avoiding a centralizing political solution, communitarians stress that only a shared ethos can pull together the various groups composing that multiform society" (2008, 367). On the other hand, Dewey is not easily classified as a pluralist of the postwar political science variety. Da Silva writes: "Dewey and Laski's theories of political pluralism comprehend normative dimensions that are completely absent from the postwar, interest-group political pluralism of Dahl, Truman and others" (2008, 361). Da Silva argues that Dewey's theory of democracy shares much with civic republican traditions.
7. Note, however, that while Weber noted variations in types of legitimacy—in fact, his whole sociology of domination is built on these variations—he did not really focus much on variations in the degree of legitimacy demanded by different organizational situations. Weber did expressly point out the tension between procedural and substantive rationality in bureaucratic organizations. But his sociology of domination does not observe that the demand for procedural legitimacy declines as hierarchical command becomes less important.
8. His argument is similar to Zakaria's (1997), who has popularly argued that the democratization of all relationships leads to a deleterious erosion of authority.
9. Unlike the dualistic sign-signified semiotics developed by Saussure or the label-object analysis later developed by the logical positivists, Peirce insisted on three basic semiotic elements: object, sign, and interpretant. He argued that the meaning of a sign that represents an object is ambiguous until "fixed" by a third element, the interpretant (which itself is a sign). This basic logic runs throughout Peirce's philosophical system. For example, when a dispute arises over a particular meaning (sign), Peirce proposed to "fix" its meaning by reference to consequences (interpretant). Peirce articulated much the same triadic developmental sequence in his discussion of signs. He also described three kinds of signs. Iconic signs are signs that have a monadic relationship with the objects they represent: they signify through resemblance. By contrast, indexical signs have a dyadic relationship with the objects they represent—as smoke represents fire. Finally, symbols are signs that operate according to a triadic logic. Their relationship to

the object they represent is arbitrary and established only by convention. Peirce believed that the combination of these three kinds of signs created the capacity for inference and reason (Hookway 2000, 97–103; 1985, 130–134).

10. Hamilton and Biggart (2004) have produced a striking claim about authority in politics. In a study of the executive branch of California state government, they find that authority is based on integrity. Officials often claim to speak in the name of the governor, but their authority depends on the fidelity of this claim, as measured over time.

11. It would be possible to draw out the parallel here with Mead's tripartite categorization of the I, the me, and the generalized other.

12. For Pragmatist views about legitimacy that draw on discourse theory, see McSwite (1997) and Box (2002).

13. These three categories of authority bear obvious comparison with Weber's tripartite classification of charismatic, traditional, and rational-legal.

14. We can put it like this: Pragmatist authority is rooted in an identity (individual or organizational), but it is an identity linked to the production of desired results (problem-solving) as interpreted in terms of broader social conventions. It is this more sophisticated compound model of authority that is implied by Follet's "relational authority" and by Dewey's concepts of "democracy" and "science." The Pragmatists did not abandon the idea of authority, only the idea of authority as based on a priori foundations.

15. A Pragmatist conception of authority would not regard it to be a static trait of a person or institution, but a quality that waxes and wanes depending on the past experience, present situation, and future expectations.

16. This argument is compatible with Dewey's understanding of morality.

17. See Carpenter's (2001) "reputational" model of agency autonomy for a similar argument.

18. Aristotle regarded friendship as having an element of publicness. It would be useful to think about how more disaggregated forms of cooperation—like social networks—can also retain a public character. Among the English pluralists, Figgis saw societal associations as having a public character (Hirst 1994). Da Silva points to Dewey's Lectures in China, 1919–1920, where "Dewey tries to supersede the dichotomy that opposes the individual to the state; his alternative points to a political model in which the state is an instrument to promote and protect other voluntary forms of association" (2008, 5).

19. The views expressed here about building bottom-up consent are very much in the spirit of the model of "empowered participatory governance" developed by Archon Fung, Erik Olin Wright, and Rebecca Abers (Fung, Wright, and Abers 2003; Fung 2004). To clarify, however, this chapter is not espousing a general model of direct participatory democracy as sometimes understood. In the approach advocated here, empowered participation is focused on concrete problems (and hence is selective rather than general), and it is facilitated and organized by public agencies (as opposed to "citizen legislatures," "citizen initiatives," or other direct forms of democracy).

20. Dewey sees the "Great Community" as expanding, but he also sees many "publics" (Smith 1964, 604). For a good discussion of local problem-solving that builds consent and creates bottom-up accountability, see the work of Edward Weber on grassroots ecosystem management (Weber 1999, 2003). Weber (1999) places his discussion of grassroots accountability in a broad historical framework.

21. See also her discussion of consent in *The New State* (1919) and in *Dynamic Administration* (1941).

22. As she writes: "When the political pluralists would allow individuals or groups to decide whether the state is fulfilling its purpose, they tend to make the state's purpose static, they are back in the block universe they have repudiated" (1924, 221).

23. Jane Addams makes very similar claims in *Democracy and Social Ethics* (1915).

24. Marres (2007) argues that Dewey and Lippman moved away from the idea that public opinion represented the democratic will and instead argued that it was associated with the formation of issues or problem-framings.

25. This is consistent with Dewey's understanding. In *The Public and Its Problems*, he argues that the state—and "special agencies and measures"—were necessary for dealing with problems of indirect interdependence (1919, 15–16). Dewey writes that the public is to become "organized by means of officials and material agencies to care for the extensive and enduring consequences of transaction" (1927, 16).

26. Smiley (1999) emphasizes that pragmatists need to think about who is included in publics: "While ... democracy for pragmatists requires full participation in the discovery of consequences, the meaning of 'full participation' is not self-evident" (1999, 641).

27. Furthermore, an argument that public agencies can help to represent more diffuse interests may seem to embody some features of what Dahl calls "guardianship" (Dahl 1985). But although the argument is that public agencies can be stewards of public values, this role is always conceived to be discharged through deliberation and joint inquiry with other public and private stakeholders. It is never meant to provide a justification for public agencies to have an exclusive decision-making role on the basis of their representation of the public interest.

28. Nor is "building consent" intended to mean that the agency will engage in marketing or symbolic consultation in order to build consent.

29. Akkerman, Hajer, and Grin (2004) discuss the concern that the state's active structuring of civic participation will undermine the authentic civic mobilization of society. They find that the Dutch version of this process—known as "interactive governance"—does not erode civil society.

30. The problem with their research design, as they note, is that they did not establish a clear pre–problem-solving baseline, which would be necessary to confidently attribute the different outcomes in the two communities to the problem-solving process.

31. See Shields (2003). Sidney Hook also saw democracy as a community of inquiry (Talisse 2001).

32. This means working in a particular way through informal social networks. Recent experience with watershed management offers some support for this strategy. Comparing watershed organization in South Carolina and California, Lee (2007) found that conservation efforts working through personal networks could be quite effective. Moore, Parker, and Weaver (2008) describe a participatory watershed project designed "around the social structure of the community" (2007, 7). This process actually enhanced local solidarity and cohesion, spilling over into other problem-solving endeavors.

33. Thomas (2003) points to the irony that the Bureau of Land Management (BLM), which has a reputation for working through the local community, was more adept at developing collaboration with local communities than the Forest Service, which had a reputation for striving to maintain autonomy (though it was often accused of being co-opted by the timber industry).

34. Close interaction with the environment has important information-processing benefits. For example, police in squad cars may be oblivious to the types of information that patrol officers walking a "beat" learn.

35. In reviewing the literature on child welfare, Noonan, Sabel, and Simon (2009) point out that family preservation strategies have not always produced the desired results, but that decentralized, customized, and integrative (team-based) management of the sort that Hagedorn advocated is now regarded as a best practice.

36. Note the parallel with the importance of maintaining intermediaries between top-level executives and street-level bureaucrats, as described in the previous section.

37. In their analysis of the contrasting "New Jersey" model, they also nicely show the drawbacks of trying to manage child welfare outcomes by specifying measurable performance standards for child welfare agencies.

Chapter 9

1. For a more general treatment of the term "collaboration," see Thompson and Perry (2006). They define collaboration as "a process in which autonomous actors interact through formal and informal negotiation, jointly creating rules and structures governing their relationships and ways to act or decide on the issues that brought them together; it is a process involving shared norms and mutually beneficial interactions" (2006, 23).

2. A Pragmatist perspective calls attention to distinctive features and contexts of collaborative governance, just as other approaches might stress distinct features and contexts. For example, rational choice scholars might construe collaborative governance as a cooperative (positive sum) bargaining game. They might then ask why stakeholders are willing to bind themselves to such a strategy, given their voluntary nature. They might set about explaining this in terms of the incentives that stakeholders face, as shaped by existing institutions. They might then observe, for instance, that collaborative governance tends to develop "in the shadow of the state" or when alternative policymaking venues are unattractive. This analysis would be selective, flowing from theoretical assumptions and concerns of rational choice theory. It would highlight some important features of collaborative governance while ignoring or glossing over others. Nevertheless, this selective interpretation would be valuable to the extent that it calls out salient features and advances critical analysis.

3. See also McSwite (1997) for an important statement on "Pragmatist collaboration."

4. Chantall Mouffe (2005) criticizes post-political visions that aim to eliminate conflict and antagonism in the name of rationalist consensus.

5. See Kelman (1992) for a good discussion of "adversarial" versus "cooperationist" institutions. He distinguishes "cooperationist" from "cooperative" to avoid minimizing the political conflict inherent in public life.

6. We should not assume that cooperation or public-spiritedness are preconditions for governance; however, cooperation and public-spiritedness might be products of fruitful conflict.

7. A "transformative approach" to mediation, they argue, suggests two dimensions of growth: the growth of "strength of self" (empowerment) and the growth of capacity to relate to others (recognition) (1994, 84). They define empowerment and recognition in specific terms. Empowerment occurs in relation to goals, options, skills, resources, and decision making. Recognition occurs in relation to the consideration of and desire for giving recognition—recognition in thought, words, and action. Empowerment is not just "power balancing" but rather is practiced with both sides (e.g., the stronger party as well as the weaker party). Recognition is not "reconciliation" but rather a form of perspective-taking that recognizes that others are not instruments of our own desires and interests.

8. As Imperial notes of a local resource management dispute: "In Lake Tahoe, prolonged conflict actually set the stage for a prolonged period characterized by productive collaborative relationships" (2005, 311).

9. Booher and Innes (2002) argue that an essential ingredient of consensus-building processes is "authentic dialogue." For a discussion of the relationship between consensus-building practices and Habermas's theory of communicative rationality, see Innes and Booher (1999) and Innes (2004).

10. For an interesting case of non–face-to-face public consultation, see De Carlo's (2006) analysis of a controversial infrastructure planning decision in France. The French state created a formal consultation process in which it met with stakeholders serially and then acted as an arbiter. However, De Carlo finds that face-to-face exchange did occur informally and was critical to the outcome.

11. Festenstein (2004) argues that there are two defenses of deliberation inherent in Pragmatism. The first, which is more Peircean, starts with the search for truth, which leads to the need to deliberate with others. The second, which is more Deweyian, argues that

deliberation is fundamental to human growth (not simply to discovering the truth). The position taken here is closer to the second than the first. See Talisse (2001) for a discussion of Sidney Hook's practical principles for achieving deliberation.

12. As Wondolleck and Yaffee (2000) write: "How can groups start focusing on problem solving? One way is to work on communication that identifies and shatters misconceptions about each other." They argue that collaboration has to be built on personal relationships. Kelman (1992) argues that face-to-face communication is the basis for the cultivation of public spiritedness.

13. As Putnam writes of transformative processes: "A common feature of these approaches [to transformation] is the way in which participants transcend or move away from the present and alter the rules of the game. Even though what is transcended is different across disputes, conflict interaction moves to a metalevel, a shift, or a qualitatively different plane of abstraction. Parties shift levels of abstraction to talk with each other on fundamentally different dimensions" (2004, 278).

14. Bush and Folger (1996) provide a broad outline of the concepts of "transformative mediation." Transformative mediation "offers individuals the opportunity to strengthen and integrate their capacities for self-determination and responsiveness to others" (264–265). Innes and Booher discuss the way that collaboration can set in motion a "cascade of changes in attitudes, behaviors and actions" (1999, 419).

15. Putnam distinguishes reframing from transformation, because "reframing rarely represents a shift in the fundamental understanding of the conflict" (2004, 290). She argues that reframing can lead to transformation if it can hold "opposites together" (2004, 291). Reframing often requires what Mitroff, Emshoff, and Kilmann (1979) call "assumptional surfacing."

16. Kray, Thompson, and Lind (2005) argue that a problem-solving style of negotiation is positively linked to "contingent contracting," which tries to build on and accommodate the differing expectations of the future held by negotiating partners. They also examine, experimentally, how preexisting relationships and accountability affect whether negotiating parties will adopt a problem-solving approach. Accountability pressures can lead to rigidity in decision making and preexisting relations can lead to attempts to minimize differences between parties. Both these factors can discourage parties from a full exploration of differences (a hallmark of the problem-solving approach, as they describe it).

17. The ability to transform a conflict into a shared problem-solving exercise requires, according to Kelman, a prenegotiation phase in which the possibility of joint problem-solving activity can be explored. This is a prenegotiation phase because the ability to transform the conflict into a problem is discouraged during the process of negotiation by concerns about reaching binding commitments.

18. Shield (2003, 2005) has argued for using the concept of a "community of inquiry" as a framework for public administration "The community of inquiry," she writes, "includes all those interested in resolving the problematic situation" (2005, 512). As Smiley reminds us, however, we should not take this "inquiry" metaphor as a mode of depoliticizing the problem-solving process: "The discovery process is itself politically charged, from its assumption of a particular community of inquirers, through its choice to focus on particular consequences and not others, to its interpretation of these consequences with symbols that are themselves powerful political tools" (1999, 642). Obviously, a problem-solving approach must be sensitive to the fact that problem definition is a political process (Weiss 1989).

19. Reich (1985) has contrasted three views of the administrative role—a pluralist interest intermediation role, a utility maximizing role, and a social learning role. He argues for thinking of the role of the administrator as one of encouraging social learning.

20. Hargadon and Bechky describe how "reflexive reframing" can occur at the collective level when "each respectfully attends to and builds upon the comments and actions of

others" (2006, 490). This idea of reflexive reframing is similar to Fernandez et al.'s (2001) discussion of "exploratory talk."

21. Reiter-Palmon and Illies (2004) provide a good overview of the literature on creative problem-solving.

22. This description is reminiscent of how open-source systems evolve (Weber 2004). An open source system "grows" through feedbacks between the growing scale and scope of the distributed open-source architecture and the increasingly focused revision of the elemental parts of this architecture.

23. In a study of 239 cases of stakeholder involvement in environmental decision making, Beierle (2002) finds that stakeholder involvement increases the quality of decisions by improving the information or analysis or by adding new ideas. Freeman and Langbein (2000) find that participants in regulatory negotiation report learning a significant amount during the process and that this was one of the most important benefits of regulatory negotiation. Saarikoski (2000) finds that a waste management dispute organized as a joint fact-finding collaboration among multiple stakeholders was a failure in several respects but did successfully produce new information that led some stakeholders to reconsider their positions. In a study of oil spill collaboration in Alaska, Busenberg (1999) found strong agreement that stakeholders had learned more about the technical dimensions of marine risks through their participation.

24. There is an interesting parallel between this discussion of uncertainty and arguments made in the literature on adaptive management. Walters and Holling contrast different ideas of experimentalism in ecosystem management: "Two kinds of science influence renewable resource policy and management. One is a science of parts. . . . It emerges from traditions of experimental science where a narrow enough focus is chosen in order to develop data and critical tests that will reject invalid hypotheses. The goal is to narrow uncertainty to the point where acceptance of an argument among scientific peers is essentially unanimous. . . . The other is a science of the integration of parts. It uses the results of the first, but identifies gaps, invents alternatives, and evaluates the integrated consequence against planned and unplanned interventions in the whole system that occurs in nature. . . . Since uncertainty is high, the analysis of uncertainty becomes a topic in itself" (1990, 2067).

25. See Fernandez et al. (2001) on scaffolding in collaborative learning in educational settings.

26. In a study of regulatory negotiations, Freeman and Langbein found that "the longer and harder the group worked, and the more they developed working or personal relationships with other participants, the more important a successful result became" (2000, 87). Lee (2007) describes the tensions between a formal, inclusive, and transparent collaborative process versus a more informal, exclusive, and personalistic one. Her study suggests two relevant points: (1) that formal agreements must be underpinned by informal agreement or they end up going nowhere; and (2) that real social transformation of preferences typically requires informal social interaction.

27. In an analysis of an EPA experiment in negotiated regulation, for example, Murdock et al. (2005) writes: "We define trust as the expectation that participants in the negotiation will be truthful and honest about their goals, intentions, and actions. . . . Our clear impression was that over time, people—primarily government and business negotiators—learned to trust other people in six XL pilots. . . . But trust grew from personal interactions, not from the formation of new institutional bridges. EPA and company negotiators suggest that prolonged face-to-face contact during negotiations helped build trust among XL negotiators from companies, EPA's regional offices, and state and local agencies."

28. Evolutionary biologists and organization theorists might call this transactional logic "co-evolutionary."

29. Fruitful conflict through communication, creative problem-solving, and recursive learning are both ends and means in this process. They are ends, because a collaborative

process should be designed to encourage these outcomes; they are means, because they provide scaffolding for more ambitious public engagement.

30. The term "enacted" is a reference to Weick's (1969) concept of the "enacted" environment, which he used to describe environments created by organizations.

31. Surveying individuals involved in a range of forestry collaboratives, Selin, Schuett, and Carr (2000) found that "recognition of interdependence" was regarded as a very important factor contributing to successful collaborative outcomes.

32. As Putnam writes: "Connecting also promotes interdependence that forms the bonds for building a different relationship instead of one centered on exchanging positions and issues" (2004, 286).

33. In a survey of American and Australian collaborative groups, Margerum (2002) found that "member commitment" was the most important factor facilitating collaboration. The weak commitment of public agencies to collaboration, particularly at the headquarters level, is often seen as a particular problem (Yaffee and Wondolleck 2003).

34. A number of authors describe collaborative problem-solving as a process (McCann 1983; Hood, Logsdon, and Thompson 1993; Thompson and Perry 2006).

35. What Hood, Logsdon, and Thompson (1993) call the "group-as-a-whole" is a partly emergent phenomenon in collaboration.

36. However, the point is not merely that all action should proceed in an incremental way, extending only marginally beyond the status quo. This is the interpretation of Lindblom's incrementalist model that led people to criticize it as conservative. Rather we are talking here of Follett's idea of "compound growth," where small wins become the building blocks for much larger wins.

37. As Margerum writes of stormwater management stakeholders in Australia: "Stakeholders emphasized that plans had to be pragmatic because the complexity of the setting required some concrete actions to build the confidence of the group, generate momentum, and help them determine their role" (2002, 245).

REFERENCES

Abbott, Andrew. 1992. "An Old Institutionalist Reads the New Institutionalism." *Contemporary Sociology* 21, no. 6: 754–756.

Aboulafia, Mitchell. 2001. *The Cosmopolitan Self: George Herbert Mead and Continental Philosophy*. Champaign-Urbana: University of Illinois Press.

Aboulafia, Mitchell, Myra Orbach Bookman, and Cathy Kemp. 2002. *Habermas and Pragmatism*. London: Routledge.

Abowitz, Kathleen Knight. 2000. "A Pragmatist Revisioning of Resistance Theory." *American Educational Research Journal* 37, no. 4: 877–907.

Ackoff, Russell L. 1987. "The Circular Organization: An Update." *Academy of Management Executive* 3, no. 1: 11–16.

———. 1974. "Systems, Messes and Interactive Planning." In *Redesigning the Future*. New York/London: Wiley, 1974.

Addams, Jane. 1915. *Democracy and Social Ethics*. New York: Macmillan.

Adler, Paul S., and Bryan Borys. 1996. "Two Types of Bureaucracy: Enabling and Coercive." *Administrative Science Quarterly* 41: 61–89.

Aguirre, Benigno E. 2002. "'Sustainable Development' as Collective Surge." *Social Science Quarterly* 83, no. 1: 101–118.

Akkerman, Tjitske, Maarten Hajer, and John Grin. 2004. "The Interactive State: Democratisation from Above?'" *Political Studies* 52: 82–95.

Albert, Alexa, and Yngve Ramstad. 1998. "The Social Psychological Underpinnings of Commons's Institutional Economics II: The Concordance of George Herbert Mead's 'Social Self' and John R. Commons's 'Will.'" *Journal of Economic Issues* 32, no. 1: 1–46.

———. 1997. "The Social Psychological Underpinnings of Commons's Institutional Economics: The Significance of Dewey's Human Nature and Conduct." *Journal of Economic Issues* 31, no. 4: 881–916.

Alexander, Jeffery A., Maureen E. Comfort, and Bryan J. Weiner. 1998. "Governance in Public-Private Community Health Partnerships: A Survey of the Community Care Network: SM Demonstration Sites." *Nonprofit Management and Leadership* 8, no. 4: 231–332.

Allen, John. 2008. "Pragmatism and Power, or the Power to Make a Difference in a Radically Contingent World." *Geoforum* 39: 1613–1624.

Anderson, Charles. 1990. *Pragmatic Liberalism*. Chicago: University of Chicago Press.

Andranovich, Greg. 1995. "Achieving Consensus in Public Decisionmaking: Applying Interest Based Problem-Solving to the Challenges of Intergovernmental Collaboration." *Journal of Applied Behavioral Research* 31, no. 4: 429–445.

Anechiarico, Frank, and James B. Jacobs. 1996. *The Pursuit of Absolute Integrity: How Corruption Control Makes Government Ineffective*. Chicago: University of Chicago Press.

Ansell, Christopher. 2009. "Mary Parker Follett and Pragmatist Organization." In *The Oxford Handbook of Sociology and Organization Studies*. Ed. Paul S. Adler. Oxford: Oxford University Press.

———. 2001. *Schism and Solidarity in Social Movements: The Politics of Labor in the French Third Republic*. Cambridge, UK: Cambridge University Press.

———. 2000. "The Networked Polity: Regional Development in Western Europe." *Governance* 13, no. 3: 303–333.

———. 1997. "Symbolic Networks: The Realignment of the French Working Class, 1887–1894." *American Journal of Sociology* 103, no. 2: 359–390.

Ansell, Christopher, and Alison Gash. 2008. "Collaborative Governance in Theory and Practice." *Journal of Public Administration Theory and Practice* 18, no. 4: 543–571.

Argyris, Chris, and Donald Schön. 1978. *Organizational Learning: A Theory of Action Perspective*. Reading, MA: Addison-Wesley.

Arthur, W. Brian. 1989. "Competing Technologies, Increasing Returns, and Lock-in by Historical Events." *Economic Journal* 99: 116–131.

Ascher, William, and Barbara Hirschfelder-Ascher. 2004. "Linking Lasswell's Political Psychology and the Policy Sciences." *Policy Sciences* 37: 23–36.

Athens, Lonnie. 2005. "Mead's Lost Conception of Society." *Symbolic Interaction* 28, no. 3: 305–325.

Ayres, Clarence. 1951. "The Co-ordinates of Institutionalism." *American Economic Review* 41, no. 2: 47–55.

Baker, Susan. 2007. "Sustainable Development as Symbolic Commitment: Declaratory Politics and the Seductive Appeal of Ecological Modernisation in the European Union." *Environmental Politics* 16, no. 2: 297–317.

Baldwin, John D. 2005. "Shibutani and Pragmatism." *Symbolic Interaction* 28, no. 4: 487–504.

———. 1988. "Habit, Emotion, and Self-Conscious Action." *Sociological Perspectives* 31, no. 1: 35–57.

———. 1986. *George Herbert Mead: A Unifying Theory for Sociology*. Newbury Park, CA: Sage Publications.

Ballard, David. 2005. "Using Learning Processes to Promote Change for Sustainable Development." *Action Research* 3, no. 2: 135–156.

Barbalet, Jack. 2008. "Pragmatism and Economics: William James' Contribution." *Cambridge Journal of Economics* 32, no. 5: 1–14.

Barnard, Chester I. 1968. *The Functions of the Executive*. Cambridge, MA: Harvard University Press.

Barrett, Brendan, and Usui Mikoto. 2002. "Local Agenda 21 in Japan: Transforming Local Environmental Governance." *Local Environment* 7, no. 1: 49–67.

Barrutia, José M., Itziar Aguado, and Carmen Echebarria. 2007. "Networking for Local Agenda 21 Implementation: Learning from Experience with *Udaltalde* and *Udalsarea* in the Base Autonomous Community." *Geoforum* 38: 33–48.

Barton, John, and John W. Selsky. 2000. "Toward an Emery Model of Management: Implications and Prospects of Emery Open Systems Theory." *Systemic Practice and Action Research* 13, no. 5: 705–720.

Barzelay, Michael. 1992. *Breaking through Bureaucracy: A New Vision for Managing Government*. Berkeley: University of California Press.

Barzelay, Michael, and Raquel Gallego. 2006. "From 'New Institutionalism' to 'Institutional Processualism': Advancing Knowledge about Public Management Policy Change." *Governance: An International Journal of Policy, Administration, and Institutions* 19, no. 4: 531–557.

Baumgartner, Frank, and Bryan Jones. 1993. *Agendas and Instability in American Politics*. Chicago: University of Chicago Press.

Beamish, Thomas D. 2002. "Waiting for Crisis: Regulatory Inaction and Ineptitude and the Guadalupe Dunes Oil Spill." *Social Problems* 49, no. 2: 150–177.

Beatley, Timothy. 1994. *Habitat Conservation Planning: Endangered Species and Urban Growth.* Austin: University of Texas Press.

Beckert, Jens. 2003. "Economic Sociology and Embeddedness: How Shall We Conceptualize Economic Action?" *Journal of Economic Issues* 37, no. 3: 769–787.

Beer, Samuel H. 1993. *To Make a Nation: The Rediscovery of American Federalism.* Cambridge, MA: Belknap Press.

Behn, Robert D. 2001. *Rethinking Democratic Accountability.* Washington, DC: Brookings Institute Press.

Beierle, Thomas. 2002. "The Quality of Stakeholder-Based Decisions." *Risk Analysis* 22, no. 4: 739–749.

Beierle, Thomas, and David Konisky. 2001. "What Are We Gaining from Stakeholder Involvement? Observations from Environmental Planning in the Great Lakes." *Environmental and Planning C: Government and Policy* 19: 515–527.

Bentrup, Gary. 2001. "Evaluation of a Collaborative Model: A Case Study of Analysis of Watershed Planning in the Intermountain West." *Environmental Management* 27, no. 5: 739–748.

Benz, Arthur. 2006. "Conclusion: Linking Research on Europeanisation and National Parliaments," in Katrin Auel and Arthur Benz (eds.). *The Europeanisation of Parliamentary Democracy.* Abingdon UK: Routledge Press. Pp. 207–220.

Berger, Peter L., and Thomas Luckmann. 1967. *The Social Construction of Reality.* Garden City, NY: Anchor Books.

Berk, Gerald. 2009. *Louis D. Brandeis and the Making of Regulated Competition, 1900–1932.* Cambridge, UK: Cambridge University Press.

Berk, Gerald, and Dennis Galvan. 2009. "How People Experience and Change Institutions: A Field Guide to Creative Syncretism." *Theory and Society* 38, no. 6: 543–580.

Berk, Gerald, and Marc Schneiberg. 2005. "Varieties in Capitalism, Varieties of Association: Collaborative Learning in American Industry, 1900–1925." *Politics and Society* 33, no. 1: 46–87.

Berk, Richard A. 2005. "Knowing When to Fold 'Em: An Essay on Evaluating the Impact of Ceasefire, Compstat, and Exile." *Criminology and Public Policy* 4, no. 3: 451–466.

Berkhout, Frans, Geert Verbong, Anna J. Wieczorek, Bob Raven, Louis Level, and Xuemei Bai. 2010. "Sustainability Experiments in Asia: Innovations Shaping Alternative Development Pathways?" *Environmental Science and Policy* 13, no. 4: 261–271.

Berman, Greg, and John Feinblatt. 2005. *Good Courts: The Case for Problem-Solving Justice.* New York: New Press.

Bickhard, Mark H. 2005. "Functional Scaffolding and Self-Scaffolding." *New Ideas in Psychology* 23: 166–173.

Bierly, Paul E., and J.C. Spender. 1995. "Culture and High Reliability Organizations: The Case of the Nuclear Submarine." *Journal of Management* 21, no. 4: 639–656.

Blackler, Frank. 1995. "Knowledge, Knowledge Work and Organizations: An Overview and Interpretation." *Organization Studies* 16, no. 6: 1021–1046.

Blanco, Hilda. 1994. *How to Think about Social Problems: American Pragmatism and the Idea of Planning.* Westport, CT: Greenwood Press.

Blom-Hansen, Jens. 1999. "Avoiding the 'Joint-Decision Trap': Lessons from Intergovernmental Relations in Scandanavia," *European Journal of Political Research*, 35: 35–67.

Blumer, Herbert. 1969. *Symbolic Interactionism: Perspective and Method.* Berkeley: University of California Press.

Boehmer-Christiansen, Sonja. 2002. "The Geo-Politics of Sustainable Development: Bureaucracies and Politicians in Search of the Holy Grail." *Geoforum* 22: 351–365.

Bogason, Peter, Sandra Kensen, and Hugh Theodore Miller. 2004. *Tampering with Tradition: The Unrealized Authority of Democratic Agency.* Lanham, MD: Lexington Books.

Bohman, James. 2002. "How to Make a Social Science Practice: Pragmatism, Critical Social Science and Multiperspectival Theory." *Millennium—Journal of International Studies* 31, no. 3: 499–524.

———. 1999. "Democracy as Inquiry, Inquiry as Democratic: Pragmatism, Social Science, and the Cognitive Division of Labor." *American Journal of Political Science* 43, no. 3: 590–607.

Boin, Arjen. 2001. *Crafting Public Institutions: Leadership in Two Prison Systems.* Boulder, CO: Lynne Rienner Publishers.

Boin, Arjen, and Tom Christensen. 2008. "The Development of Public Institutions: Reconsidering the Role of Leadership." *Administration and Society* 40, no. 3: 271–297.

Boin, Arjen, and Robert E. Goodin. 2007. "Institutionalizing Upstarts: The Demons of Domestication and the Benefits of Recalcitrance." *Acta Politica* 42, no. 1: 40–57.

Boje, David M., and Grace Ann Rosile. 2001. "Where's the Power in Empowerment? Answers from Follett and Clegg." *Journal of Applied Behavioral Science* 37, no. 1: 90–117.

Booher, David E., and Judith Innes. 2002. "Network Power in Collaborative Planning." *Journal of Planning Education and Research* 21, no. 3: 221–236.

Börzel, Tanja A. and Madeleine O. Hosli. 2003. "Brussels between Bern and Berlin: Comparative Federalism Meets the European Union," *Governance,* 16, 2: 179–202.

Boulding, Kenneth. 1961. *The Image: Knowledge in Life and Society.* Ann Arbor, MI: Ann Arbor Paperbacks.

Bourdeaux, Robert M. 1972. "John Dewey's Concept of a Functional Self." *Educational Theory* 22, no. 3: 334–343.

Bourrier, Mathilde. 1996. "Organizing Maintenance Work at Two American Nuclear Power Plants." *Journal of Contingencies and Crisis Management* 4, no. 2: 104–112.

Bouwen, Rene, and Tharsi Taillieu. 2004. "Multi-Party Collaboration as Social Learning for Interdependence: Developing Relational Knowing for Sustainable Natural Resource Management." *Journal of Community and Applied Social Psychology* 14: 137–153.

Bovens, Mark. 1998. *The Quest for Responsibility: Accountability and Citizenship in Complex Organisations.* Cambridge, UK: Cambridge University Press.

Bovens, Mark, and Anchrit Wille. 2008. "Deciphering the Dutch Drop: Ten Explanations for Decreasing Political Trust in the Netherlands." *International Review of Administrative Sciences* 74: 283–305.

Box, Richard C. 2002. "Pragmatic Discourse and Administrative Legitimacy." *American Review of Public Administration* 32, no. 1: 20–39.

Braga, Anthony A. 2002. *Problem-Oriented Policing and Crime Prevention.* Monsey, NY: Criminal Justice Press.

Braga, Anthony, Jack McDevitt, and Glenn L. Pierce. 2006. "Understanding and Preventing Gang Violence: Problem Analysis and Response Development in Lowell, Massachusetts." *Police Quarterly* 9, no. 1: 20–46.

Bratton, William. 1998. *Turnaround: How America's Top Cop Reversed the Crime Epidemic.* New York: Random House.

Brendel, David H. 2006. *Healing Psychiatry: Bridging the Science/Humanism Divide.* Cambridge, MA: MIT Press.

Bretherton, Charlotte, and John Vogler. 2008. "The European Union as a Sustainable Development Actor: The Case of External Fisheries Policy." *Journal of European Integration* 30, no. 3: 410–417.

Briggs, Xavier de Souza. 2008. *Democracy as Problem Solving: Civic Capacities in Communities across the Globe.* Cambridge, MA: MIT Press.

Brightman, Harvey J. 1978. "Differences in Ill-Structured Problem Solving along the Organizational Hierarchy." *Decision Sciences* 9: 1–18.

Bromley, Daniel. 2006. *Sufficient Reason: Volitional Pragmatism and the Meaning of Economic Institutions.* Princeton, NJ: Princeton University Press.

Brown, A. J. 2002. "Collaborative Governance versus Constitutional Politics: Decision Rules for Sustainability from Australia's South East Queensland Forest Agreement." *Environmental Science and Policy* 5: 19–32.

Brown, John Seely, and Paul Duguid. 2000. *The Social Life of Information.* Cambridge, MA: Harvard Business School Press.

Brown, Rebekah R. 2008. "Local Institutional Development and Organizational Change for Advancing Sustainable Urban Water Futures." *Environmental Management* 41: 221–233.

Brunsson, Nils. 1989. *The Organization of Hypocrisy: Talk, Decisions and Actions in Organizations.* New York: John Wiley & Sons.

Brusoni, Stefano. 2005. "The Limits to Specialization: Problem Solving and Coordination in 'Modular Networks.'" *Organization Studies* 26, no. 12: 1885–1907.

Brusoni, Stefano, Luigi Marengo, Andrea Prencipe, and Marco Valente. 2007. "The Value and Costs of Modularity: A Problem-Solving Perspective." *European Management Review* 4: 121–132.

Bruun, Henrik, and Seppo Sierla. 2008. "Distributed Problem Solving in Software Development: The Case of an Automation Project." *Social Studies of Science* 38, no. 1: 133–158.

Bryan, Todd. 2004. "Tragedy Averted: The Promise of Collaboration." *Society and Natural Resources* 17: 881–896.

Bryson, John M., Fran Ackermann, and Colin Eden. 2007. "Putting the Resource-Based View of Strategy and Distinctive Competence to Work in Public Organizations." *Public Administration Review* 67, no. 4: 702–717.

Bryson, John M., Barbara C. Crosby, and Melissa Middleton Stone. 2006. "The Design and Implementation of Cross-Sector Collaborations: Propositions from the Literature." *Public Administration Review* 66, supp. issue s1: 44–55.

Bryson, John M., Gary L. Cunningham, and Karen J. Lokkesmoe. 2002. "What to Do When Stakeholders Matter: The Case of Problem Formulation for the African American Project of Hennepin County, Minnesota." *Public Administration Review* 62, no. 5: 568–584.

Bucholz, Rogene A., and Sandra B. Rosenthal. 1995. "Theoretical Foundations of Public Policy: A Pragmatic Perspective." *Business and Society* 34, no. 3: 261–279.

Buntrock, Oliver. 2008. "Problem-Oriented Micro-Institutionalization: A Requisite Approach to Cross-National Problem-Solving." *Journal of European Public Policy* 15, no. 2: 282–299.

Burns, James MacGregor. 1982. *Leadership.* New York: Harper Perennial Modern Classics.

Burns, Tom, and G. M. Stalker. 1994 [1961]. *The Management of Innovation.* New York: Oxford University Press.

Busenberg, George. 1999. "Collaborative and Adversarial Analysis in Environmental Policy." *Policy Sciences* 32: 1–11.

Bush, Robert A. Baruch, and Joseph P. Folger. 1994. *The Promise of Mediation: Responding to Conflict through Empowerment and Recognition.* San Francisco: Jossey-Bass Publishers.

Bush, Paul D. 1989. "Institutionalist Methodology and Hermeneutics: A Comment on Mirowski." *Journal of Economic Issues* 23, no. 4: 1159–1172.

Calton, Jerry M., and Steven L. Payne. 2003. "Coping with Paradox: Multistakeholder Learning Dialogue as a Pluralist Sensemaking Process for Addressing Messy Problems." *Business and Society* 42, no. 1: 7–42.

Camic, Charles. 1986. "The Matter of Habit." *American Journal of Sociology* 91, no. 5: 1039–1087.

Campbell, Donald T. 1982. "Experiments as Arguments." *Knowledge: Creation, Diffusion, Utilization* 3, no. 3: 327–337.

———. 1970. "Considering the Case against Experimental Evaluations of Social Innovations." *Administrative Science Quarterly* 15, no. 1: 110–113.

———. 1969. "Reforms as Experiments." *American Psychologist* 24: 409–429.

Campbell, John. 1995. *Understanding John Dewey: Nature and Cooperative Intelligence.* Chicago: Open Court.

Campbell, Marcia Caton. 2003. "Intractability in Environmental Disputes: Exploring a Complex Construct." *Journal of Planning Literature* 17, no. 3: 360–371.

Carey, James W. 2009. *Communication as Culture: Essays on Media and Society*. New York and London: Routledge.

Carlile, Paul. 2002. "A Pragmatic View of Knowledge and Boundaries: Boundary Objects in New Product Development." *Organization Science* 13, no. 4: 442–455.

Carpenter, Daniel. 2001. *The Forging of Bureaucratic Autonomy: Reputations, Networks, and Policy Innovation in Executive Agencies, 1862–1928*. Princeton, NJ: Princeton University Press.

Carr, Adrian, Rita Durant, and Alexis Downs. 2004. "Emergent Strategy Development, Abduction, and Pragmatism: New Lessons from Corporations." *Human Systems Management* 23: 79–91.

Caspary, William R. 2000. *Dewey on Democracy*. Ithaca, NY: Cornell University Press.

Cassady, Joslyn D., Charles Higgins, Hugh M. Mainzer, Scott A. Seys, John Sarisky, Myfanwy Callahan, and Karl J. Musgrave. 2006. "Beyond Compliance: Environmental Health Problem Solving, Interagency Collaboration, and Risk Assessment to Prevent Waterborne Disease." *Journal of Epidemiology and Community Health* 60: 672–674.

Cavaleri, Steven A. 2004. "Principles for Designing Pragmatic Knowledge Management Systems." *Learning Organization* 11, nos. 4/5: 312–321.

Chandler, Alfred. 1962. *Strategy and Structure: Chapters in the History of American Industrial Enterprise*. Cambridge, MA: MIT Press.

Cherney, Adrian. 2006. "Problem Solving for Crime Prevention." *Australian Institute of Criminology* 314: 1–6.

Chicago Community Policing Evaluation Consortium. 2004. *Community Policing in Chicago, Year Ten: An Evaluation of Chicago's Alternative Policing Strategy*. Printed by authority of the State of Illinois.

Chifos, Carla. 2007. "The Sustainable Communities Experiment in the United States: Insights from Three Federal-Level Initiatives." *Journal of Planning Education and Research* 26: 435–449.

Chisholm, Donald. 2001. *Waiting for Dead Men's Shoes: Origins and Development of the U.S. Navy's Officer Personnel System, 1793–1941*. Palo Alto, CA: Stanford University Press.

———. 1995. "Problem Solving and Institutional Design." *Journal of Public Administration Research and Theory* 5, no. 4: 451–491.

———. 1992. *Coordination without Hierarchy: Informal Structures in Multiorganizational Systems*. Berkeley: University of California Press.

Chubb, John E., and Terry M. Moe. 1990. *Politics, Markets and America's Schools*. Washington, DC: Brookings Institution Press.

Cladis, Mark. 1992. *A Communitarian Defense of Liberalism: Emile Durkheim and Contemporary Social Theory*. Stanford, CA: Stanford University Press.

Clark, Andy. 1998. *Being There: Putting Brain, Body, and World Together Again*. Cambridge, MA: MIT Press.

Clark, Peter A. 1999. *Organisations in Action: Competition between Contexts*. London: Routledge.

Clemens, E. 1993. "Organizational Repertoires and Institutional Change: Women's Groups and the Transformation of U.S. Politics, 1890–1920." *American Journal of Sociology* 98, no. 4: 755–798.

Coaffee, Jon, and Nicola Headlam. 2008. "Pragmatic Localism Uncovered: The Search for Locally Contingent Solutions to National Reform Agendas." *Geoforum* 39: 1585–1599.

Cohen, J. M., and J. Rogers. 1983. *On Democracy*. Middlesex, UK: Penguin.

Cohen, Michael. 2007. "Reading Dewey: Reflections on the Study of Routine." *Organization Studies* 28, no. 5: 773–786.

Colapietro, Vincent. 2004. "Doing—and Undoing—the Done Thing: Dewey and Bourdieu on Habituation, Agency, and Transformation." *Contemporary Pragmatism* 1, no. 2: 65–93.

———. 1989. *Peirce's Approach to the Self: A Semiotic Perspective on Human Subjectivity*. Albany: SUNY Press.

Colapietro, Vincent, Torjus Midtgarden, and Torill Strand. 2005. "Introduction: Peirce and Education: The Conflicting Processes of Learning and Discovery." *Studies in Philosophy and Education* 24: 167–177.

Commons, John. 1934. *Institutional Economics*. New York: Macmillan.

———. 1931. "Institutional Economics." *American Economic Review* 21: 648–657.

Cook, Gary A. 1993. *George Herbert Mead: The Making of a Social Pragmatist*. Urbana: University of Illinois Press.

Cooley, Charles H. 1962. *Social Organization*. New York: Schocken Books.

———. 1927. "Case Study of Small Institutions as a Method of Research." In *Sociological Theory and Social Research: Being Selected Papers of Charles Horton Cooley*, ed. Robert Cooley Angell (New York: Henry Holt, 1930), 313–322. Paper presented at the Annual Meeting of the American Sociological Society in 1927. Published in *Publications and Proceedings* (1928): 181–191.

Cooper, Wesley. 2008. "Teleology in American Philosophy." In *Encyclopedia of American Philosophy*, ed. John Lachs and Robert Talisse. London: Routledge.

Cordes, Christian. 2005. "Veblen's 'Instinct of Workmanship': Its Cognitive Foundations, and Some Implications for Economic Theory." *Journal of Economic Issues* 39, no. 1: 1–20.

Cordner, Gary, and Elizabeth Perkins Biebel. 2005. "Problem-Oriented Policing in Practice." *Criminology and Public Policy* 4, no. 2: 155–180.

Corrigan, Maura D., and Daniel Becker. 2003. "Moving Problem-Solving Courts into the Mainstream." *Court Manager* 18, no. 6: 1–6.

Cunningham, Craig A. 1994. "Dewey's Metaphysics and the Self." *Studies in Philosophy and Education* 13: 343–360.

Cutchin, Malcolm P. 1999. "Qualitative Explorations in Health Geography: Using Pragmatism and Related Concepts as Guides." *Professional Geographer* 51, no. 2: 265–274.

D'Adderio, Luciana. 2008. "The Performativity of Routines: Theorising the Influence of Artefacts and Distributed Agencies on Routine Dynamics." *Research Policy* 37, no. 5: 769–789.

———. 2004. *Inside the Virtual Product: How Organizations Create Knowledge through Software*. Cheltenham, UK: Edward Elgar.

Dahl, Robert A. 1985. *Controlling Nuclear Weapons: Democracy versus Guardianship*. Syracuse, NY: Syracuse University Press.

———. 1957. "The Concept of Power." *Behavioral Science* 2: 201–215.

Dalton, Russell. 2004. *Democratic Challenges, Democratic Choices: The Erosion in Political Support in Advanced Industrial Democracies*. Oxford: Oxford University Press.

Damasio, Antonio. 1994. *Descartes' Error: Emotion, Reason, and the Human Brain*. New York: Putnam.

Daniels, Steven, and Gregg B. Walker. 2001. *Working through Environmental Conflict: The Collaborative Learning Approach*. Westport, CT: Praeger.

Da Silva, Filipe Carreira. 2008. "Bringing Republican Ideas Back Home: The Dewey-Laski Connection." *History of European Ideas* 35, no. 3: 360–368.

De Carlo, Laurence. 2006. "The French High-Speed Méditerranée Train Decision Process: A Large-Scale Public Decision Study." *Conflict Resolution Quarterly* 24, no. 1: 3–30.

Dehue, Trudy. 2001. "Establishing the Experimenting Society: The Historical Origin of Social Experimentation according to the Randomized Controlled Design." *American Journal of Psychology* 1114, no. 2: 283–302.

Dennis, Alex, and Peter J. Martin. 2005. "Symbolic Interactionism and the Concept of Power." *British Journal of Sociology* 56, no. 2: 191–213.

Denzin, Norman. 1984. *On Understanding Emotion*. San Francisco: Jossey-Bass.

De Sousa, Ronald. 1987. *The Rationality of Emotion*. Cambridge, MA: MIT Press.

Devuyst, Dimitri, and Luc Hens. 2000. "Introducing and Measuring Sustainable Development Initiatives by Local Authorities in Canada and Flanders (Belgium): A Comparative Study." *Environment, Development and Sustainability* 2: 81–105.

Dewey, John. 1980. *Logic: The Theory of Inquiry*. New York: Henry Holt.

———. 1960. *Theory of the Moral Life*. New York: Holt, Rinehart, and Winston.

———. 1957 [1922]. *Human Nature and Conduct: An Introduction to Social Psychology*. New York: Random House.

———. 1939/1989. *Freedom and Culture*. Buffalo, NY: Prometheus Books.

———. 1939. *Theory of Valuation*. Chicago: University of Chicago Press.

———. 1938. *Experience and Education*. New York: Collier.

———. 1934. *Art as Experience*. New York: Perigee Books.

———. 1929. *Experience and Nature*. London: George Allen & Unwin.

———. 1928 [1960]. *The Quest for Certainty*. New York: Putnam.

———. 1927. *The Public and Its Problems*. New York: Henry Holt.

———. 1916. *Essays in Experimental Logic*. Chicago: University of Chicago Press.

———. 1910. *How We Think*. Washington, DC: Heath & Co.

Dewey, John, and Arthur Bentley. 1949. *Knowing and the Known*. Boston: Beacon Press.

Dickstein, Morris, ed. 1998. *The Revival of Pragmatism: New Essays on Social Thought, Law, and Culture*. Durham, NC: Duke University Press.

Dietmar Braun. 2008. "Making Federalism More Efficient: A Comparative Assessment," *Acta Politica*, 43: 4–25.

Diggins, John. 1994. *The Promise of Pragmatism: Modernism and the Crisis of Knowledge and Authority*. Chicago: University of Chicago Press.

DiMaggio, Paul, and Walter W. Powell. 1983. "The Iron Cage Revisited: Institutional Isomorphism and Collective Rationality in Organizational Fields." *American Sociological Review* 48: 147–160.

Djelic, Marie-Laure, and Kerstin Sahlins-Andersson. 2006. *Transnational Governance: Institutional Dynamics of Regulation*. Cambridge, UK: Cambridge University Press.

Dorf, Michael, and Charles Sabel. 2000. "Drug Treatment Courts and Emergent Experimentalist Government." *Vanderbilt Law Review* 53: 831–883.

———. 1998. "A Constitution of Democratic Experimentalism." *Columbia Law Review* 98, no. 2: 267–473.

Douglas, Mary. 1986. *How Institutions Think*. Syracuse, NY: Syracuse University Press.

———. 1970. *Natural Symbols: Explorations in Cosmology*. London: Routledge.

Dreyfus, Hubert, and Stuart Dreyfus. 1986. *Mind over Machine: The Power of Human Intuition and Expertise in the Era of the Computer*. New York: Free Press.

Dryzek, John S. 2004. "Pragmatism and Democracy: In Search of Deliberative Publics." *Journal of Speculative Philosophy* 18, no. 1: 72–79.

Dubnick, Melvin. 2005. "Accountability and the Promise of Performance: In Search of the Mechanisms." *Public Performance & Management Review* 28, no. 3: 376–417.

Du Gay, Paul. 2000. *In Praise of Bureaucracy: Weber, Organization, Ethics*. London: Sage Publications.

Duncan, Hugh Dalziel. 1968. *Communication and Social Order*. Oxford: Oxford University Press.

Dunn, Delmer D., and Jerome S. Legge Jr. 2000. "U.S. Local Government Managers and the Complexity of Responsibility and Accountability in Democratic Governance." *Journal of Public Administration Research and Theory* 1: 73–88.

Dunn, William N. 2002. "A Pragmatic Strategy for Discovering and Testing Threats to the Validity of Sociotechnical Experiments." *Simulation Modelling Practice and Theory* 10: 169–194.

———. 1988. "Methods of the Second Type: Coping with the Wilderness of Conventional Policy Analysis." *Policy Studies Review* 7, no. 4: 720–737.

———. 1982. "Reforms as Arguments." *Knowledge: Creation, Diffusion, Utilization* 3, no. 3: 293–326.

Durant, Robert. 2004. "Reconceptualizing Purpose." In *Environmental Governance Reconsidered: Challenges, Choices, and Opportunities*, ed. Robert Durant, Daniel J. Fiorino, and Rosemary O'Leary. Cambridge, MA: MIT Press.

———. 1992. *The Administrative Presidency Revisited: Public Lands, the BLM, and the Reagan Revolution*. Albany: SUNY Press.

Durant, Robert F., and Jerome S. Legge Jr. 2006. "'Wicked Problems,' Public Policy, and Administrative Theory: Lessons from the GM Food Regulatory Arena." *Administration & Society* 38, no. 3: 309–334.

Durkheim, Emile. 1983. *Pragmatism and Sociology*. Cambridge, UK: Cambridge University Press.

Dutton, Jane E., and Janet M. Dukerich. 1991. "Keeping an Eye on the Mirror: Image and Identity in Organizational Adaptation." *Academy of Management Journal* 34, no. 3: 517–554.

Eames, S. Morris. 1961. "The Cognitive and the Non-Cognitive in Dewey's Theory of Valuation." *Journal of Philosophy* 58, no. 7: 179–195.

Ebrahim, Alnoor. 2004. "Institutional Preconditions to Collaboration: Indian Forest and Irrigation Policy in Historical Perspective." *Administration & Society* 36, no. 2: 208–242.

Echebarria, Carmen, Jose M. Barrutia, and Itziar Aguado. 2008. "The ISC Framework: Modelling Drivers for the Degree of Local Agenda 21 Implantation in Western Europe." *Environment and Planning A* 41, no. 4: 980–995.

———. 2004. "Local Agenda 21: Progress in Spain." *European Urban and Regional Studies* 11, no. 3: 273–281.

Eckholm, Erik. 2009. "Florida Shifts Child-Welfare System's Focus to Saving Families." *New York Times*, July 25, 2009, A12.

———. 2008. "Florida Steps in Early, and Troubled Teenagers Respond." *New York Times*, December 5, 2008, A22.

Edelenbos, Jurian. 2005. "Institutional Implications of Interactive Governance: Insights from Dutch Practice." *Governance: An International Journal of Policy, Administration, and Institutions* 18, no. 1: 111–134.

El Ansari, Walid. 2003. "Educational Partnerships for Public Health: Do Stakeholders Perceive Similar Outcomes?" *Journal of Public Health Management and Practice* 9: 136–156.

Eldridge, Michael. 1998. *Transforming Experience: John Dewey's Cultural Instrumentalism*. Nashville, TN: Vanderbilt University Press.

Elias, Norbert. 1982. *Power and Civility*. New York: Pantheon Books.

Elkjaer, Bente. 2004. "Organizational Learning: The 'Third Way.'" *Management Learning* 35, no. 4: 419–434.

Elliott, Michael, and Sandra Kaufman. 2003. "Building Civic Capacity to Resolve Environmental Conflicts." *Environmental Practice* 5: 265–272.

Elliot, W. Y. 1928. *The Pragmatic Revolt in Politics: Syndicalism, Fascism, and the Constitutional State*. New York: Macmillan.

Emerson, Richard M. 1962. "Power-Dependence Relations." *American Sociological Review* 27, no. 1: 31–41.

Emery, F. E., and E. L. Trist. 1972. *Towards a Social Ecology: Contextual Appreciation of the Future in the Present*. London: Plenum Press.

Emirbayer, Mustapha. 1997. "Manifesto for a Relational Sociology." *American Journal of Sociology* 103, no. 2:281–317.

Emison, Gerald Andrews. 2004. "Pragmatism, Adaptation, and Total Quality Management: Philosophy and Science in the Service of Managing Continuous Improvement." *Journal of Management in Engineering* 20, no. 2: 56–61.

Englund, Tomas. 2006. "Deliberative Communication: A Pragmatist Proposal." *Journal of Curriculum Studies* 38, no. 5: 503–520.

Etzioni, Amitai. 1968. *The Active Society: A Theory of Societal and Political Processes*. New York: Free Press.

European Commission. 2007. "Progress Report on the European Union Sustainable Development Strategy, Commission Staff Working Document." Commission Document 1416. Luxembourg: Office for Official Publications of the European Communities.

Evans, Bob, and Kate Thebald. 2003. "Policy and Practice LASALA: Evaluating Local Agenda 21 in Europe." *Journal of Environmental Planning and Management* 46, no. 5: 781–794.

Evans, Bob, Marko Joas, Susan Sundback, and Kate Theobald. 2006. "Governing Local Sustainability." *Journal of Environmental Planning and Management* 49, no. 6: 849–867.

Evans, Karen G. 2005. "Upgrade or a Different Animal Altogether? Why Old Pragmatism Better Informs Public Management and New Pragmatism Misses the Point." *Administration & Society* 37, no. 2: 248–255.

Evans, Peter. 1995. *Embedded Autonomy: States and Industrial Transformation*. Princeton, NJ: Princeton University Press.

Eylon, Dafna. 1998. "Understanding Empowerment and Resolving Its Paradox: Lessons from Mary Parker Follett." *Journal of Management History* 4, no. 1: 16–28.

Fabbrini, Sergio. 2007. *Compound Democracies: Why the United States and Europe Are Becoming Similar*. Oxford: Oxford University Press.

Feichtinger, Judith, and Michael Pregernig. 2005. "Imagined Citizens and Participation: Local Agenda 21 in Two Communities in Sweden and Austria." *Local Environment* 10, no. 3: 229–242.

Fernandes, Ronald, and Herbert A. Simon. 1999. "A Study of How Individuals Solve Complex and Ill-Structured Problems." *Policy Sciences* 32: 225–245.

Fernandez, Manuel, Rupert Wegerif, Neil Mercer, and Sylvia Rojas-Drummond. 2001. "Re-Conceptualizing 'Scaffolding' and the Zone of Proximal Development in the Context of Symmetrical Collaborative Learning." *Journal of Classroom Teaching* 36, no. 2: 40–54.

Feshmire, Steven. 2003. *John Dewey and Moral Imagination*. Bloomington: Indiana University Press.

Festenstein, Matthew. 2004. "Deliberative Democracy and Two Models of Pragmatism." *European Journal of Social Theory* 7, no. 3: 291–306.

———. 2001. "Inquiry as Critique: on the Legacy of Deweyian Pragmatism for Political Theory." *Political Studies* 49: 730–748.

———. 1997. *Pragmatism and Political Theory: From Dewey to Rorty*. Chicago: University of Chicago Press.

Fidélis, Teresa, and Sara Moreno Pires. 2009. "Surrender or Resistance to the Implementation of Local Agenda 21 in Portugal: The Challenges of Local Governance for Sustainable Development." *Journal of Environmental Planning and Management* 52, no. 4: 497–518.

Fine, Gary Alan. 2006. "The Chaining of Social Problems: Solutions and Unintended Consequences in the Age of Betrayal." *Social Problems* 53, no. 1: 3–17.

———. 1996. *Kitchens: The Culture of Restaurant Work*. Berkeley: University of California Press.

———. 1984. "Negotiated Orders and Organizational Cultures." *Annual Review of Sociology* 10: 239–262.

Firman, John R. 2003. "Deconstructing Compstat to Clarify Its Intent." *Criminology and Public Policy* 2, no. 3: 457–460.

Fiske, Susan T. 1993. "Social Cognition and Social Perception." *Annual Review of Psychology* 44: 155–194.

———. 1992. "Thinking Is for Doing: Portraits of Social Cognition from Daguerreotype to Laserphoto." *Journal of Personality and Social Psychology* 63, no. 6: 877–889.

Fligstein, Neil. 1997. "Social Skill and Institutional Theory." *American Behavioral Scientist* 40, no. 4: 397–405.

Flyvbjerg, Bent. 2001. *Making Social Science Matter: Why Social Inquiry Fails and How It Can Succeed Again*. Cambridge, UK: Cambridge University Press.

Follett, Mary Parker. 1998. *The New State: Group Organization the Solution of Popular Governance*. State College, PA: Penn State Press.

———. 1941. *Dynamic Administration: The Collected Papers of Mary Parker Follett*. New York: Harper.

———. 1924. *Creative Experience*. New York: Longmans, Green.

———. 1919. "Community Is a Process." *Philosophical Review* 28: 576–588.

Forester, John. 1999. *The Deliberative Practitioner: Encouraging Participatory Planning Processes.* Cambridge, MA: MIT Press.

———. 1993. *Critical Theory, Public Policy, and Planning Practice: Toward a Critical Pragmatism.* Albany: SUNY Press.

Foresti, Tiziana. 2004. "Between Darwin and Kant: Veblen's Theory of Causality." *Review of Sociology* 14, no. 3: 399–411.

Fowler, Sally W., Adelaide Wilcox King, Sarah J. Marsh, and Bart Victor. 2000. "Beyond Products: New Strategic Imperatives for Developing Competencies in Dynamic Environments." *Journal of Engineering and Technology Management* 17: 357–377.

Fox, Emily, and Michelle Riconscente. 2008. "Metacognition and Self-Regulation in James, Piaget, and Vygotsky." *Educational Psychology Review* 20: 373–389.

Frame, Tanis M., Thomas Gunton, and J. C. Day. 2004. "The Role of Collaboration in Environmental Management: An Evaluation of Land and Resource Planning in British Columbia." *Journal of Environmental Planning and Management* 47, no. 1: 59–82.

Frawley, William. 1997. *Vygotsky and Cognitive Science: Language and the Unification of the Social and Computational Mind.* Cambridge, MA: Harvard University Press.

Freeman, Claire. 1996. "Local Government and Emerging Models of Participation in the Local Agenda 21 Process." *Journal of Environmental Planning and Management* 39, no. 1: 65–78.

Freeman, Jody. 1997. Collaborative Governance in the Administrative State. *UCLA Law Review* 45, no.1: 1–98.

Freeman, Jody, and Laura I. Langbein. 2000. "Regulatory Negotiation and the Legitimacy Benefit." *N.Y.U. Environmental Law Journal* 9: 61–151.

French, John R. P., and Bertram Raven. 1959. "Bases of Social Power." In *Studies in Social Power,* ed. Dorwin Cartwright. Ann Arbor: University of Michigan Press.

Friedman, Raymond. 1995. *Front Stage, Backstage: The Dramatic Structure of Labor Negotiations.* Cambridge, MA: MIT Press.

Fung, Archon. 2007. "Democratic Theory and Political Science: A Pragmatic Method of Constructive Engagement." *American Political Science Review* 101, no. 3: 443–458.

———. 2004. *Empowered Participation: Reinventing Urban Democracy.* Princeton, NJ: Princeton University Press.

———. 2002. "Creating Deliberative Publics: Governance after Devolution and Democratic Centralism." *Good Society* 11, no. 1: 66–71.

———. 2001. "Accountable Autonomy: Toward Empowered Deliberation in Chicago Schools and Policing." *Politics & Society* 29, no. 1: 73–103.

Fung, Archon, Erik Olin Wright, and Rebecca Abers. 2003. *Deepening Democracy: Institutional Innovations in Empowered Participatory Governance.* London: Verso.

Futrell, Robert. 2003. "Technical Adversarialism and Participatory Collaboration in the U.S. Chemical Weapons Disposal Program." *Science, Technology, & Human Values* 28, no. 4: 451–482.

Gabora, Liane, Eleanor Rosch, and Diederik Aerts. 2008. "Toward an Ecological Theory of Concepts." *Ecological Psychology* 20: 84–116.

Garfinkel, Harold. 1967. *Studies in Ethnomethodology.* Englewood Cliffs, NJ: Prentice-Hall.

Garrison, Jim. 2001. "An Introduction to Dewey's Theory of Functional 'Transaction': An Alternative for Activity Theory." *Mind, Culture, and Activity* 8, no. 4: 275–296.

———. 2000. "Pragmatism & Public Administration." *Administration & Society* 32, no. 4: 458–477.

———. 1999. "John Dewey's Theory of Practical Reasoning." *Educational Philosophy and Theory* 31, no. 3: 291–312.

———. 1995. "Deweyan Pragmatism and the Epistemology of Contemporary Social Constructivism." *American Educational Research Journal* 32, no. 4: 716–740.

Geissel, Brigitte. 2009. "Participatory Governance: Hope or Danger for Democracy? A Case Study of Local Agenda 21." *Local Government Studies* 35, no. 4: 401–414.

George, Clive, and Colin Kirkpatrick. 2006. "Assessing National Sustainable Development Strategies: Strengthening the Links to Operational Policy." *National Resources Forum* 30: 146–156.

Gerson, Elihu M. 2009. "Specialty Boundaries, Compound Problems, and Collaborative Complexity." *Biological Theory* 4, no. 3: 247–252.

Gerth, Hans, and C. Wright Mills. 1953. *Character and Social Structure: The Psychology of Social Institutions*. New York: Harcourt, Brace, & World.

Gibbs, D. C., J. Longhurst, and C. Braithwaite. 1998. "'Struggling with Sustainability': Weak and Strong Interpretations of Sustainable Development with Local Authority Policy." *Environment and Planning A* 30, no. 8: 1351–1365.

Gibson, J. J. 1977. "The Theory of Affordances." In *Perceiving, Acting, and Knowing*, ed. R. E. Shaw and J. Bransford. Hillsdale, NJ: Lawrence Erlbaum Associates.

Giddens, Anthony. 1984 *The Constitution of Society: Outline of the Theory of Structuration*. Cambridge, UK: Polity Press.

———. 1979. *Central Problems in Social Theory: Action, Structure, and Contradiction in Social Analysis*. Berkeley: University of California Press.

Gilliam, Aisha, David Davis, Tracey Barrington, Romel Lacson, Gary Uhl, and Ursula Phoenix. 2002. "The Value of Engaging Stakeholders in Planning and Implementing Evaluations." *AIDS Education and Prevention* 14, supp. A: 5–17.

Glasbergen, Pieter, and Peter P. J. Driessen. 2005. "Interactive Planning of Infrastructure: The Changing Role of Dutch Project Management." *Environment and Planning C: Government and Policy* 23: 263–277.

Goffman, Erving. 1969. *Strategic Interaction*. Philadelphia: University of Philadelphia Press.

Goldstein, Herman. 1990. *Problem-Oriented Policing*. New York: McGraw-Hill.

Good, James M. M. 2007. "The Affordances for Social Psychology of the Ecological Approach to Knowing." *Theory & Psychology* 17, no. 2: 265–295.

Goode, Erich, and Nachman Ben-Yehuda. 1994. "Moral Panics: Culture, Politics, and Social Construction." *Annual Review of Sociology* 20: 149–171.

Goodin, Robert E., and John S. Dryzek. 2006. "Deliberative Impacts: The Macro-Political Uptake of Mini-Publics." *Politics & Society* 34, no. 2: 219–244.

Goodland, Robert. 1995. "The Concept of Environmental Sustainability." *Annual Review of Ecology, Evolution and Systematics* 26: 1–24.

Goodsell, Charles. 1985. *The Case for Bureaucracy*. Chatham, NJ: Chatham House.

Gormley, William T. 1986. "Regulatory Issue Networks in a Federal System." *Polity* 18, no. 4: 595–620.

Gouldner, Alvin. 1955a. *Patterns of Industrial Bureaucracy*. London: Routledge and Kegan Paul.

———. 1955b. "Metaphysical Pathos and the Theory of Bureaucracy." *American Political Science Review* 49, no. 2: 496–507.

Granovetter, Mark. 1985. "Economic Action and Social Structure: The Problem of Embeddedness." *American Journal of Sociology* 91, no. 3: 481–510.

Gray, Barbara. 1989. *Collaborating: Finding Common Ground for Multiparty Problems*. San Francisco: Jossey Bass.

Greenstone, David J. 1993. *The Lincoln Persuasion: Remaking American Liberalism*. Princeton, NJ: Princeton University Press.

Greif, Avner, and David D. Laitin. 2004. "A Theory of Endogenous Institutional Change." *American Political Science Review* 98, no. 4: 633–652.

Gunnell, John G. 1996. "The Genealogy of American Pluralism: From Madison to Behavioralism." *International Political Science Review* 17, no. 3: 253–265.

Gunton, Thomas I., and J. C. Day. 2003. "The Theory and Practice of Collaborative Planning in Resource and Environmental Management." *Environments* 31, no. 2: 5–19.

Gusfield, Joseph R. 1989. "Constructing the Ownership of Social Problems: Fun and Profit in the Welfare State." *Social Problems* 36, no. 5: 431–441.

———. 1984. *The Culture of Public Problems: Drinking-Driving and Symbolic Order.* Chicago: University of Chicago Press.

Guthman, Julie. 1998. "Regulating Meaning, Appropriating Nature: The Codification of California Organic Agriculture." *Antipode* 30, no. 3: 135–154.

Haack, Susan. 2005. "On Legal Pragmatism: Where Does 'The Path of the Law' Lead Us?" *American Journal of Jurisprudence* 50: 71–105.

Haas, Peter. 2004. "When Does Power Listen to Truth? A Constructivist Approach to the Policy Process." *Journal of European Public Policy* 11, no. 4: 569–592.

Hagedorn, John M. 1996. *Forsaking Our Children: Bureaucracy and Reform in the Child Welfare System.* Chicago: Lake View Press.

Hall, John, and Oliver Whybrow. 2008. "Continuity and Continuousness: The Chain of Ideas Linking Peirce's Synechism to Veblen's Cumulative Causation." *Journal of Economic Issues* 42, no. 2: 349–355.

Hallet, Tim, and Marc Ventresca. 2006. "Inhabited Institutions: Social Interactions and Organizational Forms in Gouldner's *Patterns of Industrial Bureaucracy.*" *Theoretical Sociology* 35: 213–236.

Hamilton, Gary G., and Nicole Woolsey Biggart. 2004. *Governor Reagan, Governor Brown: A Sociology of Executive Power.* New York: Columbia University Press.

Handler, Joel F. 1996. *Down from Bureaucracy: The Ambiguity of Privatization and Empowerment.* Princeton, NJ: Princeton University Press.

———. 1986. *The Conditions of Discretion: Autonomy, Community, and Bureaucracy.* New York: Russell Sage Foundation.

Happaerts, Sander, Karoline Van den Brande, and Hans Bruyninckx. 2010. "Governance for Sustainable Development at the Inter-Subnational Level: The Case of the Network for Regional Governments for Sustainable Development (nrg4SD)." *Regional & Federal Studies* 20, no. 1: 127–149.

Harding, R. 2006. "Ecologically Sustainable Development: Origins, Implementation and Challenges." *Desalination* 187: 229–239.

Hargadon, Andrew, and Beth A. Bechky. 2006. "When Collections of Creatives become Creative Collectives: A Field Study of Problem Solving at Work." *Organization Science* 17, no. 4: 484–500.

Hargrove, Erwin. 1994. *Prisoners of Myth: The Leadership of the Tennessee Valley Authority, 1933–1990.* Princeton, NJ: Princeton University Press.

Harries-Jones, Peter. 1995. *A Recursive Vision: Ecological Understanding and Gregory Bateson.* Toronto: University of Toronto Press.

Harris, David A. 2005. *Good Cops: The Case for Preventive Policing.* New York: New Press.

Hausman, Carl. 2008. "Charles Peirce's Categories and the Growth of Reason." *International Journal for the Semiotics of Law* 21: 209–222.

———. 1997. *Charles S. Peirce's Evolutionary Philosophy.* Cambridge, UK: Cambridge University Press.

Heikkila, Tanya, and Andrea K. Gerlak. 2005. "The Formation of Large-Scale Collaborative Resource Management Institutions: Clarifying the Roles of Stakeholders, Science, and Institutions." *Policy Studies Journal* 33, no, 4: 583–612.

Helmes-Hayes, Richard C. 1998. "Everett Hughes: Theorist of the Second Chicago School." *International Journal of Politics, Culture and Society* 11, no. 4: 621–673.

Henry, Vincent. 2002. *The Compstat Paradigm: Management Accountability in Policing, Business, and the Public Sector.* Flushing, NY: Looseleaf Law Publications.

Hepple, Leslie W. 2008. "Geography and the Pragmatic Tradition: The Threefold Engagement." *Geoforum* 29: 1530–1541.

Herranz, Roberto. 2003. "From Pragmatism to Economic Sociology through the Thought of Charles Horton Cooley (1864–1929)." Fifteenth Annual Meeting of the SASE. *Aix en Provence,* June 26–28, 2003.

Hickman, Larry A. 1990. *John Dewey's Pragmatic Technology*. Bloomington: Indiana University Press.

Hildebrand, David L. 2005. "Pragmatism, Neopragmatism, and Public Administration." *Administration & Society* 37, 3: 345–359.

Hirst, Paul Q. 1994. *Associative Democracy: New Forms of Economic and Social Governance*. Amherst: University of Massachusetts Press.

Hisschemöller, Matthijs, and Joyeeta Gupta. 1999. "Problem-Solving through International Environmental Agreements: The Issue of Regime Effectiveness." *International Political Science Review* 20, no. 2: 151–174.

Hoben, Merrick. 2000. "Clark County Habitat Conservation Planning." In Chrissy Coughlin, Merrick Hoben, Dirk Manskopf, and Shannon Quesada, "A Systematic Assessment of Collaborative Resource Management Partnerships." Master's project completed for the School of Natural Resources and Environment, University of Michigan, Ann Arbor, chap. 7, 1–21.

Hoch, Charles. 2006. "What Can Rorty Teach an Old Pragmatist Doing Public Administration or Planning." *Administration & Society* 38, no. 3: 389–398.

Hoch, Charles J. 2002. "Evaluating Plans Pragmatically." *Planning Theory* 1, no. 1: 53–75.

———. 1984a. "Pragmatism, Planning, and Power." *Journal of Planning Education and Research* 4: 86–95.

———. 1984b. "Doing Good and Being Right: the Pragmatic Connection in Planning Theory." *Journal of the American Planning Association* 50, no. 3: 335–345.

Hodgson, Geoffrey. 2007. "The Revival of Veblenian Institutional Economics." *Journal of Economic Issues* 41, no. 2: 325–340.

———. 2006. "What Are Institutions?" *Journal of Economic Issues* 41, no. 1: 1–25.

———. 2004. "Reclaiming Habit for Institutional Economics." *Journal of Economic Psychology* 25: 651–660.

Hodgson, Geoffrey M., and Thorbjørn Knudsen. 2006. "Dismantling Lamarckism: Why Descriptions of Socio-Economic Evolution as Lamarckian Are Misleading." *Journal of Evolutionary Economics* 16: 343–366.

Hofstadter, Douglas. 1979. *Gödel, Escher, Bach: An Eternal Golden Braid*. New York: Vintage Books.

Holden, Meg. 2008. "Social Learning in Planning: Seattle's Sustainable Development Codebooks." *Progress in Planning* 69: 1–40.

Holling, C. S., Lance H. Gunderson, and Garry D. Peterson. 2002. "Sustainability and Panarchies." In *Panarchy: Understanding Transformation in Human and Natural Systems*, ed. Lance H. Gunderson and C. S. Holling. Washington, DC: Island Press.

Hood, Christopher. 1995. "The 'New Public Management' in the 1980s: Variations on a Theme." *Accounting, Organizations and Society* 20, nos. 2/3: 93–109.

———. 1991. "A Public Management for All Seasons?" *Public Administration* 69: 3–19.

Hood, Christopher, Henry Rothstein, Michael Spackman, Judith Rees, and Robert Baldwin. 1999. "Explaining Risk Regulation Regimes: Exploring the 'Minimal Feasible Response' Hypothesis." *Health, Risk & Society* 1, no. 2: 151–166.

Hood, Jacqueline N., Jeanne M. Logsdon, and Judith Kenner Thompson. 1993. "Collaboration for Social Problem Solving: A Process Model." *Business & Society* 32: 1–17.

Hookway, Christopher. 2000. *Truth, Rationality, and Pragmatism*. Oxford: Clarendon Press.

———. 1985. *Peirce*. London: Routledge & Kegan Paul.

Höpfl, Harro M. 2006. "Post-Bureaucracy and Weber's 'Modern' Bureaucrat." *Journal of Organizational Change Management* 19, no. 1: 8–26.

Huber, John D., and Charles R. Shipan. 2002. *Deliberate Discretion: The Institutional Foundation of Bureaucratic Autonomy*. Cambridge, UK: Cambridge University Press.

Hughes, Everett C. 1993. *The Sociological Eye: Selected Papers*. New Brunswick, NJ: Transaction Press.

Hulswit, Menno. 1996. "Teleology: A Peircean Critique of Ernste Mayr's Theory." *Transactions of the Charles S. Peirce Society* 32, no. 2: 182–214.

Hunter, James. 2001. *The Death of Character: Moral Education in an Age without Good or Evil.* New York: Basic Books.

Hutchins, Edwin. 1995. *Cognition in the Wild.* Cambridge, MA: MIT Press.

Imperial, Mark. 2005. "Using Collaboration as a Governance Strategy: Lessons from Six Watershed Management Programs." *Administration & Society* 37, no. 3: 281–320.

Innes, Judith E. 2004. "Consensus Building: Clarifications for the Critics." *Planning Theory* 3, no. 1: 5–20.

Innes, Judith E., and David E. Booher. 1999. "Consensus Building and Complex Adaptive Systems: A Framework for Evaluating Collaborative Planning." *Journal of the American Planning Association* 65, no. 4: 412–423.

International Council for Local Environmental Initiatives. 2002. Second Local Agenda 21 Survey. Background Paper no. 15. Toronto: International Council for Local Environmental Initiatives, 1–29.

Jacobs, Jane. 1961. *The Death and Life of Great American Cities.* New York: Random House.

James, William. 1907. *Pragmatism and Four Essays from the Meaning of Truth.* Cleveland: Meridian Books.

Joas, Hans. 2000. *The Genesis of Values.* Chicago: University of Chicago Press.

———. 1997. *G. H. Mead. A Contemporary Re-Examination of His Thought.* Cambridge, MA: MIT Press.

———. 1996. *The Creativity of Action.* Chicago: University of Chicago Press.

———. 1993. *Pragmatism and Social Theory.* Chicago: University of Chicago Press.

Joerges, Christian, and Christine Godt. 2005. "Free Trade: The Erosion of National, and the Birth of Transnational Governance." *European Review* 13, supp. 1: 93–117.

Johnson, Mark. 2006. "Mind Incarnate: From Dewey to Damasio." *Daedalus* (Summer): 46–54.

Johnston, James Scott. 2006. *Inquiry and Education: John Dewey and the Quest for Democracy.* Albany: SUNY Press.

Jörby, Sofie Adolfsson. 2002. "Local Agenda 21 in Four Swedish Municipalities: A Tool toward Sustainability?" *Journal of Environmental Planning and Management* 45, no. 2: 219–244.

Jordan, Andrew. 2008. "The Governance of Sustainable Development: Taking Stock and Looking Forwards." *Environment and Planning C: Government and Policy* 26: 17–33.

Jordan, John. 1994. *Machine-Age Ideology: Social Engineering and American Liberalism, 1911–1939.* Chapel Hill: University of North Carolina Press.

Jowitt, Ken. 1993. *New World Disorder: The Leninist Extinction.* Berkeley: University of California Press.

Kagan, Robert. 2003. *Adversarial Legalism: The American Way of Law.* Cambridge, MA: Harvard University Press.

Kallinkos, Jannis. 2004. "The Social Foundations of the Bureaucratic Order." *Organization* 11, no. 1: 13–56.

Kanter, Rosabeth Moss. 1985. *The Change Masters: Corporate Entrepreneurs at Work.* London: Taylor and Francis.

Karmen, Andrew. 2000. *New York Murder Mystery: The True Story behind the Crime Crash of the 1990s.* New York: NYU Press.

Kates, Robert W., Thomas M. Parris, and Anthony A. Leiserowitz. 2005. "What Is Sustainable Development? Goals, Indicators, Values, and Practice." *Environment: Science and Policy for Sustainable Development* 47, no. 3: 8–21.

Kaufman, Herbert. 1967. *The Forest Ranger: A Study in Administrative Behavior.* Washington, DC: Resources for the Future.

Kaufman-Osborne, Timothy V. 1985. "Pragmatism, Policy Science, and the State." *American Journal of Political Science* 29, no. 4: 827–849.

Keiner, Marco, and Arley Kim. 2007. "Transnational City Networks for Urban Sustainability." *European Planning Studies* 15, no. 10: 1369–1395.

Kelman, Herbert C. 1996. "Negotiation as Interactive Problem-Solving." *International Negotiation* 1: 99–123.

Kelman, Steven. 1992. "Adversary and Cooperationists Institutions for Conflict Resolution in Public Policymaking." *Journal of Policy Analysis and Management* 11, no. 2: 178–206.

Kemp, René, and Saeed Parto. 2005. "Governance for Sustainable Development: Moving from Theory to Practice." *International Journal of Sustainable Development* 8, nos. 1/2: 12–30.

Kern, Kristine, Claudia Koll, and Malte Schophaus. 2007. "The Diffusion of Local Agenda 21 in Germany: Comparing the German Federal States." *Environmental Politics* 16, no. 4: 604–624.

Kern, Kristine, and Tina Lofflesend. 2004. "Sustainable Development in the Baltic Sea Region: Governance beyond the Nation State." *Local Environment* 9, no. 5: 451–467.

Kerr, Gerry. 2007. "The Development History and Philosophical Sources of Herbert Simon's *Administrative Behavior*." *Journal of Management History* 13, no. 3: 255–268.

Kersch, Rogan, and James Morone. 2002. "How the Personal becomes Political: Prohibitions, Public Health, and Obesity." *Studies in American Political Development* 16: 162–175.

Kessler, C. A. 2008. "Laying a Solid Foundation for Sustainable Development in Bolivian Mountain Villages." *Environment, Development and Sustainability* 10: 233–247.

Kettl, Donald. 2005. "The Next Government of the United States: Challenges in the 21st Century." IBM Center for the Business of Government Report, Transformation of Organization Series, 1–43.

———. 1997. "The Global Revolution in Public Management: Driving Themes, Missing Links." *Journal of Policy Analysis and Management* 16, no. 3, special issue: 446–462.

———. 1993. *Sharing Power: Public Governance and Private Markets.* Washington, DC: Brookings Institution Press.

Kevelson, Roberta. 1990. *Peirce, Praxis, Paradox: The Image, the Conflict, and the Law.* Berlin: Mouton de Gruyter.

———. 1988. *The Law as a System of Signs.* New York: Plenum Press.

Khakee, Abdul. 2002. "Assessing Institutional Capital Building in a Local Agenda 21 Process in Göteborg." *Planning Theory & Practice* 3, no. 1: 53–68.

Kidd, Charles V. 1992. "The Evolution of Sustainability." *Journal of Agricultural and Environmental Ethics* 5, no. 1: 1–26.

Kidder, Tracy. 2009. *Mountains beyond Mountains: The Quest of Dr. Paul Farmer, a Man Who Would Cure the World.* New York: Random House.

Kilpinen, Erkki. 2004. "How to Fight the 'Methodenstreit'? Veblen and Weber on Economics, Psychology and Action." *International Review of Sociology* 14, no. 3: 413–432.

———. 2003. "Claude Ayres Memorial Lecture: Does Pragmatism Imply Institutionalism?" *Journal of Economic Issues* 37, no. 2: 291–304.

Kivinen, Osmo, and Pekka Ristelä. 2003. "From Constructivism to a Pragmatist Conception of Learning." *Oxford Review of Education* 29, no. 3: 363–375.

Klein, Gary. 1999. *Sources of Power: How People Make Decisions.* Cambridge, MA: MIT Press.

Kloppenberg, James. 1986. *Uncertain Victory: Social Democracy and Progressivism in European and American Thought, 1870–1920.* New York: Oxford University Press.

Knight, Jack, and James Johnson. 2007. "The Priority of Democracy: A Pragmatist Approach to Political-Economic Institutions and the Burden of Justification." *American Political Science Review* 101, no. 1: 47–61.

———. 1999. "Inquiry into Democracy: What Might a Pragmatist Make of Rational Choice Theories?" *American Journal of Political Science* 43, no. 2: 566–589.

———. 1996. "Consequences of Pragmatism." *Political Theory* 24, no. 1: 68–96.

Knorr-Cetina, Karin. 1981. *The Manufacture of Knowledge: An Essay on the Constructivist and Contextual Nature of Science.* Oxford: Pergamon Press.

Koestler, Arthur. 1967. *The Ghost in the Machine.* Chicago: Henry Regnery.

Kontopolous, K. 1993. *The Logic of Social Structure*. New York: Cambridge University Press.

Kooiman, Jan. 2003. *Governing as Governance*. London: Sage Publications.

Koopman, Colin. 2006. "Pragmatism as a Philosophy of Hope: Emerson, James, Dewey, Rorty." *Journal of Speculative Philosophy* 20, no. 2: 106–116.

Kosslyn, Stephen M. 1994. *Image and Brain: The Resolution of the Imagery Debate*. Cambridge, MA: MIT Press.

Kray, Laura J. Leigh Thompson, and E. Allan Lind. 2005. "It's a Bet! A Problem-Solving Approach Promotes the Construction of Contingent Agreements." *Personality and Social Psychology Bulletin* 31, no. 8: 1039–1051.

Lach, Denise, Steve Rayner, and Helen Ingram. 2005. "Taming the Waters: Strategies to Domesticate Wicked Problems of Water Resource Management." *International Journal of Water* 3, no. 1: 1–17.

Lafferty, William M. 1999. "Introduction: The Pursuit of Sustainable Development— Concepts, Policies and Arenas." *International Political Science Review* 20, no. 2: 123–128.

Lagarde, Maria Lourdes M. 2006. "Mainstreaming Sustainable Development: Evolving Perspectives and Challenges from the Philippine Experience." *Natural Resources Forum* 30: 111–123.

Landau, Martin, and Russell Stout Jr. 1979. "To Manage Is Not to Control: Or the Folly of Type II Errors." *Public Administration Review* 39, no. 2: 148–156.

Lane, David, and Robert Maxfield. 1996. "Strategy under Complexity: Fostering Generative Relationships." *Long Range Planning* 29: 215–231.

Lanzara, Giovan Francesco, and Gerardo Patriotta. 2007. "The Institutionalization of Knowledge in an Automotive Factory: Templates, Inscriptions, and the Problem of Durability." *Organization Studies* 28, no. 5: 635–660.

Lasker, Roy D., and Elisa S. Weiss. 2003. "Broadening Participation in Community Problem Solving: A Multidisciplinary Model to Support Collaborative Practice and Research." *Journal of Urban Health: Bulletin of the New York Academy of Medicine* 80, no. 1: 14–57.

Laski, Harold. 1917. *Studies in the Problem of Sovereignty*. New Haven, CT: Yale University Press.

Lave, Jean, and Etienne Wenger. 1991. *Situated Learning: Legitimate Peripheral Participation*. Cambridge, UK: Cambridge University Press.

Lawlor, Michael S. 2006. "William James's Psychological Pragmatism: Habit, Belief, and Purposive Human Behavior." *Cambridge Journal of Economics* 30: 321–345.

Lawrence, David. 2000. "Planning Theories and Environmental Impact Assessment." *Environmental Impact Assessment Review* 20: 607–625.

Leach, William D., and Paul A. Sabatier. 2005. "To Trust an Adversary: Integrating Rational and Psychological Models of Collaborative Policymaking." *American Political Science Review* 99, no. 4: 491–503.

Lee, Caroline. 2007. "Is There a Place for Private Conversation in Public Dialogue? Comparing Stakeholder Assessments of Informal Communication in Collaborative Regional Planning." *American Journal of Sociology* 113, no. 1: 41–96.

Lei, David, Michael A. Hitt, and Richard Bettis. 1996. "Dynamic Core Competencies through Meta-Learning and Strategic Context." *Journal of Management* 22, no. 4: 549–569.

Leifer, Eric. 1995. *Making the Majors: The Transformation of Team Sports in America*. Cambridge, MA: Harvard University Press.

———. 1991. *Actors as Observers: A Theory of Skill in Social Relationships*. New York: Garland.

Leifer, Eric, and Valli Rajah. 2000. "Getting Observations: Strategic Ambiguities in Social Interaction." *Soziale Systeme* 6: 251–267.

Levitt, Barbara, and James G. March. 1988. "Organizational Learning." *Annual Review of Sociology* 14: 319–340.

Levy, Yoram, and Marcel Wissenburg. 2004. "Sustainable Development as a Policy Telos: A New Approach to Political Problem-Solving." *Political Studies* 52: 785–801.

Lewis, Herbert S. 2001. "Boas, Darwin, Science, and Anthropology." *Current Anthropology* 42, no. 3: 381–406.

Liebhafsky, E. E. 1993. "The Influence of Charles Sanders Peirce on Institutional Economics." *Journal of Economic Issues* 27, no. 3: 741–754.

Lijphart, Arend. 1999. *Patterns of Democracy: Government Forms and Performance in Thirty-Six Countries.* New Haven, CT: Yale University Press.

Likert, Rensis. 1967. *The Human Organization: Its Management and Value.* New York: McGraw-Hill.

Lindblom, Charles. 1959. "The Science of Muddling Through." *Public Administration Review* 19, no. 2: 79–88.

Lindblom, Charles, and David K. Cohen. 1979. *Usable Knowledge: Social Science and Social Problem-Solving.* New Haven, CT: Yale University Press.

Linder, Stephen. 1995. "Contending Discourses in the Electric and Magnetic Fields Controversy: The Social Construction of EMF Risk as a Public Problem." *Policy Sciences* 28: 209–230.

Linder, Stephen, and B. Guy Peters. 1995. "The Two Traditions of Institutional Designing: Dialogue versus Decision?" In *Institutional Design,* ed. D. Weimer. Norwell, MA: Kluwer Publishers.

Logsdon, Jeanne. 1991. "Interests and Interdependence in the Formation of Social Problem-Solving Collaborations." *Journal of Applied Behavioral Science* 27: 23–37.

Lowi, T. J. 1969. *The End of Liberalism: Ideology, Policy, and the Crisis of Authority.* New York: Norton.

Lubell, Mark. 2004. "Collaborative Environmental Institutions: All Talk and No Action?" *Journal of Policy Analysis and Management* 23, no. 3: 549–573.

Luckenbill, David F. 1979. "Power: A Conceptual Framework." *Symbolic Interaction* 2, no. 2: 97–114.

Lundqvist, Lennart J. 2004. "'Greening the People's Home': The Formative Power of Sustainable Development Discourse in Swedish Housing." *Urban Studies* 41, no. 7: 1283–1301.

Lustig, R. J. 1982. *Corporate Liberalism: The Origins of Modern American Political Theory, 1890–1920.* Berkeley: University of California Press.

Lynn, Laurence E., Jr. 2001. "The Myth of the Bureaucratic Paradigm: What Traditional Public Administration Really Stood For." *Public Administration Review* 61, no. 2: 141–160.

MacGilvray, Eric A. 2000. "Five Myths about Pragmatism: Or, Against a Second Pragmatic Acquiescence." *Political Theory* 28, no. 4: 480–508.

———. 1999. "Experience as Experiment: Some Consequences of Pragmatism for Democratic Theory." *American Journal of Political Science* 43, no. 2: 542–565.

MacKinnon, Malcolm H. 2001. "Max Weber's Disenchantment: The Lineages of Kant and Channing." *Journal of Classical Sociology* 1, no. 3: 329–351.

Mackinnon, Neil. 1994. *Symbolic Interactionism as Affect Control.* Albany: SUNY Press.

Macnaghten, Phil, and Michael Jacobs. 1997. "Public Identification with Sustainable Development: Investigating Barriers to Participation." *Global Environmental Change* 7, no. 1: 5–24.

Maines, David. 2001. *The Faultlines of Consciousness: A View of Interactionism in Sociology.* New York: Aldine de Gruyter.

Majone, Giandomenico. 1989. *Evidence, Argument, and Persuasion in the Policy Process.* New Haven, CT: Yale University Press.

Mannheim, Karl. 1940. *Man and Society in an Age of Reconstruction.* London: Routledge & Kegan Paul.

Manning, Philip. 1992. *Erving Goffman and Modern Sociology.* Stanford, CA: Stanford University Press.

Manning, Peter K. 2005. "Problem-Solving?" *Criminology & Public Policy* 4, no. 2: 149–154.

———. 1988. *Symbolic Communication: Signifying Calls and the Police Response.* Cambridge, MA: MIT Press.

Maple, Jack. 1999. *Crime Fighter: Putting the Bad Guy Out of Business.* New York: Doubleday.

Maravelias, Christian. 2003. "Post-Bureaucracy—Control through Professional Freedom." *Journal of Organizational Change Management* 16, no. 5: 547–566.

Marcell, David W. 1974. *Progress and Pragmatism: James, Dewey, Beard, and the American Idea of Progress.* Westport, CT: Greenwood Press.

March, James G. 1991. "Exploration and Exploitation in Organizational Learning." *Organization Science* 2, no. 1: 71–87.

March, James, and Johan Olsen. 1995. *Democratic Governance.* New York: Free Press.

March, James, and Herbert Simon. 1958. *Organizations.* New York: John Wiley & Sons.

Marengo, Luigi, and Giovanni Dosi. 2005. "Division of Labor, Organizational Coordination and Market Mechanisms in Collective Problem Solving." *Journal of Economic Behavior & Organization* 58: 303–326.

Marengo, Luigi, Giovani Dosi, Paolo Legrenzi, and Corrado Pasquali. 2000. "The Structure of Problem-Solving and the Structure of Organizations." *Industrial and Corporate Change* 9, no. 4: 757–788.

Margerum, Richard D. 2002. "Collaborative Planning: Building Consensus and Building a Distinct Model for Practice." *Journal of Planning Education and Research* 21: 237–253.

———. 2001. "Organizational Commitment to Integrated and Collaborative Management: Matching Strategies to Constraints." *Environmental Management* 28: 421–431.

Marres, Noortje. 2007. "The Issues Deserve More Credit: Pragmatist Contributions to the Study of Public Involvement in Controversy." *Social Studies of Science* 37, no. 5: 759–780.

Mathur, Gita. 2007. "Problem-Solving Interdependence in Technological Innovation: An Examination of Interorganisational Interaction in Semiconductor Component Development." *International Journal of Intelligent Enterprise* 1, no. 1: 98–113.

Matthews, David. 2006. "Pragmatism Meets Systems Thinking: The Legacy of C. West Churchman." In *Rescuing the Enlightenment from Itself: Critical and Systemic Implications for Democracy,* ed. Janet McIntyre Mills. Vol. 1. New York: Spring Science + Business Media, chap. 10, 165–121.

Matthews, Fred H. 1977. *Quest for an American Sociology: Robert E. Park and the Chicago School.* Montreal: McGill–Queen's University Press.

Mattson, Kevin. 1998. "Introduction." In *Mary Parker Follett, The New State: Group Organization and the Solution of Popular Government.* State College, PA: Penn State Press.

Mayer, Brian, Phil Brown, and Meadow Linder. 2002. "Moving Further Upstream: From Toxics Reduction to the Precautionary Principle." *Public Health Reports* 117: 574–586.

McAlpine, Patrick, and Andrew Birnie. 2005. "Is There a Correct Way of Establishing Sustainability Indicators? The Case of Sustainability Indicator Development on the Island of Guernsey." *Local Environment* 10, no. 3: 243–257.

McCann, Joseph. 1983. "Design Guidelines for Social Problem-Solving Interventions." *Journal of Applied Behavioral Science* 19, no. 2: 177–192.

McCool, Stephen, and Kathleen Guthrie. 2001. "Mapping the Dimensions of Successful Public Participation in Messy Natural Resources Management Situations." *Society and Natural Resources* 14: 309–323.

McDonald, Hugh P. 2004. *John Dewey and Environmental Philosophy.* Albany: SUNY Press.

McDonald, Phyllis. 2002. *Managing Police Operations: Implementing the New York Crime Control Model—Compstat.* Belmont, CA: Wadsworth Group.

McGowan, John. 2008. "The Possibility of Progress: A Pragmatist Account." *Good Society* 17, no. 1: 33–42.

McNary, Lisa, and Howard Gitlow. 2002. "Creating Integrative Solutions in Conflict Episodes." *Quality Engineering* 14, no. 4: 579–586.

McSweeney, Brendan. 2006. "Are We Living in a Post-Bureaucratic Epoch?" *Journal of Organizational Change Management* 19, no. 1: 22–37.

McSwite. O. C. 1997. *Legitimacy in Public Administration: A Discourse Analysis.* Thousand Oaks, CA: Sage Publications.

Mead, George Herbert. 1962. *Mind, Self, and Society.* Chicago: University of Chicago.

Meadowcroft, James. 2007. "National Sustainable Development Strategies: Features, Challenges and Reflexivity." *European Environment* 17: 152–163.

———. 2004. "Deliberative Democracy." In *Environmental Governance Reconsidered: Challenges, Choices, and Opportunities,* ed. Robert Durant, Daniel J. Fiorino, and Rosemary O'Leary. Cambridge, MA: MIT Press.

Mebratu, Desta. 1998. "Sustainability and Sustainable Development: Historical and Conceptual Review." *Environmental Impact Assessment Review* 18: 493–520.

Menand, Louis. 2001. *The Metaphysical Club.* New York: Farrar, Straus, and Giroux.

Mercer, David, and Benjamin Jotkowitz. 2000. "Local Agenda 21 and Barriers to Sustainability at the Local Government Level in Victoria, Australia." *Australian Geographer* 31, no. 2: 163–181.

Meyer, John, John Boli, George M. Thomas, and Francisco O. Ramirez. 1997. "World Society and the Nation-State." *American Journal of Sociology* 103, no. 1: 144–181.

Miettinen, Reijo. 2001. "Artifact Mediation in Dewey and in Cultural-Historical Activity Theory." *Mind, Culture, and Activity* 8, no. 4: 297–208.

Miettinen, Reijo, and Jaakko Virkkunen. 2005. "Epistemic Objects, Artefacts and Organizational Change." *Organization* 12, no. 3: 437–456.

Miller, Hugh. 2005. "Residues of Foundationalism in Classic Pragmatism." *Administration & Society* 37, no. 3: 360–374.

———. 2004. "Why Old Pragmatism Needs an Upgrade." *Administration & Society* 36, no. 2: 243–249.

Miller, Kent D. 2008. "Simon and Polanyi on Rationality and Knowledge." *Organization Studies* 29, no. 7: 933–955.

Miller, Marjorie. 1996. In *Peirce's Doctrine of Signs: Theories, Applications, and Connections,* ed. Vincent M. Colapietro and Thomas M. Olshewsky. Berlin: Mouton de Gruyter, 71–78.

Mills, C. Wright. 1966. *Sociology and Pragmatism: The Higher Learning in America.* New York: Oxford University Press.

———. 1940. "Situated Actions and Vocabularies of Motive." *American Sociological Review* 5, 6: 904–913.

Minow, Martha. 1997. "Judge for the Situation: Judge Jack Weinstein, Creator of Temporary Administrative Agencies." *Columbia Law Review* 97, no. 7: 2010–2033.

Minteer, Ben A. 2001. "Wilderness and the Wise Province: Benton MacKaye's Pragmatic Vision." *Philosophy & Geography* 4, no. 2: 185–202.

Mintzberg, Henry, and James A. Waters. 1985. "Of Strategies, Deliberate and Emergent." *Strategic Management Journal* 6, no. 3: 257–272.

Mirowski, Philip. 1987. "The Philosophical Bases of Institutionalist Economics." *Journal of Economic Issues* 21, no. 3: 1001–1038.

Misak, Cheryl. 2000. *Truth, Politics, and Morality.* London: Taylor and Francis.

Mitchell, Bruce. 2005. "Participatory Partnerships: Engaging and Empowering to Enhance Environmental Management and Quality of Life?" *Social Indicators Research* 71: 123–144.

Mitroff, Ian. 1998. *Smart Thinking for Crazy Times: The Art of Solving the Right Problems.* San Francisco: Berrett-Koehler Publishers.

Mitroff, Ian, James R. Emshoff, and Ralph H. Kilmann. 1979. "Assumptional Analysis: A Methodology for Strategic Problem-Solving." *Management Science* 25, no. 6: 583–593.

Moe, Terry. 1989. "The Politics of Bureaucratic Structure." In *Can the Government Govern?,* ed. John E. Chubb and Paul E. Peterson. Washington, DC: Brookings Institution.

Mohr, John W., and Vincent Duquenne. 2003. "Sizing up Compstat: An Important Administrative Innovation in Policing." *Criminology and Public Policy* 2, no. 3: 469–494.

———. 1997. "The Duality of Culture and Practice: Poverty Relief in New York City, 1888–1917." *Theory and Society* 26: 305–356.

Moore, Mark. 1995. *Creating Public Value: Strategic Management in Government.* Cambridge, MA: Harvard University Press.

Moore, Richard H., Jason Shaw Parker, and Mark Weaver. 2008. "Agricultural Sustainability, Water Pollution, and Governmental Regulations: Lessons from the Sugar Creek Farmers in Ohio." *Culture & Agriculture* 30, nos. 1 and 2: 3–16.

Moran, Michael. 2002. "Review Article: Understanding the Regulatory State." *British Journal of Political Science* 32: 391–413.

Morris, Debra. 1999. "'How Shall We Read What We Call Reality?' John Dewey's New Science of Democracy." *American Journal of Political Science* 43, no. 2: 608–628.

Mouffe, Chantal. 2005. *On the Political.* New York: Routledge.

Mousavi, Shabnam, and Jim Garrison. 2003. "Toward a Transactional Theory of Decision Making: Creative Rationality as Functional Coordination in Context." *Journal of Economic Methodology* 10, no. 2: 131–156.

Murdock, Barbara Scott, Carol Wiessner, and Ken Sexton. 2005. "Stakeholder Participation in Voluntary Environmental Agreements: Analysis of 10 Project XL Case Studies." *Science, Technology & Human Values* 30, no. 2: 223–250.

Murphey, Murray. 1990. "Introduction." In Thorstein Veblen *The Instinct of Workmanship and the State of the Industrial Arts.* New Brunswick, NJ: Transaction Publishers, vii–xlv.

National Commission on Terrorist Attacks upon the United States. 2004. *The 9/11 Commission Report.* Washington, DC: U.S. Government Printing Office.

Neblo, Michael. 2004. "Giving Hands and Feet to Morality." *Perspectives in Politics* 2, no. 1: 99–100.

Needham, Rodney. 1975. "Polythetic Classification: Convergence and Consequences." *Man* 10, no. 3: 349–369.

Needleman, Martin, and Carolyn E. Needleman. 1974. *Guerillas in the Bureaucracy: Community Planning Experiment in the United States.* John Wiley & Sons.

Nelson, Richard R., and Sidney G. Winter. 1985. *An Evolutionary Theory of Economic Change.* Cambridge, MA: Belknap Press.

Nelson, Rodney. 1995. "Pragmatic Validity in Mannheim and Dewey: A Reassessment of the Epistemological Critique of Ideology and Utopia." *History of the Human Sciences* 8, no. 3: 25–45.

Newton, Tim. 1999. "Power, Subjectivity and British Industrial and Organisational Sociology: The Relevance of the Work of Norbert Elias." *Sociology* 33, no. 2: 411–440.

Nickerson, Jack A., and Todd R. Zenger. 2004. "A Knowledge-Based Theory of the Firm—The Problem-Solving Perspective." *Organization Science* 15, no. 6: 617–632.

Noble, William G. 2007. "Gibsonian Theory and the Pragmatist Perspective." *Journal for the Theory of Social Behavior* 11, no. 1: 65–85.

Nonaka, Ikujiro. 1994. "A Dynamic Theory of Organization Knowledge Creation." *Organization Science* 5, no. 1: 14–37.

Nonet, Philippe, and Philip Selznick. 2001. *Law and Society in Transition: Toward Responsive Law.* New Brunswick, NJ: Transaction Publishers.

Noonan, Kathleen G., Charles F. Sabel, and William H. Simon. 2009. "Legal Accountability in the Service-Based Welfare State: Lessons from Child Welfare Reform." *Law & Social Inquiry* 34, no. 3: 523–568.

Novicevic, Milorad M., Thomas J. Hench, and Daniel A. Wren. 2002. "'Playing by Ear' . . . 'in an Incessant Din of Reasons': Chester Barnard and the History of Intuition in Management Thought." *Management Decision* 40, no. 10: 992–1002.

Nussbaum, Martha. 2003. *Upheavals of Thought: The Intelligence of Emotions.* Cambridge, UK: Cambridge University Press.

Öberg, Per Ola. 2002. "Does Administrative Corporatism Promote Trust and Deliberation?" *Governance: An International Journal of Policy, Administration, and Institutions* 15, no. 4: 455–475.

O'Connor, Ellen S. 2001. "Back on the Way to Empowerment: The Example of Ordway Tead and Industrial Democracy." *Journal of Applied Behavioral Science* 37, no. 1: 15–32.

Oliver, Willard M. 2000. "The Third Generation of Community Policing: Moving through Innovation, Diffusion, and Institutionalization." *Police Quarterly* 3, no. 4: 367–388.

Olsen, Johan P. 2006. "Maybe It Is Time to Rediscover Bureaucracy." *Journal of Public Administration Research and Theory* 16, no. 1: 1–24.

O'Neill, R. V., D. L. DeAngelis, J. B. Waide, and T. F. H. Allen. 1986. *A Hierarchical Concept of Ecosystems*. Princeton, NJ: Princeton University Press.

Ormerod, R. 2006. "The History and Ideas of Pragmatism." *Journal of the Operational Research Society* 57: 892–909.

Orren, Karen, and Stephen Skowronek. 1994. "Order and Time in Institutional Study." In *Political Science in History*, ed. James Farr, John S. Dryzek, and Stephen T. Leonard. Cambridge, UK: Cambridge University Press.

O'Rourke, Dara, and Eungkyoon Lee. 2004. "Mandatory Planning for Environmental Innovation: Evaluating Regulatory Mechanisms for Toxics Use Reduction." *Journal of Environmental Planning and Management* 47, no. 2: 181–200.

Osborne, David, and Ted Gaebler. 1992. *Reinventing Government: How the Entrepreneurial Spirit Is Transforming the Public Sector*. New York: Plume.

Ostrom, Elinor. 1999. "Coping with Tragedies of the Commons." *Annual Review of Political Science* 2: 493–535.

O'Toole, Laurence J., Jr., and Kenneth J. Meier. 2004. "Desperately Seeking Selznick: Cooptation and the Dark Side of Public Management in Networks." *Public Administration Review* 64, no. 6: 682–693.

Otto-Zimmerman, Conrad. 2002. "Local Action 21: Motto-Mandate-Movement in the Post-Johannesburg Decade." *Local Environment* 7, no. 4: 465–469.

Paavola, Sami. 2005. "Peircean Abduction: Instinct or Inference." *Semiotica* 153, nos. 1/4: 131–154.

Padgett, John, and Christopher Ansell. 1993. "Robust Action and the Rise of the Medici: 1400–1434." *American Journal of Sociology* 98, no. 6: 1259–1319.

Pahl-Wostl, Claudia. 2005. "Information, Public Empowerment, and the Management of Urban Watersheds." *Environmental Modeling & Software* 20: 457–467.

Pahl-Wostl, Claudia, and Matt Hare. 2004. "Processes of Social Learning in Integrated Resource Management." *Journal of Community & Applied Social Psychology* 14: 193–206.

Parker, L. D. 1984. "Control in Organizational Life: The Contribution of Mary Parker Follett." *Academy of Management Review* 9, no. 4: 736–745.

Parsons, Craig. 2003. *A Certain Idea of Europe*. Ithaca, NY: Cornell University Press.

Peters, Guy B. 2005. "The Problem of Policy Problems." *Journal of Comparative Policy Analysis: Research and Practice* 7, no. 4: 349–370.

Pfeffer, Jeffrey, and Gerald Salancik. 1978. *The External Control of Organizations: A Resource Dependence Perspective*. New York: Harper & Row.

Pickens, Donald K. 1987. "Clarence E. Ayres and the Legacy of German Idealism." *American Journal of Economics and Sociology* 46, no. 3: 287–298.

Pierson, Paul. 2004. *Politics in Time: History, Institutions, and Social Analysis*. Princeton, NJ: Princeton University Press.

Plummer, Ryan and John Fitzgibbon. 2004. "Co-Management of Natural Resources: A Proposed Framework." *Environmental Management* 33, no. 6: 876–885.

Polanyi, Michael. 1958. *Personal Knowledge: Towards a Post-Critical Philosophy*. Chicago: University of Chicago Press.

Pollan, Michael. 2006. *Omnivore's Dilemma: A Natural History of Four Meals*. New York: Penguin Press.

Popp, Jerome. 2007. *Evolution's First Philosopher: John Dewey and the Continuity of Nature*. Albany: SUNY Press.

Posner, Richard. 2003. *Law, Pragmatism, and Democracy*. Cambridge, MA: Harvard University Press.

Powell, W. W., and Paul J. DiMaggio. 1991. *The New Institutionalism in Organizational Analysis*. Chicago: University of Chicago Press.

Power, Michael. 1997. *The Audit Society: Rituals of Verification*. Oxford: Oxford University Press.

Prahalad, C. K., and G. Hamel. 1990. "The Core Competence of the Corporation." *Harvard Business Review* (May–June): 79–91.

Pumar, Enrique S. 2005. "Social Networks and the Institutionalization of Sustainable Development." *International Journal of Sociology and Social Policy* 25, nos. 1/2: 63–86.

Puntambekar, Sadhana, and Roland Hubscher. 2005. "Tools for Scaffolding Students in a Complex Learning Environment: What Have We Gained and What Have We Missed?" *Educational Psychologist* 40, no. 1: 1–12.

Putnam, Linda. 2004. "Transformations and Critical Moments in Negotiations." *Negotiations Journal* 20, no. 2: 275–295.

Putnam, Linda, Guy Burgess, and Rebecca Royer. 2003. "We Can't Go On Like This: Frame Changes in Intractable Conflicts." *Environmental Practice* 5: 247–255.

Quilley, Stephen, and Steven Loyal. 2005. "Eliasian Sociology as a 'Central Theory' for the Human Sciences." *Current Sociology* 53, no. 5: 807–828.

Raab, Jörg. n.d. "Selznick Revisited: Goal Displacement as an Unavoidable Consequence of Cooptation." Unpublished manuscript.

Rampart Independent Review Panel. 2000. Report of the Rampart Independent Review Panel. November 16, 2000. Available at http://www.ci.la.ca.us/oig/rirprpt.pdf, accessed April 10, 2011.

Ratner, S., J. Altman, and J. E. Wheeler. 1964. *John Dewey and Arthur Bentley: A Philosophical Correspondence*. New Brunswick, NJ: Rutgers University Press.

Raymond, Leigh. 2006. "Cooperation without Trust: Overcoming Collective Action Barriers to Endangered Species Protection." *Policies Studies Journal* 34, no. 1: 37–57.

Rees, Joseph V. 2008. "The Orderly Use of Experience: Pragmatism and the Development of Hospital Industry Self-Regulation." *Regulation & Governance* 2, no. 1: 9–29.

Reich, Robert B. 1985. "Public Administration and Public Deliberation: An Interpretive Essay." *Yale Law Journal* 94, no. 7: 1617–1641.

Reilly, Thom. 2001. "Collaboration in Action: An Uncertain Process." *Administration in Social Work* 25, no. 1: 53–74.

———. 1998. "Communities in Conflict: Resolving Differences through Collaborative Efforts in Environmental Planning and Human Service Delivery." *Journal of Sociology and Welfare* 25: 115–142.

Reiter-Palmon, Roni, and Jody J. Illies. 2004. "Leadership and Creativity: Understanding Leadership as a Creative Problem-Solving Perspective." *Leadership Quarterly* 15: 55–77.

Rescher, Nicolas. 2000. *Process Philosophy: A Survey of Basic Issues*. Pittsburgh: University of Pittsburgh Press.

Risse, Thomas. 2004. "Global Governance and Communicative Action." *Government and Opposition* 39, no. 2: 288–313.

Rittel, Horst W. J., and Melvin M. Webber. 1973. "Dilemmas in a General Theory of Planning." *Policy Sciences* 4: 155–169.

Roberts, Ian. 2000. "Leicester Environment City: Learning How to Make Local Agenda 21, Partnerships, and Participation Deliver." *Environment and Urbanization* 12, no. 2: 9–26.

Roberts, Nancy. 2000. "Wicked Problems and Network Approaches to Resolution." *International Public Management Review* 1, no. 1: 1–19.

Roberts, Patrick. 2006. "FEMA and the Prospects for Reputation-Based Autonomy." *Studies in American Political Development* 20: 57–87.

Robinson, John. 2004. "Squaring the Circle? Some Thoughts on the Idea of Sustainable Development." *Ecological Economics* 48: 369–384.

Rochberg-Halton, Eugene. 1986. *Meaning and Modernity: Social Theory in the Pragmatic Attitude*. Chicago: University of Chicago Press.

Rochefort, David A., and Roger W. Cobb. 1993. "Problem-Definition, Agenda Access, and Policy Choice." *Policy Studies Journal* 21, no. 1: 56–71.

Rochlin, Gene, Todd La Porte, and Karlene Roberts. 1987. "The Self-Designing High-Reliability Organization: Aircraft Carrier Flight Operations at Sea." *Naval War College Review* 40: 76–90.

Rodriguez-Garavito, César A. 2005. "Global Governance and Labor Rights: Codes of Conduct and Anti-Sweatshop Struggles in Global Apparel Factories in Mexico and Guatemala." *Politics & Society* 33, no. 2: 203–233.

Roeder, Philip G., and Donald S. Rothchild, eds. 2005. *Sustainable Peace: Power and Democracy after Civil Wars*. Ithaca, NY: Cornell University Press.

Romme, A. Georges L. 1997. "Organizational Learning, Circularity and Double-Linking." *Management Learning* 28, no. 2: 149–160.

———. 1996. "Making Organizational Learning Work: Consent and Double Linking between Circles." *European Management Journal* 14, no. 1: 69–75.

Romme, A. Georges L., and Arjen van Witteloostuijn. 1999. "Circular Organizing and Triple Loop Learning." *Journal of Organizational Change Management* 12, no. 5: 439–453.

Romzek, Barbara S., and Melvin J. Dubnick. 1987. "Accountability in the Public: Lessons from the Challenger Tragedy." *Public Administration Review* 47, no. 3: 227–238.

Rorty, Richard. 2000. *Philosophy and Social Hope*. London: Penguin Books.

Rosenberg, Shawn. 2002. *The Not So Common Sense: Differences in How People Judge Social and Political Life*. New Haven, CT: Yale University Press.

Rosenfeld, Richard, Robert Fornango, and Eric Baumer. 2005. "Did Ceasefire, Compstat, and Exile Reduce Homicide?" *Criminology and Public Policy* 4, no. 3: 419–450.

Ross, Dorothy. 1991. *The Origins of American Social Science*. Cambridge, UK: Cambridge University Press.

Rudolph, Lloyd, and Susanne Rudolph. 1984. *The Modernity of Tradition: Political Development in India*. Chicago: University of Chicago Press.

Russill, Chris. 2008. "Through a Public Darkly: Reconstructing Pragmatist Perspectives in Communication Theory." *Communication Theory* 18: 478–504.

———. 2005. "The Road Not Taken: William James's Radical Empiricism and Communication Theory." *Communication Review* 8, no. 3: 277–305.

Ryan, Alan. 1995. *John Dewey and the High Tide of American Liberalism*. New York: Norton.

Saarikoski, Heli. 2000. "Environmental Impact Assessment (EIA) as Collaborative Learning Process." *Environmental Impact Assessment Review* 20: 681–700.

Sabatier, Paul A. 1988. "An Advocacy Coalition Framework of Policy Change and the Role of Policy-Oriented Learning Therein." *Policy Sciences* 31, nos. 2–3: 129–168.

Sabel, Charles. 2006. "A Real-Time Revolution in Routines." In *The Corporation as a Collaborative Community: Reconstructing Trust in the Knowledge Economy*, ed. Paul S. Adler and Charles Heckscher. Oxford: Oxford University Press, 106–156.

———. 1999. "Constitutional Orders: Trust Building and Response to Change." In *Contemporary Capitalism: The Embeddedness of Institutions*, ed. J. Rogers Hollingsworth and Robert Boyer. Cambridge, UK: Cambridge University Press.

———. 1994. "Learning by Monitoring: The Institutions of Economic Development." In *The Handbook of Economic Sociology*, ed. Neil J. Smelser and Richard Swedberg. Princeton, NJ: Princeton University Press, 137–165.

Sabel, Charles F., and Jonathan Zeitlin. 2008. "Learning from Difference: The New Architecture of Experimentalist Governance in the EU." *European Law Journal* 14, no. 3: 271–327.

Sadoski, Mark, and Allan Paivio. 2001. *Imagery and Text: A Dual Coding Theory of Reading and Writing*. Mahway, NJ: Lawrence Erlbaum Associates.

Saguy, Abigail C., and Kevin W. Riley. 2005. "Weighing Both Sides: Morality, Mortality, and Framing Contests over Obesity." *Journal of Health Politics, Policy, and Law* 30, no. 5: 869–923.

Sancassiani, Walter. 2005. "Local Agenda 21 in Italy: An Effective Governance Tool for Facilitating Local Communities' Participation and Promoting Capacity Building for Sustainability." *Local Environment* 10, no. 2: 189–200.

Sapsed, Jonathan, and Ammon Salter. 2004. "Postcards from the Edge: Local Communities, Global Programs and Boundary Objects." *Organization Studies* 25, no. 9: 1515–1534.

Scharpf, Fritz. 1988. "The Joint-Decision Trap: Lessons from German Federalism and European Integration." *Public Administration*, 66: 239–278.

Schickler, Eric. 2001. *Disjointed Pluralism: Institutional Innovation and the Development of the U.S. Congress.* Princeton, NJ: Princeton University Press.

Schlager, Edella C. 2004. "Local Governance of Common Pool Resources." In *Environmental Governance: Challenges, Choices, and Opportunities*, ed. Robert Durant, Dan Fiorino, and Rosemary O'Leary. Cambridge, MA: MIT Press.

Schmidt, Luísa, Joaquim Gil Nave, and João Guerra. 2006. "Who's Afraid of Local Agenda 21? Top-down and Bottom-up Perspectives on Local Sustainability." *International Journal of Environment and Sustainable Development* 5, no. 2: 181–198.

Schneider, Mark, John Scholz, Mark Lubell, Denisa Mindruta, and Matthew Edwardsen. 2003. "Building Consensual Institutions: Networks and the National Estuary Program." *American Journal of Political Science* 47, no. 1, 143–158.

Schubert. Hans-Joachim. 2006. "The Foundation of Pragmatic Sociology: Charles Horton Cooley and George Herbert Mead." *Journal of Classical Sociology* 6, no. 1: 51–74.

Schulman, Paul R. 1975. "Nonincremental Policy Making: Notes toward an Alternative Paradigm." *American Political Science Review* 69, no. 4: 1354–1370.

Schön, Donald. 1983. *The Reflective Practitioner: How Professionals Think in Action.* New York: Basic Books.

Schön Donald A., and Martin Rein. 1995. *Frame Reflection: Toward the Resolution of Intractable Policy Controversies.* New York: Basic Books.

Scipioni, Antonio, Anna Mazzi, Marco Mason, and Alessandro Manzardo. 2009. "The Dashboard of Sustainability to Measure the Local Urban Sustainable Development: The Case Study of Padua Municipality." *Ecological Indicators* 9, no. 2: 364–380.

Scott Sagan. 1995. *The Limits of Safety: Organizations, Accidents, and Nuclear Weapons.* Princeton: Princeton University Press.

Seigfried, Charlene Haddock. 1999. "Socializing Democracy: Jane Addams and John Dewey." *Philosophy of the Social Sciences* 29, no. 2: 207–230.

Selin, Steve W., Michael A. Schuett, and Debbie Carr. 2000. "Modeling Stakeholder Perceptions of Collaborative Initiative Effectiveness." *Society of Natural Resources* 13: 735–745.

Selman, Paul. 2000. "A Sideways Look at Local Agenda 21." *Journal of Environmental Policy & Planning* 2: 39–53.

———. 1998. "Local Agenda 21: Substance or Spin?" *Journal of Environmental Planning and Management* 41, no. 5: 533–553.

Selznick, Philip. 2002. *The Communitarian Persuasion.* Washington, DC: Woodrow Wilson Center Press.

———. 1996. "Institutionalism 'Old' and 'New.'" *Administrative Science Quarterly* 41, no. 2: 270–277.

———. 1992. *The Moral Commonwealth: Social Theory and the Promise of Community.* Berkeley: University of California Press.

———. 1984. *TVA and the Grassroots.* Berkeley: University of California Press.

———. 1973. "Rejoinder to Donald J. Black." *American Journal of Sociology* 78, no. 5: 1266–1269.

———. 1969. *Law, Society, and Industrial Justice.* New York: Russell Sage Foundation.

———. 1957. *Leadership in Administration: A Sociological Interpretation.* Berkeley: University of California Press.

Sementelli, Arthur. 2007. "Distortions of Progress: Evolutionary Theories and Public Administration." *Administration & Society* 39, no. 6: 740–760.

Senge, Peter. 2006. *The Fifth Discipline: The Art and Practice of the Learning Organization.* London: Random House.

Shalin, Dmitri. 1986. "Pragmatism and Social Interactionism." *American Sociological Review* 51: 9–29.

Shaver, Phillip, and Graham Staines. 1971. "Problems Facing Campbell's 'Experimenting Society.'" *Urban Affairs Quarterly* 7: 173–186.

Sheppard, James W. 2003. "The Nectar Is in the Journey: Pragmatism, Progress, and the Promise of Incrementalism." *Philosophy & Geography* 6, no. 2: 167–187.

Shields, Patricia M. 2008. "Rediscovering the Tap Root: Is Classical Pragmatism the Route to Renew Public Administration." *Public Administration Review* 68, no. 2: 205–221.

———. 2006. "Democracy and the Social Feminist Ethics of Jane Addams: A Vision for Public Administration." *Faculty Publications in Political Science*, Texas State University. Posted at http://ecommons.txstate.edu/polsfacp/36, accessed April 10, 2011.

———. 2004. "Classical Pragmatism: Engaging Practitioner Experience." *Faculty Publications*, Texas State University. Posted at http://ecommons.txstate.edu/polsfacp/36, accessed April 10, 2011.

———. 2003. "The Community of Inquiry: Classical Pragmatism and Public Administration." *Administration & Society* 35, no. 5: 510–538.

Siebenhüner, Bernd, and Marlen Arnold. 2007. "Organizational Learning to Manage Sustainable Development." *Business Strategy and the Environment* 16: 339–353.

Silverman, Eli. 1999. *NYPD Battles Crime: Innovative Strategies in Policing.* Boston: Northeastern University Press.

Simon, Herbert. 1962. "The Architecture of Complexity." *Proceedings of the American Philosophical Society* 106, no. 6: 467–482.

Simon, Linda. 1998. *Genuine Reality: A Life of William James.* New York: Harcourt Brace.

Siriani, Carmen. 2009. *Investing in Democracy: Engaging Citizens in Collaborative Governance.* Washington, DC: Brookings Institution.

Skogan, Wesley G. 2006. *Police and Community in Chicago: A Tale of Three Cities.* Oxford: Oxford University Press.

Sliwa, Martyna, and Mark Wilcox. 2008. "Philosophical Thought and the Origins of Quality Management: Uncovering Conceptual Underpinnings of W. A. Shewhart's Ideas on Quality." *Culture and Organization* 14, no. 1: 97–106.

Smardon, Richard C. 2008. "A Comparison of Local Agenda 21 Implementation in North American, European and Indian Cities." *Management of Environmental Quality: An International Journal* 19, no. 1: 118–137.

Smiley, Marion. 1999. "Pragmatic Inquiry and Democratic Politics." *American Journal of Political Science* 43, no. 2: 629–647.

———. 1992. *Moral Responsibility and the Boundaries of Community: Power and Accountability from a Pragmatic Point of View.* Chicago: University of Chicago Press.

———. 1989. "Pragmatic Inquiry and Social Conflict: A Critical Reconstruction of Dewey's Model of Democracy." *PRAXIS International* 4: 365–380.

Smith, David G. 1964. "Pragmatism and the Group Theory of Politics." *American Political Science Review* 58, no. 3: 600–610.

Smith, Mark C. 1994. *Social Science in the Crucible: The American Debate over Objectivity and Purpose, 1918–1941.* Durham, NC: Duke University Press.

Sneddon, Chris, Richard B. Howarth, and Richard B. Norgaard. 2006. "Sustainable Development in a Post-Brundtland World." *Ecological Economics* 57: 253–268.

Snider, Keith F. 2005. "Rortyan Pragmatism: 'Where's the Beef' for Public Administration?" *Administration & Society* 2: 243–247.

———. 2000a. "Expertise or Experimenting? Pragmatism and American Public Administration, 1920–1950." *Administration & Society* 32, no. 3: 329–354.

———. 2000b. "Rethinking Public Administration's Roots in Pragmatism: The Case of Charles A. Beard." *American Review of Public Administration* 30, no. 2: 123–145.

Sorenson, Bent, and Torkild Thellefsen. 2006. "Metaphor, Concept Formation and Esthetic Semeiosis in a Peircean Perspective." *Semiotica* 161, nos. 1/4: 199–212.

Sørenson, Eva, and Jacob Torfing. 2007. *Theories of Democratic Network Governance.* Basingstoke, UK: Palgrave Macmillan.

Sowa, Jessica E., and Sally Coleman Selden. 2003. "Administrative Discretion and Active Representation: An Expansion of the Theory of Representative Bureaucracy." *Public Administration Review* 63, no. 6: 700–710.

Sparrow, Malcolm K. 2000. *The Regulatory Craft: Controlling Risks, Solving Problems, and Managing Compliance.* Washington, DC: Brookings Institution.

———. 1994. *Imposing Duties: Government's Changing Approach to Compliance.* New York: Greenwood.

Star, Susan Leigh, and James R. Griesemer. 1989. "Institutional Ecology, 'Translations' and Boundary Objects: Amateurs and Professionals in Berkeley's Museum of Vertebrate Zoology, 1907–39." *Social Studies of Science* 19, no. 3: 387–420.

Starbuck, William H. 1992. "Learning by Knowledge-Intensive Firms." *Journal of Management Studies* 29, no. 6: 713–740.

Stein, Mary Kay, Lea Hubbard, and Hugh Mehan. 2004. "Reform Ideas That Travel Far Afield: The Two Cultures of Reform in New York City's District #2 and San Diego." *Journal of Educational Change* 5: 161–197.

Steurer, Reinhard, and André Martinuzzi. 2005. "Towards a New Pattern of Strategy Formation in the Public Sector: First Experiences with National Strategies for Sustainable Development in Europe." *Environment and Planning C: Government and Policy* 23: 455–472.

Stever, James A. 2000a. *The Path to Organizational Skepticism.* Burke, VA: Chatelaine Press.

———. 2000b. "The Parallel Universes: Pragmatism and Public Administration." *Administration & Society* 32, no. 4: 453–457.

———. 1993. "Technology, Organization, Freedom: The Organizational Theory of John Dewey." *Administration & Society* 24, no. 4: 419–443.

———. 1986. "Mary Parker Follett and the Quest for Pragmatic Administration." *Administration & Society* 18, no. 2: 159–177.

Stinchcombe, Arthur. 2001. *When Formality Works: Authority and Abstraction in Law and Organizations.* Chicago: University of Chicago Press.

———. 1997. "On the Virtues of the Old Institutionalism." *Annual Review of Sociology* 23: 1–18.

Stivers, Camilla. 2002. *Bureau Men, Settlement Women: Constructing Public Administration in the Progressive Era.* Lawrence: University Press of Kansas.

Stoker, Gerry. 2006. "Explaining Political Disenchantment: Finding Pathways to Democratic Renewal." *Political Quarterly* 77, no. 2: 184–194.

Stolcis, Gregory B. 2004. "A View from the Trenches: Comments on Miller's 'Why Old Pragmatism Needs an Upgrade.'" *Administration & Society* 36, no. 3: 362–369.

Stone, Clarence N. 2005. "Looking Back to Look Forward: Reflections on Urban Regime Analysis." *Urban Affairs Review* 40, no. 3: 309–341.

———. 2001. "Civic Capacity and Urban Education." *Urban Affairs Review* 36, no. 5: 569–619.

Stone, Rebecca. 2006. "Does Pragmatism Lead to Pluralism?: Exploring the Disagreement between Jerome Bruner and William James Regarding Pragmatism's Goal." *Theory Psychology* 16, no. 4: 553–564.

Strauss, Anselm. 1993. *Continual Permutations of Action.* New York: Aldine de Gruyter.

———. 1988. "The Articulation of Project Work: An Organizational Process." *Sociological Quarterly* 29, no. 2: 163–178.

Suchman, Lucille. 1987. *Plans and Situated Actions: The Problem of Human-Machine Communication.* New York: Cambridge University Press.

Sullivan, H., and C. Skelcher. 2002. *Working across Boundaries: Collaboration in Public Services.* London: Palgrave.

Sullivan, Helen, Marian Barnes, and Elizabeth Matka. 2006. "Collaborative Capacity and Strategies in Area-Based Initiatives." *Public Administration* 84, no. 2: 289–310.

Sunstein, Cass. 1995. "Incompletely Theorized Agreements." *Harvard Law Review* 108, no. 7: 1733–1772.

Swenden, Wilfried. 2004. "Is the European Union in Need of a Competence Catalogue? Insights from Comparative Federalism." *Journal of Common Market Studies* 42, no. 2: 371–392.

Tainter, Joseph A. 2000. "Problem Solving: Complexity, History, Sustainability." *Population and Environment* 22, no. 1: 3–41.

Talisse, Robert. 2005. *Democracy after Liberalism: Pragmatism and Deliberative Politics.* New York and London: Routledge.

———. 2001. "Liberty, Community, and Democracy: Sidney Hook's Pragmatic Deliberativism." *Journal of Speculative Philosophy* 15, no. 4: 286–304.

Tarlock, Dan. 2001. "Ideas without Institutions: The Paradox of Sustainable Development." *Indiana Journal of Global Legal Studies* 9: 35, 39.

Taylor, Paul. C. 2004. "What's the Use of Calling Du Bois a Pragmatist?" *Metaphilosophy* 35: 99–114.

Taylor, Shelley E. 1998. "The Social Being in Social Psychology." In *The Handbook of Social Psychology*, ed. Daniel T. Gilbert, Susan T. Fiske, and Gardner Lindzey. Boston: McGraw-Hill.

Teece, David J., Gary Pisano, and Amy Shuen. 1997. "Dynamic Capabilities and Strategic Management." *Strategic Management Journal* 18, no. 7: 509–533.

Tett, Lynn, Jim Crowther, and Paul O'Hara. 2003. "Collaborative Partnerships in Community Education." *Journal of Education Policy* 18, no. 1: 37–51.

Thayer, H. S. 1981. *Meaning and Action: A Critical History of Pragmatism.* Indianapolis: Hackett.

Thelen, Kathleen. 2004. *How Institutions Evolve: The Political Economy of Skills in Germany, Britain, the United States, and Japan.* Cambridge, UK: Cambridge University Press.

Thomas, Craig. 2003a. *Bureaucratic Landscapes: Interagency Cooperation and the Preservation of Biodiversity.* Cambridge, MA: MIT Press.

———. 2003b. "Habitat Conservation Planning." In *Deepening Democracy: Institutional Innovations in Empowered Participatory Governance*, ed. Archon Fung, Erik Olin Wright, and Rebecca Abers. London: Verso Press, 144–172.

———. 1998. "Maintaining and Restoring Public Trust in Government Agencies and Their Employees." *Administration & Society* 30: 166–193.

Thompson, Ann Marie, and James L. Perry. 2006. "Collaboration Processes: Inside the Black Box." *Public Administration*, special issue: 20–32.

Tonn, Joan C. 2003. *Mary P. Follett: Creating Democracy, Transforming Management.* New Haven, CT: Yale University Press.

Tool, Marc R. 1977. "A Social Value Theory in Neoinstitutional Economics." *Journal of Economic Issues* 11, no. 4: 823–846.

Toulmin, Stephen. 2001. *Return to Reason.* Cambridge, MA: Harvard University Press.

Trueit, Donna. 2004. "A Pragmatist Approach to Inquiry: Recuperation of the Poetic." Unpublished paper presented at the Proceedings of the 2004 Complexity Science and Educational Research Conference, September 30–October 3, Chaffey's Locks, Canada, 241–252.

Tucker, Anita L., Amy C. Edmondson, and Steven Spear. 2002. "When Problem Solving Prevents Organizational Learning." *Journal of Organizational Change* 15, no. 2: 122–137.

Tucker, Charles W. 1988. "Herbert Blumer: A Pilgrimage with Pragmatism." *Symbolic Interaction* 11, no. 1: 99–124.

Turner, Victor D. 1986. "Dewey, Dilthey, and Drama: An Essay in the Anthropology of Experience." In Victor D. Turner and Edward M. Bruner, *The Anthropology of Experience*. Champaign-Urbana: University of Illinois Press.

Twomey, Paul. 1998. "Reviving Veblenian Economic Psychology." *Cambridge Journal of Economics* 22: 433–448.

Tyler, Tom R. 1997. "The Psychology of Legitimacy: A Relational Perspective on Voluntary Deference to Authorities." *Personality and Social Psychology Review* 1, no. 4: 323–345.

Tyre, Marcie J., and Eric von Hippel. 1997. "The Situated Nature of Adaptive Learning in Organizations." *Organization Science* 8, no. 1: 71–83.

Ulrich, Werner. 1988. "Churchman's 'Process of Unfolding'—Its Significance for Policy Analysis and Evaluation." *Systems Practice* 1, no. 4: 415–428.

Unger, Roberto. 2004. *False Necessity: Anti-Necessitarian Social Theory in the Service of Radical Democracy*. London: Verso.

Van Bueren, Ellen M., Erik-Hans Klijn, and Joop F. M. Koppenjan. 2003. "Dealing with Wicked Problems in Networks: Analyzing an Environmental Debate from a Network Perspective." *Journal of Public Administration Research and Theory* 13, no. 2: 193–212.

Vanderstraeten, Raf. 2002. "Dewey's Transactional Constructivism." *Journal of Philosophy of Education* 36: 233–246.

Vanderstraeten, Raf, and Gert Biesta. 2006. "How Is Education Possible?: Pragmatism, Communication, and the Social Organisation of Education." *British Journal of Educational Studies* 54, no. 2: 160–176.

Van Eeten, Michel J. G. 2001. "Recasting Intractable Policy Issues: The Wider Implications of the Netherlands Civil Aviation Controversy." *Journal of Policy Analysis and Management* 20, no. 3: 391–414.

Virkkunen, Jaakko, and Kari Kuutti. 2000. "Understanding Organizational Learning by Focusing on 'Activity Systems.'" *Accounting, Management, and Information Technology* 10: 291–319.

Vogler, John. 2007. "The International Politics of Sustainable Development." In *Handbook of Sustainable Development*, ed. Giles Atkinson, Simon Dietz, and Eric Neumayer. Cheltenham, UK: Edward Elgar Publishing.

Voisey, Heather, Christiane Beuermann, Liv Astrid Sverdrup, and Tim O'Riordan. 1996. "The Political Significance of Local Agenda 21: The Early Stages of Some European Experience." *Local Environment* 1, no. 1: 33–50.

Volkery, Axel, Darren Swanson, Klaus Jacob, Francois Bregha, and Lázló Pintér. 2006. "Coordination, Challenges, and Innovations in 19 National Sustainable Development Strategies." *World Development* 34, no. 12: 2047–2063.

Waks, Leonard J. 1997. "Post-Experimentalist Pragmatism." *Studies in Philosophy and Education* 17: 17–29.

Waldo, Dwight. 1948. *The Administrative State: A Study of the Political Theory of American Public Administration*. New York: Ronald Press.

Walsh, William F., and Gennaro F. Vito. 2004. "The Meaning of Compstat: Analysis and Response." *Journal of Contemporary Criminal Justice* 20, no. 1: 51–69.

Walters, Carl J., and C. S. Holling. 1990. "Large-Scale Management Experiments and Learning by Doing." *Ecology* 71, no. 6: 2060–2068.

Wang, Jessica. 2005. "Imagining the Administrative State: Legal Pragmatism, Securities Regulation, and New Deal Liberalism." *Journal of Policy History* 17, no. 3: 257–293.

Weaver, R. Kent. 1986. "The Politics of Blame Avoidance." *Journal of Public Policy* 6, no. 4: 371–398.

Webb, James L. 2004. "Comment on Hugh T. Miller's 'Why Old Pragmatism Needs an Upgrade.'" *Administration & Society* 36, no. 4: 479–495.

———. 2002. "Dewey: Back to the Future." *Journal of Economic Issues* 46, no. 4: 981–1003.

Weber, Edward P. 2009. "Explaining Institutional Change in Tough Cases of Collaboration: 'Ideas' in the Blackfoot Watershed." *Public Administration Review* 69, no. 2: 314–327.

———. 2003. *Bringing Society Back In: Grassroots Ecosystem Management, Accountability, and Sustainable Communities.* Cambridge, MA: MIT Press.

———. 1999. "The Question of Accountability in Historical Perspective: From Jackson to Contemporary Grassroots Ecosystem Management." *Administration & Society* 31, no. 4: 451–494.

Weber, Edward P., Nicholas P. Lovrich, and Michael Gaffney. 2005. "Collaboration, Enforcement, and Endangered Species: A Framework for Assessing Collaborative Problem-Solving Capacity." *Society & Natural Resources* 18, no. 8: 677–698.

Weber, Steve. 2004. *The Success of Open Source.* Cambridge, MA: Harvard University Press.

Weech-Maldonado, Robert, and Sonya Merrill. 2000. "Building Partnerships with the Community: Lessons from the Camden Health Improvement Learning Collaborative." *Journal of Healthcare Management* 45, no. 3: 189–205.

Weick, Karl. 1996. *Sensemaking in Organizations.* Thousand Oaks, CA: Sage.

———. 1993. "The Collapse of Sensemaking in Organizations: The Mann Gulch Disaster." *Administrative Science Quarterly* 38: 628–652.

———. 1984. "Small Wins: Redefining the Scale of Social Problems." *American Psychologist* 39, no. 1: 40–49.

———. 1969. *The Social Psychology of Organizing.* Reading, MA: Addison-Wesley.

Weinstein, Michael. 1971. "Life and Politics as Plural: James and Bentley on the Twentieth Century Problem." *Journal of Value Inquiry* 5, no. 4: 282–291.

Weir, Margaret. 1992. "Ideas and the Politics of Bounded Innovation." In *Structuring Politics: Historical Institutionalism in Comparative Analysis,* ed. Sven Steinmo, Kathleen Thelen, and Frank Longstreth. Cambridge, UK: Cambridge University Press, 188–216.

Weisburd, David, Stephen D. Mastrofski, Ann Marie McNally, Rosann Greenspan, and James L. Willis. 2003. "Reforming to Preserve: Compstat and Strategic Problem-Solving in American Policing." *Criminology and Public Policy* 2, no. 3: 421–456.

Weiss, Janet. 1989. "The Powers of Problem-Definition: The Case of Government Paperwork." *Policy Sciences* 22: 97–121.

Weiss, Robert S., and Martin Rein. 1970. "The Evaluation of Broad-Aim Programs: Experimental Design, Its Difficulties, and an Alternative." *Administrative Science Quarterly* 15, no. 1: 97–109.

Wescoat, James L. 1992. "Common Themes in the Work of Gilbert White and John Dewey: A Pragmatic Appraisal." *Annals of the Association of American Geographers* 82, no. 4: 587–607.

West, Cornell. 1989. *The American Evasion of Philosophy: A Genealogy of Pragmatism.* Madison: University of Wisconsin Press.

Westbrook, Robert. 2005. *Democratic Hope: Pragmatism and the Politics of Truth.* Ithaca, NY: Cornell University Press.

———. 1991. *John Dewey and American Democracy.* Ithaca, NY: Cornell University Press.

Whipple, Mark. 2005. "The Dewey-Lippmann Debate Today: Communication Distortions, Reflective Agency, and Participatory Democracy." *Sociological Theory* 23, no. 2: 156–178.

Whipps, Judy D. 2004. "Jane Addams's Social Thought as a Model for a Pragmatist-Feminist Communitarianism." *Hypatia* 19, no. 2: 118–133.

White, Harrison. 1992. *Identity and Control: A Structural Theory of Social Action.* Princeton, NJ: Princeton University Press.

White, Morton. 2005. *A Philosophy of Culture: The Scope of Holistic Pragmatism.* Princeton, NJ: Princeton University Press.

———. 1949. *Social Thought in America: The Revolt against Formalism.* New York: Viking Press.

Whitford, Josh. 2002. "Pragmatism and the Untenable Dualism of Means and Ends: Why Rational Choice Theory Does Not Deserve Paradigmatic Privilege." *Theory and Society* 31: 325–363.

Wiley, Norbert. 2007. "Znaniecki's Key Insight: The Merger of Pragmatism and Neo-Kantianism." *Polish Sociological Review* 2, no. 158: 133–143.

———. 1994. *The Semiotic Self*. Oxford: Polity Press.

Willis, James J., Stephen D. Mastrofski, and David Weisburd. 2004. "Compstat and Bureaucracy: A Case Study of Challenges and Opportunities for Change." *Justice Quarterly* 21, no. 3: 463–496.

———. 2003. *Compstat in Practice: An In-Depth Analysis of Three Cities*. Washington, DC: Police Foundation.

Wilson, Greg, and Carl G. Herndl. 2007. "Boundary Objects as Rhetorical Exigence: Knowledge Mapping and Interdisciplinary Cooperation at the Los Alamos National Laboratory." *Journal of Business and Technical Communication* 21, no. 2: 129–154.

Wilson, James Q. 1989. *Bureaucracy: What Government Agencies Do and Why They Do It*. New York: Basic Books.

Wilson, Sacoby, Omega Wilson, Christopher Heaney, and John Cooper. 2007. "Use of EPA Collaborative Problem-Solving Model to Obtain Environmental Justice in North Carolina." *Progress in Community Health Partnerships: Research, Education, and Action* 1, no. 4: 327–337.

Wondolleck, Julia Mare, and Steven Lewis Yaffee. 2000. *Making Collaboration Work: Lessons from Innovation in Natural Resource Management*. Washington, DC: Island Press.

Wood, David, Jerome S. Bruner, and Gail Ross. 1976. "The Role of Tutoring in Problem Solving." *Journal of Child Psychology and Psychiatry* 17: 89–100.

Wu, Jiaguo, and Orie L. Loucks. 1995. "From Balance of Nature to Hierarchical Patch Dynamics: A Paradigm Shift in Ecology." *Quarterly Review of Biology* 70, no. 4: 439–466.

Yaffee, Steven L., and Julia M. Wondolleck. 2003. "Collaborative Ecosystem Planning Processes in the United States: Evolution and Challenges." *Environments* 31, no. 2: 59–72.

Yanarella, Ernest, and Horace Bartilow. 2000. "Beyond Environmental Moralism and Policy Incrementalism in the Global Sustainability Debate: Case Studies and an Alternative Framework." *Sustainable Development* 8: 123–134.

Young, Iris Marion. 2002. *Inclusion and Democracy*. Oxford: Oxford University Press.

Young, Mike, and Victor Dulewicz. 2005. "A Model of Command, Leadership and Management Competency in the British Royal Navy." *Leadership & Organization Development Journal* 26, no. 3: 228–241.

Zakaria, Fareed. 2004. *The Future of Freedom: Illiberal Democracy at Home and Abroad*. New York: W. W. Norton.

Zald, Mayer. 1996. "More Fragmentation? Unfinished Business in Linking the Social Sciences and the Humanities." *Administrative Science Quarterly* 41: 251–261.

Zanetti, Lisa A., and Adrian Carr. 2000. "Contemporary Pragmatism in Public Administration: Exploring the Limitations of the 'Third Productive Reply.'" *Administration & Society* 32, no. 4: 433–452.

Ziegler, John A. 1994. *Experimentalism and Institutional Change: An Approach to the Study and Improvement of Institutions*. Lanham, MD: University Press of America.

Zimmerman, Bénédicte. 2006. "Pragmatism and the Capability Approach: Challenges in Social Theory and Empirical Research." *European Journal of Social Theory* 9, no. 4: 467–484.

Zollo, Maurizio, and Sidney G. Winter. 2002. "Deliberate Learning and the Evolution of Dynamic Capabilities." *Organization Science* 13, no. 3: 339–351.

INDEX

Barzelay, Michael, 203n18
Bateson, Gregory, 105–106, 204n27, 219n3,
    219n56
Beer, Samuel H., 141, 225n35
Behn, Robert D., 136, 224n17
beliefs, 187
benchmarking, 6, 213n42
Bentley, Arthur, 20
    Knowing and the Known, 129
Bentrup, Gary, 172
Benz, Arthur, 142
Berk, Gerald, 25
Berman, Greg, 85, 91, 92
Bernstein, Richard, 5
Betchky, Beth A., 219n63
Bettis, Richard, 80, 216n27
Biebel, Elizabeth Perkins, 96, 215n21
Biggart, Nicole Woolsey, 227n10
Birnie, Andrew, 208n25
Blom-Hansen, Jens, 141
Blueprint for Survival, 55
Blumer, Herbert, 25–26, 29
Boehmer-Christiansen, Sonja, 207n17
Bohman, James, 18, 158, 175
Boin, Arjen, 72–73, 152, 192, 193
Boje, David M., 211n22
Borys, Bryan, 222n31
Börzel, T. A., 140
Boston Gun Project, 90, 93, 94, 99–100, 121,
    188–189
bottom-up consent, 154–156
boundary objects, 48–49, 52–53, 55, 61
bounded rationality, 101
Braga, Anthony, 96
Brandeis, Louis, 20
Bratton, William, 91, 98, 105, 108–109, 111,
    225n31
Braun, Dietmar, 140, 141
Brazil, participatory budgeting in, 53
Brightman, Harvey J., 216n30
British Columbia, 179
broken windows policing, 100, 109
Bromley, Daniel, 50, 202n11, 204n34
Brown, A. J., 157, 177
Brundtland, Gro Harlem, 55
Bruner, Jerome, 88
Brunsson, Nils, 131
Bruun, Henrik, 87
Bryan, Todd, 172
budgeting, 80–81
Buntrock, Oliver, 98
bureaucracy
    and accountability, 131
    and liberalism, 3
    and oligarchy, 73
    and populism, 3
    post-bureaucracy, 222n28

and progressivism, 3
and responsibility, 224n27
and roles, 209n5
tension between procedural and substantive
    rationality, 145
Weber's model of, 16–17, 64–69, 72, 82, 91,
    191, 192, 193
    See also public agencies
Burgess, Guy, 180
Burns, Tom, 117
Bush, Robert A. Baruch, 168–169, 230n14

Campbell, Donald T., 12, 199n23
Canon, 79
capacity building, 89, 97
CAPS. *See* Chicago Alternative Policing
    Strategy (CAPS)
capture, 159
Cardozo, Benjamin, 20
Carlile, Paul, 48
Carr, Adrian, 116
Caspary, William R., 138, 225n29
centralization, 17, 71–73, 104, 105, 109, 120, 186
Central Problems in Social Theory (Giddens), 105
Chandler, Alfred, 117, 118
change, institutional. *See* institutional change
character, 25, 65, 68–69, 77–78, 82, 203n17,
    212n33, 224n26
charisma, 67, 73, 209n8
checks and balances, 139, 140, 143
Cherney, Adrian, 92, 96–97
Chicago Alternative Policing Strategy (CAPS),
    6–7, 15, 197n5
Chicago School of Sociology, 19–20, 24, 26, 28,
    200n31, 202n8
child welfare, 6, 95–96, 160, 162, 163, 164
Chisholm, Donald, 28, 85, 86–87, 88, 192
Churchman, C. West, 216n23
circular integration, 105, 115
circular responsibility, 116
Clark, Peter A., 219n3
Clinton, Bill, 134
cognitive reasoning, 218n54
Cohen, Michael, 192
collaboration, 6, 229n1
collaborative governance, 18, 166–183
    and consent, 157–158
    definition of, 167–168
    as emergence, 178–181, 182
    and evolutionary learning, 173–175
    and face-to-face communication, 170, 175, 181
    as feedback, 179–181, 182
    as fruitful conflict, 168–171, 181–182, 183
    and interdependence, 175–178, 182, 183
    and problem solving, 157, 172–183
    and public agencies, 155, 183